A Compleat Compendium

of

ACTING
AND
PERFORMING

in two parts

By

Hayes Gordon

Ensemble Press
Sydney

Published by Ensemble Press
78 McDougall Street, Milsons Point
New South Wales 2062 Australia

First published 1992

Typeset in Garamond by Setila Type Studio,
Suite 203, 284 Victoria Avenue, Chatswood, Sydney
Printed on 80 gsm Ambit
by Globe Press

Book Design by John Windus and Jennifer Sandilands

Cover design and sketches by John Windus

ISBN 0 646 06619 6

To Kati and Helen

CONTENTS

Note: The book layout makes available much blank space. This can be used for reader's notes, of which it is expected there may be many.

PROLOGUE

A good conjurer can make an audience believe in 'magic'. But the conjurer knows it isn't. He has created an illusion built with familiar materials and gimmickry handled with polished skills. The actor too is a conjurer. His materials may be a bit more ephemeral, but they should be no less familiar. And to succeed with his illusions, his skills too must be polished.

To the audience, this book may be seen as a bit of an exposé: the materials and tricks laid bare. But this should not detract at all from the appreciation of the good actor's skill in handling them. Everyone knows that pressing a piano key will produce a musical sound. But what mastery it takes to press out a Brahms concerto.

To the actor, this catalogue of materials and tools may prove even more useful. Listed here is what most good actors already use plus a few things they might have overlooked. Moreover, there are suggested exercises for improving skills so that they may conjure even more successfully.

What are these seemingly mysterious materials and tools? Most of the bits and pieces of what goes to make up a performance have been known for years. But precisely how they fit together and what goes where has – I believe – not been adequately documented. This is another attempt to recognise, analyse, classify and organise them and make them more accessible.

As so much of the actor's art is learned unconsciously, it should not be too surprising to discover that not every one is able to pinpoint or even explain what it is they do 'intuitively'. The story is told that Olivier gave a particularly stunning performance, then stormed backstage and slammed into his dressing-room. A fellow cast-member timourously peeped in to see the great actor glowering into the mirror. "Larry, you were great!" "I know", shouted Olivier,"I just dont know why!"

I'd like the story to be true. How often has one seen good actors mutilate perfectly sound characterisations in their dogged pursuit of that elusive 'Why'. Perhaps a few clues may be discovered among these pages.

Until recently, the study of acting could be likened somewhat to coming upon a pile of bones, but remaining unsure as to (1) how they all fit together, (2) how to deduce which organs were contained within which parts of the frame, or (3) how or why they all function.

I think that ***Acting and Performing*** is a step closer to providing a coherent anatomy and physiology for the professional actor, each of whom may already possess a treasure trove of dismembered fragments and organs of the actor's art.

At the same time, the book seeks to avoid partisan considerations of which style is better than what, which motivational technique is more legitimate than which and who's our favourite author.

The fundamental orientation would seem to be: given a script and a particular style to present, what tools or procedures may one best employ to deliver the results as conceived by oneself, and/or the author and director. And, having found them, know how to use them.

This follows a basic assumption that whatever the particular field of performing art one may be involved in, the tools of trade are the same. Only the application may vary.

Lest it be assumed that only the professional actor would find this relevant, the book is expected to address techniques which most of us employ in everyday life and work. Sales- business- and sports-people, teachers, therapists, lawyers, preachers and authors may find useful hints. Then, as earlier suggested, there is the art-lover who wishes to peek behind the scenes and know what makes actors tick.

Despite the occasional objection from professionals that 'we are giving away our trade secrets', the book does expose the dynamics of how ordinary people can be, and are, manipulated.

Perhaps it may be said that ***Acting and Performing*** owes as much to the spirit of Machiavelli as to Stanislavski.

This is *not* an academic treatise with balancing arguments about what others think. This is purely my own conclusions arrived at from fifty-five years in the business: brushes with extraordinary directors, famous writers and composers: studying under brilliant teachers: working with heralded actors: and fencing with ever-challenging students who, I believe, taught me the most. To all of them, my gratitude.

This would be the opportunity to also offer thanks to Arnie Goldman who helped edit that 'monstrous tome' to something a trifle more accessible; to Macquarie University's Rod Power for his advice on certain psychological matters; to Dr Carl Radeski for casting the psychiatrist's eye over it; to my final editor, Jean Cooney, who 'broke my pencil'; to my long-time associate Zika Nester; and to my wife Helen who, in addition to typing, re-editing, and translating from American to English, also led a fiendish cabal including my daughter Kati and dear friends who nagged me to risk all.

So, as we are prone to say on opening nights, with crossed fingers clutching a rabbit's foot, 'Well, here goes nothing'.

P.S. Please note: Working problems begin with chapter 5. It would none the less be useful to read the first four (three if you are already a pro). Here reside the overview and premises on which this book is based. Some of the notions are not the customary ones. Also to minimise and forestal sexist censure, most references to he and she, or him and her are interchangeable. I do draw the line at asking agents to send a woperson to audition for Lady Macbeth.

PART 1

THE MATERIALS, TOOLS, TECHNIQUES, RESULTS AND PHILOSOPHIES OF

ACTING

CHAPTER 1

ORIENTATION FOR BEGINNERS

If you are already a working (or out of work) professional actor, you may wish to skip this chapter. This is the warm-up for beginners who had better know the score before they take the plunge.

Approaching the study of acting leading to performing may be done any number of ways. One way is not to study at all. Get yourself a job somehow in the professional performing arts, and try to learn by keeping your eyes and ears open and asking a lot of questions. Just hope that what you pick up is useful, or true. Not everybody will necessarily want to tell you their trade secrets. And even the good actors you will be lucky to encounter will not necessarily be able to explain what makes them good even if they wanted to. And then again, will you know who the truly 'good' actors are?

Traditionally, most actors learned just that way: as an apprentice, learning on the job. The wastage rate used to be enormous. Of the thousands that decided to be actors, most who stuck it out ended up as fair to middling stock or repertory actors. Good enough to make up the numbers in a large cast. Experience gave them authority and facility, but not necessarily skill or top artistry. A few – very few – fought their way to the upper echelons. Those who did were often brilliant. I can't quantify it more than that.

Nor can I really quantify the other and opposite approach to learning: formal training. I can merely testify that:

- There is far less wastage. Voluntary dropouts usually recognise early in the piece that our rat-race is not for them. But voluntary. (I must admit to mistrust of that arbitrary expulsion system where teachers and other experts presume to separate 'the wheat from the chaff'. So often, the 'chaff' sees expulsion as a challenge, and goes on to win Oscars, while some 'wheat' may end up as paste in the victor's scrap-book.)
- There are more younger and better actors around now than ever.
- Even the young ones are on average better artists and crafts-people than the more mature actors of a few generations ago.

What can you learn from schooling?

Firstly, an appreciation of what to look for when you embark on your experience of performing for paying audiences.

Secondly, resourcefulness: knowing that you don't know all the answers but that there are ways of finding out.

Thirdly, a savoir faire about the performing arts that removes that overawed bewildered look you first brought with you to the theatre. Now you acquire a healthy and respectful but slightly irreverent regard for your place of work and your tools of trade.

Fourthly, if the school provides professional-type showcases as part of its training, the beginnings of some applied skills in performing.

Most actors learn from both approaches to varying degrees. But neither approach guarantees any positive assurances of achievement. It is still a very chancy profession. The nearest thing to an equation for success is; the more determined you are, the better your odds. Call it the tortoise and the hare phenomenon. Call it Einstein's "... infinite capacity for taking pains". Call it whatever you like (we will remind you often), but in the long run, it's the stayers who triumph.

You will have to cultivate the proverbial heart of a dove in the hide of a rhinoceros. Because this is a tough profession. Most of the time you can expect to be unemployed. Most auditions you must expect to fail. Most shows are flops. And still you must keep smiling.

This is, to my mind, the toughest and most intricate art form of any. You will be reminded often that learning to handle a musical instrument is a piece of cake in comparison to learning to handle the human instrument.

Look at the scene in *Hamlet* between the prince and Rosencrantz and Guildenstern. The one where the two stooges try to pump him on behalf of the queen.

They have prompted, hinted, invited, cajoled – tried their full bag of tricks to make Hamlet reveal what's seething in his brain.

Finally, Hamlet beckons a musician who had been playing the recorder, takes it from him and says to Guildenstern:

> To withdraw with you: why do you go about trying to recover the wind of me, as if you would drive me into a toil?
>
> *Guild:* O, my lord, if my duty be too bold, my love is too unmannerly.
>
> *Ham:* I do not well understand that. Will you play upon this pipe?
>
> *Guild:* My lord, I cannot.
>
> *Ham:* I pray you.
>
> *Guild:* Believe me, I cannot.
>
> *Ham:* I do beseech you.
>
> *Guild:* I know no touch of it, my lord.
>
> *Ham:* 'Tis as easy as lying; govern these ventages with your finger and thumb, give it breath with your mouth, and it will discourse most eloquent music. Look you, these are the stops.
>
> *Guild:* But these I cannot command to any utterance of harmony; I have not the skill.
>
> *Ham:* Why look you now, how unworthy a thing you would make of me! You would play upon me: you would seem to know my stops: you would pluck out the heart of my mystery: you would sound me from my lowest note to the top of my compass: and there is much music, excellent voice in this little organ: yet cannot you make it speak. 'Sblood, do you think I am easier to be played on than a pipe? Call me what instrument you will, though you can fret me you cannot play upon me.'

And with that he turns his back on them. And just as well. Guildenstern must have been a lousy actor. The fact is, a good well-trained performing actor ***can*** play upon people, from the lowest note to the top of their compass. And the first person he learns to play upon is – himself. But it takes years and years of learning and practice.

At Ensemble Studios we try to make our approach to study a bit easier.

Firstly, we acquire a preliminary overview. The material in this chapter is part of it.

Secondly, we tackle our working materials. Those parts of us we will have to call upon, we will identify and sharpen or strengthen them.

Then we learn to handle them at call. Shape them, mix them, design with them.

Next we apply those skills to actual projects. Scenes, plays and productions of various sorts.

Finally, we start learning how to sell what we have made. The marketing and putting over of the play as a performance for audiences.

There's a lifetime of work here ***if*** you really want to become expert. One will forever strive for perfection, but considering the limits of lifetimes, none of us may get any closer to perfection than 'expert'. Perhaps and rarely, 'genius'.

Actually, that moment when you have full grasp and control of all your faculties, and can arrange them imaginatively, seamlessly, economically, mixing fine and big brush strokes in such a way as to illuminate nature by flashes of lightning, that is when you can call yourself 'expert'. To be called 'genius', that skill must be infinitely greater. Never mind how hard others work or how they fare. Fulfil your own potential to the maximum. There's plenty to do there.

Now have you changed your mind about pursuing the life of an actor? If you haven't, you've just leapt a hurdle in a lifetime of hurdles. If you have – well probably just as well now as later. The prices you have to pay get steeper and steeper as you go. Among other things, you lose the fun of appreciating mediocre theatre. From now on, we are fellow crafts-people with those who perform. From now on we study what they do and how. We are no longer audiences. We are embarking on a study of the sorcery with which to enchant those audiences. We can't have it both ways – yet. Later, perhaps.

The specimens we work on for quite a while – almost a year at the Ensemble Studios – are improvisations. We don't go near written scenes, much less plays, for some time. Improvisations are usually designed to explore specific principles. But at all times they stimulate your imagination. You compose your own scene. Actors – any given number – design a given situation around the topic being studied. You generally do ***not*** decide on who will say what, then who will say or do what etc. Just decide on the merest framework – the situation, time, place, characters perhaps, special conditions, and away you go. Play it all by ear. There is a hint in that last sentence. The best improvisations are achieved when you listen (and watch) the most carefully. Keep your minds ***off yourselves*** generally. Pay fullest attention to the other person. Design conflict and make it a game as to who wins. Read the other person's mind when you are not playing a solo impro. Take in the meaning behind what they say or obviously do.

After some time, when we have acquired at least a nodding acquaintance with some elementary tools of trade, when we have at least a handful of motivational techniques to call upon, we may commence working on scenes.

Later still, full productions with the widest possible spectrum of directors and approaches. Then, acquaintance with a variety of disciplines like TV, club entertainment, film, musicals and from time to time, other more esoteric fields. A few even sample psychodrama. Often, a graduate may find that his first employment is in some sort of Theatre in Education production. Some preparation for this is not wasted.

Other than that, the only hints we should consider about acting training involve discipline – if you plan to meet for rehearsal, be prompt and reliable. Conscientious throughout. Don't waste time, your's or other's. Do have fun, but don't wreck the study or rehearsal sessions.

Really get stuck into your training studies with good working habits. These must pay off in professionalism when you join the ratrace.

Courage, courage, courage – and good luck.

WRITE YOUR OWN NOTES

CHAPTER 2

THE ACTOR

We synthesise. But with what substances? Actors start with components they have in common with everyman. And we all have much in common; usually arms, legs etc. But by the same token, each of us has uniquely distinctive characteristics that makes us different from anybody who has ever lived. Quantitatively similar, qualitatively unique. It makes surgical transplantation unnecessarily difficult. So if we want to impersonate some individual, we will start with what we have in common and then apply *their* differences.

All of which means that the actor must have the skill to recognise those differences, and the further skill to adopt them. Ultimately, having adopted, the actor must *adapt* the characterisation to the requirements of the author, director and other actors. These requirements also include the need to conjure with these results for an audience, a skill that converts an actor into a performer.

It may be fairly asserted that the range of demands on a conscientious performing actor would be greater than those on any other kind of artist. What other artist is at once the raw material and the instrument, the artistic manipulator of these, and the final product able to display every human function? What a load to place on a mere mortal! The violinist has a fiddle and produces music. We have only ourselves from go to whoa. (Or woe?)

A psychologist spends a whole career studying personality traits. A choreographer likewise, learning to design kinetic behaviour. A singer will tell you he can never learn enough about the voice in one lifetime. A salesman strives forever to competently persuade customers. Pity the poor performers who must master all these know-hows plus more in a single lifetime. Oh for fortuitous reincarnation.

What is generally not appreciated is that techniques (another name for 'know-how') that are learned (many instinctual techniques are born with us), need not necessarily be conscious techniques. In fact, most of the best ones have been committed to the unconscious, or even acquired unconsciously. We know how to walk. How many of us can describe the actual process of walking, or what it is we do moment by moment in order to walk? Reasonably the majority of performers (we must get into the habit of distinguishing between acting and performing) learn most of their techniques unwittingly, as if by osmosis. Sometimes we do find ourselves saying "that's a good trick – must try that". But perhaps more often, the things we learn most tenaciously rub off onto us from passing experience. At work, at play, domestically, etc.

But such learning has ever been a hit or miss proposition, and inevitably, bad habits are not only acquired as often as good ones, but they have to be unlearned later. Only recently has the body of knowledge relating to performing (e.g. psychology, sociology, communication, physiology) come together in such a way that all these techniques can be confronted. And only recently, with technologies racing almost out of sight, has it become particularly valuable to acquire a good theoretical grounding prior to experience, so that what could be learned on the job is discriminately absorbed at a much quicker rate. Remember radio actors trying to break into new-born TV?

What is it we can learn? How to handle *Form* and *Content.*

Form – the skillful command of and access to the body and voice. Nothing new there except in a few more up-to-date presumptions which refine the older approaches somewhat.

Content – Many a school asserts that this can *not* be taught. You have it or you don't, they insist. Perhaps it would be more true to say that until recently, the workings of the psyche were so mysterious that one could be excused for agreeing with the above disclaimers. Not any more. Content, for the actor, is all personality functions, and there are techniques for handling them at will.

In preparing our voices and bodies, we seek to cultivate them so that they can be employed readily and economically as required by our profession. Ideally, voice and speech mechanisms should be strong, free, wide-ranging, flexible, devoid of destructive and irritating idiosyncrasies, durable, resonant, with enunciation clear and pleasant. They should be capable of special conditioning such as handling (or eliminating) dialects, singing, microphone techniques and mimicry.

Also, kinetic and postural bodily requirements should include co-ordination, isolation, flexibility, durability, control and easy habituation of mannerisms, again the elimination of potentially damaging or gauche characteristics, strength, gracefulness, balance, authoritative impetus, rhythm and the ability to acquire special skills such as tumbling, acrobatics, fencing, fighting, dancing of many kinds, mime and feats of strength. A more thorough description of form will be found in chapter 42.

Every student or performer is a personality in their own right. And each has unique physical qualities. One should never minimise the aesthetic dynamics of voice and body. In conditioning voice and body, assessments and prescriptions for refining must be made individually. This has to be done *in person.* No book can tell you exactly what's needed for you because no book can see and hear you in order to assess.

We shall assume that each of you is already embarking or has embarked on courses of training that will ensure that, whenever you read an exercise in this book, you will be able to carry it out. Even the chapters on Formalising will have to assume that you have got your basic formal training out of the way. Every acting school worthy of that label must have courses designed to cater to one's physical conditioning. Would that the same could be said of content.

Remember, your work on body and voice as well as your work on content will have to continue *all your professional lifetime.* Basic training, as outlined in this book, is just that. Basic.

Another important observation: *your general good health in mind and body cannot be overstressed!* As your study and work unfold, it will be virtually impossible not to recognise the extraordinary nature of the human organism: what stress can do, how demanding is our work, how extraordinarily we must prepare, and the consequences to our health and careers if we misjudge or overload. Surely, each of us must recognise that any wanton abuse of our bodies and minds could well be regarded as demonstrable insanity!

Form and content work together. One is useless without the other.

Almost as an attempt to redress the balance with formal studies, available almost everywhere, this book emphasises content.

Now, as to the basic prerequisites for the study and application of content:

A constant supply of experience, information, artistic associations, to occupy the conscious and unconscious brain. All learning, all emotional involvements, all fantastic creations will find some usage sometime. Anything from mathematics and the sciences to music and art can be beneficial:

An almost *obsessive* determination to become an actor/performer:

A practical assessment of one's own potential and obligations:

And hopefully, a social commitment to see these formidable skills of acting used in such a way that the world has been left a little better for our efforts.

WRITE YOUR OWN NOTES

CHAPTER 3

SOME DEFINITIONS AND NOTIONS

Acting: I am biased toward Lee Strasberg's definition. Our working premise is: the ability to respond to an imagined stimulus.

Stimulus: Any phenomenon which can alter the state of an organism. Usually a sensory phenomenon, e.g. sound, light, etc. But it must be of a particular intensity. There may be noise, but if it is so quiet that it doesn't effect the hearing apparatus, it won't do anything to or for us.

Imagined: That which is not actually present here and now but which we recall or invent. For the sake of practicality we are lumping memory with imagination.

Respond: To actually change, however subtly.

Ability: Wilful regulation of the transaction. Controlled involvement. That shade of meaning implying mental competence. Psychotics may also respond to stimuli that are not actually there, but they have not invited that delusion or hallucination or fanciful belief. A razor's edge distinction may here exist between the genius actor and the out-of-control psycho.

Those who have assumed that acting needs to be on stage, as a character, with a script or expressing inspired obsessions will find this definition of acting uncomfortable. Fortunately, those assumptions can be covered by other definitions. In a moment.

According to the above definition, vivid day-dreaming could be seen as acting. It well could be. If what you imagine alters your physical or mental or emotional or intuitive state in any way, yes – that is acting. An author may pass through a moment of acting before writing something.

Fancifying about which job to choose, which partner to date, which study to pursue, which clothes to wear, all may be exercises in acting if the vividness of imagination is so keen that you can be turned on as if you were experiencing the real thing.

In other words, acting can be seen as lying to oneself convincingly.

We all have an instinctive mechanism which permits us to speculate before actually venturing. To sample in our minds before we commit ourselves. It is that mechanism which makes it possible for us to act. For that matter, it makes it possible for us to become part of an audience. Or to be moved by a book, or a painting. But more of these later.

Let's return to what we may be talking about when we expect acting to take place only on stage. Let's call that:

Performing: the art of creating illusions with living elements arranged in time – that one essential dimension.

A stage play has width, height, depth and movement (time). A film has height, width and time. Radio is depth and time. Stereo is an attempt to emulate width, depth, height as well as time. But time is the constant. A painting has height and width. But it doesn't give you its elements in time configurations. You can look at one portion of it for hours. Or at the whole thing in a half second.

The human performer (yes, other animals can perform too) contributes relevant bits of himself when needed to make the audience believe that he is a particular person or thing in a particular situation. By arranging these components in a particular way, he can give one illusion. Another arrangement of the same – or additional – components, can produce a totally different one. If a man types something, then goes to the medicine cabinet, shakes out an unseen number of pills, takes them and a moment later holds his stomach and carefully sits in his armchair, he could suggest a suicide. If on the other hand he is seen sitting in his armchair holding his stomach, then carefully goes to the medicine cabinet, takes the pills, then proceeds to type, could he not be suggesting a writer with indigestion?

Performing is illusion-building. But *not everything in a performance need be acting.* Many things are real. You sip a cup of tea on stage. It may be real tea. It may be possible to give a complete and excellent performance without acting even once. A compere (or MC) who happens to like the acts he is introducing may not have to resort to make-believe for a moment, and may give a superb performance. The illusion he creates for the audience is in the choice of superlatives used in introducing the acts.

Characterisation: creating an illusion of a being not actually that of the performer. This is what many people believe to be synonymous with acting. But one can act without characterising. And, surprise, one can characterise *without* acting. By selectively drawing on what one finds happening in real life.

We may decide to get into our best finery to attend a formal banquet. There we act politely and decorously. If an observer happens to catch us at this time, they tend to summarise those impressions and jump to conclusions. That is how we might well be characterised. They would not have had the opportunity to see us at other times when perhaps those conclusions would be tempered by other responses or behaviour.

Many a film is made this way, with the camera or director allowing us to see only those contributory bits and cutting away those when what the performer was doing could give an uncharacteristic impression.

Do we need a script? Not necessarily. Most modern theatre seems to rely on them for performances, as distinct from acting. But even in the profession, much improvisation still takes place. Most early silent films were mainly improvised. But remember, at this point we are examining preconceptions about *acting,* not performing. And as most acting takes place in everyday living or other non-theatrical pursuits, (by salesmen, teachers, flight attendants) the need for a script might be seen as non-essential.

Role playing: If you want a single loud giveaway of amateur acting, look for role-playing. Role playing is a procedure where one continuously reminds oneself of 'who one is'. The 'who' being the character. 'Always remember who you are' echoes in the ears. If you are busy watching yourself, how much attention can you give to anyone or anything else around you? Wherever your attention, is is reflected in your behaviour.

How often do we engage in conversation and detect body-language telltales suggesting that the attention of the person we are talking to has shifted elsewhere? That concern with 'elsewhere' resonates specific responses in that person which are unlike the responses they showed when they were attentive to us. People continuously aware of their identities give off such signals as we are led to believe that they are watching themselves in a mirror or admiring the sounds of their own voices. In a portrayal of such a self-centred character, then that precisely is the sort of preoccupation which will help the performer convey those characteristics.

Another problem with role playing is the tendency to package the character into confined stereotypy. Unlike freer approaches to characterisation where there is greater latitude to mix and match characteristics, it might be overlooked that a wharfie might also read Proust.

Stanislavski mentions a play in which performers represented peasants. To fill out the stage, the director hired some real peasants. Suddenly, the performers looked stagey beside the real peasants. The peasants were taking in their environment, each reacting uniquely according to his own personality: the actors were busy 'being' peasants. A peasant isn't trying to 'be' a peasant. He goes about his peasant-like business, and the observer labels him by his preoccupations (among other things) as an individual peasant. The actors seemed too confined by their stereotypes.

Playing a character (or play, or scene): It is suggested that such a term be reserved for an overall and summary view of the performer's task. It should not be seen as the actual task of the performer at any given moment on stage. Otherwise we are back to role playing. Does a builder build a building? A painter paint a painting? A singer sing a song? Yes – in time. But at any given moment, they would be putting a brick in place, a brush stroke of paint just there, a note or phrase between breaths. And if all these are judiciously conceived and each moment fused subtly with the previous and future moments, lo and behold, at the end of a certain time, a building, a painting, a song.

Living the role: Whoops! That one is tricky. A good naturalistic portrayal will contain living moments strung together to give the illusion that here is a particular person in a particular situation. And there are times – often in short phrases – where the performer identifies so completely with the character that the performer completely takes over on behalf of the character. But it can be dangerous and lead to undiscipline or self indulgence or both. Conversely it can offer moments of inspired artistry. It's chancy.

But when the character completely takes over the artist (total projection), we are usually in troubled waters. It's at times like this when we may witness the emotional disorder of multiple personality. A form of hysteria, *not* schizophrenia. Many a fine actor is reputed to have been so afflicted. Here is Identification gone out of hand.

Stanislavski is purported to have said, "When the actor begins to believe he is the character, it's time to leave the play".

We in the profession are *illusionists.* If one thinks of a good representational painting such as an illusion of a pasture with apple trees, and hills in the background, at no time should it be expected that the artist had to shrink apple trees to the size of his painting and glue them onto the canvas. A painting is a painting. You can't eat the apples.

Good: The concepts of Good and Right we shall go into more fully in a later chapter. For now, consider the premise that when one has precisely achieved what one sets out to execute, that then may be seen as 'good'. In other words, the ability to conform to arbitrary requirements. Even if it is we ourselves who have set down the requirements.

If we wish to cut a piece of timber one metre long and we end up with a piece .9 of a metre, that's not a good cut. .99 is better. One metre precisely is best. It is conceivable that in many circumstances, .99 would be near enough to not worry too many people. A popular acceptance of .99 brings us to that other parameter.

Right: Acceptability. Popularity. People like it, it's right for those people. But it needn't be good. While a show may be 'right' for you, does that necessarily make it a 'good' show? To be good as a show it should conform to certain requirements of good theatre.

This is rather like junk food. Who would say that most junk foods are good? By rules of nutrition, they are usually woefully bad. By rules of convenience they could be considered good (very convenient). But they are popular. One of the fastest growing industries in the western world. When someone needs a quick meal that smells 'good' (fried fats) or tastes 'good' (salt and spices) and fills the gut, there's nothing like them. And they may now satisfy the customers' parameters of what they think they need, so it leaves them feeling 'good'. But nutritionally the product itself need not necessarily be good, and ultimately, the customer's health may end up not so good. But at the moment of consumption, the product may well be 'right' for the customer.

This argument is at the basis of a problem which has concerned artists, connoisseurs and the general public for as long as these have existed. So often we hear 'Good is whatever I like'. Because a second person may hate that very whatever, what will the poor artist do in his pursuit of excellence? Create for the first? Create for the second? Compromise? Go his own way? Because popularity has so often been confused with quality, masterpieces have rotted while kitsch flourished. Painters and musicians of great artistry have died broken-spirited and penniless while mediocrity gloried and prospered. But at least they left behind a tangible creation which could be 'discovered' generations afterwards. Not so the actor. Particularly the stage actor. The moment he creates is the moment his creation dies. Only those immediately present may benefit, if they are discerning.

I think it is important that those for whom the art is designed can be aware of as many facets of that art as is the artist himself. Perhaps not necessarily able to do as the artist can, but to *know* when there is fine artistry afoot. Not so that we should expect to be constantly aware of the wheels turning. But rather to be able to appreciate a work so fine and integrated that those turning wheels do not impose themselves onto our attention. Also, so that when our finest sensibilities tell us that something in that performance is amiss, we can deliberately scrutinise and understand what has actually gone askew. The more judicious we are, the finer the art we must eventually get.

Shakespeare placed a premium on the judicious – *'the one of which outweighs a whole theatre of others'*.

Innovation: How different must something be to fit into our parameters of 'good'? There is a school of thought which says that *Hamlet* is better when played on ice, under water or in the nude. Alan Jay Lerner once said, "Different is not the same as good. To be good can be different enough".

Sympathy: I know what you mean or feel. I sometimes feel that way myself. Feeling *for* somebody, but easy to become detached. A 'right' performance has a good chance of generating this response in audiences.

Empathy: grunting while somebody else is trying to lift the piano. Feeling *with* or *on behalf of* somebody else, and usually deeply involving. A 'good' performance, especially one of detail and subtlety, has an excellent chance of generating this in an audience. My own favourite artists seem to usually be working to achieve empathy.

So how does one work? Or even, why should it be work? Shouldn't it all just come naturally? Intuitively? For some, yes. But hard or easy, there are always *skills* in performing predictably and consistently. This book tries to detail most of them.

In this book, when we use the term 'actor', 'performer', 'acting performers' or 'performing actors', we are talking about the same people. When we use the word 'acting', unless it is obvious that it refers to conjuring within the lively arts and therefore performing, we are most likely referring to acting skills used in everyday life or in non-theatrical pursuits. Like by sales-people, psychotherapists, teachers. Even politicians.

WRITE YOUR OWN NOTES

CHAPTER 4

CONTENT

Jung suggested that there are four psychological functions that we may operate; thinking, feeling, sensing and intuiting.
It is easier to visualise their importance if we arrange them on a cross diagram:

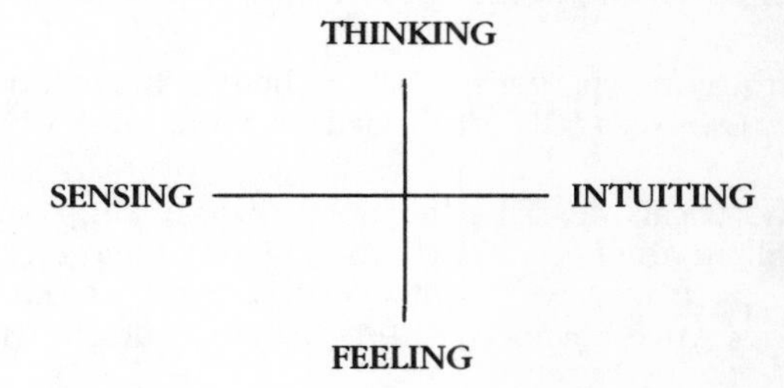

His idea was that each served as a check and balance for the one opposite, and only when all these functions operated freely (or were free to operate) could a person be regarded as a whole individual. If one or two of these, in either pair, were not doing their job, it was being left for the opposite member to work extra hard to make up for the shortfall.

You will notice that the two functions on the horizontal line could be called 'receptors'. They receive information; sensing from what is experienced by the senses, intuiting from our memory banks where information is already stored. Input functions.

The vertical line contains the interpreters or translators of the information received from the others. You could say thinking involves the logical, rational evaluators. Feeling is what we mean when we refer to 'thinking with the heart'.

If all functions are not accessible, as in an engine where three cylinders are doing the work of four, unnecessary and lop-sided wear and tear, which can impair the overall machine – human or mechanical, eventually takes place.

Fortunately, almost all of us have built into us a failsafe protection device sometimes referred to as a 'coping' factor. Its a kind of regulator which helps tide us over sudden stresses by distributing the burdens away from those functions that can't handle them to areas where some help, albeit imperfect, may be found.

The coping factor also makes it possible for us to live safely with a problem. After first assigning stress to a friendly function, it can cunningly either find a cushioned way of coming back to the problem, or at least some way of dispelling built-up steam. In time all functions can return to normal. This we could refer to as one example of 're-creation'. Theatre is one of the most effective of all re-creational devices.

By whatever means, all four functions can be accessed. In everyday life, a person who has managed to 'get it all together' (Jung would have loved that description of Individuation) is generally able to recognise happenings in his environment (sensing) and is pretty insighted in recognising what the hunches are suggesting (intuiting), is able to respond emotionally (feelings), and can weigh up and decide to act in a particular way, or ignore them, or postpone doing anything about them (thinking). Thus we are equipped to face life's problems.

The problem-facing machinery operates on all four functions. This is not to even suggest that all problems become solved. Most don't, but they can be faced. As in the creed of Alcoholics Anonymous – we need serenity to accept the things that cannot be changed, courage to change what can be, and wisdom to know the difference.

Regretfully, many human beings are not 'individuated'. And the way they go through life forcing the stronger bits within themselves to carry the weaker ones until even these may fatigue and give up, often provides us with the stuff of which plays are written and for which audiences gather.

As for instance a jilted girl who thereafter closes the door on her feeling functions altogether. All evaluating from now on will be made by her thinking functions. Such three-cylinder behaviour is asking for trouble. And in the play, she probably finds just that.

Nevertheless, whether one is together or not, the specific manner in which each of us calls on our resources falls into a pattern which describes our character and personality.

In the old days, theatricals described characters quite simplistically. The hero, the heroine, the villain, the town clown, the fallen woman etc. And the ways in which these were portrayed were equally stereotyped. Good cowboys wore white hats. Bad ones wore black. The hero strode manfully, the villain slinked or slithered.

But usually they told the audience 'what' they were rather than 'who', and they did this in broad physicalised symbols. Form was all.

When an actor was chosen to portray a hero, the odds were that;

(1) He could handle all the physical heroic trappings.
(2) That he already looked like the current stereotype.
(3) That he had already brought with him a personality which life had endowed with certain 'heroic' traits.

Item (1) could be changed by training, rehearsing, coaching, but items (2) and (3) were of the 'you have it or you don't' categories.

Thus the enormous dependence on type-casting.

True, costumes and make-up could often amend a few irregularities in (2), but mostly, what they saw was what they cast.

Then we began to understand the portion of characterisation that came from (3). That is, how Jung's four functions arrange themselves uniquely in each person in such a multiplicity of variations that *no two people who ever lived* could be exactly the same in character and personality.

With that came the understanding that a 'hero' did not have to look and behave only one way. That each of us contains personality components which, when called upon and exercised in a particular way, could effectively convey the illusion of a wide range of different kinds of heroes. Not only that, but we discovered balancing features in heroes, as well as in everyone else. The touch of fear behind the bravery. The bit of jealousy behind the magnanimity. The hidden anger behind the patience. One wonders how *Death of a Salesman* might have been staged were it a play in the nineteenth century.

A well trained actor must be able to recognise those personality traits so that they could be copied, evolved, invented, arranged and ultimately made his own in such a way that the audience doesn't see the wheels turning. In order to do this, the actor must first learn to handle his own functions. Not simply to the degree that is required by day-to-day living. Rather to a degree which goes leagues beyond the layman's capacity to handle his own nature.

Nobody would be surprised to hear that a painter's visual perception tends to be much sharper than that of a non-painter; that a musician's hearing tends to be much keener than a non-musician's: that a juggler's sense of spatial relationship, or a tightrope walker's sense of balance must be of a higher degree than others.

Then we should not be surprised to learn that an actor, whose work combines something of all of these demands must also be more sensitive with these related senses as well as all the others.

Then, when we consider how much has to be drawn from our intuitive function, wherein abides not only our spirituality but also our imagination and creativity, there should be no argument as to how much more dependent the actor must be on a rich, ranging and accessible intuition.

As for feeling, who but an actor is paid to turn on the widest and deepest emotional range on cue, at a pre-arranged design and frequency. There are times when the actor may not be required to demand any more of true feelings than a professional mourner or heavy-handed salesman. Then there are other times when only the real things will suffice, and one should have access to and control of virtually every emotional colouring in one's person.

Regretfully some of us are not able to trigger feeling responses even in spontaneous life circumstances. The actor should be a virtuoso in this department.

And thinking! Some would say that an actor thinking could be seen as a contradiction in terms. Perhaps this belief so strongly cherished in and outside the profession has contributed seriously to the delay in discovering and evolving the actor's syntax. To think was to be accused of intellectualising rather than getting on with it and *doing* it. How often have we heard actors proclaim, with mixed pride and contempt "I am an *intuitive* actor".

Admittedly, many an actor who protested that he thought, but only thought that he thought, has given the real thinker a bad name.

The actor must think, to be able to organise his behaviour split second by split second throughout the performance. To design the sequence and substance of those thoughts, the actor must know what he is *DOING* at all times. That is to say, what change he is pursuing at any given moment and what the procedure is to achieve that change. This notion of 'change' we shall explore in great detail shortly.

This purposeful pursuit of change has been found by the finest actors throughout history to be the kingpin of their performance structure. The keystone of the arch. And only recently has this become universally accepted, identified, practised and refined.

And while we all pursue some task virtually every conscious moment of our lives, the ability to design and execute such behaviour to order with discipline and in public often becomes a seemingly insurmountable hurdle to the trainee actor. But when he realises that a character's deeds (remember 'by his labours shall he be known'?) are probably the most telling devices in the entire toolkit, the actor usually applies himself for the several years it may take to acquire competence in handling them.

The deliberate deed, which includes organised thinking, embarking on and regulating deliberate tasks, is one of the hardest of all content skills to refine.

The others tend to be a shade easier.
But all are accessible!
All are developable and refinable!
All are controllable!
And all are mixable with other artistic components just as a melody line can interweave with other melody lines in rhythmic variations and harmonic relationships to give us symphonies where we might previously have only known of a whistled melody and been content with that.

CHAPTER 5

THE SENSES

Most of what we learn comes to us through our senses. And once that information is recorded in the unconscious the sensory impression is indelibly recorded for a lifetime, unless erased by certain kinds of brain damage. When we want to remember some thing, or come up with an idea, or when we have an inspiration, we draw on those bits of information stored in our unconscious. As actors – not to say as human beings – we will frequently need to turn to that sensory memory bank for memories, ideas, and inspiration: and the larger the stockpile, the more we have to draw upon. Older actors sometimes say, "You can't really act until you've *lived*", which is another way of saying that we must accumulate a wealth of experience.

The keener our senses, the more we notice: the more we notice, the greater our experience. But that's not the only reason for acquiring keen senses. When we build a characterisation, more often than not we observe models or prototypes which will help give us at least a starting point. We may even start by imitating someone or something. And the more we notice, the more we can absorb.

There is yet another reason for tuning our senses. Many motivational techniques depend almost entirely on our ability to observe. The simplest example would be the technique called Reality, where we allow ourselves to react to real objects, people, or events. Or Usery, where we also take note of what is actually there on stage, but twist the significance of the experience to suit the needs of the actor/character.

As a bonus, you'll notice how sharpening your senses affects your personal life almost beyond measure. Your new-found ability to appreciate the richness of the world around you will make it impossible for you ever to have an excuse for saying 'I'm bored', as you begin to *see* what up until now you've merely been looking at.

SEEING:

Let's try an experiment in seeing. Without warning, ask a friend to close his or her eyes and then ask them to describe as specifically as possible the visual details of their surroundings:

- what are they sitting on, and what does it look like? What occupies the space around them: objects, shapes, colours, sizes, arrangements?
- the walls or horizon: shapes, colours, relations, proportions, etc. Ask them to describe you (and others in the space): hair colour, eyes, kinds and colours of clothing, etc. How accurate a description can they make of their own clothing?

Now ask them to open their eyes and look around. How much have they omitted? How much have they got wrong? How much do they still fail to notice, even while they are looking? And, conversely, what do they notice that you didn't notice even with your eyes open? When you've finished, move to a different location and have your friend ask the same questions of you.

Chances are that you've taken in only a partial and inaccurate view of what's there before your eyes. Enough to get by with, to stay alive and perform your duties, with a little left over to notice something particularly unusual or striking, but not much of all there is to see. Such seeing may be adequate for most people under ordinary circumstances, but it won't do for an artist like an actor working in a visual and visible medium. It's no accident that some great actors and performers have also been painters, e.g. Barry Humphries, Reg Livermore, Zero Mostel.

Now deliberately select some item or person to observe and, to the count of five seconds or so, take in every visual detail there is to see, including the most trivial. Now snap your eyes shut and recite every item, its shape, colour, placement or arrangement, details of workmanship, size, proportion, highlights and shadows. Then open your eyes and check: how accurate have you been? Then try again: you should do better and better with each observation. Try observing something else, and keep trying. Then shorten your time span: how much can you take in a second or less?

Try to recall your customary environment. See if you can recall details of the front of your home, the street where you live, the store you shop in, the place you work; all those things you always look at but rarely notice. The next time you can view these, check your memory against the facts. How many have you missed out on?

You may want to practise painting and sketching, if for no other reason than to sharpen the visual acuity that every actor needs. But painting and sculpture, however much they may sharpen our visual sense, are static, existing only in the two or three dimensions of space. They freeze the image in a moment of time. Acting includes also the dimension of time. In acting, the moment is continually being replaced by the next moment. The actor, when he records life, does so on the move. Life moves, and so does the actor. To capture what a limping man looks like, a still photograph is not enough. We must observe all the evidence simultaneously and sequentially. It is important not only to note the bias of the body as it puts more weight on the good leg, but how the arms are swinging, the tempo rhythm of the ker-lomp-ker-lomp, the wince as the sore foot touches the ground, the sequence of events as one part of the body leads the movement, the side-to-side movements, the up-and-down bobbing, the swing of the hips in relation to arms, shoulders, and so on.

Most of life is perceptibly kinetic, and the actor – having observed carefully – must somehow reproduce the same kinetic design. Some fortunate people can absorb an impression of several elements in combination, virtually without having to think about it, as if by osmosis. Such people are often the ones who find themselves stuttering when they converse with a stutterer, or gesticulating uncharacteristically when communicating with someone who naturally gesticulates. Such people tend to 'fall in with' a different ambience, different customs and rituals. This is one of the actor's talents.

The word 'talent' here is used to mean what was once called Specific Intelligence: the ability to learn something special quickly.

We are all born with an instinct for mimicry, an instinct which helps us to learn many of the techniques we will need in order to survive socially. Some of us continue to develop this skill, but most are discouraged from practising it beyond a certain age, urged not to be 'copy-cats'. The exercises that follow will help to restore our skills of mimicry and to advance them to an art- form. For some students, already inclined to mimic, these exercises will come easily. Others will find it difficult to absorb and imitate other people's movements. For them it may be helpful to break down the overall moves into smaller parcels of movement.

For a start, let's take walking. How many components are there in walking? First there is the need to balance and remain upright. Second, shifting the balance of our weight to one foot – a side movement. Third, throwing the weight forward – a front and back movement. Fourth, a twisting movement as the body is set into a spin by throwing one leg forward – a rotary movement. Fifth, bobbing up and down as we step out – an up and down movement. Sixth, for each of these, the counterbalancing and compensating movements the body makes to oppose each of these motions.

When we observe this process carefully in people, we can see arms and legs swinging in different degrees and angles, hips swivelling or thrusting forward, and sequences of different parts of the body following in some characteristic kinetic design. A fashion model for instance may initiate a step by moving her hip forward, then her thigh, then her opposite shoulder, then her foot, then her opposite forearm, etc. A boxer may commence his step by tossing his shoulder forward, then his opposite foot, etc. Careful observation will detect each characteristic and the time sequence of each component, and these may be practised in combinations of two or three at a time until the whole sequence can be built up and imitated.

Watch people walk. Imitate their steps, tempo rhythms, stride, balance. What other features are there in their walks? No two people walk alike. Then check your observations: from the way somebody walks try to guess how they wear out their shoes. Do they scuff their heel? toes? swivel on the balls of their feet? hit the ground with the centre of the back of the heel? or side? walk on the outside of their soles? hit more heavily with one foot? If possible, after you've made your guesses, check their shoes to see where and how they have been worn away.

Now watch other physical mannerisms: gestures, posture, sitting, rising, turning, twisting, facial mannerisms. Work them in so that they become second nature; make them yours. In performance, physical mannerisms should be like dialogue: you should *not* have to think of them consciously unless the character is deliberately making a feature of self-consciousness. Selected mannerisms should be rehearsed to the point where they work by themselves.

Notice the difference between this and deliberate thinking when you consciously pursue change.

Then it's time to increase the speed of perception, which is most important for accepting choreography, or to acquire the adaptive nimbleness necessary to what is called 'mercurial acting'. Let's begin with a game for increasing the speed of your kinetic perception and spontaneous adaptation. Try the game of 'Mirror'. This game requires a willing partner, with whom you can take turns. Begin by imagining there is a tall mirror as wide as the room. One of you moves about in front of the mirror, inventing things to do. The other becomes the reflection, mimicking every movement, gesture, expression, etc, *instantly*. The person in front of the mirror should increase the speed and number of gestures and movements without waiting for the reflection to catch up, remembering the rule never to look away or to break eye contact.

You can invent your own perception exercises to sharpen and quicken your static and kinetic visual sense. Remember to open your eyes to both gross and detailed behaviour. Practise borrowing the behaviour of others, and making it your own. Practise also getting rid of borrowed behaviours at command, usually by replacing them with a new set of somebody else's. Don't worry yet about inventing any mannerisms. For the moment, observe and mimic.

HEARING:

Just as we need to learn to see more if we want to be professional performers, we need also to hear more of what's going on around us. As actors we must hear cues, dialogue, sound effects, musical underpinning. And we also hear the audience laugh, squirm, march out, or applaud. And again, many of the motivational techniques rely upon hearing, even distant sounds. In one show I made motivational use of the Town Hall clock in playing a certain scene of foreboding, and the chimes were half a mile away. We hear also dialects, intonations, inflections, and the music which we sing to; and we hear the reverberations in the theatre auditorium, which gives us a clue as to whether the audience can hear us.

One of the ways human beings defend themselves against unbearable assaults on their senses is called psychaesthesia. This is like anaesthesia except that it is an activity of the unconscious mind to turn off sensory stimuli. The ability of the mind to turn off undesirable sounds makes it possible to do homework in front of a blaring TV or radio. And psychaesthesia permits us not only to turn off all sound, but to turn off certain sounds selectively; it is even possible to converse quietly at a table at a disco with background music loud enough to actually deafen. This mechanism makes it easier for us to concentrate on chosen tasks if we are not to be distracted by irrelevant ones. We learn to tune out.

But – perhaps because of our need to defend ourselves against the overload of sensory stimuli in modern urban society – we may have become over-protective in our employment of psychaesthesia, cutting down on our instinctual ability to sense all there is to be experienced. The following exercises are designed to restore some of that sensory ability.

- Begin by sitting still and listening for fifteen seconds or so. How many different types of sounds did you hear? For the moment you need not try to specify which chair you hear creaking, what kind of bird is singing, etc. Call it creaking furniture, people talking, street traffic, birds singing, air conditioner humming, and so on. How many sounds did you hear?
- Now try it again. What about the sound of breathing? Or your own heart pumping? Even in the quietest environment, we discover that there is no such thing as silence except in an anechoic chamber or a vacuum. There is sound within and around us everywhere.
- Now listen for more specific detail. Take the traffic for example: what specific vehicles can we distinguish. Truck? Sedan? Bus? Sports car? How far away? How fast? Travelling in which direction. Some people have been known to refine this exercise to the point where they could guess accurately the make and model of many automobiles.
- Now back to the room. Play a short phrase of unfamiliar music on your record player and then try to whistle or hum the dominant theme. Try again, and see how few times you need to repeat the playback before being able to sing or whistle along. Take longer and longer phrases: some people can listen to a complete popular song just once and will have learned the melody.
- Here's a game to practise in class. Six volunteers come on stage; the rest of the class close their eyes. Each volunteer walks across the room and back, and the observers are told 'this is 1, this is 2,' etc. (In other words, the observers are memorising the sound of footsteps of people by number only.) When each volunteer has walked up and back once, the game begins: at random, one volunteer again goes up and back. The observers, who keep their eyes shut throughout, must guess which number it was. Then another, and then another, for a half-dozen or so crossings. Check the score.

Variations on this exercise include:

(1) Having established the sounds of the six volunteers walking with shoes on, remove the shoes and see if they can be identified barefoot. Or

swapping shoes. There should be enough distinguishing sounds in a person's tread to transcend the difficulties of detection: weight of step, length of stride, irregularity of step, etc.

(2) From the sound only, speculate on the wear sustained by the soles and heels of footwear.

(3) Listen to unfamiliar footsteps and speculate on the sex, weight, height, state of health, etc, of the person you hear. In time you may be able to identify who of your familiar associates is approaching even before you see them. I'll bet your dog can do that.

- Here is another, an audio version of the mirror exercise, called 'Echo Chamber'. One person speaks, the other echoes the sounds as the sounds are being made. Don't wait for complete sentences, phrases, or even words, but mimic the sound as it occurs. Ideally there should not be more than a quarter-second lapse from the sound to the echo, and quicker would be even better. And in echoing, go not simply for the word, but the lilt, pitch, rhythm, tempo, dialect, impediments – whatever is audibly discernible.

Actors frequently dread or resent a director 'giving them a reading' of a line. The director may require a special sound or nuance that he thinks is right for the character. We'll deal later with the general topic of accepting arbitrary direction, but for the moment it's worth recognising that as the skill to mimic is improved, to that extent one's resentment at having a reading imposed is considerably diminished.

More important, acquiring sensory sensitivity enriches our store of usable experiences, as well as helping our abilities to design, construct, and keep check on our characterisations, relationships, and performances.

WRITE YOUR OWN NOTES

CHAPTER 6

SPATIAL RELATIONSHIP

The following statement will come as a surprise to some.

Our bodies perceive through more senses than the traditional five of sight, sound, touch, taste, and smell. We're not talking about extra-sensory perception, for which a case might be made, but about two body-brain functions that are as necessary to our getting along in the world as the ability to see and hear. These are the senses that relate to space and time, our built-in three- dimensional tape-measure and our built-in alarm clock. Let's begin by demonstrating the first and the manner of its operation.

Start by standing on one leg for as long as you comfortably can. Now, standing again on two feet, raise one hand above your head, and begin spinning in place, looking constantly at your elevated hand. When you've done that for as long as you can, stop and once again try to stand on one leg. Can you retain your balance?

Try another. If both your eyes are good, find some narrow upright object, like a pen in a perpendicular pen-holder. Stand a couple of feet away from it and, with both eyes open, hold the hand you normally use most extended to the side of it, and point your index finger straight at it. Then move your hand briskly towards it, stabbing it from the side with the point of your finger. Do this again a number of times, varying the distance between yourself and the object. How many hits can you make out of how many tries? Now close one eye and keep it closed while you move so that the object is nearer or further from you than before. With your eye still closed, repeat the hand-sweeping finger-stabs as before, varying the distance each time. How many successes out of how many tries?

What we have been playing with is our sense of *spatial relationship*. This is the sense that tells us how near or far something is. It also helps distinguish up from down, and whether we are standing, lying, sitting or doing cartwheels. It also helps us to gauge the space between objects, and to some extent which direction other objects are from us. (The sense of direction is something else again, which helps us orient ourselves in relation to the earth. The scientists are still working on that one.)

Our sense of balance is one part of our sense of spatial relationship, and that was what we upset with the first spinning exercise. The receptors for that sense lie in the semi-circular canals of the middle ear, signalling the brain whether we are standing, lying, or turning.

As for gauging distance visually, the receptors are in the retina. When two eyes look at an object, two different pictures are projected onto the retinas, the difference depending on the angular impressions of distance. Objects at a great distance are seen virtually from the same angle, but as an object gets closer we begin to see it from two angles, one on either side. When the object gets within a few inches of our nose, we begin to see a different picture with each eye. The retinal cells send signals to the brain where the 'binocular cells' can interpret even the slightest fraction of an angular change to the picture, thus allowing us to perform such functions as to reach for door-knobs, shake hands, climb and descend stairs, and hop onto a moving bus. This phenomenon of seeing is called *stereoscopy*.

We could *see* perfectly well with one eye, as we could *hear* with one ear. Why two? The answer must be that two are needed to upgrade 'lookers' and 'hearers' to 'range-finders'. If a sound occurs to our right, for instance, it is heard louder and fractionally sooner by the right ear than the left; and (assuming that both ears hear equally well) when we rotate our heads until the noise sounds the same in both ears, we know we're facing the source of the sound. Also, if the sound bounces off walls, the original sound is heard louder and sooner than the echo of the sound; thus, by reading reverberations, the decoder in the brain can calculate not only the direction the sound comes from but also how far away it may be. That's how stereo sound works. With a good set-up one should be able to make out not only how far left or right each instrument is but also how far back or near.

Then there is the phenomenon of being able to locate ourselves within our own space. Even with our eyes closed, most of us can put a cup to our lips, touch our ear, touch both hands together at arm's length, and nonchalantly put our hands in our pockets. This phenomenon is known as *'proprioception'*, and the signals come and go to and from virtually every voluntary muscle in the body.

What has this to do with acting? Everything, particularly every thing to do with performing. Consider the ability to move about a stage: to aim for a chair and sit gracefully; grouping on stage without masking or upstaging other performers; taking stage; finding the light; dynamic spacing, etc. Or in working on TV: hitting the mark; filling the frame; finding the light; matching continuity; covering set areas; etc. All of these rely heavily on our ability to regulate or exploit spatial relationship. Throwing a punch, slapping, doing a fall or acrobatic turn are crucially dependent on one's spatial discipline. So likewise making an entrance or an exit.

On a more subtle level, the actor's eyeline – where he appears to be looking – can make or break a TV or film performance. In close-ups, one usually sees only one actor at a time, presumably looking at their fellow actor; usually such shots have the actor looking just past the camera. Now, if there is some compliant soul – possibly the other actor – standing beside the camera, it is relatively easy for the performing actor to focus plausibly. But what if everyone else has gone home, so that the poor worker in front of the camera has no focal point next to the camera? If he focuses onto some visible object beyond the camera, the intimate close-up will look empty or phoney. Or consider how often, when the lens is being addressed, we see the performer focusing onto and scanning the teleprompter. The TV or film actor should, with practice, be able to focus sharply and cleanly onto an invisible point in empty space if necessary.

When having to look directly into the lens, one trick is to see the reflections as some listener (the camera operator?) behind the lens. Lenses make him appear upside down.

OK, how do we develop this sense of spatial relationship? Here are a few examples of exercises, though no doubt you'll be able to think of many others:

- Locate an object at a distance of about ten metres from you, and calculate how many normal paces will get you to it. Try it, making your steps all the same length. Then try another object, and another, all at different distances from you. How well can you learn to calculate both the distance of the object and the length of your strides?

- Now, using the same objects, make yourself arrive at them in a predetermined number of steps. If, for instance, you covered the first distance in eleven paces, see how you can do it in nine precisely regular steps; keep trying until you can do it in just nine steps of the same length. Then switch and cover that same distance in fifteen steps. Then in a number of other regular longer or shorter steps. Variations of this exercise can be practised as you walk along the street. You see a light pole: how many steps to reach it? Then the next light pole, intersection, fire hydrant, etc: can you make yourself cover the distance in a prescribed number of regular paces?
- More distance gauging: locate two objects fifteen to twenty metres apart and place yourself at what you guess to be the exact mid-point. Mark the point you chose and measure the distances. Keep trying until you are spot on.
- With two other people, form an equilateral triangle. Mark your positions and measure the distance: were you at equal distances from each other? Keep trying, varying the size of the triangles.

Perhaps this would be a good time to describe stage geography. When a director asks you to move in a particular direction to a particular spot, he will usually use jargon such as: *prompt, o.p., up, down, centre, mid, pros, sight-line, up-stage, curtain-line, apron, wings, off, foots, flys, right and left.*

Caution! In the lively arts, right and left are observed from different perspectives. In theatre, these are from the viewpoint of the actor facing the audience. But the film or TV camera-operator will probably think you are stupid if, when you have been asked to move a few inches to the right you move left instead. In TV and film, the orientation is from the camera's point of view, so that camera left is stage right. But both disciplines agree on most of the other terms.

Let's start with *centre stage:* anywhere on stage which is exactly between the right and left sides of the stage. It is an invisible line which goes from the front edge of the stage back to the scenery. *Front* and *centre* is being on that line and closest to the audience. Front is usually referred to as *downstage,* and *back* at the scenery is *upstage, not* backstage, as it may be inaccurately referred to. (Backstage is behind the scenery or anywhere thereabouts, where the audience can't see you. Upstage and downstage come from the oldest traditional Italianate picture-frame stage. This was raked so that the audience could see the actors better.) Those off-stage hiding places on either side of the stage from and to which you make your entrances and exits are called the wings. You can exit into the *wing right* or *left.* But in British stage tradition, left and right may be referred to as *prompt* and *opposite prompt* or *o.p.*, the reason being that the stage manager, whose job included the prompting of forgetful actors, was customarily hiding in the wings stage left.

Two more terms we should know. One labels the actual picture frame. This is a pair of opposing columns on each side of the stage with a beam across the tops of them. This is the proscenium arch, or *pros arch* to its friends. The second word is the *flys* (yes, the spelling is correct). That is the balcony or grid way above the actors' heads and to which scenery can be hoisted out of sight via an intricate conglomeration of ropes, pulleys and counterweights controlled from an area against the wall in the wings, the gallery. By the way, the upstage wall is called the *cyclorama.* Other terms such as borders, legs, spot-bars, towers etc., we leave for you to discover on the job. We have covered enough for the tyro to understand a direction that requests three steps down right, or as Peter Pan, to know that he can fly in thanks to the strong wire dangling from the stronger flys.

Back to spatial exercises.

- Set up two chairs angled toward to an imagined audience. Sit in one, then rise and step toward the other chair with the foot farthest away from the audience (the upstage foot). Taking regular steps, walk to the other chair so that your last step is also on the upstage foot, with your right foot in front of the chair's right front foot, and lower yourself gracefully into the chair. Did you manage to do it on your first attempt? If your pace size was regular and you finished without shuffling around, then your sense of spatial relationship could be pretty good: or you might have been lucky – try it again. If you succeed in that exercise, you will be walking an odd number of steps, without shuffling and fussing with your feet, moving smoothly and authoritatively from chair to chair.

- Try variations on the above exercise. Change the distance by shifting one of the chairs a few feet either way: how quickly can you take in and adapt to the new distance? Try walking around one of the chairs en route to sitting. Walking around both. Working with another actor, both cross from chair to chair, beginning and finishing at the same time. Or try having one of you going straight across while the other goes around one or both of the chairs.
- Another two-actor exercise: two people enter from opposite sides, each stepping off on their upstage foot, and meet shaking hands, poised easily. The trick here is for the actors to end up open to the audience, that is, for both to take their last step on the upstage foot. When you've mastered that, do the same, but have them meet at some pre-arranged point on stage, like a placed chair. Move the chair around and try again. Calculate the distance and guess how many steps it will take to get from here to there: if it looks as if it would take an even number of steps, moderate the length of your steps slightly to arrive at the required odd number.

All this may seem very measured and cerebral, but with practice – that magic word! – it will come to be second nature as your own range-finder functions take over and conscious measuring needs to be called upon less frequently. After all, the practice of covering space in relation to a moving object (the other actor) is not so different from what we do when we gauge crossing a street in traffic or running to catch a ball. If you can learn those techniques, finding your way around a stage in relation to fixed or moving objects should present minimal cause for worry. You can develop your own exercises in dynamic spatial relationships such as: rushing through milling crowds without bumping: slapping and punching – without actual body contact: taking falls painlessly: acrobatics: dancing; tumbling; diving: etc.

Before we leave this subject, let's just look at one more game we play at our school. Blow up some round balloons, perhaps 25cms in diameter. Two actors face each other with a single balloon supported between the right palm of one actor and the left palm of the other, hands open and fingers pointing at the ceiling. One actor takes the initiative and moves the hand, with the other instantly following so as to keep the balloon from dropping. Don't grip the balloon or use so much pressure that you might burst it. The initiating actor moves more and more deceptively, faster and faster, and the other actor must keep up.

Now reverse roles. And when you've learned to do it without dropping the balloon, try it with two, one at each hand. As you become more expert, add another balloon to the forehead, chest, etc. And when you're really expert, play the game without the actual balloons, keeping the space intact as if the balloons were there.

In all of these exercises, and all the others you invent, learn how to use and accommodate space, how to fill the stage with movement. Discover 'your' space, which is as far as the arms can reach around and above, and as far as the legs can leap. Discover also other people's space, and relate to each other at the point of contact between your spaces. And learn how to invade those spaces accurately when called for.

While you're at it, learn to upstage. When two actors converse on stage,each the same distance from the leading edge of the stage *(the foots)* and both are cheating out so that their faces are angled toward the audience while still able to look at each other, each has equal access to the audience and the audience to each actor. In that position, the actors are level. When one actor draws further away from the audience so the other has to swing around to be able to see or converse with him, the down stage actor is denied audience access: he has been upstaged. Usually upstaging is a dirty trick which incurs the wrath of other actors and the director. But there are times when upstaging is right and necessary, as when one actor is to hold forth for a considerable period. At such moments he should be allowed to take stage. So all actors should learn to upstage, and for that matter to downstage by dropping away closer to the audience when the scene requires you to give stage to another actor. Practise both so that you never find yourself doing either inadvertently. If one day you find your fellow performer turning away from you, facing the audience and talking to you over his shoulder, chances are you've been upstaging him. Or if you find him standing between you and the audience (masking), perhaps he is signalling the same message.

On the same topic, learn to work within proscenium sight lines, so that wherever you are on stage you are able to see the entire audience, past the proscenium arch and under the top of the proscenium frame; if you can see them, chances are they can see you. Learn also not to mask or be masked by other actors. Learn to find your position on stage even without furniture or floor marks, by triangulation with fixed objects at the perimeter of the stage; this will help you to find the light, when there is particular lighting designed for you, and you must be precisely where it is focused.

Let's refer briefly to theatre-in-the-round. Several procedures of staging are favoured by different directors for this kind of stage. Some visualise the stage as a giant clock and ask the performers to come towards centre or out to 3 o'clock, etc. Another procedure is to segment the stage into a large checkerboard with each square numbered. My own method has been to number each corner 10, 20, 30, 40 in clockwise order, and the sides of the stage A, B, C, D. I have found this expedient because the Ensemble Theatre had a four-sided stage without a single proper right angle. In that theatre the most advantageous area for a solo speech was not from centre stage but from the most acute corner. And two people holding forth for any length of time would be best aligned diagonally between 10 and 30 or 20 and 40 corners, so that their backs would be to the aisles and everybody in the auditorium could see at least one face.

There is no necessity to think of upstage or downstage feet or gestures in-the-round, as there is no need to cheat out toward the audience at that cumbersome angle. Similarly in film. But in both you must learn to 'hit the mark'. In film (and often in TV), lights, cameras and scenery have been designed to create a particular composition for the camera frame, and you are expected to fit precisely into that visual composition. Chalk toe tracings of your shoes (with you in them) may be drawn and you are expected to position youself into them exactly; usually you'll have to come into those chalk marks from some distant point, and you shouldn't be seen searching for them. The story is told that Spencer Tracy's characteristic delivery of a line after his bowed head straightened up to eyeball his fellow actor was cultivated as a sneaky way of ensuring he had 'hit the mark' before he delivered his words. He made it all look as if he was searching the floor for the right words to use. Unless you want to look like a poor imitation of that fine actor, explore other techniques for finding your spot. As already mentioned, counting steps, triangulation, lining up with the light or camera, semaphored promptings from others out of range, simple distance- gauging. Whatever techniques you use, performing requires you to master space. And who knows, after that you may be ready for levitation.

WRITE YOUR OWN NOTES

CHAPTER 7

GOVERNING THE GOVERNOR – TIME

You'll remember that we said earlier that theatre in all its forms and branches is a time art. The painter arranges images and other ingredients in two dimensions – height and width. The sculptor works in three dimensions, adding depth or thickness. The theatrical performer adds motion to these. That is, the height, width, and depth of the image change according to a time pattern. And that pattern of time can be designed just as carefully as the images in a painting: first the character is seen sitting; on a particular cue, the character rises and walks to the sideboard, taking just so long to get there: then the character, on another cue, picks up a book, and so on.

OK, this raises some problems of definition. You may ask, "Is a mobile a time design, and therefore theatre?" Or, "Is a tableau on stage a static design, and therefore sculpture?" To these questions we may apply the yardstick: has the time exposure of the work been designed by humans to occur at a specific moment of time? When a mobile is hung it is moved by the wind and assumes different forms at different moments: but the artist did not design it to take particular forms at particular moments, leaving it up to wind, gravity, earthquakes, or psychokinetics to determine its shape at any given moment. In that case, it is nature or divinity which decrees the design, and not human agency: it was only in the making of the mobile that art was involved – the art of sculpture. On the other hand, if the mobile is mechanised so that it delivers certain shapes at certain times, it is a theatrical contrivance.

Likewise a tableau which is not designed for timed exposure is a sculpture using human bodies, intended to be looked at ad-lib by spectators in their own time, or re-examined at will. But if the tableau is designed to be exposed for precisely, let's say, forty-five seconds, then it is a theatrical presentation. A frame of movie film has been designed to be seen for about 1/24th (actually 1/48th) of a second, and when it is shown in that way it is theatrical. But the moment you freeze the frame to look at it at your leisure, it is no longer the theatrical art of motion-pictures, but an exercise in static study like a painting, or more precisely a photographic display.

What has this philosophic diversion got to do with acting? This answer too is: everything. For as long as performing has been known, the skillful manipulation of time – timing – has been not only the sign of the experienced performer but the very basis of every theatrical medium. Music, radio, film, TV, stage, circus, even department-store product demonstrations have the manipulation of time at the core of their functions.

And can we train ourselves to handle time, to learn timing? The answer is yes.

This is not the same as asking if we can stop or reverse the clocks. Time goes on inexorably, and what is more, each of us has a built-in circadian clock which determines when we must eat, sleep, recreate, menstruate, reproduce, be born, age, and die. These functions are not set by our wills, though our wills often get into the act as a function of interference.

In fact we live by two clocks. Human beings have decided that the day is precisely 24 hours, that each hour is precisely 60 minutes, and that the basic measuring unit for time is one- sixtieth of that minute, the second. But our circadian clock has a different basic unit, which is not as fixed as the second: perhaps the phases of the moon or even the heartbeat. As we know, this can vary from moment to moment and from person to person. Strangely enough, the averaging of the heartbeat at around 72 beats per minute is pretty universal, and music or drum-beats whose rhythm falls into that 72 beats tend to be universally affective. Yet, in spite of that natural inclination to march to the beat of our own hearts, we have learned to live with and mostly comply with that man-made clock and its relentless second.

When we do a voice-over for a commercial, or sign off on a radio or TV programme, or structure a film montage, when we have to start and finish within one, two, or 74 seconds, the skilled practitioner will do just that. But when we have to time our delivery of a line to coincide with an audience response, our time pattern follows a more flexible clock. If there is a laugh, for instance, we wait it out, and at the exact moment the coast is clear we proceed. If we are creating a laugh, we may plant the impression we want the audience to accept: and at the moment we think they are believing just and only that idea, we come in with the punchline which pulls the rug out from under their standing presumption. That too is timing. Both instances take into account the arbitrary passing of time which we sense needs to be intruded upon, and we pick the most opportune moment to intrude. It's a little like standing on a river bank watching logs drifting by and choosing the right moment to launch our canoe. When? Just as a log is passing? Or between logs? Or selecting the space between the less dangerous logs? That's timing.

Actors have long presumed there was an actual physiological time sense. And physiologists have recently confirmed that there is: a 'time gland' which is part of the hypothalamus. Practice can help us strengthen and sharpen the functioning of that sense.

Begin by tapping out the rhythm of a song. Can you guess the song from its rhythm only? Try tapping out the rhythm at varying speeds: very fast, very slowly. Are the songs still recognisable? Here we have two words which apply to our handling of time: rhythm and speed (or *tempo,* the Italian word for *time*.)

Can you see the difference? Rhythm is how you break up the beats, or design a time pattern with beats of different lengths. They may be measured in regular parcels (like bars in music) or may be unconfined to bars (like a chanted Muslim call to prayer, parcelled irregularly according to the sustained length of breath or phrase). Can you recognise 'short short short long extra-short short' as the rhythmic design of the opening bars of 'God Save The Queen'? Tempo is how quickly or slowly these beats flit by. If a comfortable delivery of a certain number of beats takes two minutes to deliver, that could be called moderate. If you crowd it all into a minute, that's fast: and if you linger over the composition so that they all get delivered over three or four minutes, that's slow.

Now listen to the tempo-rhythm of a six-foot 30-year-old man strolling across the floor. Compare these sounds with a casual walk across the floor by a small dog. (You should divide by two, as most small dogs have twice as many feet as most six-foot 30- year-old men.) Are the beats the same frequency? For a dog to walk casually and for a human to do likewise will produce different footfalls, because each has a different *pace*. Your strolling pace is different from that of a dog, a cockroach or an elephant. And your racing pace is different from their racing paces. Moreover, your racing pace is different from your strolling or your creeping pace.

In other words, pace is relative, not only to the clock, but also to the organism and to the tasks being pursued by those organisms. Think of how often we say that a show is 'slow'. In fact, when we time shows, it is remarkable to discover how often the 'slow' shows finish early and 'fast' shows run overtime. When we talk about 'slow' shows we are really talking about the pace which would have been more relevant to the total 'organism', that is the combination of the performers delivering the goods and the audience on the receiving end.

Let's consider an involving or comic show the audience regards as 'fast' or well-paced, when the stage manager's stopwatch records it as having gone overtime. It is possible that the audience was actually a 'slow' one. The performers, having taken the measure of the audience, slowed down their delivery to the rate of its appreciation. When that audience fully understands the jokes, it tends to laugh longer, and this, plus the slower delivery, extends the running time of the performance. But having been well entertained, the 'slow' audience sees it subjectively as a 'fast' show. As Einstein described the relativity of time, ten seconds spent sitting on a hot stove is a long time, but ten seconds in the arms of a loved one is all too short.

The above exercise can be repeated by trying to beat out the rhythm of some familiar song much faster than it is normally performed. Or far slower. The tempo portion of pace has been varied. Try a song at the appropriate tempo but alter its rhythm. Add a few beats here and there or remove some. Recognisable? Now try beating out the footsteps of various animals but much faster or slower, then accurately. Elephants and cockroaches, for example. When both tempo and rhythm combine in a way which is characteristic for that organism, we can say it is an optimum or characteristic pace.

This applies to different kinds of theatre. The optimum pace for a farce can be different from that of a drama or a thriller. And within each style there is some latitude for different circumstances. Imagine a Hitchcock thriller where the woman walks alone at night along a deserted shadowy street. If she walks slowly it may build tension. If she hurries, there may be more or less, depending on camera angles etc. If on the other hand she runs, it may provoke excitement. But suppose she runs at a pace more characteristic of a cockroach, it can be hilarious. Speeding up the film was one device used by the Keystone Kops to achieve humour. Pace is a contentious subject, but we expect now we know enough to engage in a discussion.

And so to a timing exercise. Listen to a metronome set at 60: each beat is one second. Let the metronome tick on and on, let the beat soak in. Now stop the metronome and, using a stop watch or sweep second hand, try to guess the passing of time. Begin with the second hand at 0, look away, and after what you think is precisely ten seconds say 'now' as you stop the watch. How accurate were you? Try again. (At first you may have to try counting the seconds, mouthing such timing phrases as 'one-chick-a-bid-dee, two ...': if that helps at the outset, feel free to use that device, but in time it will have to go.)

Now try different time periods – 18 seconds, 4 seconds, 26 seconds. You'll get better at this as you learn to relax and let your circadian network help you. And when you've become good at it, try covering distances in a given time. Pick a destination across the room and, at a regular pace, walk to it in precisely 15 seconds. Then 20, then 10. Be strict with yourself, and keep trying. As you improve, try varying the timing: to your destination in 8 seconds, then back again in 13.

Chances are that you're still trying to do it by counting, so let's introduce a bit of sabotage by adding the spatial exercise to the time one. Using a regular pace, cover a set distance in, say, 8 steps in 12 seconds. Now 12 steps in 8 seconds. 10 steps in 13 seconds. 7 steps in 23 seconds. That should interfere with your tendency to count the seconds.

Here's another practical exercise: find an item in a newspaper and read it out loud in 15 seconds, then 10, 18, 24. Read precisely and keep your pace regular at whatever the tempo. If you become expert at this one it could be worth a packet when you audition to do commercials.

Another voice-timing exercise: set the metronome going at a rate between 50 and 100 and begin talking to your partner at *one-syl-lable* to each beat. When you've driven your friend and yourself mad with that one, try one syllable every second beat. And then two syllables per beat. To make it even more interesting, have your fellow actor talk to you at one pace and you reply at another, say one of you at one syllable per beat and the other at one syllable every other beat. Then try walking slowly as you speak quickly, doing both to steady regular beats. You may want to continue using the metronome for this exercise, or you can use your in-built clock. Vary the exercise by walking quickly and speaking slowly.

One last exercise that requires no watch or metronome: talk with someone who is determined not to let you get a word in edgewise. Try to get that word in at the split second they stop for breath. Then keep going until the other person manages to squeeze their word into the slightest opening. The rule is that the non-speaker must remain silent until there is a pause, (any pause, even half a second or less).

Make time a workable tool for performance, so that you can make time seem to speed up, or slow down, or disappear altogether. This is the stuff that theatrical timing is made of.

CHAPTER 8

TOUCH, TASTE, AND SMELL

If our senses of sight and hearing have been underdeveloped through years of dulling and neglect, the three other traditional senses have suffered even more from the strictures and taboos of Western culture. Yet these three – touch, taste, and smell – are capable of subtle development, and are among the most important and useful tools in the actor's workshop.

TOUCH:

This primary sense is both the earliest and the first to be strongly prohibited. As children, how many times did you hear some injunction such as 'You may look, but you mustn't touch.' The customary rationale is that children are not aware of dangers inherent in tactile encounters with hot stoves, sharp knives, and fierce animals. More often, it's a warning against soiling or breaking precious objects, or invading someone's precious privacy.

But the injunction against touching may do more harm than good. Of all the sensory means that the young child has for learning about the world, touch must surely be paramount. Think of the phenomena that this sense can detect. Whereas the eyes can measure only light, the ears only sound, touch can measure many things. Pressure, for instance, and also weight: we can tell how much muscular effort is involved. Temperature, and friction, degrees of dryness and wetness, and with wetness viscosity. Size, as in the span of a hand or both arms outstretched; and with that, shape or contour. Movement, including vibration, not excluding the presence of live electricity. Degrees of pliability or rigidity, and thus also fragility. Texture, which is a combination of some of the above. The sharpness of pointed or edged implements, and the pain that results from abrupt encounters with them or from blunt ones. Hunger and satiation, through internal pressure or irritation: and sexual excitation and satisfaction. In conjunction with our sense of spatial relationship, touch can give us a measure of the balance of an object or ourself. It's a long list, and not a complete one.

For the actor, the taboo against touching must be overcome. The tactile sense must be encouraged to participate with the other senses to recognise clearly and respond fully to the world on and off the stage. A highly developed sense of touch helps the actor to remain alert and vital, and these exercises are designed to be practised and extended throughout your life.

- Begin by becoming more fully conscious of what's always there around you. How warm is it today? How humid? How much warmer or cooler than your hand is that table-top? The glass window? Water from the tap? Our own forehead? Any object within reach? Another person's hand?

- Now textures: feel something you are wearing. Compare it with another item, then another and another. Is it easy to detect differences? Without looking, put your hand in a closet or drawer full of your clothing. Can you recognise the items simply by touch? If this gives you difficulty, memorise certain items you see which are woollen, cotton, synthetic, etc, by how they feel to the touch, then try to identify them again with your eyes closed.
- Here's a group exercise: one person is blindfolded and volunteers numbered 1 to 6 bare their right forearms. By touching only the inner side of the forearm from wrist to elbow, the person memorises the texture of each arm in turn, being told "this is number 1, number 2", and so on. When all six have been scanned, the forearms are proffered again at random, and the person guesses which it is, not being told whether he's right or wrong until all the arms have been checked.
- Make your daily life a conscious general exercise in developing your sense of touch. As you encounter anything up close, put your hand on it and test how rough or smooth, how warm or cool, how regular, what shape, what surface contours, how thick, how heavy, what material, how rigid or resilient, where is the centre of gravity or balancing point. Use not only your skin, but your fingernails to check the smoothness or rigidity of objects. Any time is a good time to practise touch, but shopping affords ideally varied opportunities.
- Here's an exercise that develops fine discrimination in the art of hefting, of guessing weight by hand. One person hands another the same brand of matchboxes containing different numbers of matches, and the guesser places them in order of weight. Begin with a substantial difference in the number (say one with 5 matches, one with 20, one with 30), then bring the numbers of matches together. The guesser must not rattle the boxes, that would be too much assistance from sound.
- A similar exercise uses plastic cups containing varying amounts of water. Blindfolded, arrange them in order of weight. Again, begin with large variations, then work around to tiny ones.

Finally, a tactile exercise that's also a sure relaxation technique will be found in the chapter on Trouble Shooting.

TASTE AND SMELL:

These senses are so intimately related that we'll consider them together. To be precise, much of what we think of as taste depends largely on our sense of smell. The taste detectors reside in the mouth, and these taste buds can detect very little: salt, pepper, vinegar, sugar, alum, caustics, and not much beyond these. What we actually notice in food and drink – apart from textures – is mostly through the olfactory cells in the upper nasal passages. When we have a cold, food becomes 'tasteless', not because the taste buds are affected – we still can recognise sweet, salty, sour, etc – but because the cold swells the nasal and sinus epithelia over the olfactory cells and dampens the activity of their finger-like detectors, called *flagella,* which normally detect such things as the flavour of fried fat, the tang of roast beef, the garlic and oregano in the spaghetti sauce. What we're missing are the smells.

In fact, we may be affected by smells long before we know we're smelling anything. With all our senses, in varying degrees, a stimulus has to be of a certain intensity before we become consciously aware of it. It may be getting through to us on an unconscious level without our ever becoming conscious of it. To go back to sound for a moment, we could find a room so quiet that we think we hear absolutely no noise, but a sensitive recording apparatus would find the place humming with sounds. The sensitive microphones of our ears could be picking up the sounds but not sending the signals all the way to our consciousness. It's as if the information has been passed along to an unconscious substation, which decides not to worry the overworked conscious brain with trivial information. Any sound the ear picks up that you don't consciously hear is called 'subliminal', and is indelibly recorded in the unconscious. City-dwellers who have become subliminally accustomed to tune out the continual rumble of distant traffic sometimes become terrified when experiencing a silent country night because of the sudden absence of the customary 'unheard' subliminal background noise.

The range of subliminal olfactory awareness is even greater than that of sound. It is very likely that smells help to determine a major portion of our decisions in interpersonal relationships. Much of how we affect each other, where we prefer to go, what we choose to do professionally or recreationally is determined by olfactory influences. Much of what we call 'interpersonal chemistry', in real life and on the stage, is literally chemistry: it depends a great deal on how people smell (unconsciously) to each other.

In everyday life, the deliberate re-awakening of our sense of smell serves not only to enrich our conscious and unconscious memories with fresh and interwoven experience, but also helps overcome our tendency to psychaesthesia previously discussed. For the actor, there should be no limit to sensitivity. The ability to exercise a sensitive nose is crucial to motivational techniques (to be discussed in chapter 31) of Sense Memory, Emotion Memory, Aesthetic Stimulation, Usery and others. As we learn to expose ourselves more and more to the world around us, we must learn the skills of selecting and using what we can discover. The following exercises on tastes and smells should provide a pleasant – and lifelong – learning experience.

Let's have a meal, as good a one as we can afford. And let's record all the taste sensations – salt, sweet, sour, bitter, peppery, astringent – and all the flavour sensations – cooked foods, spices, herbs, degrees of doneness. What are the ingredients, the amounts, the methods of preparation? Then check with the chef, if you can find one who is willing to reveal the secrets of the kitchen.

A more accessible test is to arrange a dozen or so small containers, each holding a spoonful of spice or herbs. Smell them with your eyes open, committing each smell to memory. Now with your eyes closed, pick up a container, guess what it is, and open your eyes to check. The same game can be played with perfume, soaps and cosmetics. And a similar exercise can be performed with tasting different teas, beers, wines, soft drinks etc. Sniff the sample, chew it, roll it around on the front and back of your tongue, then spit it out, rinse your mouth well with water, and test the next sample. How many can you memorise and recognise with your eyes closed? Practise identifying all the smells in streets, restaurants, shops, lifts, public buildings, trains, cars etc.

Develop your awareness of the specific aromas of other people. All people have a natural scent, which is added to by the foods we eat, the soaps we use, the environments we work in etc. We sometimes see people reflect hostility on their first encounter, and be unaware they are responding to the faintest off-putting odour. Usually such detections take place subliminally, but a trained smeller might just recognise it. Just as you can learn to identify people by their footsteps or by touching their skin, so you can practise while blindfolded recognising your colleagues by memorising their smells. With a bit of practice, you can even recognise and name the component smells that make up the particular fragrance of each person you encounter.

So if a relationship on stage is somewhat strained, could this sense be contributing?

WRITE YOUR OWN NOTES

CHAPTER 9

FROM REAL TO IMAGINARY

Let's escape from all those real sensory stimuli for a long moment, and simply concern ourselves with feelings and imagination. This way to the plane for Fantasyland!

And as we snap on our seat-belts, we might muse on the wonders we may now experience through the magic of acting. To fly in our imaginations beyond the bounds of reality. To create and visit worlds tailored to our wildest dreams. And among these dreams we might even include a few self-serving ones, such as fame and fortune. And of course the eternal paradox: by leaving reality behind, we may yet find and embrace the ultimate 'Truth'.

And as we dream, our plane has taken off, travelled a bit and now we have landed. But what's this? We seem to be back at the very airport we left! Does this mean we are committed to reality forever? What about our imaginations?

Alas, reality is destined to be the core of most of our work. Even when we work with fantasy. Fantasy – the conscious recall of associations, or the more spontaneous recalls of imagination and creativity – draws mostly on our bank of sensory experiences. Consider: what can we imagine that can affect us? Lying on the hot sand at a beach wafted by a cool breeze? A spider walking across our face? Are these not emotive concepts because the *real things* would be emotive? Is not most of what we imagine based on what we have experienced or heard about?

The point being made is that if a factual encounter affected us, then the memory of that encounter could affect us similarly.

One more point. When real events fall together in fact, they occur as a fixed incident or experience. The way it happens is the way it is. But when our memory or imagination combines events, we can stretch and pull them around, and add or leave out bits as we wish. And the way we interpret that fanciful concoction can affect us as uniquely as would a specific real experience.

And yet another point. The channels of stimulus-response have to be operative for *any* affect to occur. That is to say, we won't appreciate the cooking flavours if our heavy colds have blocked our sense of smell. And if we hold our noses we won't smell garbage, but we won't smell roses either. So one of the best ways of ensuring that those channels are open, and incidentally one of the best ways of exercising to keep them open, is to expose ourselves to real stimuli and permit ourselves to respond freely. Even what we may refer to as artistic creativity depends on stored impressions. As does of course scientific deduction. One key attribute that distinguishes the scientist from the artist is that while the scientist measures all new experience by what he already 'knows', the artist can concoct experiences from all kinds of fragments – logical or otherwise. He measures the new experience against itself. But more of that elsewhere.

So there it is. Fancify as we may, what we imagine will continue to link with real stimuli. While there may be evidence that we may be born imagining some 'things', generally imagination does not work in a vacuum. There should be sensory impressions to draw upon.

There are a variety of ways in which real stimuli are acted upon by the imagination. And to the extent that there are, we have a variety of motivational techniques associated with them. Not wishing to anticipate our detailed study of motivational techniques, let's for the moment simply say that the imagination may draw upon:

1. Reality itself. Real stimuli.
2. Distorted reality. The delusional's device.
3. Remembered reality. Experience recalled in the mind's eye.
4. Synthesised reality. A concoction of stored fragments.
5. Ghosts of realities. Remembered realities brought forward to the present. Vivid 'tangible' memory, e.g. hallucination.

How do we cultivate a more active imagination? Let's start with the real stimuli and work on them with our imaginations. On the Jungian cruciform, our sensory and intuitive functions are on the same line. Thus it would seem that we start our drill by finding something sensory and then getting the intuitive function to participate. Remember, intuition is the pigeon-hole wherein resides imagination, memory, creativity, fantasy, spirituality, instinct and even hunches.

Let us perform a Ghost of Reality exercise. At this point we are using it to help activate our imaginations. Later under Motivational Techniques, we will refer to this as Sensory Projection for tricking out feelings. Let's take a matchbox, an empty film container or some other small simple solid object that could be enclosed in your hand. Sit comfortably at a table, placing the object on it in front of you. Look at it. Notice all its visual attributes. Tap it. Note the sound. Trace it with your fingers. Meanwhile sample the texture and heft its weight and balance.

Now with the hand which wasn't working, take the object off the table and deposit it out of sight. Keep looking at where it was and try to make it re-appear. Trace with your finger where it was. See if you can't recapture the texture on your skin. Hold your finger where you think the top of the object was. Steady ... Now with that other hand, put the object back exactly in place. Did your guessing-finger just reach the top? Did you underestimate or over-estimate its size? Try again. The whole process.

Can you just every now and then catch a glimpse of the ghost of that object when it has been removed? Can you occasionally sense the touch of it on your fingers? Just a bit? Good! Try again. But this time, try to pick up the ghost without crushing it. Or dropping it. Turn it around. Replace the ghost in a different position. Then replace the real object in that same position. Check? By now, some exceptionally endowed talents may actually begin to see and touch the sensory projection. Out there in front of you, your mind is able to create a box, a whatnot. At first in little flashes, in time, more persistently.

Those objects should be able to affect you as if they were real. At the beginning, more so. Because we will also be struck with the wonder of our magic. After a while we settle down, and that stimulus will affect us normally. To the extent that this works for you, you are now responding to the imagined stimulus!

For those who are finding some success with this drill, let's now elaborate on this Sensory Projection game. And here we join forces with Picasso and Dali. Let's pull the ghost around a bit. Let's stretch the box. See it. Touch it. Pick it up. Then let's flatten the box. Then twist it. Expand it. Shrink it. Start with another but large object and a small box. Shrink the large object so that it fits into the expanded – previously small – box.

Examine a whole range of sensory stimuli, and let your imagination play games with them. You may not go so far (unless you want to) as seeing genies spontaneously emerging from imaginary bottles, but you can turn garbage smells into perfume. A band of indigent actors used to congregate in the heatless loft of one on cold New York winter nights. There they would huddle around in a circle, conjuring up a warm Miami beach until they huddled no more.

There will be some no doubt who will decide that all this is madness: it can't be done by sane people. But do not musicians convert bird-calls and traffic noises into music? Painters can angularise curves and vice versa. Or capture several angles of view in one face. What can your imagination do with realities?

Note that we started with real objects and moved into fantasy. We can do it the other way around. But give yourself time with this one. Later we can start with a fantasy, and fill it in with substance. This can be done with pen and pad, paints or with clay. Visualise a picture, figure or design. Now bring it to substantiation by drawing, painting or modelling it. And *practice, practice, practice.*

As a continuing exercise, try to memorise random sensory impressions: bird-calls, traffic noises, visual objects, smells, tactile objects. Then later try to recapture them. At first in your mind. In time *out there in front of you.* Or at your fingertips. Or in the space around you. And don't forget to turn them off when you're through.

But please: this does *not* mean that from now on we must go about relating only to hallucinations! Nor does it mean that *unless* you can hallucinate, you cannot act! No! Essentially, the more completely we can involve ourselves with an imagined stimulus, the easier it is for, the other functions to join in. Just as when we take in real stimuli most thoroughly, we have more to think about, feel about and imagine. Sensory projection can be pretty involving.

When all the functions participate in an encounter, we tend to sparkle. However, many encounters may not require all hands on deck. Often, two or so may suffice. We are free to evaluate a stimulus cerebrally as well as emotionally. (That is an armchair. How do I like it?). Or the stimulus may trigger imaginative associations. (This object is warm; which reminds me. There are some cold children in the other room).

It is probably possible to go through life using only our senses and intellect. (This object feels warm. From its dimensions, colours, weight etc., I deduce it is a heater. Full stop.) Or senses and feeling function. (It feels warm. I like it.) Or intuition and intellect. (Most homes have heaters. I think I know how I can get us into that home so that we can get warm.) Or intuition and feelings. (Most homes have heaters. Wouldn't it be loverly to live in one!)

With all functions freely accessible we can call on them all, or emphasise those more particularly concerned with a given problem. But at least, the tools are at hand to choose from. So, to employ them all, we could say. "This object is warm and obviously a heater. There are some cold children in the next room. Wouldn't it be nice to warm them? Do I bring them in here or take this heater to them?" Once imagination is brought to bear on actualities, there is no limit as to how these actualities can be pulled around or what applications can be found for them.

Picasso has taught us much.

WRITE YOUR OWN NOTES

CHAPTER 10

THE INTUITIVE FUNCTIONS

Let's examine Jung's intuitive functions in detail, all except Spirituality. While it may be an important function, Jung suggested that its origins may be substantially inherited via the Collective Unconscious. Such a topic would be beyond the limitations of this book. We do touch lightly on it however, when we discuss motivational techniques. Also let's postpone the discussion of Instincts until we study feelings.

Firstly, ***memory*** – the conscious recall of impressions linked as they happened. In total or even snippets. But a coherent event. What I had for dinner last night or that joke I heard. We may or may not recall all the details, but those we do recall belong to the actual experience.

Imagination: fragmentary memories, often unfounded in coherent logic, dissociated impressions without necessarily cohesive links. More whimsical, often referred to as wild ideas. For example, during rehearsals an actor might say "Why don't I do this funny bit of business here", although it may be totally irrelevant to the scene. On the other hand, if we like the business, we may think of a way to work it in so it is relevant. And that we can call;

Creativity: the deliberate fusion of imaginative elements in the creation of a deliberate whole.

Inspiration: similar to creativity except the process is unconscious. When we sleep, only the conscious mind dozes off. The unconscious works overtime. So if you had been mulling over a problem at bedtime, it is quite possible for the unconscious to gather fragments from here and there in that immense storehouse of the mind and you awaken with a 'Eureka!' Of course, one needn't be asleep to be inspired. Just as often you may be fully awake. In any event you most likely will not know all the components that came together to provide the answer. Oh yes, later you may think back and speculate about what brought on this brainstorm. Sometimes you may even be accurate.

Intuition: built-in know-how. Ready made answers or habits for most occasions. Much intuition is born with us: the know-how of sucking, grasping, following bright objects don't need to be taught. This would be in the realm of that highly contentious hypothesis: ***Instinct.*** For the moment, let's just define Instinct as in-built drives and techniques.

Then a whole range of know-hows we pick up as we go. These include courteous behaviour, speech patterns, posture and the like. Here we may be innocent about the learning process; so much intuitive know-how is installed unconsciously. The actor 'born in the trunk' may indeed be intuitively expert. But he may have learned by imitation, vague instruction or often by osmosis.

Therein is both a boon and a woe. If you work with a good actor who is that kind of intuitive, and if you ask how he works, it is usually difficult for him to explain. Thus the common demurrer "You can't learn it. You have it or you don't. You're born with it." Was Mozart born fingering the umbilical cord?

There is another way of instilling intuition. By conscious application. The techniques in this book, if adopted, for some time may be expected to be called up consciously. But after considerable usage, they can hopefully become intuitive. Then the only time we seek them consciously may be when we are aware of a malfunction somewhere. It's like driving a car. Learning was deliberate and conscious enough to pass the test, but with experience driving becomes second nature. But if the brakes suddenly fail, you consciously make a decision. Emergency brakes? Brake by shifting gear? Plough into a field?

A more relevant example is the rehearsal process. There someone else's strange words are memorised and staging habituated to the point where you don't need to think of them when performing. They are expected to all fall into place, intuitively.

When habituation has been acquired by use of the intellect, not only has the intuition been ingrained but the intellect is ever ready to guide the intuition during mishaps or wild moments when it might otherwise get out of hand. Then we usually find the intellect available for creativity.

These unconscious elements with which we imagine, create etc.: can we enrich our inventory?

There are four basic considerations:

1. The range of experience we are exposed to.
2. The depth of experience we absorb.
3. The speed with which we absorb experiences.
4. How well we can relate one impression with another. The inter-connection between different parts of the brain. Associations.

Firstly, the range of experience determines the number of impressions we have to draw upon. The more we have the wider the selection of choices.

Secondly, not all impressions are deep. But the deeper one goes, the deeper the results when we call on them. There are all sorts of overtones and resonances that one can't find in a shallow encounter. Later in the Performance section, we will have more to say about this when we discuss Inspired and Genius performances.

Third, the speed with which we register the experience. Mozart had an extraordinary ability to learn quickly. Most of us may have to slog. But courage. Even if it takes us longer to learn, we can still learn. And, ironically, sometimes the slower determined learner can leave behind the more laid-back whiz-kid. Edison referred to his genius as "One tenth inspiration, nine tenths perspiration".

Fourth, the ability to associate ideas. The smooth linkage. Mental agility. Without this faculty, great imagination can seem little more than self-indulgence, or at worst, emotional instability. Schizophrenics, usually devoid of this capability, can be brilliantly imaginative, but not very coherent.

Can anything be done to refine these faculties? Indeed *yes!* You will find that every problem and technique in this book demands the application of intellect and imagination. Attack them diligently.

But beware the knockers. We are too frequently reminded that the good actor is a thinking actor or at best also an intuitive one. That creativity and inspiration are the provinces of playwrights, composers, directors, designers and even publicists. Actors are expected to be thoughtful and craftsman-like, but not creative. One director told me he regards actors as three-year-old children. Hitchcock raised the age to eight.

We disagree! Actors must always be calling on their imaginative resources, inspiration and creativity to try to make sense of some of the requirements of the author or director or both. And to integrate those often arbitrary demands into characters and relationships in such a way that the heavy hand-prints of author and director disappear into the enchantment of the performance.

What more can we do beside practice each chapter technique? We can deliberately go about perceiving more. And with each observation, noticing as many details as possible. Thus we load many more brain-cells at a time. Experience more, read more, study music, go to art galleries, museums, take up hobbies. In other words, live deeply and make the most of every moment.

For retrieving these impressions, play Charades – (sometimes called the Game). Play the Image Game. Practise lateral thinking. Create stories, make puns, tell jokes. Paint. Invent. Study maths, physics. Play improvisations.

Three of these should be described. First, the Image Game. Send a person out of the room. When they are out, conspire to name some recognisable identity, factual or fictional. Say Napoleon. Then the person is recalled. Only the sex is revealed – a male. The questions the person may ask the group, one by one, must be confined to "If he were a — what kind of — would he be?" For example, "If he were a profession, what kind of profession would he be?" The answer should not specify his actual profession such as 'soldier' or 'emperor'. The group member may reply with whatever imaginative simile he chooses. Like 'ruthless' perhaps. Or 'self-employed'. The next person may be asked, "If he were a tree, what kind of tree would he be?" 'A weed-tree' perhaps or 'an oak'. And so on. Any category of image can be explored. Smells, tastes, fruit, weather, clothing. The questioner keeps on until he thinks he knows the answer. He is allowed three guesses. It is remarkable how infrequently the questioner needs more than two tries.

Lateral thinking: an actor's exercise which was used maybe for centuries before it was given legitimacy after being labelled by Edward De Bono. Solve problems by reaching for an outlandish solution. How can a nail-file solve the problem of crossing a swift stream? How can a purse be employed to stop a swimming pool from overflowing?

Actors have engaged in lateral thinking games, such as justifying arbitrary props. A group of, say, three gets together. They are given weird, dissociated props such as a mirror, a matchbox and a railway ticket. Within two minutes or so, they must concoct a scene which makes each of these props essential to the solution. What's more, each one of the actors must prove themselves essential. If the scene can be played just as well without some prop or person, the score is low.

And of course there is no limit to the kinds of improvisations one can engage in. Wild, unplanned, built around a word, a situation, a problem, a costume – the list is infinite. As a stretcher of the imagination, this application should not be confused with Improvisation as a motivational technique. Here, any fanciful exercise will do. There, improvisations are much more disciplined and carefully tailored to the needs of the production or the acting problem.

Imagination exercises are only limited by our imagination.

WRITE YOUR OWN NOTES

CHAPTER 11

EXPEDITING THE LIE

See that girl sitting over there? Careful observation will show us that she is a nurse. How can we tell? Well, certain occupations carry with them certain telltales. For example, you wouldn't expect a concert pianist to have long fingernails.

Now this nurse. What do we observe about her? She wears her hair neatly tied back. She has a clean white blouse open at the neck with long sleeves buttoned at the cuff. She wears red slacks, no socks, flat rubber-soled shoes, a man's wristwatch, little make-up, and carries a largish handbag.

Obviously, tied-back hair is a habit cultivated by nurses because hair is germ-laden. Flat comfortable shoes are necessary for the many hours nurses spend on their feet. The open-necked blouse and red slacks may well be her reaction against the austere uniform-of-trade. And the man's watch is more legible for pulse-counting than a tiny feminine one.

Simple? Except that she's not a nurse, she's a prostitute. Those flat shoes expedite street walking. The open-necked blouse is invitingly decollete. The long sleeves conceal puncture marks of the addict, her reason for selling. And the red slacks are attention-getters. Hair tied back can be easily loosened for more sensual arrangement. And the man's watch was payment in lieu of cash.

And so it is that we can 'prove' that that girl is just as likely to be: a teacher, a concert pianist, a farm girl on a city tour, a social worker, a lawyer, a spy or whatever you say.

Note what we have done. We started with actual observations. We broke the overall picture (a girl sitting there) into particulars.Then we twisted the significance of each particular. And then with a certain amount of unresisting faith, we *believed*.

Ultimately, it all hinges on that last detail. We must believe. No matter how logical or fantastic the concept, it can only turn us on if that final surrendered acceptance of belief is working for us. The rest is intellectualisation – sterile invention or raw imagination. Only when imagination is put to work, organised in an integrated way, does it become creativity.

In the case of acting, the element of belief converts a creative idea into a creative deed. That is, before we can be expected to respond to an imagined stimulus, the imagined stimulus has to be created. Then, when we believe in it, it affects us as if it were the real thing.

Some of us would see that girl sitting there and, being told she was a nurse, would accept it wholly. Why bother demanding proof when the person who told you is known to be truthful? We may accept much on faith, and having accepted, behave proportionately. Others of us don't need to be told We may tell ourselves, and believe ourselves, and respond likewise. If and when we believe gross assumptions (she's a nurse, that man's a mugger, that boy is retarded) acting comes easy. Thus it is that many a fine actor is, either by nature or discipline, gullible. They tend to believe anything.

But there are those who perhaps would *like* to believe anything, but balk at doing so. And there are times when even the gullible draw the line. Then, acting becomes hard.

Here are a couple of hints to help us through the impasses of doubt:

(1) Particularise. Break down the 'anything' in question into small components. It may be easier to digest in small nibbles. Don't seek out particulars which go against your argument. If some undermining item obtrudes but can't be avoided, work harder in twisting its significance to support your side. In time the weight of the number of particulars will tend to swing your convictions.

(2) The magic 'if' of Stanislavski. In modern thinking, this can apply as follows: I know she's not a nurse, but *if* she were, is this not what she would be wearing, carrying, adorning herself like. And her purpose for being here could be likewise reasoned out. 'If' is a lovely can-opener, a thin edge of a wedge, a breaker-through of scepticism to which any of us may fall prey given the appropriate circumstances.

There are other techniques which we'll explore later.

If you are going to be an actor, it is absolutely essential that belief should be cultivated and refined.

Try all of the following exercises: story-telling, improvisation, games where we sell items we don't like, or ideas that we don't approve of. Try introducing people with fictitious histories, compere or M.C. acts with overblown introductions, and actually argue a case in a debate, taking the side you most disapprove of. Tell a chain story, each person taking over from the other and embellishing the tale to the extreme.

Let's accept that the actor must become a master liar. The most thorough – and plausible – lies are those which first have deceived the liar. Fool yourself first, fooling others is then a piece of cake.

What a dangerous weapon we hold, those of us who are professional and accomplished deceivers. Isn't that why we're hired to do commercials? No wonder that from time to time we are co-opted for special purposes like propaganda, or attempts are made to restrict our behaviour. There is no doubt that the adept wielder of such skills should retain a very strict ethical responsibility to society, or otherwise be prepared to accept the consequences. Nuclear weapons are as nothing compared to a well-placed plausible lie.

CHAPTER 12

AUTHORITY

Once when asked for a brief definition of 'artistry', the extraordinary performer Katherine Dunham replied 'authority'. We argued about it, but in the intervening years, that quality has more and more assumed a level of importance in my estimation which almost makes me want to surrender. Not quite, but almost.

The great Katherine, if she were describing her own artistry, could always put her skills where her authority was. When she came on stage with an aura of ... 'OK folks, you can relax now. You're in good hands' ..., she rarely broke her promise. And even if there was a momentary lapse, there was never a diminution of her power and sweep.

We have heard student pianists play with every note and phrase in place. And we have also heard Artur Rubinstein play, with perhaps the occasionally wrong handful of notes. The way he handled these only seemed to affirm the strength and humanity of the man. They never diminished the broad sweep of his intent. Which would you rather hear, the student or Rubinstein?

But there are far too many examples of 'artists' with all the apparent 'authority' under the sun and not a smidgen of substance to back up that front.

What is authority? Simply, it is an attitude which says that you have a working familiarity with the task in hand. It doesn't necessarily promise a successful resolution. And it doesn't usually draw obvious attention to the person's ego. It focuses on the work to be done. And it seems to suggest that whatever can be done will be done expertly.

How might we achieve authority? There are at least three different approaches. One is through having done the job so often that the familiarity reveals itself automatically. Another is having such a grasp of the tools to be used in solving a problem that, although the problem is new, the approach to it is assured. And the last is to inflate the ego of the practitioner to the extent that he successfully deludes himself into identifying with the first two approaches. He may have no working experience with those problems or even the tools, but he feels so 'confident' that those omissions seem not to worry him. This is the case with too many 'artists'.

It might be better if there was less chest-thumping and more of the skill-related authority. I would rather know that the surgeon who operates on me is a master of the scalpel, whatever his bedside manners, school he attended or country of origin. There is a paradoxical twist here. The more objectively one works the greater the acclaim one may attract. This in turn can tend to make the performer more self-congratulatory. Then if that leads them to watch themselves unduly, either their performance deteriorates or they find more cunning techniques for winning the audience's approval. If this succeeds they may then embark on a career of ego-nurturing under a plausible disguise of commitment to the play. And that too may be carried off with authority. But the taint of showing off all too frequently peeps through.

But what of the performer who has command of his tools and still lacks authority? He is probably being undermined by too great a preoccupation with the pitfalls in his working conditions. This self-doubt must be put aside, perhaps rationalised away, overwhelmed with positive proof of skill. Or outweighed by select motivational techniques which divert him from worrying about them: Licence, Usery, Ensemble Effect, and perhaps a dozen or so others. As an actor, you must have the authority that comes from feeling sure of yourself as a worker.

The question arises, how does one portray a character who is not sure of himself, and still retain authority? There is a distinct difference between the unsure character and the unsure performer. The unsure *performer* is doubtful of how he is going to face the audience. The unsure *character* is doubtful of how he is going to face the girl in the play. One tries to conceal his shyness from the audience, the other from the girl. They reveal different kaleidoscopic reactions. Later again please.

The surest way to equip yourself with the ultimate authority is to learn the actual know-how. Both in sound practice and in sound theory. That includes the know-how of selecting the most appropriate Motivational Techniques to help relax and reassure the skilled practitioners. The surest way is not born of an instant nostrum or magic formula. Drugs and hypnosis are seriously illusory panaceas. The ultimate authority comes from knowing how well you know your business. Then your carefully constructed performance will not be damaged by the flying bricks of doubt that can destroy artistry.

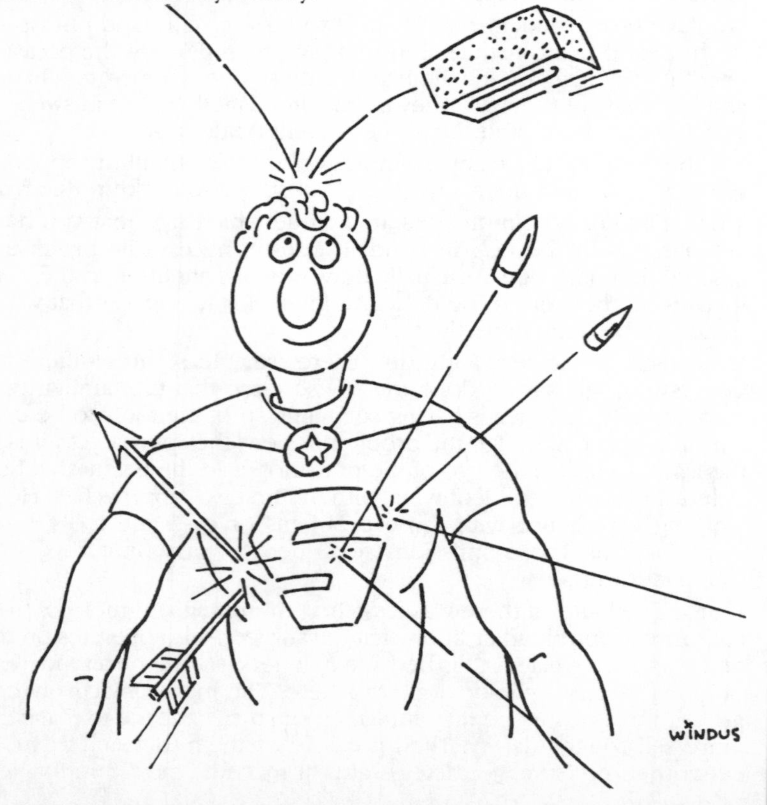

CHAPTER 13

ACTIONS AND ADJUSTMENTS

Chaplin said, "The heart and the mind: what an enigma". But from the way in which he worked, one might be more inclined to suggest, "The heart and the mind: what a partnership". In this section we'll be examining the 'mind' half of that partnership, Jung's 'thinking functions', and in the following section we'll focus on the 'heart', the 'feeling functions'. The actor's feelings are his motivations, *why he does what he does.* What he does thinkingly, his deliberately, consciously, mentally chosen behaviours are his actions. Heart and mind, feeling and deliberate behaviour, constitute a mutually inter-dependent partnership for the actor, but for the sake of clarity we'll keep them separate for the time being.

Some of the things an actor does are not deliberate: things like drinking, swallowing, or the actual process of walking. These activities come under the heading of how our intentions and feelings are involuntarily revealed. We can call these activities 'adjustments', or simply 'form', and we'll deal with them in a moment.

An action, as we define it for the actor, is a willed, planned, conscious undertaking – not automatic or habitual, but chosen by the actor. We are motivated, of course, by our feelings, but what we do about them requires a mental decision. Let's say that someone insults us. We may experience any of a number of feelings: hurt, amused, scornful, crushed, angry. If we are angry, we then face a number of choices: we may decide to do nothing, or to return the insult, or launch a physical attack, or to vent our anger on someone (or something) else, or to demand an apology, etc. In each case we have been motivated by our feeling of anger, and have deliberately chosen to do something about that feeling. The feeling will certainly colour what we do, so that whether we walk away or punch his nose we'll do it 'angrily'. In everyday life we have little choice about the feeling, but we have an enormous number of choices about what to do about it.

An action is a doing, not a being: an activity, not a state. We can usefully name actions by putting them in the form of the infinitive of an active verb: to spit in his eye, to kick my dog, to phone my lawyer. Even 'to do nothing' is a deliberate activity, subtly but significantly different from 'to be angry'. 'To be angry' is a state or condition, a feeling, and thus not an action but a motive for action: the conscious actor is always in action, even if the action is as unobtrusive, as 'to listen' or 'to wait.'

Well, how is an action performed on stage? A successfully composed action has four critically essential components:

(1) A feeling must be in motion. We'll discuss the generation of feelings fully in the section dealing with motivation, but in the meantime it's sufficient to remember that the action must stem from a feeling, and that it's on the

nature and strength of that feeling that an action is launched.

(2) An idea must be organised. Making a conscious decision and working out the details of what should be done may take a split second or five minutes. But ideation must take place, a plan must be formed, before the action can begin to activate.

(3) The action must be impinged onto a chosen object. The object may be another person ('to spit in his eye'), or inanimate ('to slam the door'), or abstract ('to count to ten'), or oneself ('to bite my lip'). The action may require movement or voice or silence or absolute stillness.

(4) The action must have a clearly-specified objective. An action is designed to accomplish a goal: I consult my solicitor *so that* he will give me advice about my traffic fine – the advice is my goal. And once that goal is achieved the action is completed and it is time to stop and move on to another action. A successful performance, whatever else it may require, certainly demands an unbroken sequence of clearly defined actions in pursuit of clearly specified objectives. At times, in a conflict of actions with another person, it becomes clear that he has won (has successfully completed his action, achieved his objective): then too it is time to stop and move on to another action. And that's true also when it becomes obvious that you haven't a hope in hell of winning after serving your best shots; time then to quit and save your energy for other things. But the mere fact that you have confined yourself to that action alone gives you full credit for playing that action.

Let's examine the formation and completion of an action in a bit more detail: take the above example in which I consulted my solicitor. What happened was that I parked my car for 15 minutes in a 2-hour zone, but when I returned there was an overtime infringement parking ticket under my wiper: that's the motivation. I got angry: that's the feeling in motion. I thought, "I read the posted sign accurately, my watch is accurate, the traffic warden is nowhere to be seen, is this a way of creating revenue for the police? Do they think I will quietly accept this? Shall I go along with it or will I fight? What chance have I of redress? Whom can I turn to? Yes, my good solicitor whose speciality it is to put legal abuses in their place": all of that was ideation. I pick up the phone and call him: that's impingement on him, the object of my action, rather than calling the police, the ombudsman, or my big brother to beat up the traffic warden. My solicitor tells me to send him a description of the incident in writing, including place, times, car registration number, etc: that advice is the objective that my action has sought.

Try this. In public, or anywhere you can observe people doing things, quickly put a verb to what it is they are doing. Avoid using the verb 'to be'. That drunk outside the pub is 'provoking a fight'; yes, he is 'being nasty', but you're interested in what he's *doing*, not what he's *being*. Then check through the four points on the list. How does he seem to feel? What seems to be going through his mind. Could it be 'this bloke humiliated me in there' or 'I hate dark-skinned people' or 'I saw him smile at my girl'. Then, 'he looks frail enough for me to take on' and 'Why not out here where everyone can see how macho I am'. What manner of impingement on his chosen victim: words? a push? a punch? And what is his objective, and does he achieve it? Is he trying to frighten his victim, to scare him off, to beat him up, to make him crawl? Everyone alive and awake is at all times performing some action. With practice you can learn to identify those actions more and more precisely.

In everyday life, the sequence of events is usually (1) motivation, (2) action, and (3) form. In theatre, the process is usually reversed: (1) form, as in the script: the words and movements we are expected to deliver; (2) the action, which must be deduced from the words and movements; (3) motivation, or what made the character decide to play that particular action. Given a script where the character goes to the door, opens it, and says to another "Get out!", this deductive process may be quite simple. But where a man says to a stranger, who is a pretty girl, "Got a match?", can we be sure that his action was to facilitate smoking a cigarette? Might it not be to strike up an acquaintance? Or, in a spy-thriller, to proffer the password? Or what?

So here's another exercise in identifying actions. Look at the script of any play, choose a single line of one short sentence, and try to deduce what the action might be. Look at what has gone before and what comes after the line for clues. You will probably come up with a wide choice of possible actions; no matter for now. Take one of the possible actions and work through those four steps. Easy? Don't be surprised if it is not. It takes most actors years of practice before the identification and execution of actions becomes second nature.

One of the difficulties you will discover is how actions tend to run into one another or to overlap. Another is how easily we are distracted from a task and find ourselves playing random actions. The ability to isolate a single bit of wilful behaviour is an acquired skill. Be patient, it will come.

Here's another exercise, a self-observing one. At any moment of the day when it is safe to do so, stop everything and ask, "What am I doing?" Give it an action name. And "What have I just been doing?" Here you not only name an action, but also can try to analyse the entire 4-step process.

Work at becoming aware of behaviour as deeds. Part of the richness of Shakespeare's plays is that he made even inanimate objects *do* things. The moon wasn't simply in the sky, it waxed, it waned, it "lingered my desires like to a step-dame or a dowager". He rarely used any form of the verb 'to be' when an active verb was possible.

Now, as to adjustments. These are all too frequently confused with actions. For one thing, they are not composed of the four- step ingredients of actions. The conscious ideation step is missing. And they may or may not pursue a clear-cut objective. Adjustments, to deviate from my teacher's definition, are anything we do *automatically*. They can be divided roughly into these categories:

(1) ***Mannerisms:*** These would include the way you walk and talk, dialects, limps, twitches, pace, characteristics of age, nationality and occupation, primary and conditioned reflexes, and even coughs and burps. Mostly they are physical manifestations, but sometimes we see specimens of mental adjustments in certain obsessives or compulsives. The automatic tendency to pray whenever under pressure or uninvitedly to price accessories your friend has purchased: these too can be seen as uninvited behaviour.

(2) ***Action adjustments:*** This is usually physical too. The formalisation of deliberate undertakings. The action 'to open the door' involves the legs for walking and the hands for extending, grasping, twisting and pulling. But there's no need to tell the limbs, "Step off with the right foot, balance, now the left ..." They behave automatically in the service of the deliberate deed. They are the means whereby the deeds are carried out, as well as the means whereby the observer can recognise what the deed could presumably be.

(3) ***Feeling adjustments:*** Similarly the physicalisation of the feeling response. Again sometimes invisible. The frown, the smile, the subtle body language of jealousy, mischief, grief – indeed almost every concievable feeling can be detected if one can read the tell-tale adjustments. Even when the adjustment is an automatic internal resonse, like responding to a surge of jealousy by spontaneously covering up with a feeling of glee, certainly the glee can be read. And if one looks closely, one might even detect a touch of grimace behind the smile.

As the design and combination of all these contribute significantly to what makes each of us unique, see the problems in fully characterising a specific person? Ideally we should have to replicate every twitch and squirm. Only the rarest actor can. Fortunately the audiences are prepared to accept enough characteristics to give the actor the benefit of the doubt, so long as there are no obvious foreign characteristics to undermine their belief. Therefore the actor must at least deliver a goodly token of the character's characteristics and be sure to filter out the other kinds. So how do we manage this?

First we must decide what the adjustments are for that character, and which of these we will go for. This can be from observation, imagination or instruction. Then we deliberately go ahead and try to produce these: the limp, the dialect and so on. This may require coaching and much trial-and-error. Finally we rehearse them to the point where they become second nature, as we do the script. This habituation process has driven many a family to the brink as the resident actor practices his gestures, dialect and other bits of homework on his helpless loved ones. Habituation may require much homework.

Then when the bits and pieces are truly automatic, the actor can then go about the business of concentrating on his actions. The adjustments, including dialogue, should fall naturally into place. Would that this were always so; some actors are still memorising words after the show has opened. Ideally, while performing, the actor should not have to concern himself with adjustments unless something goes amiss. Then, fixing the adjustment momentarily becomes an action. It can be seen that any attention paid to the *execution* of adjustments must make it an action. Simply being aware that an adjustment is taking or has taken place is not the same as making it take place. Thus, while we pay attention to working in that adjustment during rehearsals, we are at that time actually playing actions. But during the performance, a deliberate display of adjustments may be seen as self-indulgent, playing at, or at best playing one's adjustments. Like deliberately limping, staggering, vocalising or posing. They can make a performance seem show-offy, contrived or as gauche as an under-rehearsed actor reciting his lines.

Judicious adjustments give a character authenticity and/or plausibility, richness, subtlety and dimensions beyond the obvious. They can be designed as running gags or illuminating comments, like tugging at one's ear while replying to a curly question. They can provide sub-text by physicalising hidden feelings. Like when playing the action 'to reassure', a suppressed feeling might be anger, so the anger can be physicalised by absently crumpling papers from the desk. (How many of us have unwittingly doodled our feelings while on the telephone?) Or revealing supplementary actions, like holding a newspaper up to the face to implement the supplementary action 'to avoid a showdown' while the mainline action could be 'to commiserate' with his wife at having missed out on the shoe-sale. ('Supplementaries' and 'mainlines' reveal themselves in chapter 16).

Without wishing to anticipate the chapter on Formalisation, a word should be said about make-up and costume. While these too help reveal the character physically, the actor should not have to drill them. Perhaps he would be aware of the design of these, but he would not be expected to 'play' his costume or make-up. And yet, he should habituate the mannerisms that go with those. To walk like a precious ballet dancer while wearing the garb of a swash-buckler, or to display full macho behaviour dressed as the lady of the house can be the stuff from which comedy is wrought.

It should be obvious that it requires considerable talent or training or both to achieve the virtuosity of the multi-faceted actor. Fortunately, there are such actors who can testify as to the skill all this requires. All this demands a high degree of control of almost all one's faculties. Body, voice, mind, imagination, feelings, sensations, ... the works. It is not the sign of virtuosity when an actor starts a scene limping on his right foot and a few minutes later is hobbling on his left.

Exercises? Your diligent study of speech, movement, mime, acrobatics, dialects, singing, even karate, plus all exercises suggested in this book, conscientiously practised should give a solid grounding for carrying off fine adjustments. More of this when we dwell on characterisation.

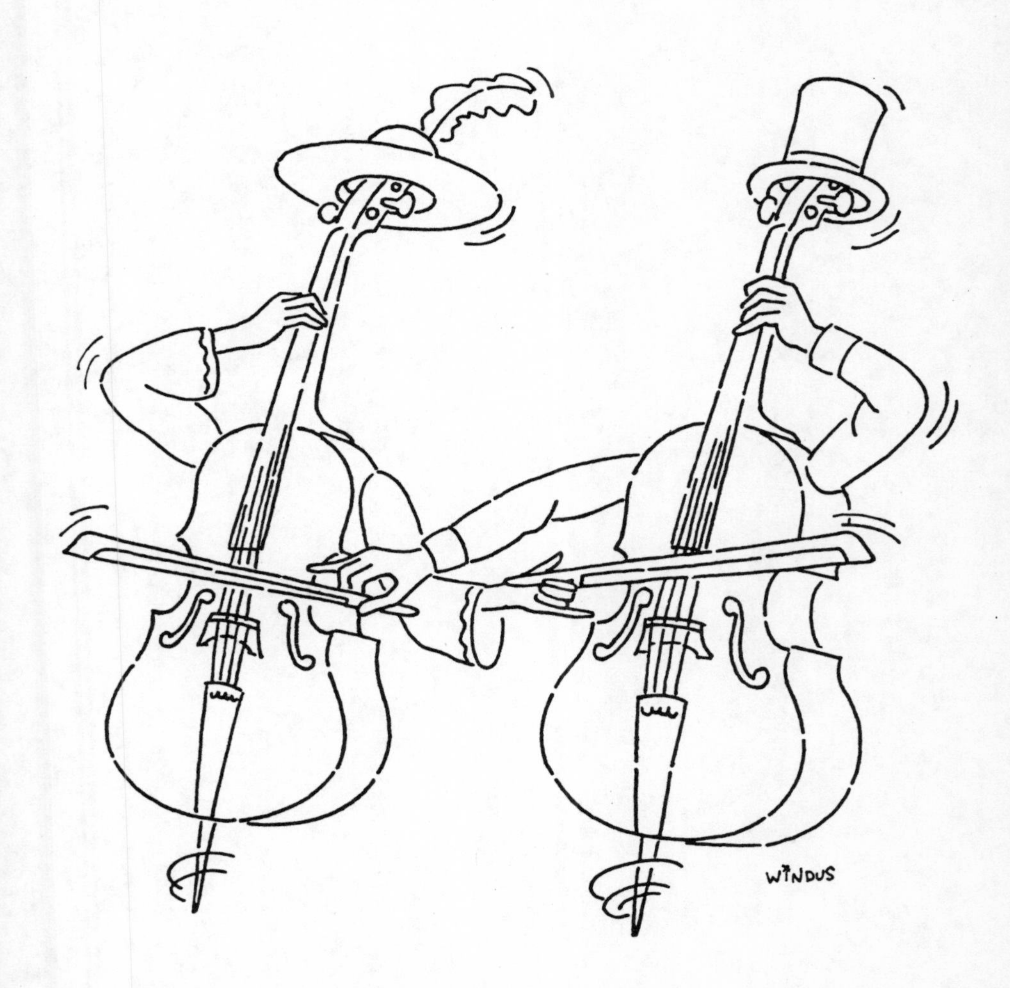

WRITE YOUR OWN NOTES

CHAPTER 14

ACTIONS IN ACTION

We spoke above of a conflict of actions. Let's consider that notion of conflict a bit further. Conflict is central to drama, there is no drama without conflict. One very useful definition of a play is: a staged sequence of events which raises and/or resolves a conflict. (And if we drop the word 'staged', it's also a good definition of most of the events of our lives.) Most theatrical impact depends on conflict.

Not all conflict, in or out of the theatre, is a conflict of one action with another. There may be conflicts of form and of feelings as well as of actions, and there may be various combinations of these conflicts. Take, for instance, two people hurrying to the movies, one tall and long-legged, the other short and stumpy. Although their feelings and their actions may be identical, their hurrying will be fraught with conflict because of the differences in the length of their legs. Here the conflict is formal. Or take a situation in which a person wishes to go to a party which might advance her career (feelings of ambition) but has to consider that the host is a pig (feelings of revulsion). Here the conflict is between feelings.

But most conflict is based on intentions, on actions. I accuse, you defend. I flatter, you minimise. I plan, you sabotage. Conflicting actions may be further emphasised by conflicts of form (the large hulking man *vs.* the small agile woman) and conflicts of feeling (he is blind with rage, she is cool with contempt). But the greatest theatrical impact will come from the conflict of their intentions as expressed in their actions: he lunges at her in an attempt to pulverise her face, she flips him over her shoulder with a deft Judo manoeuvre to dispose of him. Each has played a clean, clear, complete action on the other, the conflict has been played out and resolved, at least temporarily.

Let's try an exercise in conflict of intentions: to sell and to reject. One actor plays one, another the other. The rules are these:

(1) Prepare the given circumstances. Get together and discuss all necessary information relating to the improvisation. What is to be sold? (Let's say it is a chair.) Are we here or elsewhere? Do we work at our own or different jobs? Is the time now or when else? Is this chair as is or an antique or a mystical device from outer space? Why the sale? Work out all the details of the circumstances. But *not* 'I'll say this and you say that, and then I'll say ...' Let the words and gestures happen as the selling and rejecting dictate.

(2) Play only those verbs. No preambles, justifications or deviations. One sells, the other rejects. No mercy: each goes for a predetermined objective.

(3) Particularise the objectives. If the salesman is going to sell that chair, he

should set for himself in advance those words or deeds which would definitely clinch the deal. Try to make the victim say something as specific as 'OK,I'll buy', or 'Yes, I'll take it'. The would-be customer should also have a particular objective that will define when he has won the contest. Like getting the salesman to the point where he says 'I give up,' or is squelched to silence for perhaps 15 seconds. The moment one of these objectives has been achieved, the improvisation stops.

(4) Incorporate as much of the other person's arguments as you can to use against him. In other words, listen and put him to work on your behalf. Don't cut off.

(5) No walking through tables. If you were to open a door on the other side of the room, you'd walk in a straight line to it: but if there were a table in your way you couldn't ignore it, you'd have to walk around it. And once you were past the table you'd resume your trip to the door. Just so, in your undeviating pursuit of your actions to sell and to reject, you'll need to be conscious of obstacles, to deal with them as efficiently as possible – but not to ignore them. And then to return as quickly as possible to the pursuit of your objective.

(6) Don't worry about adjustments. The pursuit of an action (deliberate behaviour) requires a lot of adjustment (spontaneous automatic behaviour). Remember, an action such as to close the door includes walking toward it. Walking in this instance is *not* an action: it is part of the spontaneous automatic process of getting to the door. Raising your hand to the doorknob is not an action either: it is equally automatic. Stick to your action and let the adjustments take care of themselves.

If the scene breaks down prematurely, check out the quartet of action components. Was your behaviour adequately motivated, did you need to pursue this action? Was the ideation reasonable and imaginative enough? Did you concentrate on impinging your action onto an object (in this case the person you were selling to or rejecting), or did you sometimes play to the spectators? And did you pursue your objective, always keeping in mind what you wanted your opponent to do?

On the other hand, if the scene does not break down, you'll know it from these results: first of all, the more clearly matched the energy and purposefulness of the actions, the longer the scene will go on and the hotter the sparks that fly. Second, usually one or the other will win the contest. If you lose cleanly, and if you haven't deviated throughout the exercise, remember you still get full credit for playing your chosen action.

DYNAMIC ACTIONS:

We've said that an action is a deliberate undertaking with a clearly defined objective, and that we know the objective has been achieved when we've brought about a change, generally in the object of the action. Much of the time actions have observable consequences. If our action has been to open the door, we know we've achieved our objective when the door is standing open. When our action is to sell a prospective purchaser the chair, we can see that the action is successful when the prospective purchaser agrees to buy it. Once we see the change we have wrought, we can reasonably stop: no sense in flogging a dead horse – or any horse, for that matter.

Usually the change will be clearly observed in the object of our action. But sometimes the task is trickier, as in the action 'to read the newspaper'. What change do we actually perceive in the newspaper? Even if the newspaper is left crumpled and disorganised, that is no proof that the paper was actually read. Perhaps the answer to this question is suggested by the second example above; the object of the action 'to sell the chair' is not the chair, but the buyer. We might rephrase that action to be, 'to persuade the customer to buy the chair'. However, the real object of the action 'to read the paper' is indeed the paper *but* the change has occurred in us: we are the wiser for having read the news. To put it another way, the object of an action may not be where we look to see the objective: the chair that has been sold may not have under-gone a change, but the buyer's mind will have. A simple way of conceiving it is to add the words 'so that': I sell the chair *so that* the customer will agree to buy. In this case we will check the customer, not the chair.

Think of other possible objectives for the action 'to read the newspaper': we might be reading the words aloud. The verbalised words could be an end in themselves. Once the words are proclaimed or enunciated, the objective would have been arrived at within this meaning of the action. Or yet another meaning might be possible for the action 'to read the newspaper': you might be reading the paper aloud to another person, in which case that person is the object of the action, and the objective is reached when that person signals acknowledgement that the intelligence of the information has registered with them.

In that case, what is a newsreader on TV doing when he reads us the news? The simple answer would seem to be that his action is to inform us. But how can he check us to know if we are informed? Unless there is a talkback hookup, which is unlikely, the best he thinks he can do is 'broadcast': the news is read out loud to be picked up by anybody who may be listening and attentive. The only objective he can check is that the words and inflections are intelligently enunciating the news dispatch. He can't even be sure that the words are going anywhere: the station may be off the air, or nobody has tuned in, or noone may be paying attention. The TV newsreader's situation is the one faced by actors in films, radio, and television when they are playing scenes solo: they usually 'broadcast,' and imagine that there is an audience whose reactions they cannot check. But if, as occurs with the best of such performers, they can vividly visualise the audience's responses, they may be no longer broadcasting but communicating. The lesser-skilled reader may choose the script as the object of the action, with the objective that it be read out loud precisely and intelligently.

One implication of this for the stage actor is that broadcasting is *not* communicating. Communicating implies that the information is shared *with* someone: even a phantom someone. So the exasperated protestation, 'I made it perfectly clear that ...,' usually means merely that they have made a statement which *should* be clear, but may not be. If the object of the intended communication remains confused, that may well be evidence that the statement is not sufficiently clear.

The point of this apparent hair-splitting is that the choice of a particular verb does not restrict us to any single objective. One may choose from a whole range of objectives to be arrived at via the chosen verb. Thus, the verb 'to confront' may seek to achieve in the object a feeling of guilt, or defensiveness, or intimidation, or defiance. Likewise, a particular objective may be arrived at by way of any number of verbs: for instance, the feeling of guilt may be generated in the object by employing the verbs 'to accuse', 'to insinuate', 'to tease', or 'to confront'.

In deciding which verb and which objective, think of the action as a contract binding one of each. Take a simple one: to go shopping for a pair of socks. There we have bound the verb with its objective. But we could just go shopping, in which case we may buy socks, but we may buy dozens of other things along with or instead of socks. There's no limit to the possible objectives. Or we might say that our objective is a pair of socks, but not specify the verb, in which case our action could be to buy or borrow or steal or knit. There's no limit to the kinds of actions by which we achieve an objective. It's important to note, however, that any choice we make will alter our characterisation: stealing socks makes you a thief.

Think of the objective as a goal, and the verb as the chosen way of getting to it.

There is an important difference between the ways we carry out actions in everyday life and in the theatre. In everyday life, the determination with which we play actions tends to undergo random fluctuations. For example, if we are going to reprimand a flat-mate about leaving clothes strewn all over the place, we might set about to pursue the objective that they feel guilty and/or that they resolve to be more neat in future. We may begin with a strong resolution to have it out with them, but we ease off when we notice that they seem bewildered at the onslaught. Then they gather their wits and begin to retaliate, so we come on strong again. Something we say makes them laugh, so we join in the joke and ease off again, until it occurs to us that they were laughing at us. So we come on again, perhaps too strongly, and they start to cry, and we end up apologetic and consoling. Our action 'to reprimand' blew hot and cold and finally petered out.

In the theatrical arts, however, one phrases an action. Where and how we start a moment of behaviour depends on what occurred a moment before, and how it evolved. Since the last moment is a springboard for the next, building each action to a higher point than where we started it helps us to connect actions in an ascending sequence of dynamic phrases, each time building the phrase upward to a possible climax. If we played that flat-mate reprimand scene on stage, it would finish low in dynamics: the next phrase would have to build from nowhere.

So what can we do in theatre to ensure that the next scene begins on something of a plateau? We need to keep up the energy, as we might not do in everyday life. Stage energy, as Bobby Lewis repeatedly reminds us, is not the same as everyday life energy. Just as time is telescoped or stretched on the stage, so are the other dynamics, including drive or energy. How can we play the scene to reprimand our flat-mate and ensure that the energy will be dynamically higher at the end than at the beginning of that scene?

Consider a spaceship headed for the moon. If we think of the enormous energy required to launch the spaceship and bring it up to speed, we know that once the rockets are turned off, the spaceship will go no faster, may even slow down if there is atmospheric friction. But once it gets into the gravitational field of the moon it starts again to accelerate, and even requires strong retro rockets to slow it down and keep it from crashing. In advertising this phenomenon is called 'push motivation' and 'pull motivation'. Hitler knew this well when he activated a whole nation. He exploited a ruined economy (push). Then by providing his people with distinct enemies and scapegoats, he gave them something to zero in on (pull): which, as we know, they did with almost unparalleled ferocity.

We can make use of this homing-in energy in scenes like the one with our flat-mate.If during our ideation we decide that we will only be satisfied that our objective is reached when the flat- mate reveals sufficient remorse by bursting into tears, we will find ourselves actually pursuing that result. We will not be put off by all the blandishments and distractions along the way. We will note them and use them, but all as reinforcement toward those tears of remorse. And as we see signs that we could be succeeding, we zero in for the kill as if it were a game. Which it is. And with the tears, the moment ends on a triumphant high rather than an abashed low.

Of course the characterisation would have to be such as to accommodate such an image of a person. The point is, one chooses whatever objective one thinks is characteristic. And then pursues that objective with full – and ruthless – dynamic energy. In the drive for the finish line we start out strong and we can finish strong or even stronger.

PRODUCT AND BY-PRODUCT:

Sometimes we achieve our objectives by going energetically for them, but sometimes they're achieved in other ways.

Imagine a scene. An actor is driving past a newspaper building when he sees a critic who has always given him bad reviews. As the critic steps off the curb, the actor says to himself, "I may never have such an opportunity again". He presses down on the accelerator and, thud, there beneath the wheels is a dead critic.

Now imagine the scene again, only this time the actor doesn't see the critic. Observing a friend across the street, the actor turns to call out and wave to her when, thud, there beneath the wheels is the unfortunate critic.

And again. This time the actor does see the critic and feels the urge to run him down, but his civilised sense tells him, "If I do him in, all the world will know why. So I'd better not". He steps on the brake pedal, but the brakes fail, and there once again is the critic under the wheels.

And once more, and more cunningly. The actor knows from observation that the critic leaves his office and crosses the street at precisely the same moment every day. The actor makes a detailed study of the route and the timing of the relevant traffic lights, and using his computer determines that if he leaves home at a certain time and travels the route at a certain speed, he will arrive at the point of impact at the precise moment, without having to stop or slow down even once. So he invites his policeman neighbour to ride into town with him, secretly greasing his brakes before departure. As they approach the point of impact, the actor tells his neighbour, "There's so-and-so, the famous critic; wouldn't want to ruffle his feathers." Ostentatiously the actor steps on the brake pedal, but the car keeps going and, thud, there's the dead critic again.

In each of these four scenes, the end result is a dead critic. But only in the first and fourth was the action played 'to kill the critic'. In the second, though the result was a corpse, the action was 'to greet my friend'. And in the third, the action was actually 'to stop the car'. The difference between one and four was that the first was a single bit (or beat) and the latter was a scenic action made up of many bits. All shall be revealed about this distinction in the next chapter.

Although an event may occur as a result of human endeavour, that may not always clearly tell us what the action was that led to it. An event may occur as a by-product. Much that happens in theatre, as in life, is a by-product of an action designed to achieve some other objective. Romeo steps in to prevent Tybalt and Mercutio from fighting, and Tybalt fatally stabs Romeo's friend Mercutio: "I thought all for the best", says Romeo.

Often by-products are better ways of arranging events than direct products of actions. Take the action 'to ignore'. If we were to play that action directly on the ignored, we'd have to focus our attention on him, and a spectator could be forgiven for not understanding that the ignored was being ignored. So we might arrange a by-product process. As the ignored approaches, the ignorer plays the action 'to window-shop'. He involves himself in an examination of the goods on display to the extent that he doesn't notice the victim walking by. The victim is ignored, although the window-shopper does not play the action 'to ignore': and the snub is unmistakably clear to the audience. The ignorer's motivation told him to avoid contact, but the action he chose achieved that result as a by-product. And if that way is more effective, why not?

Now – does all this action-playing sound like manipulation? You're right, it is just that by another name.

WRITE YOUR OWN NOTES

CHAPTERS 15

BIT, SCENIC, AND SPINE ACTIONS

When the Moscow Arts Company first toured the United States, American actors were so impressed by the quality of the performances that they asked their Russian counterparts about the methods of their rehearsal processes. "Ve break de scenes into leetle beats", they heard the Russians say. American rehearsals were transformed overnight, with actors playing – and talking about – 'beats'. Later, interpreters pointed out that what the Russians had been trying to say was 'bits', but the earlier name stuck, and to this day many actors still refer to 'beats'. Or so the story goes.

Both names have their merits. 'Beats' suggests an analogy with music, the rhythmic moment, the play conceived as a complex musical score. 'Bits' is less metaphorically suggestive, but it has the advantage of accuracy: acting was an activity that could be designed and executed a bit at a time. Practically everyone is now aware that that's how almost every film is made, but not many people, including some actors, are aware that stage plays may be constructed in the same way. Although we understand that all other artists – painters, composers, musicians, dancers, architects, sculptors – must concern themselves with individual details and execute a small task at a time, many audiences and even actors still cling to the belief that actors play roles, scenes, whole plays: that the conception and execution of a performance is an holistic concoction conceived in talent and delivered by magic.

Of course, long before the advent of the Moscow Arts Company it was known that productions were planned, that scenes went to make up the overall production, and that bits were designed and rehearsed to make up the scenes. But before the Moscow Arts, these procedures applied chiefly to the physical and formal aspects of the show. Now at last it was possible to give the content of the production similar consideration. Now we could pinpoint precisely the wilful pursuit of a character at any single moment of a performance. Now it was possible to describe the conscious intention and the emotional colouration through a single active verb with an adverb attached.

Thus, Hamlet can 'confront' Rosencrantz and Guildenstern 'mischievously', or (in the "To be or not to be" soliloquy) he can 'consult' the audience 'philosophically'. Once we have decided what the character's determined response to a situation is, all we need do is to distil that response to a simple verb (with the welcome help of Roget's *Thesaurus)* and away we go.

Moment by moment adds up to a scene. Scene by scene adds up to a play. The momentary intent can be referred to as a bit action. The intent of each character in a scene is their 'scenic action.' It is their "What did I come here to do?" Note that it is not their motivation, not "why did I come here?" What does Cassius intend to do in the scene where he waylays Brutus coming from the Forum? It could be to enlist Brutus or to put a flea in his ear: or to sow the seeds of rebellion. The 'why' could be because he is jealous of Caesar; or because he believes that Brutus is manipulable; or both. But let's stick to actions for now. Within that scene, bit by bit, he plays such individual detailed actions as 'to invite', 'to tantalise', 'to insinuate', 'to flatter', 'to appeal to his patriotism', 'to undermine', 'to ally', etc. The sequence of bit actions adds up to the scenic action.

An important implication of what we've just said is that one does not play the scenic action. One *plans* the scenic action, but plays each bit with the scenic action in mind as one of the *reasons* the bit is being played. Cassius invites, tantalises, etc., so that he can carry out his overall scenic intention of making an ally of Brutus. In other words, the scenic action is one of the motivators (or references) for each bit within the scene. But the scenic action itself is not played, unless ones scene is made up of only one bit, like a butler announcing that dinner is served.

A grouping of bits within a scene, constituting a subdivision or mini-scene, may be called an 'event'. This is where some small pursuit takes place, contributing to the scene and made up of a string of bits. For instance, there is a scene in a supermarket. Your scenic action is to shop. Accidentally, your trolley nudges some precariously arranged display, which plays its own action, 'to crash to the floor'. You now engage in a mini-scene (an event) 'to rectify' perhaps. You try to collect the broken glass that used to be a jar of strawberry jam, apologise to the buyer who arrives with a tolerating air, you offer to pay for the damage, make jokes with some commiserating fellow shoppers, and stoically retreat from the scene of carnage to resume gathering groceries. This incident needs to be carried out as thoroughly as any other scene, though it is a small hiccup in the greater scene, 'to shop'.

When a group of scenes culminates in a play, that too may be described as an action, sometimes called the 'through line,' or the 'spine'. It is what we are trying to engage in from the beginning to the end of the play. Every character has a spine action. The play's script has a spine. And the production has a spine, sometimes hopefully the same as the spine of the author's play, although that depends on the director. The objective of the spine of the production answers the question, what are we trying to do to the audience? It could be to leave them with a message like 'crime does not pay', or 'all's well that ends well'. It could be to relax tired businessmen, to promote a riot, or to bring insight to a community. Every play, film, musical, TV show, circus has a spine; it couldn't hang together without one. Sometimes the spine and its objective have the same name. In vaudeville for example, the customary verb could be 'to amuse' or 'to divert'. Here the payoff – the objective – will most likely be that the audience leaves amused/diverted. They'd better: the cardinal rule in vaudeville is, "Thou Shalt Not Bore".

Take a possible spine for the film *Butch Cassidy and the Sundance Kid.* The verb portion could well be 'to make crime and danger seem to be fun'. But the objective could just as well be to prove that crime does not pay.

Let's look at another classic, Ibsen's *An Enemy of the People.* What happens at the end? The doctor who has tried to expose water pollution is mobbed, his house stoned, the community he tried to save has turned against him. How that leaves the audience depends on a number of factors. How was the doctor portrayed: as a deluded fanatic or a brave, balanced, socially dedicated humanitarian? If the latter, we should be sorry, or even incensed, that things turned out that way. Unless of course the audience is one big theatre party of land and industrial developers. Even so, all audiences might still share the thought, "That's what happens to stirrers".

To arrive at such a message, how was the production handled? Was it a cunning display of political wheeling and dealing? Did it seem that the good doctor was angling to rally the locals and march on the offending factories? No, he confronted all the relevant parties with 'the truth,' as though that should be all that was necessary. Perhaps the spine was, 'to let the truth speak for itself': or 'to bring out the truth and all problems will solve themselves'. Of course the ending of the play shows the opposite effect: nonetheless, the process the play pursued was to inspire Quixotic courage and dedication in the audience.

Take any play. Having read it all, consider the ending. How would you say it is likely to leave the audience? Then look to see how this impact can be made from the details within the play. Do they seem to invite disarming the audience? inciting the audience? exciting them? amusing? confronting? shocking? teaching? impressing? What verb could describe the overall process of creating that impression? That then is the name of the spine action.

The actor and the character he plays may – and frequently do – have different spines for the production. The character's spine is presumably what the character believes it is pursuing. The actor may also plan another spine on behalf of the character's unconscious goal, for the actor knows what the character may not know about himself. Thus in a play where the character may be unconsciously drinking himself to death but believes that he is living life to the full, the actor may plan the slow suicide as the sub-textual development: a sub-textual spine action 'to drink himself to death'. But the manifest spine for the character would be: 'to live life to the full'. As might be imagined, the skill of planning and executing textual and subtextual spines is not easily achieved.

A spine cannot be played any more than a scenic action can be played. But whereas one keeps the scenic action in mind while playing a bit action, one need not keep the spine in mind as one plays bits. Playing the spine may be useful in portraying certain characters, particularly those who have long-range visions or aspirations, or those who are so obsessed that they see every moment in their lives as one step toward a life goal. But in most instances, being constantly aware of the spine can lead to traps. So much of theatre is based on surprise, discovery, and adventure. So much is based on encounters where the character suddenly realises that the course they were pursuing did not lead to their truest goal, and we see a change of mind amounting to a conversion. It is all too easy – and prevalent – for the actor to anticipate, to play results before the events actually lead to them. Too frequently we see plays going stale even during rehearsals. Take a situation where a man tries to win a girl, but the play is resolved with someone else marrying her. For the first few rehearsals he pursues her energetically, but after a few run-throughs, repeatedly missing out, a little voice within tells him he's beating his head against the wall, and he begins to work more and more dishearteneddly, anticipating the outcome of the play from the beginning. To avoid this situation, it is better for the actor to focus on the immediate goal at hand, to concentrate on the battle and let the outcome of the war reveal itself in its own good time.

On the other hand, if your character is that of a chess player, the kind who characteristically thinks, 'If I move here he should move there, in which case I will force him to take this piece, in which case I then ...' Then, sure, you will think far ahead as you go. No wonder some chess players may take days for each move.

Since characters do a good many things in the course of a play, how do we identify a spine action? Look at how the play resolves. What happens to your character, and how does the character feel about it? Does the character end up with a mate? Happy with the outcome? Then perhaps the objective of that spine was to get that particular mate. Not happy with the outcome? Then perhaps the spine's objective was to get some other mate, or no mate at all. The rest of the script should add evidence, as to what the verb could be.

RADIAL, LINEAR, AND TACKING ACTIONS:

Let's consider several types of bit actions. Here is a rather common type. Imagine that you've picked up a splinter in your finger, and your objective is 'to remove the splinter'. You try scraping it out with your fingernail, but it remains. So you try to pinch it out, using your fingernails as tweezers, without success. Then you try to bite it out, but that doesn't work. Metal tweezers, nope. A strong magnet, in case it is steel. A needle to dig it out. None of these works. Then you dab antiseptic on it and cut it out with a razor blade; success at last.

Many of our actions in life and in the theatre are of that kind. We face a problem and attempt to solve it. When one approach doesn't work we try another and then another until we find a solution. Any one of those approaches might have succeeded, and we believed each time that success was only a step away. When we found that it wasn't, we approached it from a different angle, and then another angle, each approach converging on the problem from a different point on the radius of the situation. We can refer to this design of a scene as a radial (or catch bucket) action. In an action movie car chase, for instance, at any moment, with any corner turned, escape or capture is possible, the objective could be achieved with a single stroke: the dramatic excitement of such a scene is a result of each bit's not quite working – the escaper's turns don't shake off the pursuer, the pursuer's ploys don't cut off the escaper. Not until the final, climactic moment, which might have come at any point.

Radial actions are useful in improvised scenes, where almost anything goes to achieve an objective that is always potentially only one step away. Not knowing in advance which way one will have to proceed, the actors have to keep on their toes all the time. Thus they can count on a high degree of spontaneity. The problem with such an approach comes when the first attempt does the trick: one actor tries to sell the chair, and the other immediately says 'Yes, I'll buy it'. Faced with instant success, the actor must either end the scene, or go for more success of a slightly different kind: perhaps reconsider the price and/or suddenly demand an import charge, tax, or some unexpected commission.

Most scenic actions, however, are more systematically organised. In these scenes each step sets the stage for the next one until finally the scenic objective is reached: in other words, reaching step number 4 depends on step number 3 which in turn needs step number 2 to be taken. There are two procedures available for playing these systematic sequences of actions.

The first is quite straightforward, like climbing the rungs of a ladder or claiming a parcel at the post office. At the post office, first you queue up at the parcels window to await your turn. Then you present the card that notified of the parcel's arrival. Then you sign for it. Then you collect it. There's no mystery about what you were there for: neither you nor the post master acted as if there were any devious purpose. Still, the objective could not be achieved by leaving out any of the steps. (Yes, you could have jumped the queue or snatched the parcel and run, but there would have been a ruckus: better to take each step as it comes.)

This kind of scene may be called a 'linear' scene, and every bit in it is a linear bit. There are no real surprises in such a scene, though each bit has to be played completely and thoroughly. The apparent ease of such a scene is a trap for the unwary actor. The actor, having read the script, knows that the scene will be played through without a hitch, but the character is usually not endowed with such hindsight (or foresight).

When the character gets into the queue, does he know who will be there, how long it may take, how hot or fly-infested or smelly the post office will be? Will they close for lunch before he gets to the counter? And when he is asked to sign, is that really his consignment or is it for somebody with a similar name?

Does he have adequate identification? What if the contents are embarrassing and the postmaster insists on the parcel being publicly opened? What if it contains a bomb? To watch a real person – or a fully realised character – in such a situation is to observe a multiplicity of reactions, all of which contribute to make the experience plausible.

What most actors find themselves doing in such a scene is anticipating the wrong expectations. That is, they anticipate what they know happens to the character according to the script because they have read it, rehearsed it, and played it. When one anticipates what actually happens in a play, the scene becomes stale.

One of the best antidotes to staleness *is* anticipation, but anticipation of another sort. Take a situation where you have to cheerfully open the closet door and a corpse falls out. The first few times at rehearsal, the startle reaction is powerful, but after a while you may actually find yourself moving aside to let the body fall past you even before you open the door. The cure is to try believing, say, that a special Christmas present for you has been hidden on the closet shelf: if you are sneakily anticipating the discovery of your present, the falling body will catch you by surprise every time.

Another important practice in making linear scenes fresh, energetic, and involving is to achieve each bit's objective as fully as possible before moving onto the next bit. Every objective firmly established is a firm foothold from which to step to the next. Make each step authoritative and definite: a well scored objective will build your confidence for proceeding toward the next.

The second procedure for playing a planned sequence of actions is more devious, and is less prone to the trap of staleness. This pattern is in answer to an assumption of difficulty from the start, as if you were trying to sail a boat to a point directly upwind from you. Since no boat can sail directly into the wind, as every sailor knows, it is necessary to sail a planned zig-zag course at an angle to the wind, until the goal has been reached. This manoeuvre is known in nautical circles as 'tacking,' and we've appropriated the term for those actions where we must move in oblique ways to achieve our objective.

Imagine that you want to borrow fifty dollars from an acquaintance. You should be able to accomplish your objective in a single bit action: when you see him, you simply say, 'Lend me fifty dollars until payday'. If he is friendly and has the money, that should do it. But if you know that although he has the money, he is not so friendly, because you have never repaid the $100 you borrowed from him some months ago. Getting a quick and easy loan from him would be like sailing directly into the wind. So you devise a plan that will make it difficult for him to refuse, by not showing your hand until the last moment. First you play the action to gain admission to his home: you ring the doorbell,wait for him to answer, and step in when he invites you in as he is bound to, (especially if you sidle in as soon as he opens the door). Secondly you pass the time of day, to put him at his ease. Third you get the lay of the land: how's his business going? family all well? no large hospital bills or other conspicuous debts? Fourth you win his sympathy, with a tale of how your spouse is on the verge of blindness for want of new spectacles. Fifth you come in for the kill with sincere promises of repayment of new and old debts and vows of gratitude in anticipation.

None of the first four bits were aimed directly at borrowing. Each could have been heading in any of a number of directions. But what you were doing with each bit was tacking, moving diagonally closer at each step to your ultimate objective. Each bit was a tacking bit, and the scene itself a tacking scene. This device is common where characters must conceal their real pursuits, as in whodunits, soaps, farces: in fact it is hard to think of any play where some tacking does not take place.

Skill in playing tacking actions lies in the ability to imply a decoy direction, to make others think that each bit is leading somewhere other than where it is actually going, to misdirect them. But such misdirection should remain ambiguous. After the final bit, the observer should think, "I thought you were leading up to somewhere else, but now that I look back on it, you could have been heading in this direction just as well". A variation of this technique is the 'double-entendre' or double meaning, except that with the double-entendre we do want the observer or the object to instantly recognise there are two possible ways of taking the action. In the lyrics to Rodgers and Hart's ***"Bewitched, Bothered,*** and ***Bewildered"*** from ***'Pal Joey',*** the middle-aged Vera has taken young, despicable, but virile Joey as a lover. She scornfully refers to him as "a laugh" but confesses that "I love it, because the laugh's on me". There's no need for her to spell out the two meanings of the phrase.

ASIDES, BACKTRACKS, AND TRANSITIONS:

Sometimes a script – or the events of our lives – requires us to depart temporarily from the pursuit of our objective. Such momentary departures from the mainline scenic action are called 'asides', and they come in a variety of forms and serve a variety of purposes. An aside may provide a chorus-like comment, explaining background and bias to the audience. It may reveal traits of personality, like a villain winking at the audience over someone's desperation. A string of asides may serve to reveal the sub-text.

Asides may be performed in character or out. They may be verbal or gestural. They are usually short, but some long and complex soliloquies like Hamlet's "Oh what a rogue and peasant slave am I ...", are asides. Aside actions may be played on any object: yourself, another person, an animal, an inanimate object, an abstraction, the audience or some part of it, even the same character you were just talking to in the mainline action. The aside may take us anywhere *except* in the direction of the mainline action: if the aside were removed, the scene should still be able to continue smoothly. And the aside should be consistent with the style of the presentation: a single aside in a full play may be out of place, while a pattern or string of asides may look as if they are part of the style. While the aside is being played, others on the stage may do any of a number of things: keep going about their business, freeze in time and space, leave the stage or be blacked out, or conduct their own asides simultaneously or in conjunction with yours, depending on the style of the production.

An aside is an action, and it has all the usual action components, including clear-cut and cleanly-pursued objectives. It should be smoothly executed, with no fumbling, no marking time, no wasteful filling-in. It should start almost as if it were still the mainline, and the end of the aside should smoothly and unerringly return to the mainline without a pause. No repeating the word you left behind before going aside, no 'where was I?' The trick with aside actions is to think ahead: even as you recognise the need for switching, don't interrupt yourself until you round off the current thought, then without missing a beat make a smooth transition into the change, both going into the aside and returning to the mainline action.

The most common failing in the execution of the aside is the reluctance of the performer to follow through to the aside's objective. If we veer off from the mainline to appeal to heaven, let's give heaven the opportunity to return some sign that it has heard, not hit and run. Another major weakness is in the tendency some actors have of putting asides into scenes where they have no business. Such actors may suffer from one or more of these problems: (1) insufficient discipline in concentrating on their prescribed sequence of actions, allowing their attention to wander out of control: (2) lack of concern with integrity of detail or structure, like trying to break up fellow performers by whispering jokes to them: (3) ego-building impulses which alter strict designs to cater to momentary whims of milking approval from audiences or fellow actors, like subtly changing a plotted action so as to seek to impress the audience with the actor's cleverness, appearance, vocal quality, etc. Flashing glances at the audience, or delivering to the audience lines which were obviously designed to be addressed to others on stage. These are common examples of self-serving asides.

Another action which requires special treatment is the 'back track', or acquiescent action. Suppose that you have two pages of persuasion to deliver to another character. What can you do if, no sooner than you've embarked on the persuasion, your opposite number nods his head as if to say 'O.K. I'm convinced'? The wind has been taken out of your sails: the persuasion scene is virtually finished. Since there's no drama without conflict, where are you to find the conflict? If the actions are non- conflicting, it will be necessary to find some other conflicting or abrasive ingredient, in order to justify continuing.

The solution is to use one of the other major tools of the actor: motivations (which regulate feelings) and adjustments (which contain all non-deliberate, habitual, or spontaneous forms of behaviour). Consider the action 'to invite' matched opposite the conceding action 'to accept'. You couldn't keep such a scene going without the introduction of some additional abrasive component. But if the accepter were to play his action with such an emotional colouring as 'doubtfully', the inviter could continue to invite until the doubt disappeared. This means of course that the inviter would have to choose as his objective not a simple 'yes' but an enthusiastic 'yes'. Or for that matter, the inviter may proceed 'doubtfully', as if to suggest that if the invitee does come, he may meet someone who could be embarrassing. The implication here could be, 'Are you absolutely ***sure*** you want to come?' Or if one sought to resolve the problem by means of a formal component (adjustment), the inviter might suddenly acquire a coughing fit, and continue inviting between coughing spasms and through barely intelligible hoarseness.

It should become obvious during rehearsals when a backtracking exchange is occurring, and that is usually the time to decide who will provide the shades of conflict, and how they will do it. But despite the careful plans, when a show has been running for a while and begins to get a bit stale, one of the participants may forget, and find themselves too totally in agreement too soon. Then what?

In ***The Wiz*** the mother sings a song of caution to Dorothy. Presumably Dorothy should remain unconvinced until the end, when mother no longer finds it necessary to go on. But in the performance I saw – it was towards the end of the season – no sooner had mother begun to caution when her daughter nodded her head vigorously. Now, with her task apparently achieved, what was mother to do with the remaining 93 bars of the song? Fortunately, the mother was a skilled actress who renewed the vigour of her persuasion as if to say, 'You are simply nodding your head to make me believe that you are convinced. I don't care if you think I'm nagging, but I'm not letting you off the hook until I see a truer sign of surrender. Perhaps a warm smile and a cuddle'. The mother's singing and acting deserved special praise; Dorothy deserved a talking-to, if not a complete refresher rehearsal.

WRITE YOUR OWN NOTES

CHAPTER 16

THE SUPPLEMENTARY ACTION

This type of action requires a chapter to itself, for this is the action that separates the virtuoso performer from ordinary. To learn how to play the supplementary well is to acquire absolute control over performance values. It is the deft playing of supplementary actions that creates the illusion of a richly truthful performance. It is the action that most affects the audience's response. It is the action which people who grew up in show business ('born in a trunk') acquire as if by osmosis. It is a difficult action to play, but it can be learned and refined.

The supplementary is the action that allows us to seem to do two things at once. If we become very adept, we may juggle three, four, or even five actions at the same time. It is, of course, an illusion: strictly speaking, we cannot do two *deliberate* tasks at precisely the same time, but we can quickly alternate between two tasks in such a way as to created the illusion that we are doing so.

If we wished to roll two hoops with one hand, we'd give one a shove and when it rolls evenly give the other a shove. Then, as the first slows down or veers, we give it another push, while the second coasts by momentum. Then back to the second, then the first again, and so on. Likewise, we might concern ourselves with reporting an accident by phone while at the same time mixing ingredients that must be added at specific times to an elaborate dish we're cooking. If we are slow on the uptake, we obviously cut down on one task while we gather our thoughts on the other: then a cumbersome gathering of wits while we get back to the first.

But consider that the average intelligent person unencumbered by chemicals or undue stress or fatigue can make two value judgments per second. Should it not be possible to flick backward and forward nimbly enough so that, having measured out a teaspoonful of cinnamon we could keep the spoon going by momentum from spice jar to cooking pot while we clarify what the ambulance people have misunderstood about the address. We don't have to keep the spoon poised in mid-air for the half-second it takes to correct the operator with 'High Street' when she thought we said 'Bligh Street'.

Each of us has a short-term memory bank where what somebody has said to us rings in the mind's ear for some time after we heard it. We recognise this phenomenon when for example we look up a phone number, then repeat the number out loud before we dial it in order to create a short-term retentive impression. Often in fact it is not so short term: we may retain it unconsciously forever. But the conscious retention can be counted on for a brief time at least. This conscious retention is often referred to in the theatre as 'funding,' like an account in the memory bank of our mind. And the same applies to our other senses; we can have instant replay of what it was we just saw, touched, tasted, smelled.

This funding works for us even while we are more fully devoted to another task to which we have become diverted. If we miss a word or two from the operator while we're removing a lump from the sauce, not to worry: we can hear it on instant replay in a moment when we're ready. If we count on being able to switch within half a second, we should be able to give the illusion that we are performing two tasks simultaneously. If we can smooth over the jerkiness of transitions we can perform like virtuosi, like the pianist improvising on the piano while chatting up some person of interest, or the reporter keeping two phone calls going at the same time.

Experiment with such exercises as playing a game of cards while at the same time describing some event of the day. No faltering jerkiness, keep both pursuits flowing smoothly. Or memorise a newspaper item while you're talking on the phone.

It is important to keep in mind that a supplementary action is still an action, with all its attendant bits and pieces. A supplementary is not an adjustment, which is an automatic bit of behaviour. Thus putting on your coat while instructing the babysitter is probably not supplementary action playing, since for most of us donning coats is an automatic operation. Of course, if the coat fastens in an uncustomary way that requires deliberate execution, then the process could be seen as an action. But playing an action that coincides with an adjustment does not add up to supplementary action playing, though it may seem so to the casual observer. Some actors, aware of the rich impression created by multi-level behaviour, try to fob off an adjustment for an action, but that ruse usually lacks the many-faceted sparkle of the real thing. We'll have more to say about adjustments later.

We have been assuming that the actor is the average human being who can be expected to make at least two value-judgments per second. But if you are a trained/experienced actor, you should be able to handle three or four per second. Then if you wish to acquire the mental nimbleness of a racing driver you will need five. And not a chance of becoming an astronaut until you have acquired six. Many exercises can help to improve nimbleness. Fencing is one such.

One question that arises when both a mainline action and a supplementary are performed with equal vigour is: how do we know which is the mainline and which the supplementary? Well, some times we aren't meant to know, so that the mainline may later seem to emerge from the jumble. But when in doubt, we might say that the mainline is that action which best serves the scenic action.

Think of the TV, film and stage performances you most enjoy. They are likely to be those that seem 'human,' 'natural', 'multi faceted'. Or put it another way: we are dissatisfied with those performances that seem blinkered, tunnel-visioned, either/or types of behaviour. Simplistic acting is 'either/or'. It is like a person who acts as though at any given moment the only thing in the world that exists is precisely what he is looking at. Think of the character in a TV drama who sits at a restaurant table accusing his friend of getting off with his girl, apparently totally unaware that the restaurant is full of people capable of eavesdropping. Watching this, even if we allow some dramatic licence, we find we must suspend disbelief a bit too much for reasonable plausibility. We'd be more likely to accept a character who accuses, but at the same time tries to ensure that the conversation may not be overheard. That is, who plays a supplementary action. (Unless of course he actually intends that the accused be exposed to everybody in the restaurant. And even there a supplementary action should be played: to make sure that everybody in the restaurant *does* get the message.)

'Either/or' behaviour is so apparently stiff and artificial that it is often exploited in comedy and fantasy to distance audiences from complete acceptance of the character or situation. And of course there is the need, at climactic moments, to be able to deliberately blinker, to focus our all on a single task no matter what else is happening around us. But the ability to make such moments count, to point them up as more important than what has gone before, may well depend on the ability to soft-pedal what has gone before. And that softening can often be done with supplementary actions.

Imagine a scene in which a mother comes home to her daughter lying on the sofa reading a book. 'Has anyone called?' asks mother. Without looking up, daughter reports, 'Dad phoned and said he'd be late. Also you'd better call Marjorie. She wants us to go to the beach on Sunday'. (Here reading is probably the mainline action, and reporting could be the supplementary. By splitting her concentration, the daughter diminishes the importance of both actions.) 'Has anyone been here?' continues the mother while organising and stowing groceries she came home with. 'Nope' says the daughter, still seeing herself as the girl in the book. 'Then what's this red stain on the carpet?' asks mother. Now daughter puts down the book, gets up and inspects carefully. See how the narrowed focus is emphasised by the putting aside of the other activities so that a single task may be served?

Watching performances by accomplished performers who are able with ease to manipulate two or more objects, or achieve two or more objectives from the same object, can be a magical experience. The ability to play supplementary actions makes it possible to select and impinge upon a whole range of objects. But for the performer, one object constantly looms large: the audience.

To do your finest and most intimate and colourful work on stage with total disregard for the audience's capacity to share in any way must be regarded as selfish and counter-productive. For those concerned that the products of acting be arranged and dispensed in a manner best designed to serve the needs of audiences, the supplementary is an indispensable tool.

There are times when we address an audience directly, in which case the audience becomes the object of a mainline action. But usually we are supposed to pretend that we don't know there is an audience on the other side of the imaginary 'fourth wall'. In these cases, the audience are treated as objects of such supplementary actions as: to get them on side, alienate, confuse, set up, misdirect, lull or disarm, shock, provoke, rally, excite, appeal to, fool, divide, unite, silence, amuse, inspire, and – need we say it – impress.

How, for instance, might we get an audience off-side? Take the example of the villain who behaves 'sincerely' to those onstage, but still wants the audience to be aware of his ratty hypocrisy. In the old days, the scoundrel might turn to the audience, twirl his mandatory moustache, and chucklingly mutter some dastardly aside, like "Little does he know ..." Today's techniques are somewhat more refined. We may establish in the audience's mind some bit of business which they come to identify with nasty thoughts, like crumpling or shredding a piece of paper or casually examining a room while condoning some bit of cruelty early in the play like having the cat tortured. (Of course the play must be such as to allow for it.) This then can become a leit-motif as distinct as the creepy music sometimes still used to underpin a nasty scene. Then, later, while 'sincerely' reassuring the widow that she will not be evicted, he can at the same time size up the room or do the paper bit. Remember the character played by Frederic March in ***Executive Suite,*** who wiped his hands with a handkerchief whenever he lied? With all the inventiveness available to us these days, it's no longer necessary to twirl the mo to show our evil intentions.

The chief problem in playing supplementaries on audiences – the trap inherent in handling all supplementaries – is that of proportion. A supplementary should never overpower a mainline action. Indeed, most supplementaries should be kept to such a low profile that the audience generally is unaware of them. We don't want to parade before the audience the fact that they are being manipulated. And yet, how often supplementaries get out of hand, particularly on occasions like opening nights, when we are tempted to neglect the integrity of the production for the desire to look good to the critics and first-nighters: the supplementaries to watch out for here are such actions as 'to impress,' 'to one-up our fellow performers', 'conceal our nerves from the audience', where these tasks may divert from the play.

And many performers are familiar with the 'road phenomenon', the way a show gets corrupted when it goes on tour without its director, and the actors – tired of doing the same old bits over and over again at every performance – succumb to the flattery of laughter and applause. It is then that they are liable to start playing mainline actions on the audience, like: 'to woo', 'to milk,' 'to compromise,' 'to cheapen', 'to spell out', 'to nudge': or, when frustrated and annoyed, such actions as 'to punish,' 'to deprive,' 'to send up,' and 'to neglect'.

How often have we seen performers walking indifferently through a performance? They may be going through the motions as directed, 'working to rule'. But their attitude toward the audience seems to be, "You're too dumb to appreciate my genius: why bother putting myself out for you". Such attitudes almost inevitably result in a range of supplementary actions such as to ignore the audience, send them up, or even punish them. I once heard a famous actress come off stage after her first scene, muttering, "To hell with them. They're not worth working for". Obviously the audience had not received her as she felt was her due, so for the rest of the performance she actually emphasised certain words as one might to a slow child, virtually saying to the audience, "The only thing you would understand is baby-talk". Regrettably, such behaviour is not uncommon.

Invent for yourself a pair of actions, e.g. to find a particular number in the phone book and at the same time explain to a fellow actor why you were late for an appointment. Play each one separately at first. (Be sure there is opposition to the 'explain' action. The phone book will provide its own difficulties.) Now try combining the two unhesitatingly. And *really* play those actions. Especially paying attention to the objectives.

Now play the mixture again, but this time putting more emphasis on the phone-number. Now once more, but making the explanation more important. Once again, only this time we cross-fade. Start with making one of them the mainline action and gradually allowing it to recede into the supplementary, while what was supplementary now becomes the mainline. Now cross-fade back and forth.

Having acquired some proficiency with this sort of exercise, let's now make the object of one of the actions ('to explain' for example) the audience. Repeat the above ritual. First one at a time, then combining them. While the audience may not actually reply to you, simply imagine that they do.

Just in case you find these exercises no challenge, why not try one mainline and two supplementaries. Three? Four? I know of one actor who once juggled five.

Skill in supplementary action playing will prove to be absolutely essential in tackling performing.

CHAPTER 17

EMOTIONAL RESPONSES

Imagine a game we often play in classes at Ensemble Studios. A dozen or more small covered boxes are brought in, each big enough to contain objects the size of, say, a finger-sized doll or a dead spider. A student opens one of the boxes, carefully inspects the contents without allowing them to be seen by the others, and closes the box. The others are then asked to guess what was in the box.

Although I've repeated that experiment dozens of times, I am still astounded at the persistently high degree of accuracy in the guesswork. Even when the volunteer attempts to keep a poker face while examining the box's contents, the observers can usually identify the sort of thing that was examined, and often can pinpoint the actual item spot-on.

Does this happen through mental telepathy? Perhaps we can allow for some small measure of this, but the percentages of accuracy and the universality of the phenomenon suggest that other forces are at work, particularly since the signals cannot be transmitted from another room: they have to be seen then and there.

What I believe is that a universal language is at work here, perhaps the only language which transcends reading, writing, and the precise expressions of a learned tongue or mimicry. Let's call it the language of emotional responses. Wherever you travel, whoever you meet, it is almost impossible not to discern when a total stranger is feeling friendly or hostile, happy or sad, worried, jealous, sensual, indifferent, compassionate, angry, frustrated. Sometimes you don't even have to see the person: you may simply hear their voice, even over the telephone. Feelings are hard to conceal.

So what happens when you open a box is that an emotional reaction takes place which changes your body-signals. And the more you peruse the object, and recognise the different special characteristics of the object, so your reactions change with each fresh discovery, and so your body-signals alter.

Perhaps a description of a fairly typical experience will help explain how the language of emotional response works: One of the women in the class is handed a box. We see that she approaches it with an attitude of whimsy mixed with tentativeness. She sits, holds the box steadily for a moment, looks at us and laughs, holds the box at arm's length, then slowly opens it. When nothing jumps out she turns the box towards her face; her laughing ceases and is replaced by a raised eyebrow and a reaction of mild surprise and curiosity. She then reaches in and strokes whatever it is with her forefinger while wrinkling the corners of her mouth with the look that says "How silly it was to feel apprehensive", and she smiles childishly as she seems to tease the object by lifting and lowering some part of it. Shielding the object from us, she takes it from the box and examines it closely: suddenly a look of horror appears on her face. After a while, she slowly replaces the object in the box and looks accusingly at us, glancing occasionally into the box. Then she closes the box, rather sadly, but with a look of feigned indifference, as if – oh well, it's just a game.

In the box was a tiny celluloid doll such as one finds in cereal packets, with movable limbs and without clothes, pink, smiling, and with arms extended as if inviting a cuddle. But when the student went to pick it up, she discovered, trailing from it, a cord tied around its neck in a hangman's noose.

The observers guessed: "a toy", "a doll", "a game", "something sweet": then, "something horrible happened to it that could only be seen when it moved," "its head fell off", "it displayed a rude word", and so on.

In everyday life we are affected to some degree by everything we encounter. At first we seek to recognise or comprehend the encounter, and as we do we also make an evaluation of it. If the encounter is of normal interest, we respond with ease and some proportional familiar reaction. If it seems relatively unimportant as measured against our current circumstances or feelings, we respond with feelings of indifference or impatience. If the encounter is highly meaningful our response will be great and relevant. If it's too full of meaning we may pause a moment before doling out a sort of careful response. And if we can't make it out at all, or feel that it is out of place, we may respond with feelings of confusion or indignation. In other words, ***whatever we perceive will produce some sort of emotional response in us.***

And someone watching the sequence of our emotional responses as we perceive a sequence of stimuli is in a good position to deduce what it is we perceive. Even if we attempt to repress our feelings, the observer may ask, "What is so significant in what they perceive that they are making a deliberate effort to conceal their reactions. It must be extraordinarily important". Any good spy knows what every good actor should learn: whatever you relate to turns you on in a very special way. The degree to which our emotional reactions are understood depends primarily on the acuity of the person who is 'reading' us. Some people can believe that someone is a nice person because they smile: while the more perceptive can make out an avaricious gleam in the eyes that says, "I'm smiling because I'm about to swindle the day-lights out of you".

How does it happen that there is a cause and effect relationship between perception and emotional response, between this input and output? For that matter, what are 'emotions' or 'feelings' anyway? Since psychologists and other experts are either silent or in disagreement with each other, I join the fray by offering my own explanation. My presumption is that emotions are our instincts' psychological yes-no responses to stimuli.

For example, we have an instinct to survive: any stimulus which can be interpreted as a threat to our survival makes us feel afraid, and any stimulus which we interpret as securing our survival makes us feel safe. Likewise, the stimuli which gratify or deprive our sexual instinct can make us content or frustrated. Robert Ardrey (a playwright incidentally) and Conrad Lorenz write of an aggressive instinct which determines the amount of drive behind our endeavours: thus when we strive and succeed at a project we feel dominant, and if we don't succeed we feel ourselves to be failures.

We could have a lot of fun listing and linking emotions with possible instincts, but a word of caution is in order. Consider that the earliest stimulus to an instinct produces the 'raw' emotion, the kind of response we see in children and others unable to impose social controls on their behaviour. Let's for the moment assume a pleasure instinct: A very young child is given a toy: it gurgles and plays with pleasure. Then, if the toy is snatched away, what anger! The infant screams, hits out, would kill if it could. We may regard these as primary responses. Even if it is a loving parent who is the toy-snatcher, the anger is no less ferocious. But if the child is cognitive enough to equate parent with source of food, comfort, affection, etc., and reasonable enough to work out that if it killed (or even upset) the parent, its supply of food, comfort, affection, etc. could be threatened, then the child is likely to modulate its emotional response.

When the child brings a number of instincts into conference it arrives at a response which is neither the hatred of having his pleasure frustrated nor the security of anticipating a meal. Rather, we see a compromise reaction, one that we might call 'disappointment'. What has happened is that the emotion of hatred has been politicised, and we have a conditioned emotion, or 'feeling'. It is by such a process that all of the emotions are tempered to give rise to a whole range of secondary, tertiary, etc. responses, which are the feelings.

Feelings are to emotions what conditioned reflexes are to simple reflexes. More interestingly, some feelings may become so diluted or shallow that they become manipulable by our conscious will. It is of course almost impossible to summon a primary emotion by direct command, or even most feelings – try telling yourself to 'be murderous,' or 'be disappointed'. But one shallow area of feelings can be ordered on cue: attitudes. We can tell ourselves to 'to calm down,' 'to cheer up,' 'to be pleasant', or 'to be careful', and often the command succeeds, although rarely on anything more than the most shallow level.

So there we have what we may call a Stratified Instinct Response Capability Theory *(sircat)* which will serve to go on with. The deepest and most vigorous responses are the emotions, like the dark dense currents close to the sea-bottom. On the surface, like the waves and ripples, are the superficial attitudes. In between are the feelings, and they are as rich and plentiful as the sea. Although we try to pigeon-hole feelings into accessible groups for purposes of description, there may in truth be many more subtle combinations of feelings than there are adverbs in the language.

What word is there to explicitly communicate the complex feelings of an Ethiopian mother watching yet another of her children dying in her arms? And yet, who cannot read her clearly? For we read not only her grief at her inevitably impending loss, but the degree of stoicism that comes from her having experienced such loss before and from having observed the losses of so many others. Then there is the faint glimmer of hope that the tide may turn, that perhaps the well-fed photographer will offer her something for her infant. Add to that the inevitable anger that maybe nothing will be done in time to help. And pride and challenge that she will not go to pieces in front of those looking on, as well as traces of resignation, and camaraderie with others around her in similar straits. Is there also some guilt about having brought her child into this situation? And if so, a degree of vindictiveness, perhaps directed at the husband who may have suggested that they leave their village. Is there perhaps a stifled resolve of vengeance which could one day explode into armed revolt?

Shades upon shades of emotional nuances, each of a different weight and duration, each constantly on the move and interweaving with others. What word could adequately describe the mother's feeling-situation? Grief-stricken? Stunned? Outraged? Surely no words could suffice, particularly when we consider the wealth of associations accumulated at each living moment: for that mother the experience must carry infinite traces of affect usually too subtle to separate and too fleeting to note. And hers is only one of the unique personal situation-responses on this globe of five billion people. The next mother in similar circumstances will have responses as subtly different as their fingerprints: our gross perception will see them as alike, our trained awareness will see the all-important distinctions.

All these ingredients, obvious and subtle, must add up for a particular kind of behaviour to ring true. When we observe behaviour in which not all the bits and pieces seem to belong together, we may doubt the truthfulness of that behaviour. Likewise, if certain ingredients should be there but seem not to fit, (even as seen under the microscope of the judicious) we'll tend to doubt the truthfulness of that behaviour as well. If, as we observed this specimen mother, we saw her drop her baby so that she could more freely shove other women aside in an attempt to snatch a cheap bangle from a box of trinkets, we well might suspect the depth of her grief. Coping is natural and necessary, but there are limits. And beyond these limits, we tend to disbelieve.

This raises – finally – the issue which is central for the actor: can real feelings be faked? Would it be possible for a skilled actress to be planted among the genuinely distressed and to fool us into believing she's a real Ethiopian mother? Well, a good actress could generate similar real feelings, and could perhaps fool even the judicious. But somebody going through the motions without truly feeling grief, despair, etc, can usually be unmasked. That's because, although each feeling has a plethora of special responses, all feelings have at least three telltale signs in common, and the deeper the feelings, the more marked the tell-tales:

- ***Ambivalence.*** Strong feelings are usually accompanied by a strong effort to hold them back, to keep control. Of course one may lose control of feelings, but not from lack of trying. So when we see emotional behaviour that seems forced or too eagerly forthcoming, we may well be suspicious. Remember that the drunk does not try to stagger.
- ***Kaleidoscopic responses.*** Behaviour fluctuates rapidly as now one feeling dominates, now another, and as feelings and attempts to control them alternate. The to-ing and fro-ing of mixed feelings are revealed as obvious physicalisations.
- ***Retention.*** A real feeling takes a while to dispel. Even after the stimulus has been removed, it takes time to rid oneself of the signs of the feeling. It may convert to an active manifestation of a different sort, as tears may be transformed into laughter. Agitation takes a while to settle down as adrenalin or other endocrine secretions take time to leave the bloodstream. An abrupt and complete turnoff of strong feelings is suspect.

Unless all of these telltales are present, we may well suspect that feelings and emotions are merely 'played at' (indicated). With practice, we may soon get to recognise common patterns in the play of kaleidoscopic reactions: the momentary smile before the tears, the arrest of conversation in the struggle to contain upsurges of feeling, the flattening of the voice and difficulty in enunciating, or giveaways of suppression like controlling the hands and upper body but feet moving agitatedly.

It isn't only performers who can pick out the difference between a real and an indicated appearance of emotion. Audience members, although they may not be able to analyse specific symptoms, are frequently capable of knowing 'with their hearts' when they are in the presence of true emotion in a performance. Particularly if they are not jaded by repeated impositions of what they should believe. Schoolchildren above all have been assaulted by the fake and unfelt performances of thrown-together companies who supply Shakespeare as if it were patent medicine. No wonder the kids sometimes assault the actors in turn with Jaffas, fruit, and insults. On the other hand we've seen the same groups of kids arriving rowdily at a theatre, prepared to practise mayhem, and then – after a few minutes of integrated performances, with real feelings in place – find themselves carried along like the audiences performers have wishful dreams about. Schoolchildren notoriously do not countenance gladly what is fake and unfelt, and neither should adult audiences. When the Emperor appears before them, he had better be well and truly clothed.

CHAPTER 18

THE CASE FOR FEELINGS IN ACTING

Not every role is naturalistic in style. That is, not every role requires the portrayal to reveal the gross and fine details of behaviour we would find in the Ethiopian mother of the last chapter. Some roles require sketchiness: political satire, burlesque, caricature, etc. Some call for mismatching components of behaviour so that attitudes or feelings don't fit with actions or formal designs of voice or body: comedy frequently depends on this kind of absurd incongruity.

But all roles, naturalistic or absurd, are composed of building blocks, those components which the audience sees as clues to the identity of the character. And since, as we know, the character is an illusion concocted from parts of the actor like a Frankenstein monster, what are these component-clues that the audience behold?

The answer is: everything we say or do that the audience can detect. If we speak, the audience hears a voice. If we take a cup from a saucer and put it to our lips, they assume that the character is preparing to drink. If we walk across the stage with a limp, they assume a limb defect or injury in the character. If they see tears, they have a clue as to the character's feelings. But if we perspire, their intuitive computers begin to whirr, and a small readout whispers, "the actor is nervous."

Had we been able to contain our nerves, to control our perspiration, perhaps the telltale sweat would not have provided a clue about our flawed workmanship to detract from our designed characterisation. What we're saying is that everything in the performance that is there to be detected is in a position to help or hinder our characterisation. And if we can put appropriate discernible ingredients to work to build a character, then each of these becomes a building block: if we could learn to sweat only on cue, the audience might then think – as we wish them to – that "the character is nervous".

Feelings are noticeable: body language gives them away. So we need to integrate our feelings in such a way that – even if they don't illuminate the character or situation – they don't hamper or damage the effect we wish to achieve. In a naturalistic portrayal of a character locked in a dungeon, it would be unwise for the actor to allow the audience's laughter, gasps, sobbing, or applause to affect him. To bask haphazardly in the varying reactions from the audience would be to reveal subtle responses which will be detected, and which will cause the invisible fourth wall to collapse. That subtle acknowledgement of the audience can become a small flying building block to dent our carefully assembled characterisation.

Likewise, any deliberate attempt to draw attention to his craftsmanship rather than to the character can totally unmask the actor. The 'Hey-look-Ma-I'm-acting' approach which some actors take will totally destroy the integrity of a performance. Even in a caricatured portrayal, where the character is expected to take himself seriously, any comment on the character by the performer is destructive. We've all seen some supposedly deadpan comic laughing at his own jokes, and we know how deadly that can be to the performance. A flying brick?

In the Japanese theatrical tradition called Bunraku-za, human-size puppets are operated by a puppeteer dressed in black, standing right alongside or behind each puppet. Years of training and experience help these puppeteers to achieve such illusions that even discerning audiences are led to believe that the puppets are actually people. Since not all puppeteers are equally skilled, not all puppets are equally plausible. In one company, while most puppeteers wore black hoods to conceal their faces, the master wore no hood and revealed absolutely no feelings, but all eyes were drawn in profound pathos to the puppet he operated. It seems that when a puppeteer has achieved perfect mastery of his puppet and can at the same time control the show of his own feelings so as not to intrude on the stage magic, only then is he entrusted to unmask.

This applies to our premise that feelings are primary building blocks of performance in several ways. We might see the Master Puppeteer's performance as an act of suppression, the ability to control his feelings so that nothing showed to support, comment on, or otherwise undermine the illusion conveyed by the puppet. But another way of looking at it is to see the puppeteer as deliberately introducing a feeling, the feeling of detachment: not an act of suppression but of induction or substitution.

What is relevant here is that the puppeteers are so knowledgeable about feelings – their control as well as their physical manifestations – that they can mask their own while they provide their puppets with the body language of feelings so that they look more lifelike than many human actors.

You might think that a puppet could never seem truly lifelike, since one of the things that makes human appear human is the infinite number of subtle bodily responses that speak the language of the feelings. But as an illusionist, a performer is not required to provide every single nuance of detail, only a selection of those details that are the giveaways of the character's feelings. This does not mean that all a performer needs to give us is a single giveaway detail of two for us to believe in his characterisation. Would that it were so easy. The problem is that we also tend to show other details which may be counter-productive as a result of: (1) being on stage, (2) having an audience or camera looking at us, (3) our survival instincts in relation to these, (4) our professional pride and commitments to the job in hand, and (5) other influences relating to work. A performer virtually cannot avoid some of his or her own emotional responses to the circumstances of performance. And each of these stimuli tempt us to reveal telltales of nervousness, self-satisfaction, over-reactions to difficult bits of acting, staleness, anticipation, and more.

So when performers work live, they must provide hints of positive characteristics and play them with greater than normal energy, in order not only to put across the image of the character but to neutralise the effects of those irrelevant personal responses which are the sabotaging giveaways of performance. Feelings – both the character's and our own – need to be regulated as deliberately and artistically as actions, voice, and kinetic behaviour. All are part of the total illusion, each contributes its own dimensions, and each is capable of bringing the performance unstuck when abused or ignored.

Actions can be carefully executed. You can accuse, flatter, condemn, annoy, tease, amuse: name almost any verb and it can be performed. Form – in voice and gesture – can likewise be meticulously produced through rehearsal and habituation: indeed it may often be too easily produced and used as an empty substitute for actions (by going through the motions) or for feelings (by pulling faces or display of the outward signs of emotion). But feelings, since they are by-products, can't be substantially forced to our will. We have to trap them by using our imaginations to make ourselves believe that we are encountering certain select stimuli which will release in us related and useful emotional responses. And – we hope – will eliminate or minimise the sabotaging emotions produced by our actual situation.

What is more, a real feeling arrived at by that imagination offers us a rich bonus. It usually triggers more imagination. Remember how we assumed that imagination is a vast pool of bits of information waiting to be called upon? How do we actually call them up? We can use our conscious thinking function of course. But we may also excite them with our feeling function. 'Let's go on a picnic!' 'Why?' 'I feel like one'. Again,'Why?' On close and frank inspection it might be revealed that the idea came out of an unconscious boredom. If such a low grade feeling can give birth to an idea, what might a strong feeling do? Any psychologist can testify how much of our everyday behaviour may be a result of unconscious feelings.

We'll discuss the nuts and bolts of feelings-management in the long section on Motivational Techniques. But first, there's more to be said in a general way about the significance of feelings to theatrical performance, and we'll say some of that in the next chapter.

WRITE YOUR OWN NOTES

CHAPTER 19

'WHY' AND THE IMAGINED 'BECAUSE'

The emotive component of a performance is both the source of propulsion and the colour of the deed. Let's explain that with an example. Suppose we wish to play the action 'to scold'. The person to be scolded is there, and so are the words to be used in scolding, but we need a 'why': why are we scolding that person? Because that person dropped a vase? That may be a reason for the person to be scolded, but not yet reason enough for US to scold them: there's nothing in the dropping of the vase to link us into the action.

Perhaps it is the additional 'because' we bought that vase with our holiday savings, and 'because' that person had been behaving thoughtlessly to us in other instances, that the broken vase now becomes a 'cause' for us to take issue. Because now we feel angry: so we find it easy to launch into a blast called 'to scold'.

But is not the actual blasting – whoops – scolding loaded with emotion or feeling? The fact that the word 'blasting' sneaked in testifies to how a cool dispassionate 'scold' can be elevated to something more colourful. It has acquired a special quality from the details of the 'because'. The anger triggered the scolding, so the scolding is done angrily. The deed is propelled and coloured by the emotion.

There is a single term we use which covers the concepts of 'why', 'because', 'springboard', 'launching pad', 'motivator', 'driver', 'propellor', 'fuel', 'commitment' and others of the same kind. We call it a *reference*. "What is your reference?" means in effect, what are you using to get going emotionally, not just to get you knowing or talking?

And the ensuing colour – the quality of delivery or execution – we may refer to interchangeably as the 'emotion', 'feeling', 'mood', 'colour', or 'adverb': e.g. angrily, happily, frustratedly and so on.

It is essential to remember that *colours are not played!* Actions are played. Colours are generated by the appropriate choice and acceptance of the reference. They fluctuate as the action is being played, now tentatively, now aggressively, and the colours dance around the deed like fragrance around a bouquet of flowers. We arrange for colours by designing appropriate references. We shouldn't bung on angry voices if we don't feel angry. Not if we expect to be believed by the judicious.

Generating and controlling feelings is particularly crucial when we design 'inner conflict'. We have seen how actions can be made to conflict. So too can feelings. And conflict within ourselves if we seek a rich deep characterisation. Karen Horney described inner conflict as "the difference between what you'd like to do as opposed to what you have to do". If they are both the same, there is no inner conflict. And the performance looks relatively shallow. What you see is what you get.

But when one designs opposing feelings, much richness results. Not only may we see the usual tug-of-war between characters, but within them as well. And they may all interact. With skill, we can cleverly interweave those threads of feelings with threads of actions and adjustments, much as a composer may do with a symphony. Thus, great acting!

At Ensemble Studios we have attempted to discover and classify emotional references into technical categories. Each category might contain literally thousands of references, but they have been grouped under a particular technique because they share certain notable characteristics in common. They may share a common approach, be useful for certain common types of responses, and/or may share common side-effects – some useful, some detrimental.

In any event, we have designed a catalogue of 45 motivational techniques which we believe contains all of the references any performer is likely to use. If something has been left out of the list, it may be either because we never thought of it, nobody ever mentioned it to us, or it's probably such a self-evident technique that we have not thought it was worth mentioning.

The complete list of motivational techniques is described and discussed at length in the following chapters. In this chapter, to help make it easier to grasp the next section, we want to discuss only the first technique. Here it is:

Yes, the line was blank. The first technique is no conscious technique at all. It is probably the ultimate technique. As the meaning of technique is 'know-how', this is the know-how devoutly to be wished by all of us. It is the already built-in know-how that works for us without our having to call upon it consciously. If we need a name for it, we might call it Inspiration. Some prefer to call it Intuition. But it's the same operation.

When the director says 'scold' to an actor whose intuition is helping out at that point, the actor actually seems to spontaneously generate supportive anger to help launch the 'scold' action, and colour it as well. To be sure, there is a lot of nerve-signal twitching going on under the skull so that the appropriate anger emerges. But the actor may not be even remotely aware of what association is locking in with what. It all simply emerges as anger.

Inspiration may spontaneously produce any of the required ingredients. It may produce concepts of form. Or inventive ideation. Or detached feelings. Or recalled sensations. Or, for that matter, clues as to which resource could most likely yield any of these. But for our purposes now, we are simply pursuing inspired references to help generate feeling, or simply the spontaneous feelings themselves. Later we can call on inspiration for other assistance.

The following instance may strain credulity but I will testify to it. One terrible actor of my acquaintance once gave a magnificent performance. The role required him to defend himself from a charge of attempting to kill his wife. When I went backstage to congratulate him, he gloated that he used no 'technique' at all, and how contrived my brand of actor must be, going to the expense and effort of consciously identifying techniques, etc. He knew he'd given a great performance, and probably wasn't aware that all else I'd seen him do was awful. But he did not seem to associate his performance with the fact that several years before, he faced a charge of attempting to kill his own wife.

Many a psychiatrist will have had experience with this kind of thing. Whether he had actually blocked out that experience, I don't know. But he did *not* consciously associate the two factors. Yet his intuition was re-enacting the earlier experience, albeit with different words and names.

Well, if inspiration or intuition is that good and so effortless, why bother with anything else? As Stanislavski puts it, "conscious techniques begin where inspiration fails". And it does fail: for everybody sometimes, for some of us often. So we must return to more deliberate key-fumblings to unlock the store of feelings.

And there's a bonus inducement. When we have worked at a conscious technique well enough and often enough, it may become part of our intuitive approach. It can become an unconscious technique. Thus another source of inspiration is born.

How do we develop inspiration? Primarily by taking on work: projects, scenes, plays, productions – any theatrical or non-theatrical pursuits that require you to apply yourself to problem solving. Then trust yourself to make a stab at it. Exercises like those outlined in De Bono's *Lateral Thinking* are great to cultivate imaginative problem-solving.

And another magic word: 'Let'. 'Let' it happen. Don't push. Don't force. Don't worry. Relax. Ease up. Tackle the problem matter-of-factly. And if it doesn't happen this instant, conditions permitting, sleep on it: how often one wakes with a Eureka!

The intuitions of most of us are well stocked with impressions. The brain is a prodigious computer. We have but to tell ourselves, "Here is the problem". Outline as much as we can, then leave it. No panic. And more often than not – Presto! Of course the resultant idea may not work as intended. But it will be a start. After that, another idea perhaps. In time, one may have to resort to deliberately teasing ideas out of one's unconscious. But give inspiration a chance first. It's usually the easiest approach and often yields the best solution.

We could leave the issue of inspiration at this point, without probing further the mystery of its beauty. But as we plough through the list of motivational techniques, some of us may be provoked to wonder something like, "I think I see how the cause and effect relationship of this particular technique works. Shouldn't I be able to relate equally clearly to Inspiration?"

So let's try, by likening the process of inspiration to a great librarian who can lay his hands on any book in the library. When approached nicely, he may hand us any book or simply some information from it, or summarised information from several books. But no matter how competent he is, his abilities are wasted unless there is a well-stocked library he can turn to.

Almost every one of the motivational techniques is the equivalent of a librarian. Some are better than others, and some are specialists in certain fields. But all are quite accessible. We might imagine them standing at the front counter. Inspiration, on the other hand, has an office at the back.

We can do two things to make feeling-retrieval better for ourselves. We can cherish and pamper our librarians, and give them lots of experience. And we can provide the library with a constant supply of more and better books, and we can ensure that they are kept in good condition.

There are very few libraries anywhere with as many and as varied books as there are recorded impressions in the mind of the average urban young adult. Every experience we have ever had would have left its fragments in out unconscious memory. Deliberate or highly associated sensory exercises embed experiences more deeply. Our unconscious personal library is probably the greatest store of random and organised information that one can find. The best computers are imbeciles by comparison. We may not know exactly how our Inspiration actually goes about riffling through our mental file cards to ultimately laying his hands on that idea we asked for, but we do know that he gets better with practice.

Our other-technique librarians are a little less mysterious. But if we exercise them enough, they may be promoted to an office adjoining Inspiration. In fact, it may be the same office. Won't it be nice to know that we are on first-name terms with some of our back-room operators?

WRITE YOUR OWN NOTES

CHAPTER 20

MOTIVATIONAL TECHNIQUES

At last we come to a discussion of the techniques with which we can fuel the emotional qualities of a performance, the motivations which provide actions with their impetus and quality. It takes a certain degree and shade of bottled-up anger before someone will punch the postman, kick the cat, or bash the baby. The specific sources of accumulated frustrations may vary, but the resulting emotions or feelings might be similar. That is, it matters little what sources we use to create an emotion for performance, so long as they produce precisely the kind and degree of emotion needed for playing the action convincingly.

I recall one instance where a novice actress was called upon to react in horror as a response to seeing a body washed up on a beach. A simple but specific facial reaction was all that was necessary, but despite prolonged coaching and many takes she was unable to produce it. Finally the frustrated director quietly asked the camera-man to "roll 'em", stepped up to the actress, whispered some uncustomary obscenities into her ear and quickly stepped out of the picture. The stunned look of horror on her face now matched the requirements of the dramatic sequence.

Yes, it was trickery, but so what? What the director did to the actress is what we usually do to ourselves to release the appropriate feeling responses that motivate the desired action and thus create the desired illusion to be conveyed to the audience. It is not the audience's business that we have rehearsed for weeks to make the dialogue sound like it was our own, freshly invented for this moment. Nor is it their business how long we sat in the make-up chair, bickered over the costume fit, haggled over salary, politicked over billing. What matters is the bits that construct the final illusion, and how cleverly they are pieced together for ultimate plausibility or acceptance.

Finding and tailoring those bits so that they are proportionate is one of the actor's biggest tasks. Sometimes we see an action played where the conviction and feeling seem askew, and we're tempted to say that the action was 'unmotivated': strictly speaking, that's not true, since no action can be played without motivation. Even if the action was played only because the director said 'Do it or you're fired', then fear of losing his job would be the actor's motivation. And if the results don't match what is required, our criticism will be, not that the action was unmotivated, but that it was not *proportionately* motivated; that there was a mismatch of motive and action.

It is of course possible for the director's threat to produce a perfect match. If for example the scene is one in which the wife threatens to leave her husband unless he asks for a rise in salary, the director's threat could be used to induce in the actor a feeling of anger or reluctance, so that he plays the action 'to apply for a rise' with the appropriate colouring 'angrily' or 'reluctantly'. Film directors have been known to construct masterpieces using actors who had responses tricked out of them, the actors often not even aware of the story line, much less what was expected of them moment by moment. More to the point, actors have constructed masterpieces of characterisation by tricking responses out of themselves, more frequently and more surely than arriving at a performance by 'believing in' the script.

The bits and pieces the actor must produce mostly reside in the actor before even reading the script. To create the illusion of the character, certain of these components must be released and arranged in such a way as to make the illusion complete. Since no two actors contain precisely the same components, when one calls upon, say, a moment of grief tinged with awe, it will not look precisely like another's grief tinged with awe. For that matter, each actor has a whole repertoire of grieving moments tinted with various shades of awe, or alternatively some appropriate reaction of grief and another of awe which can be combined: the actor's objective is to find the precise combination which will satisfy the director and the discerning audience. We can't be sure that the quality being sought will be arrived at by believing in the situation in the script. In my own experience, the precise components we seek can rarely be relied on to occur from simply believing in the script.

This is not to denigrate believing in the play's situation as a way of psyching oneself to feel as the character feels – it is an effective technique which has its strong points and its negative side-effects, as has every technique. Which is precisely our point: believing in the situation created by the author is just another motivational technique, in itself neither better nor worse than most others.

What is a motivational technique? It is a specific means of changing one's feelings, altering one's moods, psyching oneself to give a particular emotional colouration to a particular action. Sometimes we already feel the necessary feelings to embark on a given action, and if the way those feelings colour that action is right for the character, then that's it, there's no need to employ a deliberate motivational technique. But if we need to play an action and the only feelings we can readily muster make the combination of action and feeling wrong for that character, we must look around for some way to ensure a more suitable feeling. (We could look for a different action to match the feeling we already have, but such a cop-out usually ends up making us look more like a different character.)

Now here is a problem. No matter how useful it would be to be able to will a feeling on cue, there are very few feelings which can be commanded as readily as an action. These are shallow attitudes. Deeper feelings to order must be tricked out of us. Feelings are products of stimuli. And when we have to pretend those stimuli, feelings are then by-products of our efforts to pretend. Those triggering imaginary or selectively-chosen stimuli we can refer to as 'references'. If we invoke the right reference, we can usually find the sought feeling emerging. So though we know which feeling is expected, we don't dwell on it but rather relate to the chosen reference which will produce it.

Whatever we imagine and believe will induce a feeling response. Thus, even actors who tells us (a) it is unnecessary to 'feel', and/or (b) they can fake it when necessary, are imagining and believing those assumptions. And the consequences can range from smugness or contempt through to nerves or over-acting. Of course if the scene calls for such feelings, the results can appear properly proportionate. Those beliefs are their 'references'.

With a box full of different motivational techniques, each technique loaded with sometimes thousands of references, we should always be able to produce a suitable feeling for the required action. Given the forty-five or so techniques we catalogue here, there should be enough possible references for an actor to be able to change techniques and references for a particular action in a show that ran for ten years and never go stale. Some otherwise great actors have said they run out or get bored by seven months: chances are that they have latched onto a small handful of techniques which have been reliable, and perhaps they are reluctant to examine others. What others, and why bother classifying them? Whey bother identifying these techniques individually when indefinite batches will do? Indeed they well may, on the job. In fact, they always did serve.

Throughout the history of theatre, actors have restorted to motivational techniques but didn't worry too much about dissecting them. If something works it works and who cares whether it is made up of two parts something and three parts something else.

By the same token, there was a time when the total contents of the abdominal cavity were referred to as 'guts' or sometimes more politely, 'viscera'. In the case of animals' guts, it was discovered in time that certain parts were edible and had distinct flavours. Other parts weren't edible. And other parts could be made edible with special culinary cunning.

As to our own viscera, we learned that a heartburn was usually an ailment of the digestive tract. Or the liver. And we learned to distinguish a belly ache from a heart attack. Tidying up the generalisations helped no end in extending our life-spans.

With motivational techniques, it would be surprising to find that we are not very much benefited from knowing one refined technique from the other. Even if in practice we mixed them, we can count on the mixture having certain flavours, because each has a number of features special to that technique.

Each may have its optimum preparation time, durability, side-effects, depth capability, eradicability. Knowing this, we may choose more wisely.

Having studied and acquired a certain range of techniques, some more deeply than others, within our working habits there is also a built-in scanner. It helps search for the appropriate tool for a given job. That is to say, I know how to use a pen and I know how to use a fork. If I am invited to sign my name, I automatically reach for my pen. This I would not do if I were asked to taste some ravioli.

One might ask if, as a working actor and cataloguer of all these techniques, have I made all the forty-five techniques my own? Am I now the expert in all of them?

No.

Life is too short. One could spend a lifetime exploring and perfecting any one of them. I have simply become somewhat adept at a handy few – those that seem to suit my talent limitations or those that could be relied upon for the sorts of jobs I do mostly, or both. As to the others, I know about them and could restort to them consciously and systematically when and if needed. Even with those with which I have a certain facility, I would not have spent a lifetime perfecting any single one. But if it is found that some uncustomary technique could be particularly useful in a scene somewhere in a show, during rehearsals and performance of that show, there is the opportunity to apply oneself with enough zeal to acquire a bit of special expertise. Here then is what we mean by resourcefulness. Recognising that a special technique could be useful, we know where to search for it. And having found it, we then know how to check it out and acquire proficiency with it.

One develops an affinity for certain techniques. One tends to turn to a special sequence of possibilities. We each have our favourites, our techniques of choice. When these seem inappropriate, we tend to search out something else down the list. Obviously, some on a list are totally inapplicable for a given job, so we skip them and scan on.

When we first begin working in new techniques they tend to be self-consciously laborious, like first learning to eat with knife and fork, or to type, or to drive a car. With time and practice they become second nature. Best to work through the catalogue of motivational techniques slowly and patiently, practising until each becomes familiar. Ultimately, pay more attention to those that seem most natural and most useful to you, and as you become more comfortable with them, move on to others.

Another word or two about references. Since a reference is a key for unlocking a feeling, it is not enough merely to *know* it: one must *believe* in the reference – imagine it, have faith in it, surrender to it, let it happen. And in the event that we find it difficult to believe, there are even references that help us believe in our references. Which brings up another point: no action can be invoked based on a single feeling: there will always be two or more contributors to drive and colour an action. One of these contributors is likely to be a built-in supervisor which may say "OK, let it fly" or, "Put it aside, it is too painful". In any event, an action is unlikely to be motivated simply from a single feeling.

If, for example, we are pushed in a crowd, we may have a knee-jerk reaction to shove back. After all, we suddenly felt imposed upon, and on the urging of that single feeling we may react without thinking. Such impetuous behaviour can be seen as an adjustment, which can indeed be born of a single emotional reaction. But if, before you shove back, you notice that the pusher is a ferocious-looking muscular six-and-a-half-foot drunk spoiling for a fight, you might now feel cautious (or cowardly) and decide that on second thought it might be better to ignore the push and look the other way. That final – deliberate – choice was not born of the feeling of imposition, nor even the feeling of caution, but rather of imposition tempered with caution. Here then is an action impelled by two feelings.

But the number of references motivating that complexity of feelings is irrelevant: it can be one (as in a friend in terminal agony has finally died), or many (like giving a lecture with a bad case of laryngitis before rushing off to a funeral). References are the triggering devices for liberating or generating feelings. When we talk of motivational techniques we are actually talking about references. These can be classified according to usage, advantages and disadvantages. The following chapters do just that.

Once you have learned to employ motivational techniques easily, you'll find that some of them (e.g. Imagery or Improvisation) serve not only to affect your feelings but to provide hints of what your actions might be – and your staging, business, props, or total characterisations. It's good to know that we can turn to motivational techniques for help in these other areas when we need such help, but in the catalogue that follows we'll focus on the changes they can make in our *feelings*. And just as we found that feelings are usually mixed, shaded, and combined in many ways, so the references and techniques can be mixed and designed imaginatively to produce multitudes of unique and subtle creations.

CHAPTER 21

BELIEF IN THE SITUATION

I live just outside the city but work in it, part of the ratrace. My life is governed by the clock and by the rules of my company. I can see the reasons for the company remaining in operation, but what about me, do I exist merely to keep the company going? What am I doing here? On my next holiday I think I'll get away from it all and give my mind a good overhaul. Maybe I'll go to the highlands of Scotland – it's an isolated place, but at least they speak English there in case I need to talk to somebody.

Such is the background situation for Tommy in ***Brigadoon,*** and – aside from the difference in name – it's the situation of thousands of people who might conceivably play the part of Tommy in the musical: we'd have no difficulty in accepting his situation as our own. After all, there's nothing in this outline which tells us about Tommy's age, background, tastes, friends, marital status, personality, etc. What we know about Tommy, apart from the circumstances he finds himself in, is that he questions them and decides to go for a trip. Accepting that these are ***our*** circumstances, how does it make us feel? Restless? In limbo? Adventurous? Suicidal? Some combination of these or other feelings? If the director finds us responding in a way which he deems to be appropriate for the role, ***Belief in the Situation*** has been working for us. We need prepare our moods no further.

When Tommy finds himself lost in the wilds with his friend Jeff, here is another bit of make-believe. No problem: I can easily believe being lost in the woods, so the technique of *Belief in the Situation* is still working for me. But suddenly a strange unmapped village arises through the mist. Can I believe that? No: too hard for a realistic person like me to believe that non-existent villages can materialise out of nowhere. Yet I have to respond with a complex feeling including relief that I can now orient myself, and awe at this uncanny event: so what am I to do? Then I recall a moment when I was fishing before sunrise in a rowboat on Puget Sound, a calm dawn with the mist so thick around me that I couldn't tell where I was, didn't know west from east, was lost, disoriented, and anxious. But in a moment the rising sun caused the mist to lift from the calm water, and gradually the awesome snow-capped mass of Mount Hood emerged, towering just above me. Close as it was, I could hardly see it for the tears of relief and awe in my eyes.

Back to ***Brigadoon.*** I couldn't believe in pop-up villages, but I could recall the almost magical apparition of Mount Hood. What I did at that moment of the play was to switch techniques from 'belief in the situation' to other techniques. As if Mount Hood was being unveiled before my eyes. In doing so, I momentarily departed completely from the situation. The technique worked for that moment in the play. Had I persevered with trying to believe in the author's situation, I doubt – in fact the director confirmed this – that the results would have been as suitable.

'Belief in the situation' is so primary a technique that it must come at the head of our catalogue of deliberate motivational techniques: but as the above example may show, it is a technique of limited effectiveness. As a pure technique it means that *You The Actor* must be able to believe that you find yourself in this situation, and you must find yourself responding to it as the character would. Please note that we're not saying you identify with the *character* finding himself in that situation: identification with the character is an altogether different technique, which we'll discuss later. Belief in the Situation requires, first of all, that we believe the story: and second, that what happens to us when we believe is also what happens to the character in the situation. The results of the motivation must match the situation.

For myself, while I can most likely go along with such makebelieves, the results I achieve are rarely what the characters call for, which is one reason that 'belief in the situation' is very low on my personal list of techniques.

If I were committed to this technique as the be-all and end-all of motivation, as some schools espouse, I might have to use a large number of supportive techniques to help me believe in the situation. That is, when I was unable to believe in the miraculous appearance of the village, I might have forced that belief by thinking, "It's not on the map because maybe this is an old map – that is a new village": or "I'll bet it's a film company shooting an historic film and they built a special location village set". Either of these reasonable-within-the-situation excuses might have inspired me with some awe and enthusiasm, perhaps once or twice. And here is a crucial defect inherent in that technique: belief in the situation tends to stale easily. When we live with a situation, after a while we tend to take it for granted.

The technique of Belief in the Situation, where it works for the actor, is most useful in short-run plays, TV episodes, film, and some repertory work. But long-run shows need techniques which avoid staleness. We mentioned earlier the play where a woman opens the closet door to get her coat and a body falls out. For a while her scream sounded convincingly startling, but after a while she was actually stepping aside even before she opened the door. Relying on belief in the situation not only makes the circumstances become too familiar, but makes the responses to the circumstances habitual as well.

Understanding the situation can provide us with a plan of details, not unlike an architect's blueprints, which we might expect to find in that character. Then we may go about ensuring that each detail is duly arrived at. But relying on belief in the situation so that my responses emerge looking like those of the character I find more often than not a wasteful means of accomplishing what other more predictable, controllable, and refreshable techniques can do better and more directly.

Before leaving this technique, let's mention certain situations that may benefit from the inherent side-effects. Given a situation such as that of an old married couple bored with each other, time is on the side of the actors who can believe in the situation: the longer the run, the more familiarly predictable the responses.

Exercise: Try these. Imagine you are in a dentist's waiting room. Imagine you are in a sunken submarine. Imagine you are baby-sitting one night when you had arranged a previous engagement. Do any of these affect you? Whatever you imagine must involve *you,* not the one in the play. This distinction is crucial when building a character.

Remember those indigent actors huddling in the wintry attic? They actually were using a combination of sense memory and this technique. It obviously worked for them.

CHAPTER 22

IMAGERY OR IDENTIFICATION

Let's approach the motivational technique of ***Imagery,*** or ***Identification,*** by looking at how it differs from Belief in the Situation. Take the situation where I am cast as a man who motors into a small town and finds himself arrested and charged by the local sheriff on a trumped up charge of speeding. Belief in the situation would be that I (H.G.) find myself arrested on a bogus charge. My response is frustration/anger/indignation – all fortuitously combined so that the director finds it unnecessary to instruct me any further.

Had he asked me, he would have learned that it was *not* a response of imagining myself to be *somebody else* driving into town: rather it was *my* response to a set of unjust events. That was Belief In The Situation. That is, I know that if this was happening to me, no doubt this is how I would feel. Since our task is to build an illusion, there is no need for me to identify with the character, so long as the emerging results look like those of the character.

This is worth re-emphasising. Belief in the situation does not include fictionalising the people, only the circumstances and events. It is I, in a fictional situation.

Pretending to be the character is a different kind of activity, a make-believe in its own right. Traditionally, it has been used together with Belief in the Situation, but it is useful to regard it as a separate motivational technique independent of Belief in the Situation or any other technique.

Consider a scene that calls for me to step onto the stage and announce to the audience that the second act is about to commence. The situation is the end of interval. I step before the curtain. How do I feel? Since I am an experienced professional, generally at ease and authoritative, I am likely to feel considerate of the audience's needs, patient as they take their time quietening down, perhaps amused as a latecomer scurries furtively to their seat. "Wrong!" says the director. "The script says that you should be self-conscious, terrified, half-choked, faltering." In which case, since I am a professional, I give the director what he wants by identifying with an inexperienced amateur forced to do this. If it works, what has changed? Not the situation, which remains that of a performer announcing the start of the next act. Only the image of the performer has changed, from that of confident professional to that of terrified amateur.

This technique, which we call Imagery, is one of the big ones. Imagery is another name for what psychologists might call 'Identification', meaning personal identification, or who one sees oneself as. We define it as putting oneself in a position of, or seeing onself as an extension of:

(a) A person:

(b) An animal:

(c) An inanimate object:
(d) An idea or abstraction:
(e) A token image, such as make-up, wigs, costume, masks, expressions, props, adjustments, business, etc.

Identification is the taking on of characteristics from influences around us, as opposed to 'projection', a procedure whereby we read into others characteristics borrowed from ourselves. Projection moulds the other person. Imagery (or Identification) is a self-building process.

The technique involves two crucial ideas which can be labelled 'put' and 'let'. You must 'put yourself in the place of X' and 'let yourself respond from the vantage point of X'. But before you have made firm your concept of 'X' you will have studied the play carefully. 'X' will be the distilled embodiment of everything the author, director, and your own creativity see in the character.

Take (a) above, a person: it makes no difference whether the image we draw on is a real person or a figment of somebody's imagination, for in either case we still have to imagine how they would respond. So let's take the person of Hamlet, since he is a figure known to most of us. Let's assume that what we know about him (or believe we know) provides a picture clear enough so that we don't at this point have to engage in research. All right, put yourself in his place. If that is easy, we may proceed with no reinforcing techniques. Now, through Hamlet's eyes and ears, through all his senses and his mind, look at what he has to put up with. If there is no bottleneck, we may now be feeling what could be Hamlet's feelings when he/you see the Ghost: when he/you suspect there is a 'nasty' hiding behind the curtain: when he/you see the skewered body of Pololius emerging from the same curtain.

By now you could be producing an unbroken string of feelings on behalf of Hamlet. But they would remain *your* interpretation of Hamlet, and *your* responses determined by what you have in your own personal repertoire of responses based on the life you have led. Another person performing the same procedures will inevitably come up with responses based on *their* interpretation and accumulation of responses based on their own lives.

Identification requires that we know enough about the character in some detail, and that we are capable of appreciating their confronting circumstances. If we don't know, we may have to resort to any of a series of preparations to ensure that we do. (Research may be necessary, particularly if the character was a real person, see chapter 29.)

As for imaginary people, the background you decide upon will only be limited by the will and imagination of the author, the director, and yourself. There is lots of fun to be had in deciding on personality traits, though ultimately they must be consistent with what the character has to do in the play.

Identification with real or imaginary people, however difficult and demanding it may be in practice, is straightforward enough. But what about sub-heading (b): Animals? Can we put ourselves in the place of an animal, and can we let ourselves experience the world from its vantage point?

Begin with animals you have known, your dog, cat, or budgie. Those of us who have pets frequently find ourselves anthropomorphising them and, if you happen to be hungry, putting words in their mouths like, "I'm hungry. When do I eat?" Some of these ideas might sometimes be true, but the process involved in putting words in their mouths is basically 'projection': we are imposing ourselves on them, saying in effect, "You are speaking my thoughts".

Identification is the reverse. It says, "I speak on behalf of my cat", And while the words "I'm hungry. When do I eat?" may be the same, the associated feelings can be quite different, since we are now trying to see things through their eyes. If we say those words while *identifying* we might feel, on their behalf, "Stupid humans. If only you could appreciate what a favour we do you by living with you. Now come on – get cracking – I want food *now!*"

Of course we can't be sure we are thinking as animals do. After all, we are imagining. But hardly more so than in the case of Hamlet. And there are a number of plays where the characters are obviously human, but each has animal characteristics. Perhaps the best known is Ben Jonson's ***'Volpone,'*** where the characters are named for – and behave like – a fox, a crow, a fly, a parrot, etc. Then there's ***Under the Sycamore,*** which has humans behaving as ants, ***The Insect Comedy*** (Capek), where the characters are assorted insects: we can look back to the Greeks with ***The Frogs*** and ***The Birds*** (both by Aristophanes), or forward to Andrew Lloyd-Webber's ***Cats.*** Some of these plays call for complete animal characterisations. Some, like ***Volpone,*** get their power from the combination of animal feelings and attitudes with otherwise human characteristics.

Try using animal imagery. If nothing else, it will help break down some inhibitions. Mix pets, zoo animals, wild animals, insects in improvisation. In a group, have each person image a different animal, then let them relate to each other as those animals. Now have them relate to each other as they would when all are threatened by external circumstances. Work up to this complex exercise in stages of identification. At first just imitate the animal, as totally as you can, and have your group guess which animal you imitate. Then provide the animal with human means of communicating. Then get the animals to try to pass themselves off as human, still thinking and feeling like their animal, but showing very few of their obvious animal traits. How did Tarzan think, having been raised by apes as an ape? As you work on these exercises, perform actions, especially conflicting actions: how do these make you feel?

If you feel comfortable enough with animal imagery, it is time to move on to inanimate imagery, (c) above, the technique that has drawn most of the jibes directed against modern acting methods by a skeptical public. Peter Finch was said to have cringed from such baiting as, "And what kind of typewriter are you today?" Yet we often in everyday life talk about people and ourselves in the imagery of the inanimate. We hear that someone has a mind like a steel trap, or a garbage-can memory, someone who bulldozed our plans, someone who is a walking computer or encyclopaedia.

Suppose we were called upon to portray such a person. By using a technique like Imagery, we might be lucky enough to come up with a completely suitable package of feelings.

For example, how might a rock feel if it could feel anything? Under what circumstances? You see it is easier to visualise when the image is being acted upon, as in a conflicting situation. So, how would the rock feel buffeted by waves? Or basking in the hot sun? Or burrowed under by lizards? Or chipped away for specimens?

Or a chair. How old, firm, what kind should of course be first be established. Now how might a rocking-chair feel being sampled by a nice old lady? How about an oversized overweight man? Or a scantily dressed nubile model? (A male chair of course.) How about being knocked about or even knocked over by playful children? Play the game while physically assuming the appropriate form as much as possible. Imagine any of the above. You would be a rarity if you were not somehow affected.

And the same observations apply to (d), abstractions. Much theatre history is tied in with the practice of portraying abstract forces. Victorian melodrama was generally about such abstractions as the struggle between Good and Evil.

In the Middle Ages, morality plays such as ***'Everyman',*** had one person portraying Greed, another Lust, another Gluttony, etc. And in conventional Hollywood Westerns, the black-hats and the white-hats are representatives of evil and good.

How would 'Goodness' behave in a pub? at a political rally? in a torture chamber? in a brothel? Practice identifying yourself with such tangibles as Authority, Kindness, Democracy, Famine, Death. These abstract forces are familiar enough in their effects. But how might we identify and personalise them? Somehow, children can generally seem to do these effortlessly.

The early Group Theatre, obviously hoping to restore childish innocence, devised many exercises of which this is one. One actor started from his sleep, brushed his teeth while showering, dressed while eating, combed his hair while rushing to the bus-stop, avidly devoured the newspaper while strap-hanging, rushed into his workplace, darted up three flights of stairs, dropped into his chair, put his feet up and went back to sleep. What he had chosen to portray was the word, 'America'. Incidentally, this actor metamorphosed into the playwright Clifford Odets.

Borrowing this game, how would you portray Australia? family? politics? friendship? loyalty? happiness? Once we grasp the many facets lurking in any concept or what that concept means to you, it is a small step to identifying with them and thus engage in asserting or defending the image. Have we not seen somebody described as the embodiment of bravery? Or persecuted for what seemed its absence?

The final sub-heading, 'Token imagery,' requires us to modify slightly the procedure of putting and letting. In this instance, we put ourselves in the place of somebody who wears/ looks like/ dresses like/ carries, etc., this token: and we let ourselves be affected by the environment we have put ourselves in. Token imagery is what many of us resort to when we ask to rehearse in the shoes (or skirt or wig or make-up) of the character. Many actors tell of how a character only came to life when at last they saw the finished make-up in the mirror, or when they actually started walking around the set, using the furniture or props.

The Greek masks of comedy and tragedy could be seen as token images. Today masks are used in some rehearsals, but unlike the Greek masks these may be neutral masks that remain open to multiple interpretations, or specific masks which suggest specific individuals or types of people. Dr Arnie Goldman suggests there is a name for this phenomenon: synecdoche, or the part-for-the-whole.

Less esoterically, we know this phenomenon well from everyday living. Walk around the house in old slippers and dressing-gown. Wear your best clothes. Don a funny hat. Play tennis in gumboots. Wear dark glasses. For that matter if you have several pairs of glasses with different frames, try one and then the other. Women particularly (feminists, gnash your teeth but I'll say it anyway), I am told, respond more sensitively to different hairstyles, make-up, perfumes or jewellry. Do not these tokens colour our behaviour?

Tokens are tangible touchstones that assist our imaginations to get going or keep moving. Some actors won't work without props – and the pun is intentional, since props (properties) have propped up many an otherwise disoriented and collapsing performance.

Try engaging in an improvisation between two people whose actions are in conflict. As the impro proceeds, each person in turn picks up or puts on some token – a knife or gun, scarf or hat, drink or cigarette, sword or whip, phone or crucifix, hood or mask or make-up: or pulls a face, hunches their back, etc. Any one of these tokens should alter your feelings sufficiently to make a change in your performance. And the token needn't be seen by the audience to be effective. Knowing you carry a pistol in your pocket may be enough.

Many performers around the world rely on two techniques only: Imagery and Belief in the Situation. And it makes sense, for these techniques represent the most central activities of dramatic performance: to apparently identify with the character, and to place that character in the situation of the play. Indeed, some teachers argue that if you can't do and rely on these two techniques alone, you have no business in show business. I don't go so far. These techniques are very useful and important, but I've seen some superb performances which totally ignored both these old faithfuls.

The advantages to Imagery: first, that it is a 'package deal': by pressing one button (if it is the right one), you may come up with a full characterisation with lots of interwoven feelings. Also, it can be very quick. And it is a technique which is easy to doctor, using other techniques to help patch over misfitting moments. Detailed preparation (such as research) can turn imagery into a very substantially-based product. Since the image can mature with time and repetition, so can the feelings, so it's a useful technique for a long run. Finally, and most spectacularly, it can free us from inhibitions by allowing us to hide behind the mask of the Image while we perform actions we would personally disapprove of or be embarrassed by. The customary explanation is, "Its not me, its the character".

But there are disadvantages as well. The image I identify with may generate a parcel of feelings that may be a gross mismatch with what the author and director had in mind, and no matter how I doctor or patch it, it will still not sit comfortably. Or there may be certain blocks in the actor that won't permit such Identification: an ex-prostitute portraying a prostitute, a closet or latent homosexual portraying a homosexual, a lapsed Catholic portraying either a devout Catholic or an atheist. We once had to abort the production of a play because, unbeknown to us and himself, the leading man was re-enacting his own life on stage, and he broke down at the confrontation with his own personality. In such instances, the characterisation could be better served being built up characteristic by characteristic via other techniques. This might prove less cumbersome than the number of band-aids needed to patch over the disintegrated product of a forced identification: and in this way contributing techniques could be carefully selected to ensure the appropriate feelings with less chance of backlash.

Another disadvantage is that the results of Imagery are frequently shallow. The character is only as old as from the start of rehearsal, and by opening night the character has experienced perhaps only four weeks of living – hardly time enough to acquire attitudes to the world at large, not to mention attitudes to one's own attitudes. Of course, most motivational techniques invite associations from deep in our psyches, but my own observations suggest that frequently only the tips of those conscious and unconscious associations come into play to assist in composing the image, and that the deeper portions are left unused.

Thirdly, if the actor is of an hysterical disposition, the technique of Imagery may trigger an attack of the affliction known as multiple personality, which results in the actor going over the brink and actually believing they are that character. Once in that state they become totally undisciplined and unmanageable, engaging in certain obsessive or otherwise over-reactive behaviour onstage or carrying the role offstage. This can be dangerous: pity the Desdemona with an actor who believes he is Othello. Presumably this is the problem Stanislavski had in mind when he said, "Once you begin to believe you are the character, it is time to leave the show".

Fourth, there is a tendency to undiscipline. Even when the identification is not pathological, there is a tendency to subordinate other elements of the play to fit in with one's own image, though the results may be inappropriate for the production. This is where many an argument takes place between director and performer who says something like,"I know how this character reacts. Don't tell me what I should be doing". When the characterisation becomes the centre of the world for this performer, such matters as plot, detail, relationships, etc., have to be bent to accommodate the image. This may lead to Telephone Boothing – as the name suggests, giving a private performance as if isolated in a telephone booth.

Fifth, unless the practitioner is extraordinarily skilled in this technique, there is an obvious tendency for one to watch oneself inordinately. This behaviour is referred to as 'role-playing' or 'image-playing'. We all know people who, while talking to us, seem to be continually glancing at reflections of themselves in anything shiny or listening to the sounds of their own voice: people so inclined seem to have a marked appetite for fleshing out what they may intuitively recognise as a skimpy ego. Often such behaviour is a misguided response to the well-known edict, "Always remember who you are": an arguable concept at best.

One safe and general employment of Imagery, or Identification, is as a technique used by many skilled actors during the early stages of rehearsal, in order to acquire a list of components they think should be seen in the character. Having made the list, they may then go about ensuring that each of these is in place by means of other techniques. During performances they go nowhere near Identification, and their performances seem not to suffer a whit.

Some general exercises to flex functions which are required for Imagery: from then on invent your own.

(1) The Game (Charades). A most universal and useful way of having to find symbols with which to communicate ideas.

(2) Play the Group Theatre Image game. Act out what some particular abstraction means to you. Make it a succinct distillation which encapsulates the idea as you see it. Even stereotype will do. This exercise helps make abstract ideas tangible and releases feelings associated with them.

(3) Two people improvise with conflicting actions. But character A assumes he is character B, and vice versa.

As a technique – or family of techniques – Imagery is extremely popular and universally accepted, but it is not without its critics. For me, while I believe it is an extremely useful and broad-spectrum technique, and most effective in the hands of the very skilled, it is after all just one more technique. It so frequently requires so much augmentation from other techniques that there is a strong case for simply using the other techniques by themselves.

CHAPTER 23

IF – AND AS IF

Sometimes – at different times for different actors – it's impossible to believe in the situation. You look at a 'tree' on stage and you see not a tree but papier-maché covering a chicken-wire frame. What can you do at those moments when you look at what is supposed to be a romantic scene and see only a paper moon, hanging over a cardboard sea?

This is where the magic ***If*** comes in. OK, you tell yourself, it's not actually a tree, but ***if*** it were a tree, would I be prepared to lean on it? That magic ***if*** can encourage natural skeptics to play a game. And once they have begun to suspend their disbelief, it is often possible to take their fantasy a stage further. ***If*** puts a foot in the door: ***If*** encourages the fantasy-shy to dip a toe in the water. ***If*** can put a great wedge into the lives of emotional Scrooges. Indeed, what helped spike Scrooge's 'humbug' might be regarded as an ***if***.

The soft-sell ***If*** goes as follows: "We know the make-believe is just that. But if it were true, how do you suppose you might feel about it?" Upon saying that, it should not be expected that the skeptic instantly starts to feel all over the place. It may simply help the skeptic leave himself open to further suggestions. Then, even if the skeptic does no more than go through the motions of what he believes, it's a start. Then he might be invited to elaborate on the reference. As he does, he will bring in personal associations which will usually and gradually cause him to reveal obvious feelings. And from then on it is a case of steering.

To ask 'How *would* you feel?' is less confronting than 'How *do* you feel?' But in time it could lead to the same results. No wonder Stanislavski referred to it as the "magic if".

If can help transform the fake but relevant trappings of the setting and situation into emotional realities. But ***As If*** is no less magical, and it can take us further. ***As If*** refers to relatively irrelevant circumstances, the belief in which we know can affect us.

From time to time we speculate on things that might happen to us, or that have happened to us, without necessarily recalling a specific single instance. The idea of going to a party can associate a joyous anticipation without necessarily reminding us of any single specific party.

What would it be like to have somebody shove slivers of bamboo under our fingernails, then light them? Does the idea fill you with dread, make you shudder? File the idea away. Some day a director might say to you, "Open the door and there stands a beautiful woman who for some reason fills you with terror". Now how is a doorway full of beauty expected to make you feel dread? Try As If. How easy it will be to open the door, see the woman, then imagine that your hands are forced open and bamboo slivers ...

Of course, it has nothing to do with the woman. Or the play. You may or may not find it necessary to tie her in with the torture: you may imagine that it is she who will be pushing in and lighting the slivers with the aid of two accomplices who are out in the hall. But ***As Ifs*** don't need to be tied in if you don't want to. You may simply choose to conjure up the bamboo fantasy the moment you open the door.

Many fine actors have relived on ***As If*** to motivate and enhance their performances. Bobby Lewis tells of Benno Schneider's terrifying scene of impending suicide, for which Schneider visualised himself about to take a cold shower. And Charles Tingwell has performed in the widest range of media, relying, he asserts, virtually on ***As If*** alone. For instance, when he needs to add urgency to a scene, he simply accepts ***As If*** there is a taxi waiting for him, the hungry meter ticking over. His performances are rarely less than exceptional.

Theoretically, an ***As If*** is a totally make-believe situation, based on nothing we have ever experienced before. (Mutilated hands up, all those who have actually experienced the Lighted Bamboo Fingernail treatment.) But in practice ***As If*** is frequently mixed with sense or emotion memory. Most of us at some time have collected a splinter in the finter, or even under a fingernail. So we may be wincing at the notion of a splinter magnified many times by our imgaination to the size of a bamboo sliver. To the extent that we do this without consciously recalling the actual event, we may regard the idea we imagine as the mythic ***As If.***

Belief in the Situation also relates to an imaginary situation. The difference between it and ***As If*** is that ***As If*** may have nothing to do with the play. It's an irrelevancy that we call on only to provide us with a momentary feeling. True, we can string a whole lot of ***As Ifs*** together for a string of momentary feelings, or conjure up one moment to underlie a whole scene. For example, if a scene needs to be played in slow motion, we might say "as if we were living under water". Of course we haven't walked, talked, or cooked under water, but we can imagine it, and aside from affecting our movements, it also slows down our feelings.

Or you want to come into a scene depressed, so you choose "as if I have just been fired from my job". This could give you the precise degree of depression you require, even if you have never been fired. But suppose you once did get fired. You might still call it an As If, provided that the details of the actual event do not stare you in the face. Once they do, you have mixed in either Sense memory, Emotion memory, or both. If in fact you have been fired, today or very recently, and if you want the benefits that go with As If, it would not be advisable to employ that experience as an As If: it would be too vividly fixed.

This helps explain why we are going to such great pains to distinguish the mythic As If from the actual Sense or Emotion Memory: sometimes it is necessary to avoid vivid reminders of actual experiences. One of the great advantages of As If is that it can be pulled around, added to, subtracted from and mutilated to a degree which is only limited by our imagination. Whenever we need to modify a certain portion of our feelings, we can doctor the equivalent component in our fantasy to suit. Do I need panic? As if I was pursued by a hungry lion ... Greater panic? ... And in escaping the lion I fell into a pool of piranhas. The great Australian swimmer Stephen Holland said he attributed much to the belief that he was being chased by a shark as he swam.

But once you vividly recall a specific true incident, as by Emotion Memory (chapter 32), particularly one which carries a strong and complex emotional association, you are faced with a finite experience that is hard to distort and amplify without disturbing those delicate elements that in fact made it an emotional experience. Look again at that Brigadoon mountain unveiling. It was impressive because it was precisely what it was, appearing precisely when, how and where it did. Suppose that by clever imagining I turned it into an iceberg, or a ghost ship, or a mermaid, or saw it from land in the company of a rowdy crowd in the middle of the afternoon? Sure, I would feel something, but not the awe that moved me to tears. And yet, when we shall look at Emotion Memory, we will discover how to *append* an As If to it to give it a twist.

So let's leave actualities to work their own magic in their own ways. For the moment, we luxuriate in the unfettered world of mythical imagination where almost anything goes. And note that in the examples above we have typified some sub-categories of As If:

(1) I was fired – it happened in the past, thus an historical As If. A background motivation. More often a means of preparing the start of a scene. Not necessary to reinforce with present evidence.

(2) We are under water – it is now happening, thus a present As If. During the scene it may become necessary to reinforce that belief, since much that is happening around us in the scene may cause us to doubt it. For instance, if we are underwater, why aren't we making bubbles as we talk?' This class of As If usually works best in conjunction with other techniques, or some elaborate combination of As Ifs.

(3) We expect to go to a party – thus a future As If. This should be the easiest type to play, since the future is always open to guesswork and imagination. Just remember that the invention need have nothing to do with the situation in the play.

If concocting As Ifs the mythical beliefs should be as particularised as possible. Thus six-inch slivers of bamboo, rather than just slivers. So if we anticipate a party, specifying what or who will be there can make all the difference: your favourite food or musicians, the beautiful person you've been trying to meet for months, your old arch-enemy, a Hollywood casting-agent – all will make particular differences to your specific expectations.

The strength of As If is that being virtually pure imagination, it is limited only by your imagination.

The weaknesses: chiefly that one must select the As If so that the ensuing combination of feelings is not too abrupt or unlikely for the character in the scene: you must select the sorts of references that produce feeling which can be reasonably integrated. The consequences of an inappropriate motivation may be too abrupt for the flow of the scene: you wouldn't want to use winning the lottery to motivate joy at meeting your prospective in-laws. Whatever the As If, the integration of the feeling into the emotional flow of the scene should be as smooth and subtle as the integration of a beat action into the scenic action.

Another caution: preparing an As If in the middle of a scene can sometimes take an unnecessarily long time. In which case, it might appear that an inappropriate beat action – such as the action 'to motivate' – is being played. Consider that, before one plays an action, that action needs to be motivated. How long does one take in preparing actions? Ideally, less time than is taken in performing the action. So if motivation takes as much or more time than a beat action in a scene, you may be accused of playing the action 'to motivate'. To be seen taking time to motivate is to call attention to one's techniques, like saying "see how cleverly I am putting the bits together". Of course that can be very impressive: watching the theatrical conjurer produce a string of feelings out of a hat can be a matter of great sensation – audiences get pleasure from seeing actors cry real tears or blush on cue. But the ultimate art, as a wise person once said, is the art that conceals art.

So your As Ifs should be done surreptitiously. On the tail end of a previous action as it is coasting to a conclusion. During transitional beats, if you can work cunningly and swiftly. During someone else's long speech, where the As If can be covered by listening. Or before coming on stage.

As If is a rich technique. It can trigger shallow feelings quite easily. And it can often be used to stoke deep emotions as well.

Exercises: Imagine you have not eaten for two days. Shake hands with someone as if they have just handled a pustulous ulcer. Shake the same hand as if they are palming a $100 bill they wish to hand you. Imagine a traffic warden is at this moment writing out a summons for you. Complete a discussion as if your pet has been seriously injured and needs to be rushed to the vet. (I saw a scene powerfully played this way although the motivating actress actually didn't possess a pet.) Need we detail the list of As Ifs you can imagine? Your imagination is uniquely yours. Let it fly.

CHAPTER 24

THE ELASTIC CIRCLE

Both If and As If operate not only as motivators in their own right, but also as techniques for facilitating other techniques, methods of dispelling feelings of skepticism and doubt. Now we turn to another such auxiliary device, one which assists other techniques as well as functioning as an independent motivator. The *circle of concentration* works as a dramatic palliative, and as an unsurpassed aid in focusing concentration.

We refer to it as a Circle of Concentration, but it is rarely a circle: more often it can look like a shapeless, free-form amoeba. Here's how it works: first, visualise yourself standing in a crowded brightly lit room: notice how busily your attention may dart from one person or group to another in relatively random sequences. Now focus a concentrated pin-spot on one person alone, and turn out all the other lights: where does your attention turn? OK, move the spot away from that person and onto yourself: where now is your attention?

Usually your own attention will confine itself to all that you can see within your own lighted area. Even if you try, you may not be able to see what is outside your lighted area. Although you may remain curious about what is going on out there, in time you will have to be content with the knowledge of what you can see. So let's imagine that we have opened the lighted area to include you and one other. Notice how easy it is to relate to that one other person and to ignore the rest.

That is how the Circle of Concentration works, except that most of the time we have to light the area with our imaginations rather than with pin-spots. If you imagine a line drawn around just the two of you, and believe that only what is inside that line is worth concentrating on, you will have a containing area which can affect you in much the same way as the area illuminated by the spotlight.

If you have ever experienced a sense of panic on entering a crowded and fully lighted room, you will appreciate how the isolation created by the spotlight of the Circle of Concentration could not only calm you down, but perhaps even make you feel like someone special and above the crowd. On the other hand, if you are one of those who can't avoid associating isolation with panic, don't use the Circle of Concentration – that is, not unless you need to generate panic. There are some who feel that to be lighted and surrounded by darkness could be tantamount to a third-degree interrogation: then it still could be motivationally useful. But not for relaxation or concentration.

There are times when a scene is to be played low key or privately. Certain film or TV close-ups on quiet intimate relationships are helped by the feeling of privacy derived from being involved only in a tight area of interest. In such a scene, your concentration may be helped if the lights concentrate only on your area, particularly if they dazzle your vision so that you can't see even as far as the camera. Likewise onstage where the audience is blacked out and the dazzling front-of-house lights prevent you from seeing them.

But with practice, you will find that you don't need the assistance of actual lighting. You can learn to extend or confine your area of concentration at virtually a moment's notice. At first there are two of you. Now a third comes into the room: hit them with one more light, as it were, and spread it out until it joins yours in a pattern with bulges like a cumulus cloud. Now include yet another: more bulges to the cloud. Now one person leaves: one less bulge.

And here lies one of the problems involved in confining your concentration to a small area. Perhaps you have noticed what happens to your voice when you converse with somebody on the other side of a large room: and again what happens when you move closer to each other. Likewise, when you meet or dine with someone in a small booth, do you not also tend to lower your voice? Unskilled use of the Circle of Concentration can bestow on you more privacy than you might care for: so much that your audience may not have a clue as to what's going on. This intimacy could be great for certain close-up film or TV shots, but possibly deadly for theatres except the most intimate.

Yet, some performers, myself included, thrive on this technique even in mega-seat auditoriums with the most expansive musicals. That's because of the elasticity of the Circle. It need not be limited to merely embracing people on stage: it can embrace the entire audience or some part of it. On several occasions my circle included the town clock on the other side of town. I relied on its chiming the quarter-hour to help motivate a certain scene.

Sometimes the sky is the limit. In the midst of a relatively quiet scene, a noisy aeroplane passes overhead. The craftsman in you tells you the audience may have difficulty hearing. What to do? Speak up? Wait for the plane to pass? Break into a tap dance? Whatever course of action, it will have been born of your awareness of a machine miles from the stage. You have quickly included it in your circle.

As with all specific techniques, it is your choice as to whether you make yourself open to all sound and other stimuli or selectively shut some out. Many actors use the Circle of Concentration to delineate tightly-confined areas. These actors, however, frequently complain that they were thrown by somebody in the audience coughing or a stagehand clumping across backstage: they feel their concentration intruded upon, violated. Others use no selective boundary within which they confine concentration. Any stimulus from anywhere is noted, so that their performances, while lively, tend to jump about in coherence, rather like Ronnie Corbett in one of his famous erratic monologues.

Then there are others who continuously move the boundaries of that circle. Whatever they feel needs or invites inclusion is nimbly enclosed; what is unnecessary or intrusive is excluded. That is my own habit with this technique. The trick is to go about one's business but leave oneself open for visitors. But not to split one's concentration by anticipating the other actor who may come in at any moment. That's like setting the alarm for an early rising, then losing sleep by lying awake waiting for it to ring.

Rather your philosophy should be more like going about your business at home. The time to recognise that we have a visitor is when someone knocks on the door. The time to worry about an incoming call is when the phone rings. Normal alertness – tension is a saboteur here – can be counted on to tell you when the circle needs stretching.

Selective concentration is closely linked with tension, and they can impair or help each other. If we enclose ourselves in a friendly, familiar or interesting area, we tend to feel more secure. We know how a crying baby can be distracted and calmed by some dangled attention-getter: selective concentration can be helpful at any age.

But if we feel imposed upon from outside our circle, we may feel threatened. The antidote is to embrace those threats in some way, to befriend them and enclose them in your circle. I once worked as a counsellor at a summer camp where the campers were city kids, unaccustomed to the country and so terrified of the night that they would rather wet their beds than cross the ten paces of grass to the latrine.

One night we talked. They were ashamed but the terror was greater. "Of what?" "Spooks!" they chorused. Just then we heard an owl. Cries of horror, blankets pulled over heads. "Do you know what that really is? An owl" "You mean one of them wise old birds with the big eyes?" incredled one. Murmurs all round.

Suddenly there was a crack of a twig. More screams. "That could be a rabbit!" I lied hopefully. More murmurs filled the dormitory. Then a muffled twang. Not so many cries. "A frog". And so on, listing fauna that city kids knew only from their alphabet primers or Disney movies. Lights out on a dormitory full of whispers.

On my next hourly round I found that nobody wanted ferrying across to the toilet. Nobody needed to go. Nobody had wet their beds. In fact, nobody was in the dormitory. They were all off in the distant sinister jungle, pinpoints of lights from their torches busily scanning for the wise old owl, the bunny rabbit, and the twanging frog. Their Circle of Concentration now embraced the entire night forest.

Those who cultivate an ability to extend freely their Circle of Concentration need never fear the audience. They are the people we not only work for but also with. They can be embraced, ignored, put on hold, teased, startled – in fact whatever we feel we may do with friends, acquaintances or guests. They are not the enemy! But even if they were, embracing them from time to time within our Circle of Concentration could turn them into friends.

Sometimes tension causes us to huddle in an enforced mini-concentration camp. Indeed it can be so mini that we withdraw into ourselves. Performances born of such isolation tend to be self indulgent. Masturbatory. The kind of performance Rouben Mamoulian referred to as an 'orgy of self-expression'.

We don't want to let any stimuli force us into involuntary isolation. The ability to handle a Circle of Concentration is a controllable tool for involvement. Which may remind us that everybody on stage has their own circle of concentration. When someone overlaps their circle of concentration on where you have placed yours, there's a reinforcement, like two people being illuminated by two strong spotlights instead of one. When you and they encircle the same area, the effects on yourselves and the audience are multiplied.

The ancient prank by a group of people who stand in a small bunch looking up at a building never ceases to fool some innocent who must stop to see what they are looking at. One prankster has some effect, two will double the impact, and five can be irresistible. So it can be with the performer's concentration. In a later chapter, when we go into details about directing and misdirecting the audience's attention, we can think back to the Circle of Concentration as a practical technique for involving the audience so strongly that they find it hard to look away.

Exercise: Try this. You are alone in the living room reading an interesting book. Draw the circle tightly around you and the book. You have been expecting a private phone call at 9p.m. Now extend the circle to include the clock. It is 8.45. Then back to the book. It occurs to you that mother/father/friend could be within earshot. Listen for their presence. They could be just a thin wall away. Now include the phone, wishing it not to ring just yet. You think you hear the potential eavesdropper going to their room. Settle back with your book. Notice how you didn't concern yourself with what else was in the room other than the book, clock and phone. Concentrate on a picture on the wall. Now include the wall. Then the whole room. And back to the picture. Your turn!

CHAPTER 25

JUST LIKE

When we began developing our list of motivational techniques, two popular procedures seemed just other ways of using As If. In time, we recognised enough differences to justify our giving *Just Like* and *Identity* pigeon-holes of their own. As If relates to a situation, a happening, a series of circumstances that can be added to or modified. But 'Just Like' is an image of a person, projected onto another person, and it can't be modified to any substantial degree though it may be qualified. He is or he isn't just like my uncle but he can be the happy uncle or sad. Identity too, as we will see, superimposes images, but these are synthetic: products of imaginative concoctions and easily modified.

We have come to believe that the *just like* phenomenon is based on a deep-rooted instinct – the instinct that makes it possible to learn, the one that is the basis not only of scientific thinking but also of bigotry. This presumed instinct contributes to our habits of summarising, integrating and classifying, and to our tendency to generalise, hypothesise and prejudge. These are but a sophisticated version of some conditioned reflex like to shy away from what could be a repetition of some earlier unfortunate occurrence, 'once bitten, twice shy'. Since even amoeba can behave that way, we may presume that it is a very primitive and universal instinct. And what a busy little instinct it is.

We learn about the world around us by sticking labels on any thing or concept that can be seen as a contained entity or group of entities with characteristics in common. When we think of the label, we associate the common characteristics. Once the male parent has been labelled 'Dada' for the baby, he is Dada and not Mummy. 'Maleness' equals 'Dada'; an association which can sometimes prove most embarrassing for Mummy at the supermarket.

Later in life, nameplates are attached to specific people. Thus, if Mary is the name of the neighbouring child who always grabs and smashes our toys, then the nameplate Mary comes to represent not only the name of the child but also the associated destructive qualities. So when one day we meet another child called Mary, we will necessarily make the assumption that we can expect destructive behaviour from her, and it will take some considerable unlearning before we can trust Mary-2 with our toys. Associations are hard to eradicate. And if you think this is true only for small children, try to imagine yourself becoming un-selfconsciously friendly with a perfectly nice person named Bruce Hitler. When someone we meet reminds us of someone else, it is hard not to treat the new person somewhat the same as the other. This also applies to people we may never have met but have strong associations about via literature, newspapers or hearsay. To wit, the above Bruce Hitler. One of the positive implications of this phenomenon is that meeting new people can be an adventurous encounter measured against old acquaintances or associations.

The Just Like phenomenon can be employed as a motivational technique. We can specify for ourselves similarities between the character we're playing opposite and some familiar person. Then if we *believe*, we can generate useful emotional results in ourself. He is 'just like my uncle'. She is 'just like my first history teacher'. He is 'just like Napoleon'. To use this technique you must find people for whom you have strong and definite feelings, then superimpose their image onto your fellow actor. Note that in using the technique of Just Like it is the other actor (not the character) on whom you superimpose the image: and that the image you superimpose is that of someone for whom you already carry an emotional association (not the fictitious character of the play). By selecting a suitable Just Like, it could indeed look like you are relating to the character in the play.

Just Like is a phenomenon we see virtually every day in ordinary life. Introducing young children to tigers, the teacher tells them that tigers are 'cat-like', and draws the children's attention to the similarities between the family cat and the unfamiliar wild animals. The simile allows the children to make the necessary visualisations and associations. How easy it is to abuse this marvellous learning phenomenon. In wartime, this technique is imposed on people as a means of making them hate the enemy. One technique of several.

As a motivational technique, as with *all* acting techniques, its use is a matter of personal choice. Does Just Like turn you on at all? In what way? As a primary or a supportive technique? Would it be one of the first or one of the last alternatives to be explored? And of course as with all techniques, does the resulting response suit the play?

As a primary technique, Just Like invites a range of supportive techniques to help you reinforce the super-imposition. Three of the most useful are As If, Usery and the Ensemble Effect. We'll discuss the last two techniques in later chapters: As If may be used when our acting partner seems to be doing something that could undermine our belief in them as Just Like. For instance, if our partner is behaving more glumly than we might expect of the uncle he is supposed to be just like, we may alibi for him by thinking it is as if uncle has had a rough day at work.

Practise projecting particular people's personalities that have some significant emotional connotation onto others you are meeting for the first time. Let it work for you for a while, then switch projections by imposing a different somebody onto your victim. In time you should neutralise all these projections so that you can get to know the person for what they actually are: you could be missing out on a potential close friend. Even if you discover that this technique is not for you, the mere awareness of it should help you to see through the techniques of bigotry, propaganda, and spurious advertising that we meet all too frequently. Advertisers usually take great care to ensure that actors they choose represent some identifiable image.

A recurrent hybrid application of Just Like was brought to our attention by a student who came up with a particularly warm response during a practice session. She told us later that she had projected not a relative or famous person onto her partner, but rather her best friend, her kitten. Can a kitten be a person? Well, why not: after all, what we are inviting when we employ Just Like is a package of responses based on a familiar association. With a single triggering mechanism, we can respond in a complex manner built up over a period of time and endowed with many shades of colouring. It is reasonable, if one relates to a cat as a dynamic and multifaceted living being, that the group of responses it can engender will be like those stimulated by a human. Perhaps we should change the definition to imposition on another performer of another being not actually the character in the play.

The major advantage of Just Like is that it can help one generate a complete complex of affects in one hit, with each affect richly multi-faceted. A second advantage is that it tends to keep us related to our partner during both action involvement and motivation process, while other techniques may disrupt the flow. For example, As If sometimes requires a momentary blanking out in our action-relationship while we cut away mentally to concoct the mythical incident. We re-focus and pick up where we left off, but that small gap may be undesirable. But with Just Like, the object of our action is also our key motivator. The reason we feel this way about our partner is because of our already built-in feelings for our parent/aunt/teacher/lover/whoever, who is also the person we are playing the action upon. Since there is no need to cut away from the source of our feelings, we tend to remain in contact more constantly.

Disadvantages: Just Like often needs reinforcing. From time to time, the personality of the actor surfaces sufficiently so that it becomes a strenuous effort to see them as someone else we know. Conversely, our attitudes toward the source of our feelings may change during the run of the show, and thus affect our attitudes toward our fellow actor. This was seen recently when one actor, in the flush of blissful romance found it useful to impose a 'just like my boyfriend' on her stage partner. Everything sparkled until one day there were vibes of hatred and anger where there shouldn't have been. She had broken up with her boyfriend, and her stage partner paid for it.

These warnings aside, Just Like is a generally useful technique for both long seasons or short appearances. It is worth trying, and if it works for you, it can be a warm colourful device.

WRITE YOUR OWN NOTES

CHAPTER 26

IDENTITY

Identity, as with Just Like, also requires superimposing a character onto your fellow actor. But this character is totally (or largely) fictitious. You can create a character to order. The character can be conveniently designed to fit whatever you, the author or director, think should show itself in your relationship.

I once knew someone in a stock company in the U.S. whom I identified as a good friend. A few years later when I was doing Air Force basic training, I ran into him again and my friend became also my confidant. One day, when I was letting fly with some particularly vitriolic denunciations of the military higher-ups, he whispered to me to shut up, because he was actually a member of G2, Internal Military Security, and he was required to report me. As if my magic, my friend ceased being my friend. He was now ... a spy! A summary simple label, whereas before that he had been a label enriched by much detail. And since then I doubt that we've exchanged more than a few brief pleasantries. Come to think of it, tipping me off could have been a token of true friendship. But at that paranoidal time I chose to see it differently.

By now you should be asking 'but what's the difference between this technique and Just Like?' Thank you. Remember, Just Like is a superposition of a specific person (or animal) and is difficult to alter. Identity concerns an invented one. Therefore he is as unlimited in characteristics as your imagination allows. Most importantly, he is usually a label. A doctor, lawyer, soldier, etc. Lenny was no longer Lenny: he was a *spy*. And as a spy, he was capable of any traits I could want him to have.

How summary or specific detail should we go into with the Identity technique? That depends on how deeply we wish to relate to that identity. Are we satisfied to settle for a label or do we seek a more fulsome identity? Consider first the more superficial.

A good starting place for imagining the character is with the picture that the authors or director describe for us in the first place. Often they will have provided a good deal of detail, either in their descriptions of the characters, or in what the characters say about themselves or each other, or in what becomes evident from their behaviour in the play. Perhaps these clues can be summarised into some accessible and succinct identity. Like he is a bitter, frustrated, spiteful man.

Sometimes, when a play has not provided enough clues, we may find ourselves turning for help to the book or film on which it is based. Be careful about this one: a book is not a play is not a film, etc. Each may be conceived in different terms with different emphases. Sometimes the only thing they have in common is the title. Sometimes not even that.

Sometimes the image comes to us in a flash, sometimes it slowly emerges as we plough through rehearsals. In any event, having arrived at a picture of who he or she is, we proceed to accept it and even believe it. This final stage is when we crystallise the Identities of others in the cast.

When you believe in another person as a total identity, as with Just Like, results occur for both yourself and the other person. But what we are concerned with primarily in our discussion of these two techniques (Just Like and Identity) is the effect on ourselves. Whatever happens to the other person is a group benefit of the same kind as that of the Ensemble Effect, which we'll discuss in the next chapter.

Identity, on its most superficial level, simply labels a character with a summary image or with a mixture of summary images. "She is a friend", we might think, or "She is a good friend". We should be able to define a character's Identity fairly succinctly, since it works as a package deal approach, like Just Like and Imagery.

The blanket concepts of friend, spy, pilot, policeman, headwaiter, etc., carry with them emotive associations, some of them quite powerful. So in a play we might have the hero, villain, ingenue, soubrette, character man etc. – images so generalised that the classifications can embarrass those of us who pride ourselves on our non-biased thinking. Nevertheless, these conjure up conditioned packages of responses. To test this, watch a bunch of unconstrained swearing revellers as you introduce a stranger to them as Father O'Brien.

The instinctual basis of Identity (as with Just Like) is summary thinking, as it is also of both bigotry and science. Some of the chief differences are that in order to generalise or summarise, the scientist needs much evidence, the bigot a very small amount, and the actor virtually none. For the actor a mere assumption will do. Thus we can look at and relate to another person on stage as a labelled human being, one whose label defines his relevance to us. As long as we believe in the label or image, we can be turned on in the particular way we need. A parliamentarian. A hero. An author. A journalist. A Nobel Prize winner. A cop. A priest.

In *Once a Catholic* there is a scene in which the girls are committed to a day of total silence. One restless and mischievous girl (X) has a classmate (Y) who she knows likes to stick by the rules. To alleviate her boredom, X embarks on a game of getting Y to talk to her. All X needs of Y is to see in Y the Identity of a zealous student-religionist. (Of course that's not all there is to this scene, and we'll look at it from another angle in the next chapter.)

Practising Identity can be like the game we played earlier to help sharpen our imaginations. If we are accustomed to stereotyping people, or if we were raised in families or communities where social, religious, cultural or occupational delineations are a fact of life, we should find it easy to ascribe Identities. Any class system is a boon to actors who rely on Identity, and so is religious exclusivity.

Everywhere in our society we see how labels can induce perfectly decent and fair human beings to mete out special treatment to their fellow humans. Along with group identification, it is probably the greatest source of such things as titles, uniforms, fashions, degrees, and snobbery. As with Just Like, when abused, this technique can be destructive.

For those of us to whom labels need some justification, we still may use Identity with a little help from Usery, As If, Improvisation, and quite a few other supportive techniques. And the Ensemble Effect can help turn Identity into a powerhouse of a technique. It is usually with the assistance from these others that a shallow label could be fleshed out to a rich, multifaceted full image of an identity. He is a cop, my neighbour whose kids go to my kids' school. He worries about his mortgage. He often parks his car across my driveway. Last year when my wife was sick he was a real pillar of support. And so on. Here we have gone beyond the simple labels of cop, neighbour, friend or inconsiderate bastard.

Among the advantages of this useful technique are ready access, strong associations, and a capacity for touching us superficially as well as deeply. It affects both the Identifier and the Identified. It can be played by both individuals and groups. And – unlike Imagery – Identity keeps us in contact with our reference. Imagery tends to invite us to cut off and play by ourselves, but Identity is particularly helpful in sustaining contact.

Since the source of our motivation and the object of our action are usually the same person when we practise Identity, we may find it easy to observe a rule dear to some of our finest performers: *wherever possible, the object of your action should be your key motivator.* (Why am I fawning on that man? Because he is the richest man in town. Why am I doing this to you? Mostly because of your need for assistance.)

Identity is a technique that can help create strong bonds, vitality, colour, variety, and even humour in our stage relationships. It is ironic that so powerfully useful a tool should be born of a practice which, in society, is so often destructive.

And unlike Just Like, it can be easily amended. Thus there is less tendency to staleness.

Disadvantages: a certain shallowness of *relationship* if unsupported by other techniques, though not necessarily a shallowness of *feelings*. Like a fan meeting a star. Here the bond between people tends not to be deeply committed. That is another difference from Just Like.

It also tends to be affected by the passage of time perhaps more than other techniques. For example, identifying my fellow actor as a mathematical wizard may fill me with awe at the first rehearsal, but after I've got to know him a bit, by later rehearsals he's just another nice guy. But by the same token, because it is limited only by the imagination, this should be easy to remedy. I might now consider him a great foot-baller.

But this time-effect can work in the other direction as well. Two students can play a game in which they agree to see each other as some other person (Just Like) or professional (Identity) without revealing who it is each imagines the other person to be. This game may be extended for weeks. A gradual change will occur to both, to the point where often each recognises who they are in the eyes of the other. The results can be startling.

Who knows but that conscious insight into these techniques may one day help us to avoid its everyday dangers. And surely even help us to be more civilised.

Repeat that exercise where you identified a woman as having different professions. But this time, see if you can label her with conviction without deliberately seeking corroborative evidence. If you can do this readily, see how easy it can be for others to label you.

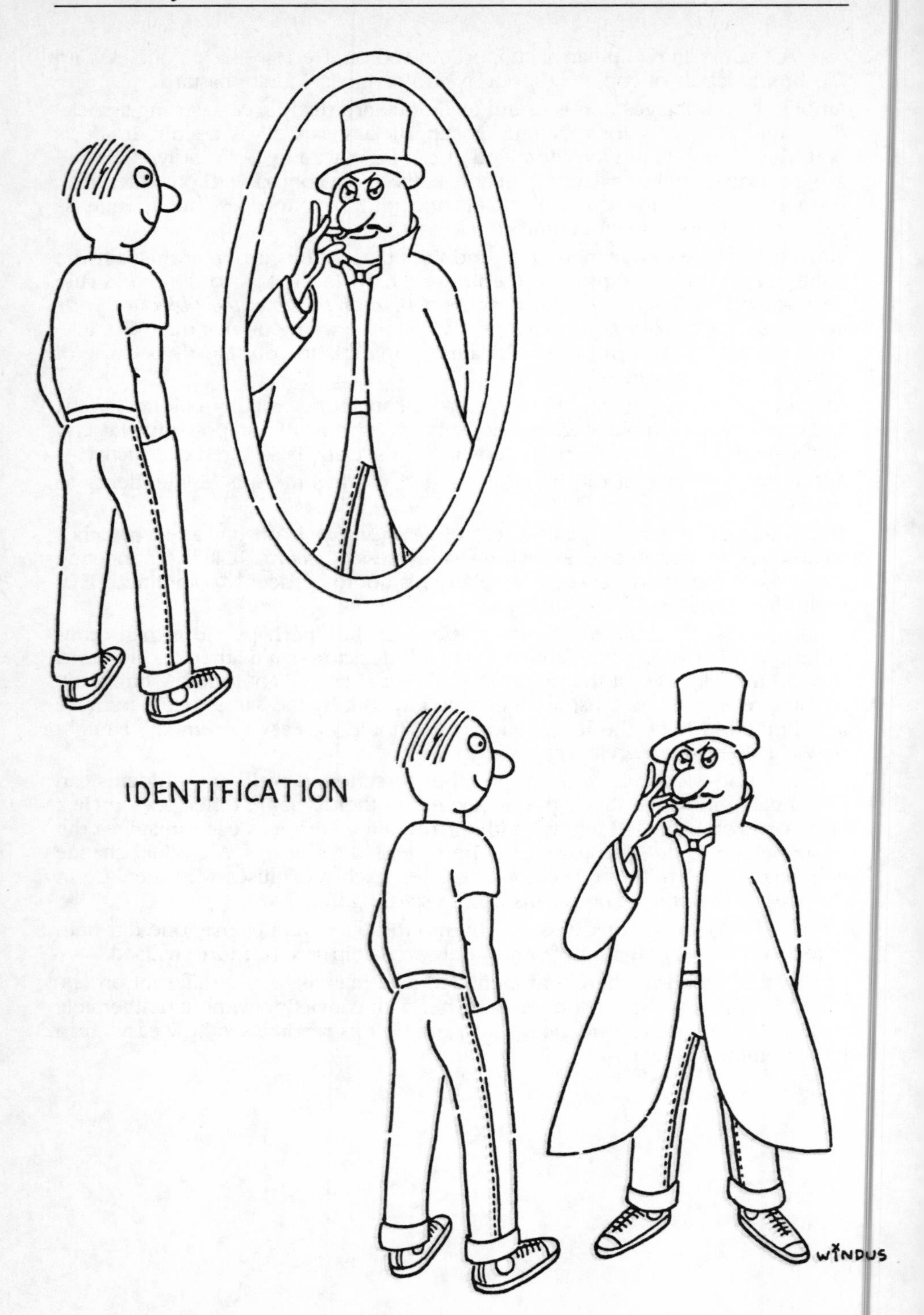
IDENTIFICATION
IDENTITY
WINDUS

CHAPTER 27

THE ENSEMBLE EFFECT

An egoist is reported to have said "But enough talking about me – let's talk about you. What do you think of me?" Thus far our techniques have involved self-seeking and self-serving. But what about the other fellow? Let's talk about him.

Having mentioned the *Ensemble Effect,* we might as well examine it now. We find this technique so formidable that we named a theatre after it. 'Ensemble' is a word to which we give a meaning more special than the more common definition. To some it means playing or working together, which is simple enough. But that definition seems thin to those familiar with the magic of the Ensemble Effect – and 'magic' does not exaggerate by much the swaying power it can have on cast and audience.

Let's use an example to examine the effect of this technique. We send one student out of the room, asking her to prepare an improvisation. When she returns she will organise the group for some activity like a party, barbecue, sports event – anything she wishes.

While she is out the group conspires to treat her as wise, competent, friendly, good-humoured. We aren't to say as much, just believe that she has those virtues, and to discuss her plans with her in that light. But after a certain amount of time, at some subtle cue like dropping a book, we will all regard her as devious, hostile, foolish, dishonest and boring. Once again, there will be no heavy cues or accusations, just thinking and believing her to be so.

When the victim returns there is at first some slight guardedness; after all, we have been talking about her. But after a while she relaxes as the friendly group discusses her plans. She opens up, glowing, relaxed, chipper, colourful, nimble, good humoured. Then the cue, and the group turns. Within a minute or so the victim feels defensive, recriminative, impatient, hostile, and a whole range of other than pleasant feelings. She has changed, but usually won't know why, because her change of feeling was not controlled by herself but was manipulated by the group. Her identity remains unchanged. Only her feelings were modified.

The Ensemble Effect is based on the concept that you will respond according to how you are treated. We should know this one well from our experience of everyday life.

Picture yourself arriving at a party you've been looking forward to: the hostess greets you with a large smile and freindly welcome. Others stop what they are doing and come to greet you, hand you a drink, offer food, introductions all round. How do you feel? Now replay that. You arrive with the same anticipation, but this time the hostess' face drops when she sees you at the door. She pauses for a moment too long, sighs and says come in. Others glance at you, then rapidly find a renewed interest in the conversations they've been in, or the contents of their glasses. Nobody greets you, you just stand there. Do you suppose you'd have a ball? Only the extremely strong or daring would stick around longer than necessary.

When the Ensemble Effect is used on stage, the audience may see an actor transform before their eyes, but unless they have unusual expertise they will look in vain to guess how the change occured. It is an effect which is activated by reading certain detailed personality traits in another person.

Originally we saw the Ensemble Effect as the consequences of a whole group of people treating an individual in a certain way. It was conceived as a motivational technique *imposed* upon an individual. We thought at first that unlike such techniques as Belief in the Situation, Imagery or even Identity, where we are primarily concerned about what our references do to *us,* the Ensemble Effect aimed to change the other fellow.

After a while though, we found that even starting with a technique like Identity, although we were to be the chief beneficiary of, say, associating with a strong friend, our friend got something out of it too. We might benefit, for instance, from asking him to help us recover some money from the bully who has stolen it: we couldn't have dared to confront the bully without his support. Our strong friend, on the other hand, feels useful, noble, and has his feelings of physical prowess endorsed once more. But with the technique of Identity, I invited the strong friend primarly for *my* benefit, and anything accruing to him was a by-product.

With the Ensemble Effect, if I make my friend feel good by employing and complimenting his strength, my direct intention is to bolster his ego. And if I too subsequently feel good, that's a pleasant bonus. By the same token, I can make 'my friend' (the identity) feel guilty, defensive, aggressive, or anything I choose. He still remains the same identity, 'my friend', and I too get a bonus benefit from the way I treat him.

The Ensemble Efffect is a tricky one in other ways. Remembering that drama depends heavily on conflict, can you imagine the non-drama occurring as a result of a strong action-player having to oppose a wishy-washy one? The Ensemble Effect is capable of elevating a most subservient partner into a formidable opponent. Suppose we use an analogy where we make 'money' represent 'dynamics'. Let's imagine we earn, say $400 a week, and we employ a part-time housekeeper for $100 a week. That makes us three times richer than our employee. But now let's say we are sharing a house with eight others, and each of us earns $400, and each of us forks out $100 for the housekeeper. Suddenly our housekeeper is three times richer than each of us, earning $900 a week.

Unified group attitudes to another person can elevate that person's dynamic status to the point where she becomes a worthy adversary in a dramatic conflict. But we need not assume that only the combined weight of a group may do this. It is possible for one individual to enrich an associate by raising their status by way of the Ensemble Effect. Then when we cross words with a now formidable opponent, the conflict will be greater. What difference that they acquired their power from us.

Take the instance, mentioned in the last chapter, from the play *Once a Catholic.* The mischievous girl (X), having induced the girl who was sticking to the rules (Y) to speak, then decides she will extend her efforts to bait the victim. X challenges Y about her morality, making her feel wicked and turning her into a centre of the other girls' attention. But this change in status makes Y feel important for the first time in her life, and she discovers untapped inner resources. She goes beyond her accuser's charges and submits evidence that she *has* committed a mortal sin: and in her bragging revelations she also reveals a capacity for one-upmanship which deflates X and send the others into a frenzy.

And all this from the way one strong persecutor endowed a relatively vulnerable person with importance.

A good con-man, salesman, politician, or preacher is expected to have this skill almost as a mandatory tool of trade: the ability to make somebody feel whatever we want them to feel by the way they are treated.

When we considered Identity, we noted that it was designed to create an image out of presumptions or generalisations, whether the generalisation was simply assumed in one hit or built up from fragmentary bits of evidence. In any event, inevitably a bit of Ensemble Effect can come into play even if we make a general character assumption about the victim. Even more so if we project onto her a whole stack of particular characteristics. But we will find that if we must deal with a person for their detailed personality traits instead of their summarised identities, we might just as well start with the Ensemble Effect and let the identity take care of itself. Given enough detail, complex identities tend to form themselves.

We often see productions where a character is first seen as a generalised identity: a gangster or a priest, say. But as the play unfolds the identities become more fleshed out, often surprisingly. We soon learn that the gangster has a heart of gold and the priest is actually a nasty. New characteristics have gradually revealed themselves, and these may have been generated by — yes, the Ensemble Effect. It would seem to be a technique for all seasons: perhaps the only one some companies rely upon.

But why should we adhere only to the Ensemble Effect? Why should we confine ourselves to any technique? Too often, actors reject a piece of direction because they can't make it conform to their limited range of techniques. "I can't believe it, so I wont do it". Or "Sorry, this situation won't make me cry". Theatre is *not* about displaying techniques, but rather choosing and using techniques to serve the plays.

Nevertheless, that Ensemble Effect is temptingly potent. In particular it is a most effective partner with Identity. An identity arrived at by way of the kind of detail the Ensemble Effect can provide will have depth and go beyond the ordinary label of such an image. This then creates a character identity in the fullest sense of the word.

The Ensemble Effect strives to generate its own parcel of feelings and traits on the target person economically and efficiently. It may impose one attitude or several – perhaps a whole batch of attitudes at the same time. When, as in performances, we seek to structure specifically predetermined personality traits in our partner, we should choose our treatment carefully so that whatever happens to our partner is what is actually required to be seen. Any imposed traits that are irrelevant can alter his image.

Now let's go back to the example of the improvisation where a student tried to organise a group which in turn gave her the treatment. Let's look this time at what happened to the group, for there can be no doubt that the group itself underwent an emotional change. When they treated the 'organiser' with friendliness, it seemed to bring out a whole range of warm qualities – consideration, compassion, goofy humour, the works. But when they turned we were looking at a lynch mob expressing spite, vindictiveness, hostility, anger, outright cruelty, and other usually dormant or repressed emotions. Had any of the group been confronted with their responses at that moment, they would have been shocked. But they were not looking at themselves, which is one important reason why they could release such hostility. They were busy with their victim. Moreover, they had group reinforcement. As well, they were only 'playing a game'. And even the initiation of the game was someone else's, so there was little inhibition or guilt associated with the attack. And afterwards there was no remorse, but rather congratulations on a group project well done. We need not pursue the moral, social and political implications of this phenomenon, except to ask if this is also what a lynch mob might feel.

The Ensemble Effect is repeatedly used to colour the feelings of the treated and the treater. Many a show has been rescued by – if not actually structured on – the Ensemble Effect. The story goes that in the original *West Side Story* the performers portraying the Sharks and the Jets were dissuaded from socialising with each other. And I am sure that one of the chief contributions to the magic of the original *Oklahoma!* production was the Ensemble Effect. Everybody built everybody else, there were no selfish 'star' perforemances.

One production of *Kismet* was saved from disaster by an Ensemble Effect rehearsal. After a disastrous preview, the cast got together and discussed how they saw each other. The emphasis was thus off themselves, and they generated vitality and other responses in their partners. And of course each was their partner's partner.

Regrettably that show subsequently destroyed itself by that very same device. It became clique-ridden, with each clique treating other cliques contemptuously. In time this could be seen on stage, and what was conceptually a beautiful production fell apart. Like other techniques, Ensemble Effect doesn't play favourites. It can destroy a show just as readily as it can build one.

In sum this is a technique that can be employed by individuals or groups. It can be self-initiated or imposed by a director. It can be supported by other techniques when and if it seems necessary, and in return may support them. It is so strong and mult-effective that as often as not it may stand by itself as the only technique necessary for many a scene.

One more sub-division of Ensemble effect should be noted. Besides modifying the feelings of others or of ourselves as individually separate entities, it is often employed in cultivating bonds of mutual trust. For very often performers believe that a production is a conglomeration of soloists, each perhaps thinking that this is how the show will best be served, perhaps believing that others in the show will not be able to – or will not care to – match their own skills in performance.

So we've developed some *group* Ensemble exercises, designed to deflect the mistrust. We can play improvisations wherein the projected qualities of each actor on the other are of trust and dependability. We assume that the other person will always be there to accommodate our needs: and of course the others assume this of us too. For instances, you sit back into empty space and someone can be relied upon to either catch you or tuck a chair under you before you hit the ground. You fall backwards into each other's arms. You let yourself be carried or tossed around. You leave sentences unfinished and trust that someone will complete them for you. You even believe that by putting a cigarette in your mouth (must you?), someone will come up with a light.

Trust exercises can be invented and lib, depending on whatever aspects of mutual sensitivity and responsiveness are required. Here's how such trust applies to working: let's say that the scene requires you to leave the room when you are stopped at the door by the other actor who calls out "Wait". If you trust the other actor to stop you just in time, you go to exit with all the drive and determination of someone who is about to do something specific elsewhere. When the word "Wait" comes, you don't freeze instantly, but coast while you struggle for a moment thinking: "I'm late for my appointment, but that 'wait' sounded so urgent that I can risk delaying a bit longer". Of course, the urgency of your exit will determine how long you deliberate. Your decision to halt will be – and look – well motivated.

But suppose you don't have complete trust in your acting partner. You may well find that you don't approach the exit at full tilt, but begin to slow down before you get to the door, almost as a nudge to your associate which hints, "Now! Stop me now". So when you do stop, it is abruptly, with no trace of momentum, as if you were anticipating and preparing for it.

Which of these would be the most plausible arrest of an exit? Obviously, if you trust your fellow worker, you got to exit with full conviction, leaving it entirely up to them to stop you. And even if you are not stopped in time, you can keep going and leave it up to them to get you back, trusting their skills to extricate you both from this mishap. (Of course, if where you are going is over a cliff, we might have to reconsider the remedy.)

Advantages: great subtlety in arriving at emotional change. Broad range of feelings. Mutual benefits. Can be used most effectively for setting up feelings of trust. Where the audience *can* see cause and effect, a great invitation to empathy. Deeply effective. Often induces long retention of feelings. Easy to play on audiences. Easy to help motivate supplementary actions. An effective springboard for launching other techniques. Avoidance of need to stereotype. And in particular, an excellent motivator where mercurial acting and nimbleness are required.

Perhaps that last requires a word of clarification. You are playing a scene with three others. You feel differently about each of the others. You are expected to turn to one, say something coloured by how you feel about him. Now you quickly talk to the second, this time coloured by what you feel about him. Then perhaps quickly back to the first, then the third. Each time your attitudes are expected to colour your actions.

Assuming that spontaneity is not working for you sufficiently, and each nimble exchange needs its own preparation, most techniques will slow you down, since most techniques may take anything from a few seconds to hours or even days in order to motivate you adequately. The mark of a mercurial actor is extreme nimbleness in changing from one fully prepared action to another. The Ensemble Effect can provide that. Having decided a string of personality traits for each of the three, merely turning to them tends to associate what you feel about them and reveals that feeling immediately.

Watch a sensitive person perusing faces in a crowd. As their eyes scan from one to the other we can see them undergoing attitudinal changes. At their best, the changes are kaleidoscopic. The moment you believe certain qualities to exist in another, you change your attitudes to these qualities. And when you have pre-programmed your attitudes to certain people, the change is mercurial.

Disadvantages: not helpful if you are portraying a character who is cut off from the world in some way. In fact it could be sabotaging. It may inadvertently create attitudes which can be too revealing or disarming unless handled carefully. Some ego-frail or hypersensitive actors may never forgive you for having induced in them a feeling they would rather not have shown, or having manipulated them when they would rather have had complete command of their functions with no presumptuous interference from you.

Also, mixtures of feelings may produce side effects or secondary responses which may be counterproductive. The theatrical equivalent of a faux pas. It is an empirical technique which needs to be sampled or otherwise tried out before one can rely on precisely what to expect from pressing each button.

It should be emphasised that whereas some see Ensemble Effect as some vague form of togetherness, our definition is based on treating each other in specific ways. Not simply on dutifully picking up cues, but generating in each other specific feelings and attitudes. The premise is always, "One responds as one is treated".

Remembering that a motivational technique is concerned with inducing changes in feelings, what we use to get those feelings in motion is limited by the specific technique. For the Ensemble Effect the devices we use to treat our partner can be virtually anything. We can play specifically selected actions on him. We can maintain certain feelings towards him. We can use form, like by-passing him as we carry a tray of drinks, or looking through him. We can use any kind of treatment, so long as what comes out at the other end are the feelings we wish to see generated in him.

Looking at it from the point of view of characterisation, we can recognise that a characterisation can change almost instantly as a result of ambivalent relationships. Two people treating you differently will produce in you two differing sets of responses. You might even behave like two different people in the same room with two others. This effect is surely familiar from experience of everyday life.

It cannot be too emphatically stated that in every way, the Ensemble Effect is a powerful technique. So much so in fact that for years this device has been the secret weapon of the so-called star system. It often occurs that by cunning promotion and other manoeuvrings, some person is assigned the position atop a plastic totem-pole. And the rest of us – theatricals and audiences alike – tend to believe it to the extent that we accord them extraordinary deference. And when we do, they are affected by our treatment so that they actually come to believe in their own specialness: almost like believing their own publicity. *No* ... this is not to imply that extraordinary skill may not of itself exalt a performer to a well-deserved stardom. Even here, our respect for them may help them overcome moments of uncertainty which even real stars are prone to, for example Judy Garland. But be it stars who earned their status or stars synthesised for the box-office, it is ultimately the Ensemble Effect at work.

So if one person can be made to shine in a production, why not a whole company of stars. Again ... that old Ensemble Effect ...

CHAPTER 28

REALITY AND USERY

Not everything that happens in a performance is make-believe. Sometimes we deal with reality. Rather than embark on a philosophical treatise on what reality is, for stage purposes we can leave it as anything you can actually sense, have just sensed, or are about to sense with a reasonable degree of predictability.

I really did just come on stage from those wings, and barring accidents, will really be leaving by that doorway to return to my dressing room. This is a real stage, those are real lights, the wall is a real canvas flat stretched on real wooden frames, painted with real paint and supported by real braces and real cord lashing them together. That is a real sofa, real chairs, real cups. The tea is real tea, and the Scotch filling the real glass is real water tinted with real Coca-Cola.

My headache is real, as are the rumbles coming from my real stomach. My dry mouth, the frog in my throat, and my frail memory for the third line in the long speech are all honest and truly real. But then so is the invisible electricity going through the filaments of those lamps, and if a fuse blows the scene and my feelings can certainly be altered. The people on stage are real, as are their costumes, make-up, and most of the props. The cigarettes they will smoke are real, and the poison one of them swallows is real powdered sugar.

Every one of those real elements can affect me. The ones we just listed are generally planned-for realities, deliberately included to affect efficiency, viability, or plausibility of the production. But like the blown fuse, accidents do happen. And most accidents are real: they too must be included in our list of realities.

How do we make realities work for us as motivational aids?

Firstly by arranging for them to be there. If I know there will be a strenuous routine after which I might feel exhausted, I might arrange to have a chair there to fall into. With this reality I can now feel replenished, restored, happier. Some actors arrange for a cigarette to be smoked or a cup of tea to be served at a strategic cue when they think they could probably use one.

Secondly, there is the simple device of finding an appropriate reality as it is needed. As everything within our circle of concentration is real, we can select what will be convenient to relate to. If for some reason I ran out of reasons for crossing upstage on a particular cue, I could simply do a furtive preliminary scan to find out whatever is to be found upstage. A bookshelf? A phone table? Photos on the wall? Wouldn't it be interesting to check out what the props department decided to put there and why? Sometimes these are private jokes between departments and some of the items are too obscene to mention here. Sometimes the prop man has put a photo of himself up there. Or his mother-in-law. Doesn't this sound enticing enough so that in a small gap in the scene, which just happens to coincide with my cue to cross upstage, it would be worth having an innocent exploration?

And accidents? Many a show has come to life due to the reality of accidents. A momentary lapse of dialogue has been known to bring actors together in warm relationship as, with the subtlest of promptings, one actor helps the other out of the blockage and the other acknowledges with silent gratitude. Likewise the way actors share acknowledgements that a prop is misplaced, or a door jams or a flat shudders. These can be like a warm breeze wafting through a cold room.

The means by which one relates to reality vary depending on whether the audience may share your reference or not. This in turn may depend on whether your relationship with reality can be incorporated into the integrity of the production or not. Obviously the audience can see and would accommodate your character flopping into the comfortable chair, lighting a cigarette, or even crossing upstage to inspect the photographs. But they shouldn't see one performer rescuing another from a mental block of dialogue, nor should they know how I count on hearing the town clock as a scene marker.

Sometimes realities occur that challenge our resourcefulness, as when a wrong backdrop is lowered into the middle of a scene, or when a stagehand has inadvertently backed out onstage checking the overhead lights. How does one capitalise on such realities? The axiom must be that simply because a reality exists does not necessarily make it useful as a reference. The performer has to make a quick correlation between:

(1) What feeling do I need, and is there a reality around to help trigger that feeling.

(2) Given an unexpected reality, can I exploit it to:
   (a) serve my needed feelings at this moment:
   (b) conceal the mishap from the audience by including or incorporating it to make it support the play or appear only a small detour from relevance.
   (c) in the event that the mishap is too obvious to hide from the audience, acknowledge the real laughter from the real audience, even joining in as a last resort. Then after they've got the laugh out of their systems, to tactfully escort the real audience back to the make-believe on stage.

Note that in 2(b) and 2(c), the primary purpose is not to exploit accidents to help us motivate what we need to do, but rather to keep play going for the audience. What we probably end up doing is taking on board additional feelings which, while they are more than we need, won't harm the play for the slight embellishment.

We can look at this as an issue of enforced motivation. We don't actually need it, but since the audience already sees it – so what's the sense of pretending that *we* don't see it – we can put the mistake to work to keep the show going. It's not an excessive price to pay for unbroken plausibility.

Advantages of reality: feelings of many colours, conducive to relaxed presence, nimble transitioning. Easy relationships. Helps us avoid Grim and Earnest intensity. And usually it's a reliable technique.

Disadvantages: It may be hard to mix with more fictional techniques unless the performer has great discipline. At one moment we have to recognise the reality that we are on stage, a moment later we believe that we are in a dungeon, and then back on stage again – and we haven't moved. Not everyone would be happy mixing techniques like that.

But otherwise there aren't too many disadvantages if one decides that the vehicle is one where reality would be beneficial. Some highly fantastic productions would, on the face of it, not be very conducive to even small amounts of reality.

Since most motivational techniques are useful for only a moment or a scene at a time, and one doesn't necessarily commit a play to one technique only, reality is one technique which helps provide a production with touchstones of rich human responses. These can create a sense of credibility in productions where much else all too frequently looks like truncated, overly edited behaviour.

In one play I recall, the last scene of the first act was intended to be fast and driven, but the actress involved couldn't avoid dragging the scene, making every moment 'significant'. Direction made no impression, and by the end of rehearsals the producer had resigned himself to a flop. But on opening night the scene came to life. The show was saved thanks to the leading lady having to constrain a fortuitous attack of diarrhoea towards the end of the first act.

If there is so much richness to be found in ***Reality,*** its cousin ***Usery*** is richer yet. 'Usury' may put us off because of the associations of the word with loan-sharks or negotiating a second mortgage. But Usery is nothing like that. Usery is a reality gone wrong. Or rather, we start with a reality and add a small lie. Or even a big lie. But the untruth is essential. In Usery, we twist the meaning or significance of a reality. The technique is a piece of cake for anybody with a paranoidal predisposition. And I must admit that it happens to be my own first port of call.

Let's begin with a small example of the possible flexibility and range of this technique. In the middle of a scene I am supposed to have a burst of anger. But intuition tells me the usual build-up is kind of flat tonight: perhaps I will have to fake the outburst. Suddenly somebody behind the drop can be heard clumping across the stage. Perhaps the reality of that sound at this time should be enough to get angry about. But experience tells me there are many possible extenuating circumstances behind that sound, and one shouldn't get too uptight about it. But ... Suppose that clump came not from a stagehand but from my understudy who would like to take over my role. Immediately I drop all civilised forgiveness and understanding. I think, "The bastard! He can't wait to take over. He wants to see me give a bad performance as well". And I'm away. Angry as needs be.

Or try a different scene, a tender moment in which I must feel worry and compassion. Once again the juices are not flowing proportionally, and I need help. Suddenly those same clumping footsteps. But this time I choose to think, "Nobody in this company would knowingly do anything upsetting. There must have been an accident. Perhaps the old stage manager has keeled over and people are rushing to his assistance". There's a good chance that the right juices will flow.

Those footsteps can be used for colouring virtually any situation. We are limited only by the nimbleness of our imaginations.

Usery may be seen as Reality with an As If attached. But Usery is unique enough for it to be recognised separately. As If is free ranging and unlimited in scope. Usery is confined by the core of reality to a limited area. As If invites us to disengage contact with our surroundings. Usery usually forces engagement. As If exploits the schizoid part of our nature, Usery the delusional paranoid side of us.

In everyday life the constructions we make of events or objects or behaviour or people are very convincing to ourselves. If we see somebody stop walking, stoop and reach down, we tend to make assumptions about why they have stopped and reached even before we see what they are reaching for. And we will tend to do so in a manner closely related to our own feelings and needs at the moment. If I happen to be broke, I may construe the stop-look to mean "There's a coin on the pavement". If I am concerned about a negligent town council, I could just as well say, "There's a dangerous crack in the footpath".

We tend to project our thoughts onto someone else. Thoughts that would match their behaviour. As we have seen, the same behaviour can have many matches, each of them plausible.

A game we sometimes play is to have someone strike a pose like a mannequin in a department store window. We imagine a balloon over her head as in a newspaper cartoon, and we call out the words with which we'd fill in the balloon. Some of the suggestions are wildly amusing. The same game can be played as you pass shop windows with mannequins in them. And whatever we project as a caption, we can be sure it is something from ourselves, usually related to what is dominant at that time in our unconscious minds.

But another way of finding the captions may be based on our consciously-recognised needs and our resourcefulness in fulfilling these. Imagine that we're handed a walnut but no nutcracker: how to get to the kernel? If there's a split in the nut we may try prying it open with our fingernails, or a pocket knife or nail-file. If we're still not successful we look around, what will crack it without smashing it? The quick discovery of an appropriate tool marks our resourcefulness.

When we are on stage and discover the need for help in motivating a moment, both the conscious and unconscious mechanisms may work for us. Our conscious searches for some help in any likely category of aids. The unconscious process helps put the specific interpretation onto whatever it is we find. Usually it isn't necessary to find the reference object, then stop and say, "Now let's see what As If shall we impose on it?"

The whole process of Usery is relatively instant. That stagehand clumping noisily backstage wasn't the only sound or viewable object in the vicinity. But the conscious resourcer did a quick scan and said, "Now that's the kind of reference I can capitalise on easily, because one thing that makes me angry is a noisemaking understudy sabotaging my performance". It is instantly recognised for what it isn't. The local paranoiac getting drunk at the pub demonstrates the process well. If he is spoiling for a fight, he has only to catch somebody looking in his direction to interpret an innocent look as a challenge to fight. It is a similar process we cultivate to practise Usery.

You may find this aspect of Usery particularly useful in working with partners who 'give nothing back', performers who don't respond as you need them to in order to justify your next move. The answer is that there is *always* something to be seen in them, even if it's a deadpan expression.

The scene calls for you to amuse that character, and you do your bit but he remains stony-faced. Great! You have succeeded, because that stony look proves to you that he is so amused he doesn't want to let you think you moved him. Or if he looks withdrawn and introspective. Again great, because you can see him searching for his best funny story to top you because yours amused him so much. No matter what you see, you can construe it to suit your needs.

Advantages: freshness, openness, involvement on several levels. Deepest range, depth and breadth of access to feelings. Mixable with almost any other technique. Rarely conducive to disengagement with things around you. Useful for mercurial acting, relaxation, authority.

Disadvantages: sometimes performances doctored by Usery acquire slight implausibility, so it must be used carefully to avoid this. For example, I can read amusement in a deadpan actor's face and that gives me authority and drive to persevere. But the audience may see only the expressionless face and wonder what I see that makes me bother to go on. Although it's true that our authoritative perseverance may seduce our fellow player back to life, it doesn't always follow. And we should be prepared to 'use' mostly those responses which the audience could accept as valid.

Exercises: for Reality and Usery these are often the same sort of game, and similar to those used in honing our imagination. Solve theoretical problems like relocating one's place in a book, leaving a warning for a friend, gaining someone's interest, confusing somebody – do these with the aid of objects to be found in your pocket, purse or wallet, or bits of clothing. That is, invent a linking sequence employing that prop in such a way that they help solve the problems.

Try solving problems starting with realities as far removed from obvious solutions as possible. For instance, how would you get a cat out of a tree with the aid of a book? Some might suggest they throw the book at the cat. Another might suggest setting fire to the book, and when the firemen arrive ask if you can use their ladder. How else might you rescue the cat? (Lateral thinking again.)

Painting and sketching are good aids for relating to realities. Draw or paint anything you can perceive. The more you examine objects, the more they can affect you. Then, looking at these objects, imagine what any of them could be used for besides the most obvious. The still-life bowl of fruit is filled with fanciful implications. The bowl itself now contains fruit. It could be used for making a salad – pretty obvious. Serving a drink to a dog – not very imaginative. A helmet during magpie nesting season – that's better. A receptacle for catching nuts as a party game – hmmm. A cover for germinating seeds. A trap to place over the spider you find on the living room floor prior to slipping a cardboard under it and relocating the spider. There's lots more you could do with a bowl. You fanatasise.

Play the game of 'I Spy'.

There's a game where we imagine some famous person has died. There he or she lies on the bier. We line up to bid them a last farewell, but a moment or so before you arrive at the coffin, you are handed a surprise prop to be given as a parting gift. You have a few seconds to justify, in your farewell speech to the cadaver, what you are giving him and why.

Some hilarious and some moving scenes have eventuated when a president or prime minister was presented with a lipstick, box of matches, pair of shoes, sanitary pad, keys, or whatever else is found in pocket or purse. And such personages as Hitler, Marilyn Monroe, Liberace, and your acting teacher tend to kindle such associations as to scorch the printed page. It's a game where students may relate to these props either as Realities – ascribing to them their most obvious functions – or as Usery – where functions are conveniently deformed with a twist of the imagination.

Reality and Usery in the hands of a skilled practitioner can be wide-spectrum and powerful. They can be used to refute the arguments of those who believe that only Belief in the Situation and Identification will give the so-called true results. Some extraordinarily good performances have been given by those who, once it is clear what is expected in order to create the necessary illusion, have relied on virtually nothing more than Reality and Usery. For myself, whose usual employment has been in long-running musicals, I only occasionally look beyond them.

WRITE YOUR OWN NOTES

CHAPTER 29

RESEARCH

When we're preparing a role, how do we decide which personality traits should accompany each moment of behaviour?

Sometimes one simply invents and imposes a characteristic. The decision may be clued by the play. Or by a whim. It may be a favourite trick that the actor can do particularly skillfully. Or some popular or otherwise special audience-titillator. The result may be integrated or appear forced – as might occur when I'm quite arbitrarily deciding that "at this point I'll sing something". Sometimes characteristics occur as a natural consequence, like an unpremeditated outburst of frustration arising from a clash of actions. And sometimes an accident occurs during rehearsal or performance which create results that lead the director to say, "Leave it in".

But a most effective source of detail may be the result of research. When one portrays an historical or living character, research is the most natural avenue of information. Books, films, photos, painting, biographical references, newspapers, interviews with authorities or with relatives, friends or acquaintances of that person. Or with the actual person.

If the character is derived from literature, the library or perhaps the author may provide insights. Note the word 'may'. As we said, a book is not a play or a film, and a dramatic interpretation could well distort the character beyond its literary meanings. Moreover, several people reading the same book may come away with different interpretations of the character. Is the author's interpretation the last word?

If the character belongs to some particular classification, research includes studying that classification. For instance, you may recall that ***The Effects of Gamma Rays on Man in the Moon Marigolds*** has a character who suffers from epilepsy. Not only did the rest of the cast acquire attitudes toward an epileptic, the woman playing the role consulted in great detail a specialist in epilepsy, studied various aspects of epilepsy, settled on one particular form of the disease, and rehearsed its specific symptoms. So in the scene where the character has a seizure, she portrayed it most effectively.

If we decide that the character is paranoidal, or alcoholic, or whatever, we can again consult the experts. There may be certain characteristics that are distinct and consistent enough to be virtually diagnostic of such a personality's behaviour. Likewise for certain occupations, nationalities, cultures, educational levels, etc., where certain patterns of behaviour could seen as characteristic.

This all relates in general terms to finding a character's characteristics, which may be physical, vocal or mental mannerisms or preferences. But in a dispute, for instance, people of certain professions or levels of education may incline toward dispassionate discussion, others toward pugnacity. So as this chapter is concerned with research as a motivational technique, let's leave other aspects of characterisation aside for the nonce.

The most obvious application of research to the motivational process is as an aid to map out how the character is expected to feel at any given point in the script. Research may suggest that here he could feel amused, there angry, here kindly disposed, there jealous, etc. Then in the playing of each moment, one might call upon appropriate techniques to generate feelings on cue.

The process of research may lead us to actually identify with the character. Subsequently, in the playing, it will be the Identification process which motivates us on cue. Or our research may give us an intimate insight into the problems the character faced. Now in playing we may implement our Belief in the Situation, or As if, or Just Like processes.

Apparently research is a valuable aid for employing other techniques. But how does it find its own way as a primary technique on stage during the scene? It does so firstly by drawing upon the adventure of the research itself. Normally when we respond to a sequence of references here and now on stage, it may be that research helped us choose these references. And in that case we are not so much affected by the research as by what the research pointed out to us that we should relate to.

But we may find ourselves hearkening back to certain impressions we experienced while we were doing our research, and we may find it useful to do so right on stage, in the manner of Sense or Emotion Memory. If we researched a particular ambience and were moved by its beauty, or if we read about Mozart and Salieri and found ourselves affected by their relationship, then – if we need, say, a preparation of compassion – we can muse for a moment on the rough time Salieri gave Mozart and commiserate with Mozart, if that's how the episode affects us. Or even feel sorry for Salieri, if that's what our research has made us feel. This can work even though we are portraying neither Mozart or Salieri: even if the play has nothing whatever to do with either. It is like remembering a book that affected you, and you exploiting that memory. Having been through the experience, we can think back on it. And if that process turns us on as the scene demands, then research is working directly for us during the scene. A shallow variant of Emotion Memory.

The second approach is exemplified by the occasion a woman playing a 16-year-old prostitute visited a brothel, not to work but to gain information. This we could call 'Field Investigation'. The women who worked there were helpful in informing her about all manner of things relevant to her portrayal: and she saw the line-up of men at the door, the way they were greeted when they were admitted and how everyone behaved as they left. No damage was done, and her portrayal was a minor masterpiece.

Thirdly, there is what might be called 'Experiential Research'. This is a procedure which does, unlike the above approach, invite some personal risks. It may be safe enough to work for a while as a fruit-picker or barman, if you're preparing to portray one of these occupations. The story goes that actors for ***On The Waterfront*** had to pass themselves off as wharfies in New Jersey bars as part of their research. All survived. But picture the actor who insists on swimming in crocodile-infested waters because he wants to prepare himself for that kind of film. A friend joined a bikie gang as background research to a film, and shortly after he disassociated himself there was a bloody gang fight where more than half a dozen lost their lives.

Experiential research is one of the few techniques whereby we may acquire new emotional responses. And although there are few feelings we haven't experienced by the end of our teenage years, among those few may be one or two an actor needs for a particular role. Mature and responsible love, some forms of sexual experience, the awareness of inevitable and imminent death – these may be foreign territory to the youthful actor. The question must be asked, is the experiential knowledge really worth the experiential research?

Some types of experience, especially if prolonged, may change one's feelings permanently and pervasively. It is not unusual for someone sampling cigarettes, drugs or alcohol to get hooked. Some attend religious or cult assemblies and become converted. Perhaps some types of transformation could even be for the better. But that should not obscure the fact that involving oneself in experience for the sake of a single characterisation or show exposes one to risks of enduring or permanent change.

Still, the most frequent use and value of research remains to provide us with cool understanding of where in the play certain responses should take place. A map, that is, as an adjunct to other techniques. It is a rich technique. Few serious actors would not employ some kind of research before embarking on a heavy project. You can hardly avoid it unless the role has been written about yourself.

Drills and exercises for the three types of research we've discussed should be self-explanatory. Take a sample role and find access to the character's feelings by any of the above. And in using the experiential, keep a weather eye open for sudden wind shifts. Some unpremeditated discoveries have led to moments of genius.

WRITE YOUR OWN NOTES

CHAPTER 30

IMPROVISATION

"So I said to him you can't fire me, I quit!"
"Yes. And what did he say?"
"He didn't say anything. Not at that point. But you should have seen his face. He flushed and his eyes wandered all over and ..."

From the suppressed glee in the voice and the authority and colour as this incident was further described, there was no doubt that such an event had actually taken place. What a pity he had to give up his job just so that he could perform this scene in a play with such conviction. When he talked about the boss, he not only responded to each image with a proportional feeling, he was able to apportion most of his attention on communication rather than recollection. The memory was fresh and he had merely to impress us with his bravado at challenging the boss. Everything he said seemed so true that it would have passed the scrutiny of a fine psychiatrist.

Actually, he hadn't lot his job. It was all a lie, but so convincing that we might protest, "But he seemed to have intimate knowledge of what he was talking about". And indeed he had intimate knowledge of that very incident and conversation. But not with an employer. Rather with a fellow actor. Earlier he had been criticised for sounding as though he wasn't really describing anything tangible. He was just giving a colourful 'radio reading', with all the right inflections in place but empty of specific colours which would give a special matching to the deeds referred to. So he went away to lose a job he worked at between shows, or so we believed.

But he hadn't. Instead he and a fellow actor improvised a scene, with the other fellow as the boss, well briefed but not rehearsed. They acted out a situation where the boss calls him in for not appearing more frequently at his desk. And all the words that he later reported that he said to the boss, he had said. And the reactions of his boss had been the reactions of his friendly accomplice. He had heard and spoken those words, and he could report them with the ring of truth. *Because he did hear and utter those words.*

Here is one application of improvisation. It can do almost all the things the real situation could do by way of motivation. In addition, it is safe, inexpensive, malleable, fixable, and if necessary repeatable. Whereas participatory research may occasionally skirt dangerous terrain, improvisation is usually as safe as game playing. Moreover, as improvisation is limited only by imagination, there is no limit to where one may go in time or space, nor whom or what we may encounter. That wouldn't be the case with participatory research. And although academic research could provide detailed information about a situation in another time or space, it couldn't provide living experience. Improvisation can do that.

The technique of improvisation is to assemble the necessary participants, describe the given circumstances, assign identities, and then inter-act. Each character may (or may not) undertake to play a specific action. Then go for broke until some acceptable conclusion is reached. You don't write or say what each says or does, you simply provide a framework and let the behaviour happen. How much you pre-plan will depend on what you seek to discover from the improvisation. The impro may be designed to gain insight into actions, motivations, or adjustments. In this chapter we are limiting our search to uncovering feelings. If we were seeking other results, we might modify the process somewhat.

An improvisation is an original scene played extemporaneously. It can be based on:

(1) ***The author's script:*** if there is difficulty in making sense of the author's words in rehearsal, you may gain an insight into what the author intended by putting it in your own words. You can improvise a few lines, the whole scene, even the whole play. Many a Shakespearean production has come to life when approached this way. Saying it in your own words tends to permit associated feelings to flow more freely. Then of course, having gained insight we return to the words of the author.

(2) ***Parallel situation:*** the author's situation may be hard to grasp, and the performers may not be sure or agreed on what the author is driving at. Someone (the director?) who is sure can set up an improvisation of a situation which goes in the same general direction as the author's, but which is more accessible to the cast.

To use a slightly ironic example, a group of youngsters studying contemporary history were to dramatise aspects of the Jewish Holocaust. They acted out soldiers bursting into homes, taking out the fathers and mothers and shooting them before the eyes of the children. Although this telescoping of events was intended to horrify the youngsters, generally it didn't. Perhaps they'd grown so accustomed to similar scenes of violence on TV that they couldn't associate it with their parents, or perhaps they didn't mind having their parents disposed of thus.

So the scene was reconceived. This time police burst into the home and carried out the pet dogs and cats, to be shot before the eyes of the children. This time it worked, there were tears and anger all around. A concept which had seemed far fetched now began to make sense because it had been put into a form capable of being personalised. The parallel approach to improvisation can do this.

(3) ***Rearranged roles or situations:*** in one primary school, there was an enormous amount of suppressed hostility toward teachers, particularly when problems of school discipline arose. We arranged an improvisation between teacher and pupil around a disciplinary issue, but they reversed roles, with teacher portraying pupil and pupil portraying teacher.

By the end of it the pupil had a greater appreciation of the teacher's viewpoint and feelings, and so did the other pupils watching the scene. What is more interesting perhaps is that the teacher gained insight into the pupils' behaviour. One could be certain that when disciplinary problems arose again, they would be approached with an awareness of the other person's needs, sensitivities, and point of view.

This kind of improvisation is useful for actors who tend to act by themselves, who don't make contact with others on stage, or who do so only in terms of "What can I get out of you for my purposes?" Whenever one relates to another in terms of "What do *you* need?" or "what can I do for *you*?" a degree of warmth and compassion, even charm, is introduced, and a sensitivity to the situation of the other actor which can lead to more genuine on-stage relating.

A similar application involves situation reversal rather than role reversal. You turn the tables, so that what has been happening to someone else now happens to you. How does it feel to be on the receiving end of what you dish out to others? If the scene has needed an element of moderation or compassion, such an improvisation may be useful. In ***Finian's Rainbow,*** the Southern racist turns black.

Arrange an impro where characterisation remains the same but situations are reversed. Retaining your characterisation may bring out values closer to home, therefore more dramatically. "Fred was caught in bed with his secretary", we gloat. But what would it mean if we were likewise discovered? Our families, our neighbours, our social status – how would they be affected?

(4) ***Background or historical:*** like the incident at the beginning of this chapter, where the actor could talk with conviction about losing his job because an improvisation gave him the background to talk about. Whatever we have to relate to as a past incident can be vivified by acting it out first. Then it slots into our memories as a deed in fact, even if we arranged the deed.

(5) ***Anticipatory improvisation:*** as above, we can vivify the specifics of what we expect in the future. In a scene of preparation for a party, the actor is to play with elation and energy that shows how much she's looking forward to it and fantasising about it. But the way the actor is now playing it suggests that her energy owes more to the fact that she has rehearsed it for three weeks than that she has dreamed of it for forty-three. So we act out the party scene with all she could wish for happening to her. Then we go back to the play and find the preparation scene much more full of enthusiasm, because she now has particular pleasures and delights embedded in her mind, and she can look forward to those specifics as she dresses for the party.

This type of impro has been used to give vocational guidance to young people contemplating careers as, say, receptionist, pharmacist, nurse or engineer. Sample incidents expected in these careers are acted out by those contemplating the job. It gives them a chance to explore work experience of a dozen careers in an hour.

(6) ***General mood preparation:*** we can act out As if as an improvisation during rehearsals or before the show, rather than merely thinking or talking about it. This technique can spectacularly enhance the impact of the make-believe. This applies particularly to when you have to come into a scene already loaded with a specific feeling. If there is time to prepare, and available people and facilities to improvise, you can generate precisely the right mood or colour for the start of the scene.

Advantages: generally improvisations have all the advantages that go with experiences, without the disadvantages that come from paying the price of those experiences. And many of the things we can experience via improvisation often couldn't possibly be encountered in real life.

Another advantage is that it can provide the entire company with a common reference. The play is to commence with everybody talking about the church service they just came from where a woman got up and accused the minister of fathering her unborn baby. If all have witnessed it as an improvisation, they have something substantial about which they can compare notes.

Improvisations can be treated like a game. Of course not every performer agrees to mixing games with work: Ralph Richardson is said to have walked out of a rehearsal where improvisations were being used.

The impressions they make in one's unconscious tend to endure, almost as Experiential Research can. They can be shaped, coloured, mixed with other techniques. But they can't be easily erased. The kinds of feeling responses they may induce can range from the shallowest attitudes to the deepest emotions.

Disadvantages: some performers seem allergic to impros, and when they are asked to participate as part of a team they sabotage the proceedings, making the whole attempt useless. If, for instance, we're preparing a situation designed to leave everyone sombre, and one clown sends it up, everyone breaks up laughing. What's worse is that this association will tend to stick with us, and when we play the scene on stage we may break up then as well.

It's even more important with impros than with other techniques to design them to assist with specific problems, not to use them randomly just for the sake of the exercise. I have watched too many classes where random exercises were inflicted on vulnerable students with no one having an inkling of what specific benefits were to be derived from which exercise. The teacher had a repertoire of exercises that could look impressive, so that the students might think they got their money's worth from an hour full of activity. And sometimes actors engage in random exercises before a rehearsal or performance on the general pretext of the need for a warm-up. But doing that is like reaching for whatever medication you first grab in the medicine cabinet.

Physiologically, if our fingers need strengthening, finger exercises are called for. The mountain climber whose only weakness is in his fingers will benefit little from an hour of deep knee bends. Every improvisation can exercise some function. Further strengthening of what is already strong while neglecting what needs attention is both foolish and wasteful. But when judiciously employed, improvisation can be a powerful general purpose tool.

CHAPTER 31

SENSORY MOTIVATIONS

Sensory Stimulation, Pornography, Sense Memory and Sensory Projection

SENSORY STIMULATION:

Reality and Usery depended upon some stimulus being actually present, then our thinking function applied itself to steer the stimulus toward an emotional reaction.

Now let's look at some techniques where the thinking function may not come into it at all. Or when it does get into the act, it may be only to set up the stimulus where needed. For example, the thinking function can arrange to have certain background music playing during the scene. This can then have its own direct affect: *Sensory Stimulation* takes over.

Such techniques tend to work more smoothly in bridging transitional actions. Also they are easily employed as preparation for a scene. A sniff of perfume before going on, for example – depending more on unconscious associations or instinctual pleasure principles than intellectualising.

You remember that we recognise at least seven senses, and each sense can be affected by a whole range of stimuli. And each stimulus can give a different result depending on its quality or intensity.

For example, a persistent sound frequency not strong enough to affect our conscious mind can make us uncomfortable without our recognising what stresses us. Turn it up until it's audible and it may soothe us. A bit louder and it may annoy us. Louder still and it can deafen us or drive us crazy.

Certain sounds may have multiple effects. They may lull us, excite or alienate or unite us, simultaneously. Sometimes they do this because they remind us of specific events when there may have been mixed feelings, like the song I heard on my first date, or the one played at my father's funeral. What we felt then, we feel again when we hear the sound: "They're playing our song!" But let's leave this reminder-sound for our discussion of Emotion Memory. For Sensory Stimulation, let's dwell on stimuli that don't automatically conjure up specific origins.

Obviously we can explore the widest range of possibilities, testing which sensation does what to us. This isn't a technique we could learn, or even catalogue, in a day or two. Rather, it is to be explored, analysed and refined over a lifetime, and the time to start is now.

Listen to music. Different compositions, each played by different artists, heard at different volumes. Listen to traffic. Birds. Wind. Street calls. Market calls. Construction work. People talking. Singing. Domestic appliances. Keep a notebook in which you record as accurately as you can how each sound affects you.

The same applies to exploring the gamut of things to see. Smell. Taste. Touch.

Place yourself in different spaces: beside massive buildings, in open fields, in parks, art galleries, furniture stores, offices, home, etc.How does each affect you? Toy with time: hurry to keep an appointment, be late, be early, be prompt. How do these experiences affect you?

Sensation is a powerful process by which to access feelings. We can't begin to list emotive sensory stimuli. Anything in your life which turns you on through your senses can be considered for your list. And how many such sensations are there in each minute?

Through sight alone, what do we experience walking from one room to the other? The change of light: satisfying. Last night's unwashed dishes: yuk. Fly buzzing around: how did it get through the screens? Grey spider up in the corner: brrr. Fly heading towards spider's web: watch it! Fly trapped: oops. Dust on ledge: guilt. Painting askew on wall: compulsiveness. Unopened morning mail: impatience.

And of course smells. Perfumes, spices, flowers, mustiness, body odour, petrol, stale beer, a roast dinner – the list is endless. Some say the association of pleasant food smells might appreciably account for the popularity of theatre restaurants.

All these exercises are primarily means of 'sensitising' ourselves to stimuli: how can we possibly bring a freshly-mown pasture into the theatre? But by alerting ourselves to sensations per se, we can contrive to bring some more portable and applicable devices.

In performance, a whole panoply of feelings may be on tap from the sensory ambience we arrange for ourselves. Even the costume we wear next to our skin or the weight distribution of hat, belt, sword – these can provoke our senses. Can't we arrange to wear sensation-appropriate substances? The hot dressing-room, the cold breeze on stage can affect us. The way we decorate our dressing-room, the colour and condition of the walls, these can affect us. And even in the dressing room, we can alter and arrange things to suit our emotional requirements for the performance.

The details of your dressing-room can prepare you for a scene, but your chosen perfume can affect you on-stage. Music in the dressing-room or on-stage underpinning can work for you. Many a love-scene in the shooting of the silent films was performed to the accompaniment of an off-camera violin. And who of my generation can forget watching those films to accompaniment of the pit piano?

Notice how reassuring it is for many actors to be holding, elutching, fondling some on-stage prop. A glass, a cup, a cigarette, a purse, a handkerchief, a lorgnette, spectacles, a pen – the list again is endless. All tactile stimuli.

Do all you can to open yourself to new sensory experiences. Look, touch, listen, taste , sniff, move about. Go on outings. Read poetry. Commune with nature. Listen to music. Meet people. Sail a boat. In other words, come alive, more alive than you just were. Dame Sybil Thorndyke was an expert in this: she opened herself to new experiences every day of her life, and when she died in her nineties she was younger than many we know in their teens.

The only real disadvantages of Sensory Stimulation come from exposure to dangerous levels. Lights too bright can blind us, weights too heavy can herniate or crush us, touches too hot can burn us, sounds too loud can deafen us. But handled sensibly, sensations can only enrich us. And the effectiveness of this technique is limited only by the range of our conscious experience.

PORNOGRAPHY:

The late Irving Ackman, one of Broadway's best musical directors, sometimes joined in the game of Trickery (see chapter 34). As the leading lady and I, arm in arm, slowly duetted down across to the footlights, Irving's left hand surreptitiously flashed a choice pornographic photo at us while his right continued the beat as usual. He always insisted that it helped phrase the scene toward the more romantic, though it mostly made us want to laugh.

Nevertheless, with the passing of the years, and Irving, it became obvious that whereas in our case it was assuredly no more than a prank, in other circumstances it could be something else. *Pornography* is a motivational technique in its own right. It can change people's feelings in ways that other techniques can't. The nearest might be sensory stimulation or sense memory, but close examination of these confirms that they are each too distinctly exclusive. Arguably, this technique warrants a section of its own.

In scenes where one needs to appear lustful, or to insinuate hot passion in a relationship, Pornography can supply the erotic stimulation that inspiration may fail to bring. How often we hear it said about a scene in a film or play, "He seemed to undress her with his eyes"; or she him. In some TV soap operas, it would seem that this is what transpires most of the time.

But why bother to resort to borrowed equivalents when you could simply and directly undress your partner with your eyes right then and there? Most experienced performers could tell you that although the audience believes the illusion that these two are perfectly matched as lovers, the actual performers may in fact turn each other on like a cigarette dropped in a cup of coffee. Sometimes the leading man and lady barely manage to be civil to each other offstage. They work closely enough to each other to see past the make-up and padding, and are able to smell, touch, and sometimes taste sensations that are tolerable only because of pay day.

That idealised perfectly compounded interpersonal chemistry (chapter 39) is a state more often desired than realised. The passionate stage lovers may be more likely to be in other relationships, or homosexual, or monastic, or indifferent. But they must create the illusion that they are dripping and bursting with lust.

In these circumstances, pornography often works. Not always, of course. Exposure to pornography can induce a range of responses extending from prim shock to a complete turn-off, by way of other responses such as the giggles, scholarly detachment, embarrassment, guilt, feelings of inadequacy, bravura, jitteriness, and sometimes quiet withdrawal. It is a technique that needs to be pre-tested. Eroticism (polite pornography) has so many personal and social ramifications that we can hardly generalise about what stimulus can be counted on to produce what result.

Some actors find it hard to address the issue of eroticism either as a basis for their own motivation or as a topic for public performance. Quite a few recoil from displays of passion that go beyond a longing look or, in extraordinary circumstances, heavy breathing. They insist that the community and they have survived for centuries before the advent of explicit displays of intimacy. Today, it's hard to find a film without its mandatory explicit love-scene.

In fact, theatrical erotica has a long history, and has never left us. True, the degree of explicitness tends to come and go in cycles, but sex-play has been part of theatre since the beginning. For many in our community, eroticism is appreciated only when heavily disguised or suggested by inference. So in the older movie conventions, boy and girl would kiss and the lights would fade, or there'd be a cut to the following morning, or the camera would roam out the window to show us fireworks exploding or waves breaking on a beach.

In Ballet, a very socially respectable entertainment, the highly erotic is likewise conventionalised. Male dancers traditionally stuff their cod-pieces with tissues, as the ancient Greeks danced with giant strapped-on phalluses: and female dancers wear tutus, like skirts lifted as if preparing for sex. And many of the dance movements may be seen as kinetic elaborations of the positions found in the *Kama Sutra.* The origins of dance as fertility ritual may still be seen even in so polite a form as ballet.

By whatever devices we manage to make erotica officially acceptable, the fact remains that it is basically erotica, and the range of responses to which an audience finds itself stimulated (the more acceptable word is 'excited') may be random.

Performers, on the other hand, require specific rather than random responses. And the technique of pornography can create very specific responses, though the performers must explore the stimulus-response question for themselves.

Advantages: given a successful choice, the loading can be powerfully dynamic. It can be mixed with other techniques, and regulated for duration. It can be readily quenched. For what it is designed to do, it can be the technique of choice.

Disadvantages: it is useful usually for a narrow range of feelings. Also, it isn't always easy to have access to the picture or figure of reference. Easy enough before a scene, but during the scene one must be ingenious. Another problem is that the attitudes of others in the company to your use of this technique in such a way may affect your and their performing.

A point of clarification: pornography refers to erotic stimulation derived from writing, pictures, movies, carvings, etc., – in other words, to a depiction of sexual involvement, not to actual and direct participatory involvement. Direct involvement may work too. Couples deciding to look amorous on stage by actually engaging in sex-play before or during the scene are using the techniques of Sensory Stimulation or Reality. The stimulation may be somewhat similar, but the resultant loadings will usually be different.

SENSE MEMORY:

How does one bring a pasture into the theatre? In your memory of course. As you become increasingly open to and aware of Sensory Stimulation, you build up a store of *sensory memories* to draw upon when you need them, even those experiences you've had only once. In this chapter we begin to draw upon those memories.

You begin by trying just to name the stimulus. A spider on your lap! If you have been affected by a spider, it holds certain sensations in your memory, and that may help you to picture it in your mind's eye. And if you can visualise it – or even think of it – on your lap, you may respond accordingly. The memory image will have been created in your mind.

If the name or thought hasn't conjured the image, let's try drawing or mimicking or animating it in some way. You may find that a gesture of imitation will help the image to form. And if that doesn't help, try a photo, painting, story, description or some other reminder of that spider.

Need more help? Perhaps instead of trying to see the whole spider you could break it down into its details. Let's just visualise the abdomen – shiny, oval, bit of hair, black, no markings. Now the thorax – about this big and also black. The head with palpae reaching out like two walking sticks. The fangs! Slightly hidden but enormous. Then the eight legs, shiny, jointed, ending in hairy sharp feet.

And even if that hasn't worked, the last resort aside from hypnosis is to encounter the spider once more and familiarise yourself with it in greater detail. And if this isn't possible, or if it still doesn't affect you, it's reasonable to give this attempt at Sense Memory a miss.

This technique in its various forms is not everyone's bag. Some people are highly resistant to emotively-associated Sensory Memories. Some acting schools will not on principle dabble with sense memory or its relatives. Those are often the schools that either (1) see Sense Memory as simply As If: (2) contend that the only way to act is by Identifying and Believing in the Situation: Sense Memory being seen as an irrelevant intrusion: (3) it is so closely allied to Emotion Memory which itself may be regarded as Taboo: (4) it's some more of this airy-fairy method: (5) it is seen as the same as Sensory Projection, which demands that 'the actor must be nuts'. Fair enough. There are more than enough techniques available to be able to forego those that don't work for you, or that you don't want to work with. But you may choose to explore for yourself whether this technique may be useful for you. There are many skillful performers who wouldn't be without it.

Because of its simplicity, Sense Memory is a useful tool for mixing motivational ingredients carefully and predictably. Complex associations tend to bring with them a whole range of colours, like calling up a rainbow when all we need at the moment is a small touch of a particular hue of green. Do we need a flicker of disgust? Perhaps the memory of a splash of vomit will do it. Only a splash. A whole puddle could bring in a number of side-effects which might be not only extraneous but misleading.

What works with Sense Memory for some may seem totally inappropriate to others. One actress generated her raucous laughter on cue in every performance by visualising an eyeball popping out of its socket. We never asked whose, nor would such an image be able to provoke even a smile in most of us.

Let's now look at fragments that can be used to prompt Sense Memory. In fact, we used such fragments when we were easing our way into vividly recalling some sensation. One such 'prompter' was the word. A word in fact is a squiggle on a page or an arrangement of sounds, but its significance is monumental. It is not only the symbol of an idea, it may also be evocative of sensations associated with the idea. As we say "roast beef", for instance, we don't just think of the idea 'roast beef': we trigger memories of the sight, smell, taste and texture of a delicious meal. Thus the term 'roast beef' is a partial sense memory, a prompter to remind us of the sensation.

Another partial Sense Memory would be a photo of the object (if it is visible), or a drawing. Other prompters might be mimicked gestures or imitations, like crawling your fingers, spider-like up your arm.

But one of the most obvious and useful – though least noted – symbols or prompters we find in theatre are props. Of course the 'tea' we drink on stage *may* be real hot fresh tea. Where it is real, we can use the technique of Reality to motivate our pleasure in the drink. Where it is not real tea, we use partial Sense Memory.

One very talented actress despised sense memory exercises, refusing to do them in class, or sending them up when pressured to do them. But one night, in *Orpheus Descending*, when she was supposed to down several glasses of neat bourbon, we noticed that she was actually getting drunk on what we knew was coloured water. At the end of the first act she staggered across to blast the prop man for spiking her drink, but we checked it and found it was indeed coloured water. She was so gifted an actress that sense memory worked all too well for her. Perhaps she knew it and dared not toy with it in class. In any event, she did need several cups of coffee during interval.

I still remember a rehearsal of the Australian production of *South Pacific*, when Billis hands Emile's bouquet to Nellie Forbush after Emile has stormed out. The rehearsal 'bouquet' was a rolled newspaper, which Lenny Stone, as Billis, handled as if it were indeed a bouquet of precious blooms. The impression was so powerful that Mary La Roche was caught by surprise and burst into tears.

Some performers are terrified of props. Sadistic directors sometimes require these actors to open their scenes while sipping a cup of tea. Even if the rattle cannot be heard throughout the theatre, there is every likelihood that the performers may slobber or choke themselves into humiliation.

But most performers welcome them. Not only can they occupy you during the long pauses – you know, the ones when the other actor is talking – but they can stimulate sense memories which evoke a whole range of feelings. If the props are carefully chosen, the results can illuminate the play, characters and relationships.

One good group exercise to develop a nimble Sense Memory is to roll a small towel into a bundle and toss it from person to person, calling out what it represents as you toss it. As you toss the bundle, call out "cat". If the recipient is quick enough, they may even catch the bundle as they would a cat. Otherwise, they treat it as a cat after having caught it: then toss it to another, calling "vase" or whatever.

There's a particular performance problem that should be given special mention here, though it will spill over into the next technique as well. The problem is the monologue, and its close relative the soliloquy, and the prompting device we can use to confront the problem of our old friend the telephone.

In the ancient Greek theatre when the audience needed insight into what a character was thinking, or if he had to fill in some non-evident detail, he would address the audience directly and, in poetic speech or song, tell them what was on his mind in a monologue. The risk, of course, of direct address to an audience is that it might talk back to you. In the theatre of Elizabethan England, which came a step closer to realism, the actors' pretence was that we didn't know the audience was there. So instead of talking to the audience, the actor talked out loud to himself, in a soliloquy. But this device soon came to seem implausible, as well as an invitation for the performer to indulge himself. And then on through the various stages of theatrical history – including puppertry, where the puppeteer splits himself into two or more voices or characters – authors ultimately provided us with an alter ego, a friend or confidant with whom we could share our thoughts.

But with the exigencies of theatre economics, and perhaps other pressures as well, rather than use another actor to hear one's inner work-out, playwrights began to rely on Alexander Graham Bell's nifty little prop, the telephone. By talking to a friend on the other end of the line – who , by the way, doesn't need a salary – you could bring the audience up to date, reveal, conceal or insinuate your private thoughts and set the scene for whatever was about to happen.

The problem here is one we've all encountered in the theatre: abominable portrayals of phone conversations. "Hello-who-sorry-he-doesn't-live-here-anymore", with nary a pause to suggest that the actor has heard another voice on the line, much less registered what it was saying. The other person needs time to be heard. And not only time, but all manner of things about their personality. Male or female? Cultured, rough or what vocal quality? Grammatical speech? Friendly or what? Emotionally distressed or what?

Now, if we had to address another non-existent actor on stage, we would have to concern ourselves with not only these aspects of their personality, but also the visual, spatial, tactile and possibly olfactory aspects. We'll deal with that hefty problem under the next heading. But the telephone can get us, as it were, off the hook. We need only imagine the voices. Or better yet, rehearse the conversation with someone, and while performing remember their voice. In preparing a phone conversation, it is often best to script it, and rehearse with a partner, using the same words and voice coming at you each time. The sense memory of the repeated experience will stay with you in the actual performance,

What's important to remember is that telephone conversations are almost always dialogues, and the performer has to *listen* as well as speak.

Incidentally, some of the best soliloquies I have observed were in fact treated as dialogues between two parts of the character's own personality. And at this point in the history of theatre, when we don't mind piercing the imaginary fourth wall occasionally, soliloquies can sound plausible as monologues once more. When Derek Jacobi brilliantly portrayed his version of Hamlet in Sydney in 1980, he shared "To be or not to be" with his own conscience, and from time to time consulted the audience as group advisers and probably friends whose philosophies he loved to challenge. I imagine that that was how, at their best, the addresses of the Greek protagonist to his chorus might have been handled. Who says the wheel doesn't come full circle?

SENSORY PROJECTION:

In the days when we grouped this technique with the two previous ones, it marked the highest achievement of Sense Memory, and by justifying it held it together. And many an actor rejected all aspects of sense memory because of difficulties with this component. Now by classifying it separately we not only recognise its uniqueness, we also make it possible for the squeamish to come back in. Now they can use Sensory Stimulation and Sense Memory without having to deal with *Sensory Projection*. Because in truth this is a touchy one.

Another name for Sensory Projection is 'hallucination', and hallucination is so deeply associated with mental derangement that it is almost futile trying to discuss it with some actors. These actors find nothing disturbing about being able to weep or have outbursts of anger or violence on cue: they seem not to see that such behaviour might also be symptomatic of emotional disturbance. Just as it is possible to grieve on cue, why should we not be able to hallucinate on cue as well? The psychotic person manifests the same functions found in the healthy person, a psychosis being actually, to oversimplify, a disaffection in which otherwise healthy functions run out of control.

A few years ago, there appeared in a scientific journal an item about a woman who could project images in space: whereas most of us customarily see things in our mind's eye, she could see them out in front of her as if projected on to a screen. She was tested and retested, using colour dot charts where two charts fuse to make one picture. Yes, she could and she did: and she seemed perfectly healthy. Then the report suggested that it was after all not so unusual, there were surely many people who could do the same. The psychologists even have a name for that sort of thing: *Eidetic Imagery*.

And it's a practice that actors have been using for thousands of years while remaining perfectly healthy. Well, at least they all don't go off the deep end. My own experience with accomplished actors suggests no undue psychopathology afflicting them. If anything, they seem healthier than a sample of the general population. Perhaps that's because they have to be extra healthy to handle Sensory Projections effectively, or perhaps it's because the work they do constantly exercises their physical, imaginative, intellectual and sensory faculties.

Maybe the technique itself is good for them. Maybe they have been unwittingly practising it whenever they memorise a script and visualise the words on a phantom printed page in front of them.

You may have had similar experiences. Have you listened to somebody describing a new restaurant they'd discovered: when they went into fine detail, has it happened that you could smell the food. Or a piece of music: have you ever recalled it so concentratedly that you could actually hear it? Have you ever looked at a garment and felt it on you? Those are all hallucinations.

A very plausible phone conversation can be performed by hallucinating the voice of the other person. This level of auditory hallucination can often be achieved in a relatively short time. The visual one is harder to accept: we depend so much on our eyes (seeing is believing) that we are reluctant to fool with them.

This is a technique that can be learned. All we need is the will, determination and perhaps thirty years of practice. We can pick up glimpses and smatterings within a few weeks, but most of us will need a lot of time to develop the skill to the point where we can depend upon it.

So many beginners flake out after a few feeble forays. It might be a better idea to rely on other techniques while making a longtime study of this one. Perhaps during the early years some occasions may arise where Sensory Projection seems worth a try: it may not work, but if it does it can be money in the bank. Literally. Because this skill is often seen as a special mark of virtuosity. If your Macbeth can see a dagger, if your Lady Macbeth can see a damned spot, if your Tevye can see 'God' clearly enough for a chat, the greater the salary you can command.

The basic approach to practising Sensory Projection is the same as for the study of memorising objects we discussed in Chapter 11. Concentrate on the object in fine detail. Put it aside and see if you can recapture it right there where it was before. All visible features, tactile features, sounds it made when tapped, smell, proportions. At first there will be only faint glimpses of sensory retentions. Then bit by bit the impressions linger longer.

At first practise against a neutral background: intrusive backgrounds can make for additional handicaps. In time, any background need not be distracting. Although I do remember some show I was in where I used the dark background of the audience upon which to project the face I talked with. One night, just as I asked it a particularly confronting question, a square hole suddenly appeared in its forehead. When I recovered from the jolt, I realised that an usher in the first balcony had opened the door to the foyer which lined up exactly in the middle of the brow. Thereafter I positioned the face with greater care.

Advantages: all the kaleidoscopic reaction that one normally generates in real experience. Excellent preparation for one person shows. And a great antidote for working with dull partners or overcoming the occasional bout of boredom. Yes, it can be used for fly-catching (chapter 51), as in the well-known but perhaps apocryphal story of the great Chaliapin, who distracted the audience from the singing of the tenor on stage by visualising a mouse walking across the footlights. The story goes that he visualised so well that many in the audience stood up to see what he was looking at.

Disadvantages: until one can instantly conjure up the desired sensations, there's a tendency to withdraw from contact with real objects on stage. This shows up as a moment of being cut off. Some performers show an obvious and awkward transition as they shift attention from real people to phantom to real again. Some performers blank out in shifting from real to phantom as do people programmed to perform under post-hypnotic instructions: for this reason, some believe there could be a kinship between willed hallucinations and suggestion or hypnosis.

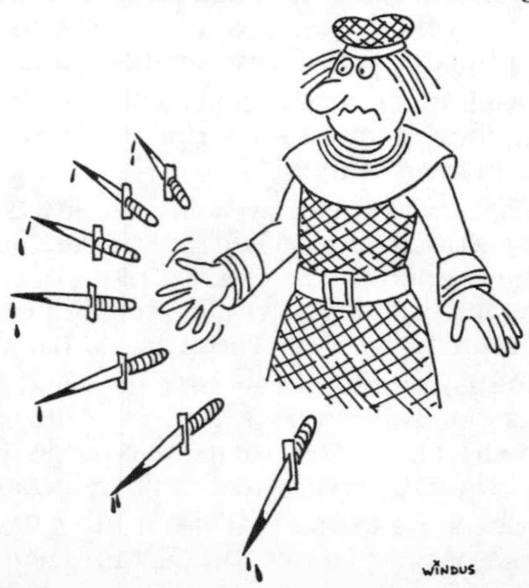

CHAPTER 32

EMOTION MEMORY

Not long ago in a newspaper interview, a popular and quite good actor vented his spleen on 'Method Actors'. Then he described his own favourite approach to a role. What he described, in detail, was ***Emotion Memory.***

Often seen as the rallying point for many of the 'Method' schools, and hotly denounced by others, this technique remains the Big Bertha of our motivational artillery. Simply described, it is capitalising on what you felt as a result of some earlier identifiable experience. Somewhere in your past you know of an emotional incident. It may be recaptured, and what you felt then may be repeated now. And while the result is an emotion memory, the process of making it happen is actually a sense memory.

Certain variables that will affect the result of emotion memory should be noted:

- Repression: If the incident was suppressed, or better still repressed, the better chance of a dramatic result.
- Impressionability: The earlier in life the incident took place, usually the more emotive the result.
- Privacy: If the incident was never revealed or discussed, the fuller the response.
- Depth and detail recall: The deeper and more detailed the recollections, the fuller the response.

Here's the technique: Begin by relaxing. *Don't reach for the feelings!* Having found an incident (more about this later) we quietly visualise the physical features of the ambience in which it occurred. Outdoors: were there trees? where? how big? what kind? colours? benches? grass? people? what doing? how did they sound? and so on. Or indoors: furnishings? light from windows? lamps? carpets? wallpaper? ceiling? smells? sounds? temperature? animals? people? peculiarities? food? objects? and so on.

Then, how did the incident start? Who said or did what? How did they look or sound? Then who did what? Continue until the entire episode has been acted out in your memory. Remember not to reach for any feelings! Simply let whatever happens happen. Be honest. And the more vividly you can recapture the details, even to the point of Sensory Projection, the more certain you can be of results. If you have chosen a suitable incident and have let your sensory memory do the work, you should be rewarded by a surge of strong feeling or emotion.

Certain emotive experiences work better than others. Those that were traumatic, associated with fear or guilt, anger or remorse could be buried deeper and carry strong loadings. But by the same token, they may be buried so deep that it is hard to remember or retrieve them. For some reason, old humorous experiences don't seem to work very well, but recent ones do. The most frequent and useful application for Emotion Memory is in retrieving strong, tenacious, and usually heavy, serious feelings.

The first time we wish to draw upon a particular heavy reference, the ritual of recall may take three to five minutes. But thereafter we can manage to shorten and speed up the ritual, so that if it has to be used nightly it takes less time and less detail each night. After a while we may only need a token signal for the full wave to swamp us. Three to five seconds, a single word or image to set it off.

If an Emotion Memory reference is kept private and unresolved, it may be good for years. But it can be lost forever if (1) one talks it out then has some abreaction, or (2) the scene being played gives the performer the opportunity to work out the traumatic fixation and resolve it. This has led to the technique of Emotion Memory being used by psychotherapists as a tool to treat deep-seated repressed traumas.

Advantages: Capable of dredging up deep strong emotions. Since these emotions tend to persist with the actor for a long time, they are re-usable in a variety of situations. They can be mixed with other techniques, often to provide an antidote. For example, if the memory of a parent humiliating you brings on tears and a moment later you need laughter, you might add an 'As if'. Like, then he tripped and fell into the pigpen.

Disadvantages: Once generated they flow, and you may get more than you want. And because they flow, they can't be kept on ice for later, because they'll either be suppressed again or heavily colour the time between when you generated them and later when you expect them to surface. So there's no point in preparing an emotion memory before a scene and expecting to be able to trot it out on cue five minutes into the scene. If you are, say, to begin the scene happily and then receive bad news and burst into tears, what will happen is that for four minutes and fifty nine seconds, instead of looking fresh and happy, you'll look as if you're fighting back tears. Then on the fifth minute, you may realise that most of your grief was used up in the battle.

Another disadvantage is that they usually stick around for a long time. If you have a short, sad scene and the next scene is to be happy, and if you can't find the appropriate antidote, you may not be able to shake the sadness in time. And there's also the problem that Emotion Memory tends to withdraw the actor from relationships with others on stage. If the scene calls for that it's fine, but if not it's hard to retain contact.

It is a powerful weapon, perhaps the most powerful of those controlled by the actor. Some regard it, like strikes, as a weapon of the last resort, to be used sparingly. My own vote would go that way.

How can we find these buried experiences that might be tapped for their emotional contents? The casual ones are easy to remember. The block-busters are hidden very deeply, and may take patient probing. Often years of psychoanalysis. However before embarking on such a worthy but protracted endeavour, you might try the following group game as a land-mine detector.

Form a comfortable and relaxed ring to play a word association game. Someone starts with any old word, and the person to their left immediately says a word associated with it. The third person quickly says a word associated with the second word, and so on around the circle. Each person tries to blank out any words except the word immediately to their right. Sooner or later, somebody will block, unable to think of a word.

Stop the round, noting the word just before the block – 'blood' or whatever. Then begin the round afresh, starting with the person who blocked. As soon as they say the new word – 'father' or whatever – stop again. Now ask them to say to themselves – and it should be nobody else's business – what word they would logically use to link 'blood' with 'father'. They usually say 'none', but then a smile creeps up on their lips. They have found a word. We say, "Dig under that word and you may find a repressed traumatic experience". There almost always is, and one which the actor may ultimately put to use.

The game goes on until most or many have detected personal land-mines.

There are other times, particularly when practising Sensory Stimulation, when a flash of an associated specific experience may occur to you. Make a note of it, try it out, and if it is useful include it in your catalogue of Emotional Memories.

It should be mentioned that actors calling upon repressed trauma are exploiting a built-in personality defect. Some might say, "See, I told you that you have to be a little mad to be an actor". Perhaps that's true, but this technique can't be used as substantiating evidence. Exploiting Emotion Memory is more a case of "If the monkey insists on clinging to my back – and which of us is without monkeys? – I can at least put him to work to earn his keep".

Actually, I doubt that the monkey would mind. It's often the only exercise he gets.

WRITE YOUR OWN NOTES

CHAPTER 33

PSYCHOLOGICAL GESTURE

We have borrowed this term from the great teacher Michael Chekhov, who meant something else by it. What we have referred to in this book as supplementary actions could cover most of what he described. Subtextual adjustments might account for the rest. We hope his ghost will forgive us.

Years ago a certain school of psychology pronounced, "We do not run because we are afraid: we are afraid because we run". There's enough wrong with that argument for the theory to have been long since superseded. But perhaps if those psychologists had peered a bit more closely, some of their theories might still be around.

We can demonstrate for ourselves that screaming fast and loud can generate feelings of panic, that stamping our feet on the ground persistently can generate feelings of anger, that punching a pillow can make us begin to feel pugnacious. And a perfectly calm person, asked to run away very fast, will generate not only adrenalin but noradrenalin – the 'flight or fight' hormone.

Perhaps a fairer formulation of that old theory might have been: "We run because we are afraid: but the process of running may also engender fear". Our thesis is that when we run we associate early experience of running which may have been because of fear. Then, the body/unconscious remembers and spurts some more hormones into our system to keep us going.

So when we improvise a sparring match with the stage manager in order to generate pugnacity for the scene we are about to play on stage, we are employing *psychological gesture*. Be careful that the increased enthusiasm does not culminate in a really hard punch. I believe that how Brando's nose was broken.

This technique is based on the powerful expressive effect of the random or habituated gestures of our infancy and early childhood. For example, if we suck our thumbs now, we may unconsciously remind ourselves of a time when we sucked our thumbs as an act of desperation because the desired nipple was not offered. Try it now and see what emerges... from your feelings, not your thumbs.

Of course, doing so at this time of our lives in the presence of our peers could invite ridicule. So try it in private, perhaps in your dressing room. Behave as a baby would behave. Lie on your back and grasp the air at random. Poke your fingers tentatively at various objects. Thump the table with your hands or a spoon. Smile and chuckle at people. Curl up in a corner in a fetal position.

Do any of these do anything to your feelings? Particularly when they are accompanied by the more violent infantile activities such as screaming, stamping and punching, they should turn on some emotional juices. But if they don't, no worry. What works for one may not work for another.

Try out a whole range of random or habitual behaviour acquired early in life. Just get stuck into the behaviour. Never mind the actions or why. The overall why is to see what works for you. So if you hit pay-dirt from any, make a note.

For performance, generally they should be included in the warm-up before the scene. You'd rarely have the opportunity to suck your thumb on stage. And yet ... when we look at some of the sensory stimulants that turn us on, we may discover that many are in fact slightly disguised infantile gestures made socially acceptable: they do find their way onto the stage. The thumb has given way to cigarettes. Sucking milk has given way to sipping cocktails or tea. Squeezing mother's breasts has given way to clutching a purse. In fact, many of our adult gestures – even the most sophisticated of them – may be versions of emotionally-loaded infantile behaviour. So, in effect, a whole range of psychological gestures can be worked into performances, as business or other adjustments.

Perhaps this gives us a clue as to why highly stylised forms, such as musicals and pantomimes, remain the most popular kinds of theatre. Much of such theatre is evocative of our pre-rational infantile development. The associations trigger such raw and unguarded responses from us that we can truthfully say, "When I hear the music, I suspend critical judgment". The associations are pre-rational, thus pre-critical. Audiences are generally judgmental in emotional terms – I like it, or I don't: but they may not be critical in an analytical, rational sense.

Advantages: Psychological Gestures are useful for blanket feelings covering longish scenes. They can also be mixed with other techniques. In raw form or in varying disguises, they can provide an additional layer of feeling, complementary to whatever else is introduced.

They also tend to produce package results. If a gesture is called upon to lend, say, shyness to a scene, it may also bring with it a whole parcel of associated feelings that may prove beneficial to the scene. Or they may be irrelevant, superfluous, or even misleading. Trial and error is the way to find out.

Disadvantages: The above-mentioned clutter, also a slight tendency to withdraw from contact when employing certain early gestures. Also, they're not always readily accessible during the scene. And it's not everybody's tool: some people just won't allow themselves to try, while others have tried and found them useless. See for yourself.

CHAPTER 34

SNEAKY TECHNIQUES

Ambience, Faith, Dedication, Licence, Alibi, Procrastination, Contagion and Trickery

The groups in this chapter might not seem like techniques at all. Don't we resort to most of these almost by nature? Notwithstanding, however we learned them they are still techniques (know-hows) and we can handle them, even refine them, deliberately.

AMBIENCE AND FAITH:

Here we have a pair of non-dynamic techniques offered up as a gift to the lazy. No need to bestir yourself much in implementing these, since they are concerned more with a state of mind than they are with procedures. But nonetheless, they are procedures.

We describe the first, *ambience,* as 'avoiding disturbance of the feeling you came in with'. In other words, the practice of leaving it alone.

Suppose, for instance, that in your first scene you are supposed to be on a hypermanic high, happy, enthusiastic, etc. Now it just so happens that before you left for the theatre, a phone call informed you that you'd just had a big win in the lottery. You'd have to be an idiot to suppress your real feelings of the moment, in order to invoke some far-fetched As If that worked pretty well for you last night. You don't need anything else! Leave it alone, and avoid any influences that would stifle your elation.

Therein is the technique: a fending off of all distractions. How you do it will depend on the circumstances and your resourcefulness. But the aim is to avoid interfering with whatever you feel, *if* what you feel is appropriate for your scene. It's a technique that puts to the test the old aphorism: warm heart and cool mind. Keep your wits about you and it can be simple. One tip: keep your experience to yourself. To share it is usually to dissipate it.

Faith, on the other hand, owes nothing to accident. Faith takes advantage of the experiences you have acquired, not only through the period of rehearsal and the length of the run so far this season, but through your lifetime of experiences, and through all the skills you have acquired throughout your career.

We may describe Faith as "a coalition of intuitive associations". The fundamental thought behind this one is "she'll be right". It is the belief that all your techniques are so deeply ingrained that whatever is required will just pop up on cue, that there is no problem so great or unexpected that you can't find some simple and adequate solution. This is often the claim of the so-called intuitive actor.

It's a great way to induce or bolster authority. If you recognise your own skills and capabilities, you can use this technique to generate a narrow but strong range of responses: composure, authority, attack, openness, that sort of thing.

By the same token, an over-inflated or unfounded belief in such capacity, based on ignorance or foolishness, may well lead to underestimating the requirements or pitfalls. When the crunch comes for such a performer, the result is usually a decisive crumple: the authority and the performance disintegrate.

Faith is a useful technique in those situations where an understudy is required to go on. If the understudy has practised and rehearsed, and is without reputation, we can sometimes almost feel the growth of the "she'll be right" attitude. And why not? The excitement of getting a crack at the role, and the possibility that this may be "a step up in my career" may provide the motivation. And "The worst that can happen is falling on my face, in which case my career may have to wait a bit longer". And "The others have been playing the show for a while, they'll pull me through if anything goes wrong. So – here goes nothing".

The process of thorough rehearsals, and a well-integrated sequence of performances can also contribute to an attitude of Faith. It worked yesterday, the day before, the week before, so why not tonight?

Advantages: Faith is a mighty inducer of the feeling of authority, particularly when backed up by actual professional competence. It helps us to expand our circle of concentration with extreme facility. A capacity to help others on stage, a great sense of openness, even vulnerability, often a generator of warmth, charm and persuasiveness. It is particularly useful when established performers become increasingly nervous of losing their big reputations.

Disadvantages: when it is poorly based or handled, Faith may induce cockiness, arrogance, indifference, selfishness, contempt. It may tend to set us on automatic, so that we walk through performances. And there's the possibility of distorting the play and undermining others' performances. A double-edged sword.

The practice of Faith as a motivational technique is arrived at both experientially and philosophically. The experiential influences work in their own good time: the longer you work, the greater the experience. Philosophically, we should consider that the audience has come for what we have to offer them: that we have been chosen from among many as the person to handle this job: that we have been briefed, prepared, and tested so that our work is as effective as we can make it under the circumstances: that we can't control all the circumstances, but we can in all circumstances do our best. And we can accept that in extreme circumstances we may have to admit frankly that we are beaten and not suffer loss of face: we are artists, but we are also human, and the audience as well as our peers can acknowledge that there are limits beyond which no reasonable human being – or artist – should be expected to cope.

So, what's to lose? There's more we can expect to gain through Faith. And the more confidently we approach the production, the less chance there will be of problems requiring strenuous coping.

DEDICATION AND LICENCE:

Here are two more relatively easy techniques. Let's begin with an example of the first. One long-running show was looking tired: the actors were stale, morale was low, the audience was cheated. As the company prepared for a matinee one afternoon, the stage manager announced over the PA system that the curtain might be a bit late as there was some difficulty getting the wheelchairs in, and he muttered something about the Children's Hospital. Of course, that matinée performance was probably the most inspired since opening night, and the company waited around expecting some of the disabled children to be wheeled backstage for a look-around and a chance to meet the cast. There were no wheelchairs nor children nor had there been. But the company had been reminded of what a conscientious performance could be. They had practised, even if they weren't about to name it, the technique of *dedication:* they would give those kids a show they would never forget.

One of my earliest professional associates, Rodion Rodionoff, who had danced with Pavlova's company, taught me much through occasional tactful hints. He had one device, however, that I thought was amateurish: his practice of peering through a hole in the curtain at the audience as they were arriving. One day he explained that he would find one face in the crowd, and that performance he would dance for her. That too was Dedication, and it kept him from ever flagging in his conscientious professionalism, even when others in the company were larking about.

How to practise it? Find people or a cause you can champion. If they are present during the performance, so much the better, but it is not strictly necessary. When one performs in a benefit for flood relief, the wet victims need not be in the audience. Then present the efforts of your performance as a selfless offering. It needs no more rehearsing than that.

Advantages: warmth. Blanket motivation for one's supplementary actions on the audience. Dedication is almost a must if one is to be a conscientious performer with integrity.

Disadvantages: there's a possible tendency to limit the audience relationship to a small section of the audience. It works best if the objects of dedication are scattered throughout the audience – or better still that the object be the entire audience.

Be careful not to slip into the trap of obviously playing *to* the audience instead of *for* them. Theoretically, the target of dedication is not so much the object of action as a reference for motivation. But in all performing, the audience does become the object of a supplementary action. Here we remember to observe the principle "Wherever possible, the object of your action becomes your key motivator". So the audience has always been both: a reason for doing what we do on stage, and the object of a secondary action which ensures that they are duly swayed. With the motivational technique of dedication, they become a bit more important as both object and reference. So to keep the show from swinging its emphasis away from the onstage happenings, we have to work just a bit more powerfully on stage. That will keep the balance. In other words, if we are giving the audience more attention, we'd better do at least as much for our fellow performers. Thus we get a more committed and vital performance all around.

The second technique, *Licence,* is designed not so much to overcome occupational tedium as occupational reticence.

At some time in our careers, often near the beginning, we stop and ask "Why?" Why do I think I have the right to preach to, or set examples for, people who are no doubt more wise, experienced, mature than myself? How can I get away with anti-social behaviour on stage when others get arrested for doing some of the same things even in private? Why is my photo in the papers over concocted stories when worthy causes can't get a mention? And why is my private life invaded? When I work onstage, why don't I simply face my partners naturally instead of talking to them via the audience, angled and side-wise? And whatever created me a 'star', with free plane trips and people demanding my autograph?

The cumulative effect of these and many other self-doubting questions tends to undermine our authority on stage. Sensitive, intelligent performers are sometimes tempted to apologise for being part of this enormous sham, this public hoax. Abner Dean once had a book of cartoons entitled ***What Am I Doing Here,*** and many of us theatricals have asked that. When we do, it tends to undermine us and weaken our work.

One antidote is to remind ourselves of a very special social contract. We have been licensed to provide certain goods in exchange for certain remuneration. Part of what we provide includes the surrendering of a whole range of normal rights and commitments, including some of our privacy. We have inherited the mantle of the Court Jester, and our licence says we're stuck with the conditions. Almost.

It is just as well that today the licence remains a mental fiction. What would it be like if in fact we couldn't perform unless the government issued us with an actual permit? The nearest we get to such conditions is perhaps qualifying for an Actors Equity card. Or maybe the Soviet system of recognising only those who have graduated from authorised acting schools. On the other hand, it should be remembered that had the Court Jester transgressed, there was always the risk that both his contract *and* he himself could be expunged.

However, now in most countries there remains a more tolerant implied contract when by some fluke or by dint of extraordinary effort one becomes recognised as a professional performer. And so many aspects of behaviour we might otherwise regard as impertinent are not only permitted but demanded of us, and we are required to do them without holding back. So as John Casson once said, "Put on the red nose and get out there".

ALIBI AND PROCRASTINATION:

Who do we know that has not developed a cold, or laryngitis, or a sprained ankle or a twisted back before an opening night. Or else pranged their car, or quarrelled with their spouse, or – what was yours, toothache? Who doesn't need an *alibi?*

Our psyches arrange for most of us some fail-safe program so that what goes wrong will not be seen to be a result of our inadequacy. Oh no, we are quite capable, we could do that show on our ear: it is only because, you see, as I was coming home late I tripped on this garden hose ... So the garden hose is to blame if I blow my lines.

We seem to have an instinct that concerns itself with our effectiveness, how good we are at the things we undertake. Some people often undertake nothing so that they need not worry about how well they score. If they don't try, they can't fail, and prove to themselves what they fear. But those of us who try our darndest are really putting ourselves on the line. "I have rehearsed, been directed, assisted, encouraged, promoted, received everything that success requires. Everything is geared for triumph. What if, in spite of my best efforts, I fail?"

So we build in some Alibi to cushion the possible disappointment. Some performers deliberately prepare some controlled Alibi. Better a controlled one than falling down a flight of stairs. Controlled Alibis include other jobs or projects during rehearsal, so that one didn't have enough time to learn dialogue or dialect. Or we moved house during the rehearsal period. Or prolonged visits to sick friends, arguments with the director or producer, or ... the list is entertaining if not endless.

It is at least as useful to recognise alibi as an influence over the feeling of confidence, as it is to practise it. One can celebrate the moment a 'spontaneous' alibi occurs. One can then say, "Right, I can relax now, I'm well insured with a face-saver just in case". Given such confidence, "just-in-case" rarely happens.

A well-prepared performer usually delivers most of the goods as rehearsed. One can reasonably expect that almost everything that was prepared to happen now comes together in a happy confluence of influences. No Alibis are needed. But something in the performer doesn't necessarily see it this way. The reasoning mind well might, but the instincts have their own reasons. So if shortly before a crucial performance you decide to rescue the theatre cat stranded on the catwalk, and your bad cold causes you to sneeze and overbalance, so that you fall though the ceiling above the auditorium and impale your leg on the spear protruding from the chandelier – rejoice. You have your Alibi, and you can risk failure: moreover you have a special bonus. The audience will love you for going on in the wheelchair, all splinted and bandaged up.

If Alibi is psychosomatic, its cousin *Procrastination* is relatively un-neurotic. Procrastination in everyday life derives from somewhat the same insecurity as alibi. The longer I can put off deciding or doing something, the longer I can forestall having to test myself against success or failure. That's one reason why people put off tackling or finishing a problem. Laziness or indifference can also induce procrastination, as can uncertainty of the need to attempt the problem at all. Lack of preparedness, the complexity of the problem, or its low priority in a busy schedule can all justify stalling.

But for the performer, there is one use for procrastination which has been known to produce brilliant results. Letting an idea marinate, or sleeping on it. In other words, giving inspiration a chance to join the decision-making panel. It may take a long time: some actors will not essay the role of King Lear until they have thought about it for years. There is much to be said for a performer who, after a multi-faceted examination of a problem, says, "Let me think about it". Assuming there is time for such percolation, saying "Your turn" to the unconscious can make the difference between a half-baked interpretation and one of genius.

If you haven't the luxury of days or years in which to decide, you can usually hold out for at least one overnight: "I'll sleep on it". Of course if you are on a film set costing thousands per minute, few directors will tolerate such a request: but you might use the time it takes to set up the shot. Any pause might be usefull. Sensitive directors know this. After the fifteenth take of an extra-close-up on a film set, when the actor's eyelids are flapping like trapped butterflies, the director may wisely announce, "OK, take a break".

When you are in doubt about how something should be approached, if there is time, take it. Relax. Let the ideas wash over you. Don't force. Don't panic. 'Let' – that magic word.

As a motivational technique, Procrastination is primarily an aid in tracking down other motivational techniques, including Inspiration. "What will help motivate this bastard of a moment? Nothing will come to mind". Before you demand that the moment be rewritten to accommodate your inability, let time work for you. I once spent eight months looking for a satisfactory trigger.

You might say, "Today we are trying to solve too many problems at once. You are too uptight. Relax, get a good night's sleep, we'll look at it again tomorrow". In the morning, refreshed, you may be able to tackle the job. The night functions as an anxiety-eraser.

A break can be particularly useful as a consolidator of what could be multiple references: the director gives a bewildering number of details of what should occur emotionally. "She should be happy but in a quiet way, and yet in the quality of her smile you can see this worried look that she suddenly becomes aware that others can see. So she converts this worried look into a joke-type response and then pretends that she is not really frivolous". Even without instantly grasping the director's full meaning, it sounds as if an unmanageable number of techniques might have to be called upon. Could we simplify?

Perhaps one needs a bit more time to get those ingredients to mix in one bowl. After a night's sleep you might wake and say, "I'm meeting my prospective mother-in-law for the first time. She thinks theatre people are shallow and frivolous. My fiancé tried to convince her differently and hopes he'll prove it with me there. If Mum says 'No', we may not be able to get married". As you see, an As If. That should take care of the smiles and the worried cautious looks or whatever, all under one set of references.

Perhaps there should be a less negatively-emotive name for this technique. Contemplation? Cogitation? Stewing it over? Rain-check? If we leave it at Procrastination, you'll know what we mean.

Advantages: one may discover rich detail and clever invention. Comparable to Research, except that the sources are in our psyches. Tends to produce richly-layered results. And of course, it can even give us more time for research.

Disadvantages: it may take more time than is practicable. There's the possibility of missing the moment. The time comes when all the ingredients of a performance – the others, the technologies, time of day or month – come together in that fortuitous confluence of influences, only you are not ready.

The risk of over-fixing. One can, by an over-zealous commitment to perfection, continually seek to improve the product forever. Or never attempt it at all. As the Muslim carpet-weavers assert when they put a deliberate imperfection into the rug, "Only Allah is perfect". Over-fixing usually results in spoiling the product.

Notwithstanding, Procrastination used judiciously can work for the broadest range of problems and at all levels of feelings.

We can't end without mentioning an aspect of Procrastination that seems to owe much to Gamesmanship (chapter 39). This is the putting-off process often seen in rehearsals, where performers postpone showing their hand to other performers. They walk through the rehearsal, mumble their lines, conserve their energies. The others in the company are neglected. Relationships remain undeveloped.

Comes the night, and the 'procrastinator' may come up with a bucket of bright surprises, fitting in nicely with what he knows the others are prepared to give. But the others may be thrown. Hardly a technique for fostering friendliness, this epitome of "I'm all right Jack, bugger you!" is a time bomb in most companies where it is found. Whether born of insecurity, meanness, or whatever, while the results for that performer may be startling, the effect on a company can be devastating.

CONTAGION:

There is little about this technique that would not be known to virtually everybody. Is there a host or hostess, receptionist, nurse, or any human being who at some time in their career did not have to set an example of cheerfulness? What happens is that one person exudes a certain feeling and others pick it up. The process of *Contagion.* Any real feeling is contagious.

For a while, good manners in driving in traffic were generated by the campaign slogan 'Courtesy is Catching'. And it was. People do tend to reciprocate a cordial gesture made by another driver. So total behaviour, not just feeling alone, can be made contagious. As can be surmised, Contagion is primarily a means of altering behaviour of others, but it can benefit you as well. Once the result has started, you get swept up in it. For example, finding yourself laughing at your own joke is usually because somebody else is laughing.

If we want to affect others so that they will behave in a certain way, we may set the tone by behaving that way ourselves. If we are genuinely authoritative in carrying it through, inevitably others will fall in with it. On the other hand, if we are not sufficiently authoritative, we may just as easily cultivate perverse reactions.

Some observations: Firstly, you will have to take into account the prevailing mood and possibly the reason behind it. The mood you're hoping to introduce might be wrong for the occasion. If you come in overbearingly cheerful and do not recognise the cause of the prevailing mood of gloom, someone is likely to resent the abrupt incursion, particularly if they are mourning the death of a child.

Given the right ambience and approach, Contagion can work in stimulating certain responses which may resist other techniques. We just referred to laughter. That is usually a tough one to generate. But in the right scene, where one person can get a real laugh going, others may pick it up quite readily. Then you find yourself laughing all the more. Deep depression is another example.

We know how all too easily that monstrously undesirable feeling of nervousness can spread through a company, largely due to contagion. In its way, that should be an example of how this technique can be put to good use. If the director, stage manager, leading actor can exude confidence and good cheer without overdoing it, that can go a long way toward instilling similar feelings in others. Note the compere-MC approach to warming up an audience. If he is unsure of himself or his material and does not feel truly jolly, then making jolly faces and jovial sounds will not kindle joviality in the audience. They'll see that he is trying too hard, and are more likely to be infected by his contagious feeling of worry. We see it in opera and other music theatre, when a song may be started by a singer worried about a top note. The audience worries with her until she hits the note satisfactorily, after which she tends to relax. And so does the audience.

Sometimes we must conceal or disguise Contagion. If we want the audience to worry on behalf of the character, but the performer secretly feels he is so capable there would be no need for worry, the scene may not play properly because the deeper feelings of confidence may shine through.

One performer portrayed an ineffectual character who turns at the end and exacts high vengeance for having been kicked around. We did everything to make the man look totally vulnerable: a club-foot prosthetic, shabby clothes, gauche staging. But he was so good at it that during rehearsals everybody flattered him into a state of confidence approaching arrogance. When he came on stage, although he limped and cringed, he exuded such authority that he looked as though he could take care of himself very nicely thank you. So after every performance, the director (I) tore his performance to shreds. The performer felt completely undermined and exuded that uncertainty when next he came on stage. All went to schedule until curtain call, when he was given an ovation. The process had to be repeated every performance throughout its twelve-week run. We are assured that the actor never did see through the trick.

If there ever was a justification for cliques in a company, one might be that a small band can often raise itself to a high energy state because of how its members affect each other. Among the motivational devices available to such cells is Contagion, which they may use not only to build their own energy level but to kindle similar responses in the rest of the company. The clique may become known as a 'ginger group'.

Sometimes the company is blessed by having somewhere high on their totem pole a person of integrity, who commands universal respect. Such people are capable of setting the tone for the most effective and constructive use of contagion. They often do. As do wise managements and good directors.

Advantages: Like the ensemble effect, the effort is minimal for big results. contagion between actors doesn't reveal itself easily to the audience. But between actor and audience, Contagion can be very telling. We often hear the public enthusing about some mediocre show with the words, "They looked like they were having so much fun!" That often displaces critical faculties. It can be habit-forming. Because it is designed primarily to benefit the other person, any benefit to ourselves is a by-product.

Disadvantages: it can't easily be faked. Requires an amenable group or enough members of the group. It must be tailored more carefully to the prevailing circumstances than some other techniques. Because it imposes on others, we are to some extent invading their motivational procedures and we could be inadvertently interfering. There are people who prefer to prepare in private, and along comes Mr Party-Game-Organiser interrupting and cheerfully roping in Ms Privacy. Resentment all round.

Any technique which imposes itself on others, like Ensemble Effect, Trickery,

Gamesmanship, or Contagion should be handled with great sensitivity.

TRICKERY:

Here is one more device designed mostly to affect others.

Trickery is primarily a director's device. Recall the example of the film director inducing a shock-horror response on the face of the starlet in the chapter on Supplementary Actions? Or the example in the preceding chapter, where the actor's propensity to be contagiously affected by an audience was countered by directorial trickery.

Certainly some directors like to play Svengali, but should they need to? Shouldn't the performer be able to take direction succinctly and accurately? We know that directors and editors sometimes find it necessary to cut away from some film actors when the results are not what is desired. And often a director may not know what he wants until he sees something interesting. He may simply trust the actor to come up with a performance, grab what seems useful, and discard by cutting those bits that are not the best.

But if the director needs quite specific responses and the actor fails to provide them, the director often feels justified in using tricks. In ***Moulin Rouge,*** there was a touching vignette of a drunken old woman rummaging in a garbage can. This was no clever impersonation by a sober member of the Screen Actors Guild, but a genuine Parisian derelict whom the director had discovered doing just that. The crew kept her around drinking until they could set up, then stowed a bottle deep in the garbage can. She was then filmed searching and finding the bottle, in a scene that few actresses could simulate. And as we mentioned earlier, the legend is that Victor McLaglen was not always aware of his behaviour during filming of ***The Informer,*** and again alcohol provided the necessary tranquilliser. These examples could be deemed callously cruel, but they are used as extreme examples of how far some directors presume to go.

Hardly a film is produced that doesn't involve Trickery. The medium is a natural for such a technique, since the responses to being tricked are likely to be strong and spontaneous. They are also likely to work only once, and they are unpredictable. So if we get the wrong response, we can re-shoot the scene and try again another way. One good take is all we need.

But Trickery is not exclusively a film device, nor is it solely the property of directors. It can be used by one actor upon another. One example I know of risked an actress's stage career. She was in her first Broadway show, which was in its last weeks, and a director was coming to see if she was suitable for another show he was casting. And she was very nervous.

In addition to nerves, she had other disabilities to overcome in a hurry before the director's arrival. She was beautiful and she had a great singing voice, but she was very young and had been coached by her mother. The result of this was that she had never demonstrated any outstanding acting ability, never looked at anybody on stage, but was always posing out front and hadn't a clue who or what was on stage with her. She had become something of a performing joke.

Her leading man impertinently used Trickery to help her, in a sink-or-swim risk. Her big number involved a wedding reception in which he and she were the newly-weds. Before going on, he made her aware that the 'flower' in his lapel was a water-squirter, but refused to answer when she asked if he intended to squirt her while they were onstage. So they went on, with her eyes virtually never leaving him. And each time a knowing smile was needed, he simply moved his hand toward the pocket that held the bulb full of water. The scene went beautifully, she was cast in the new show, and went on to a radiant career.

Fortunately, she was able to contain herself sufficiently to avoid breaking up. More importantly, she subsequently found herself a good coach to replace a backstage mother. But what a gamble! And what presumption!

Of course the theatre is no stranger to Trickery, but usually actors use Trickery to play practical jokes on each other. Often it does overcome some of the tedium which may set into long-run shows, and sometimes the audience may see a brighter and more loaded performance because of it. But usually the audience is left wondering and often offended by what seem to be private jokes passing between performers at the expense of the show and the spectators.

The advantages of Trickery are as suggested.

Disadvantages: as we mention under Alteration (next chapter), there is a traditional hi-jinks performance (closing night) which usually invites Trickery. If the general acceptance of such a performance endorses such by-play, then it is virtually open slather. Pranks everywhere, and the boundary between Alteration and Trickery is blurred.

The distinction we make between the two is this: Trickery is a device to affect another person, hopefully helpfully, and any personal benefits are a bonus. Alteration is primarily a self-serving technique, and any effects induced in our work-mates are regarded as secondary. Trickery aims carefully to achieve a specific result, like shooting at a target with a rifle. Alteration aimlessly attempts to escape personal boredom, like amusing yourself by scattering firecrackers at random. Alteration usually uses the same basic material slightly rearranged, like small changes in dialogue or entrances made through a window instead of a door. But Trickery frequently introduces elements that were not there in the first place: the inactive prop phone which now rings, cellophane tape encasing the apple to be eaten onstage, messages written onto the bottoms of teacups.

These may be fine distinctions. But one hopefully wouldn't expect to see a film director wasting creative ideas or precious time on Alteration when Trickery is available.

WRITE YOUR OWN NOTES

CHAPTER 35

MORE SHORTCUTS

Indication, Imitation, Diversion, Alteration and Distortion

INDICATION AND IMITATION:

The whirring, gnashing sounds you hear are from the grave of Lee Strasberg. If there was one stage behaviour he despised, it was *Indication*. He never spoke the word, he spat it. It seemed to be the antithesis of all he stood for. He would say there are two kinds of acting: acting for effect, and acting for inner truth. He aspired only to the latter. The former was Indication: going through the motions.

Indication means knowing what the feeling is expected to be, but instead of generating the actual feeling, one goes through the motions of what one thinks will give the effect of that feeling to the audience. You've seen it: the boo-hoo-hoo-gasp-shaking-shoulders-wiping-away-pretend-tears school of acting. In a bygone time, the Delsart method taught such poses as hands-to-the-head-chin-high to indicate grief.

Indication can also refer to going through the motions of action playing instead of actually playing the actions. But let us confine ourselves to the emotive aspects of Indication.

Why bother with Indicating when one could produce the real thing? Well, sometimes, with the best intent, the real thing is not forthcoming. We can hardly stop the play until it comes. If the next line is "Why are you crying?", it is necessary for us to appear to be crying, to keep up the illusion and the pace as best we can. Sometimes we may just have to fake it. We try to be as clever and convincing as possible, but fake is better than nothing. (Yes, Lee, that's what you heard.)

Another reason for faking is that some actor-performers do not believe we should resort to real feelings. Why bother with real feelings when indication will do? Harold Lang, who did much to make action playing acceptable to actors on several continents, would not have a real feeling on a dare. Mental justifications for actions, trappings of feelings, not the real thing. He told me that he'd been put off by some humiliating experiences while learning to act, and never got over it. He believed that real feelings were self-indulgent, unnecessary and uncontrollable. Nevertheless, his productions were very popular, and his proselytising to action-playing was unimpeachable.

Some actors might welcome a real feeling if it should happen upon them one day, but in the meanwhile they prefer to 'act' their feelings. We often hear this referred to as 'falling back on technique' (sic). And there are those who mistrust the real feeling to be clear enough, or strong enough to carry to the far corners of the theatre. So they lay it on or spell it out, overlaying a real feeling with layers of indication. Gilding the gold or painting the lily.

So why are we including indication among motivational techniques, when it would seem to be a device for *not* producing feelings? Well, one argument runs something like this: "I would love inspiration to occur. Until it does I will simply provide its shell, its form, its outline. And when it comes, it will fill in this outline". This belief is more prevalent than one might at first imagine. Such a motivational use of indication is an invitation for the feeling to occur. And sometimes it actually does that. I did say "sometimes". Actually and more frequently, Strasberg's thesis proves itself: Indication tends to stifle any incipient inspiration.

One precondition for ensuring that a feeling won't come is panic: the more you tighten up, the less chance a feeling has of squeezing through. But when you say, "Why worry? I give a good indication of a feeling. I'm sure the audience doesn't feel cheated", you tend to relax. And that could be the very moment the real feeling decides to get into the act. There may be other explanations, some of which may touch on psychological gesture or contagion, but for whatever reason, Indication can work. Not as a reliable motivational technique, I admit. But as a performing device to keep the show going, it is certainly a tool of the professional. But accurate indicating please. Study real people in the throes of real emotions. Note your observations, and rehearse them until you can fool people.

As a performance tool, indication is useful in certain plays that demand abrupt transitions, where profound grief may have to give way to gregarious relaxed glee within 15 seconds. As we know, deep feelings tend to carry over for quite a while, and a brisk change within 15 seconds is the sort of problem even experts find challenging. Often, the audience is better served by a good actor indicating one – or perhaps both – of those feelings. But it should be *good* indicating: blatant face-pulling won't qualify.

Given the choice, I much prefer a good indicator keeping the drama building than a 'truthful' performer interrupting the flow while struggling for the motivation. You're not on stage for the purpose of exercising your techniques. If the feelings emerge without disturbing the phrase, beautiful, that's best of all. But if I have to go into suspended animation while watching an actor revving his motor, the illusion can be shattered much more manifestly than with skillful indication. Plays are about illusions, not about clever actors displaying their techniques.

This is not to negate those instances we see, particularly in films, where the dynamics depend on our being able to see a feeling change take place before our eyes. At such moments the action to be played may actually be 'to motivate': or perhaps some more passive action, like a strongly motivated 'to sort out' or 'to weigh up' or some other transitional action. Here the actor may actually be encouraged to take their time generating an emotional response. If the resultant 'reaction shot' is too long, some of it may end up on the cutting-room floor.

We shall again touch on indication in chapter 42.

A kindred device is *Imitation,* whose qualifications as a motivational technique we might also challenge. It is sometimes known as 'Understudy Disease', since it is the recourse many an understudy has resorted to in the absence of good clear direction or other guidance.

It can be quite disconcerting during a performance to glance into the wings and there see your understudy mimicking every move and gesture you are making on stage, like a side-wise mirror exercise. Chances are he hasn't a clue as to what each gesture physicalises. Is the hand going this way helping to implement my action, or is it formalising a feeling, or is it physicalising a supplementary action?

The understudy does it because when he must go on, he can slot right in with the rest of the company without disturbing the well worked-in pattern of the production. So that I will not be missed. Never mind that my gesture is born of an emotional explosion, and is body language saying, 'Better hold your tongue or you will regret it'. He simply makes the gesture, and there are no explosions anywhere.

We know that mimicry is an excellent communication device. And it is a useful means of acquiring characteristics for characterisation where we seek to impersonate wholly or in part some person or animal. But does it set the actor's juices flowing? The surprise is that sometimes it does. Perhaps again by touching on similar associations that work for Psychological Gesture, or it may kindle Imagery associations, or Indication, or Contagion, or a little of each. Whatever the reason, Imitation is sometimes the door to real feelings.

We see imitation in other forms. Often when a director can't get through to an actor any other way, she may give him a reading of a line. The actor imitates and maybe, Eureka! The penny drops and feelings well up to fill in the form of speech. Even if not, a good parroted reading may give the audience a chance to fill in for themselves. The reading should be backed up by appropriate feelings, but if they aren't there at first the actor may some day stumble on an appropriate feeling. Whether he welcomes the incursion is another story, and will be dealt with more in the section on Performing.

Another manifestation of Imitation is to be found in the road company or import-export production. Often it is the stage manager who prepares a road company version of a successful show, seeking no more than accurate imitation: "Never mind why: just do it. That's what the original did". The same is true for overseas shows, except that frequently that director is the replacement of the replacement of the stage manager, with the accompanying dilution or loss of the original motives for stage behaviour. I was once 'directed' by a third-generation stage manager, who at least had the good grace to admit that he hadn't a clue about what he was doing.

In rehearsing the original production of ***Oklahoma!***, Lee Dixon, as Will Parker, was working in his dance for "Everything's Up to Date in Kansas City". A wonderful performer and tap-dancer, he was taking in a good sweep of stage with one of his 'how's that?' variations. As he approached me I mischievously swept my foot across his path to trip him up, and he jumped over my foot without missing a beat. Everybody thought it was a good touch and it was left in.

Would you believe that in the countless reproductions of ***Oklahoma!*** I have forced myself to see, the jump was still in the dance routine? But nobody was putting their foot out to trip him up. It has become a ritualised but unmotivated movement.

We may never know how much of opera's traditional stagings could be due to signals the feuding tenor and soprano were using to degrade each other, or the clumsiness of some original not being able to move freely in a new costume, or simply the need to find some place to spit. (Legend has it that "Visi d'Arte" in Tosca may be sung lying on the floor because the original soprano tripped.) But generation after generation will rehash the 'traditional version', each copy growing fainter or more distorted.

The painful irony is that from time to time flashes of real feelings break through. Not necessarily the feelings sought, more often feelings irrelevant to the performance. And there is the key distinction between these rather flimsy techniques.

With Indication, you do know what the feelings are, and go through the motions as a means of attracting them. With imitation, chances are you do not know, and use mimicry as a means of physicalising the performance. Of course you may combine the two, if you know what it is you pursue, and believe that mimicked business will help you find it. Which may or may not be an improvement on inventing your own indicated face-pull or head-in-hands. In any event, both techniques share the common belief that whatever it is we are giving the audience should suffice for now. They won't know the difference.

These techniques are worth practising. We should sharpen our perceptors, then try to replicate what we have observed in great detail. However we may disparage these devices as motivational techniques, they are extremely valuable processes to aid characterisation and in gaining insights into relationships and much else theatrical. Certain forms of theatre rely heavily on skills derived from such practices: mime, burlesque, caricature, vaudeville, puppetry, to name a few. In almost every performance of even the finest actors, we may find moments in which they are going through the motions. Audiences generally are prepared to accept those if they are well done. Even if they do not induce empathy, they can still stimulate sympathy.

DIVERSION, ALTERATION AND DISTORTION:

Here is a little triumvirate that do their best work as auxiliary techniques for other motivational techniques. Though each of them can trigger perhaps one or two feelings in their own right, they can free up the widest range of other techniques. And as they are quick and easy to comprehend, we group them here together.

Let's say that opening night is upon us and you approach it with great apprehension. That is the last feeling in the world that will help you through such a trial. The stimuli generated by that prospect are both real and imaginary, hemming you in from all quarters. You feel trapped. You can try *Diversion* (alternatively referred to as Distraction). Become involved with anything at all that could be captivating enough to distract you from all quarters. Suddenly the curtain is up and you are away, too busy with actualities to allow much speculation on dire possibilities.

In the days when TV was becoming crucial in determining 'image', I was employed to coach some politicians. Almost everyone political was assumed to be a crook, and any politician who looked the least bit furtive or uncomfortable on TV was certain to be seen as one such.

Now there's a critical time in the TV studio, during the countdown before going to air, when even P.T. Barnum might have been discomfited. The floor manager calls "Quiet in the studio please ... quiet please! Rolling ten seconds from ... now!" Then the countdown, 10-9-8-7-6-5-4-3(-2-1) ... we're on the air. And while the viewers watch, there sits a guarded politician coping defensively with intimidation and waiting for the interviewer to castrate him with the first trick question. And that 10-second pause certainly didn't help.

The audience could well have made up its mind at this stage. Even if the questions are responded to with competence, the audience might not have forgotten that guarded look at the beginning.

One of the best antidote techniques was Diversion. On a table beside the politician was a water carafe and a tumbler, items of possible interest, which allowed him to get busy with something ***irrelevant*** to the interview. "That's an interesting tumbler. Real cut glass too. Any indication of place of manufacture? It is not the same style as the water carafe. That too is cut glass, but see where this pattern describes circles, this one describes squares, etc." Suddenly there is the first question, and the lens picks up an alert, vital, un-furtive face.

Diversion is a very effective technique. Merely saying "Get your mind off it", or "Don't think of it", presents no possible substitute. It is like saying, "Don't think of the word 'elephant' while I count to ten". But finding some positive object of involvement helps us by-pass that negative. Even a crying baby responds to a dangled bunch of keys, and usually stops crying.

Advantages: it works for relaxing and offering a clear field to your other preparations. And it is useful for long-range preparations as well as short immediate ones. If you've been working too hard in rehearsal, divert yourself with a night out at the movies – but don't go to see one about an actor worried by and tired at rehearsals. Diversion is also used in the art of mis-directing, which we shall encounter in the section on Performing.

Disadvantages: Your entrance preparation may require a heavy involvement with references relevant to the play. Like preparing telltales of where you are coming from. Diversion could sabotage it.

And Diversion is very open to abuse as an instrument of sabotage, especially when used by bored, clever, malicious performers. This can be seen as the naughty side of mis-direction. Remember Chaliapin using the Sensory Projection of a mouse walking along the footlights, in an attempt to sabotage the performance of the tenor? Such misbehaviour is called 'Fly-catching', perhaps because once some actor chose to catch a fly just at somebody else's peak dramatic moment: here we divert others' attention. You can generate real feelings if you become involved in some irrelevancy on stage just at someone's crucial moment, but the feelings are likely to be in the other actor, and they're not likely to be friendly. In someone else's big scene, if you have a quick flash that suggests that this is the moment to yawn, scratch, step on a cockroach, go looking for a cigarette, swat a fly – extinguish that flash instantly. No, not even a smile, glance or wave at the audience. And no mugging. I once saw an actress fired for licking excess lipstick off her teeth during a tense, still, stage-full-of-actors scene. The director was at the matinee, and noticed several of the audience turn their heads momentarily in her direction. Fired!

As for *Alteration,* one aspect of this technique is known as the Coward's Castle. Can't come to grips with the play? Haven't memorised the script? Get it rewritten so that it fits in with what you *are* able to do easily. If the performer is a 'star', some authors or directors are too ready to conform to the often over-rated capabilities of certain crowd-pleasers. Some actors demand the rewriting or merciless cutting of an author's rich work. Then they re-fill the moment with their stale stock of readily available tricks or feelings.

We know so many theatricals who are more than ready to extend themselves to provide the author's intent, who welcome the challenge, that the script-changers seem a paltry lot. Yet, there are times in every career when a rewrite is advisable for the noblest of reasons. The play may be lacking in conflict, or opportunity to build the phrasing of the play or ... many reasons.

The other aspect of this technique involves changes in performance. You don't ask for a re-write, but during the performance you paraphrase the script, change the staging, even alter characterisation. Occasionally the altering performer is courteous enough to warn the cast or stage manager of the changes, but more often than not he doesn't. After all, one of the main reasons one does this sort of thing is the belief that some surprise change will ginger up the performance by startling others in the cast to a new high of alertness. Or maybe we can get a bit of private fun going: to hell with the audience, we need cheering up too!

No doubt Alteration of this kind can serve as an antidote for boredom. Some audiences in certain conventions have come to expect such behaviour and even look forward to it, as on closing nights when a tradition of horsing about with the play is tolerated by the management, director and author. Many an audience comes for the express purpose of witnessing the more or less integrated hi-jinks. And other audiences expect a show to grow or improve, to become richer and more mature as it changes over time. This expectation has been seen by some performers as an invitation to usurp the author's and director's functions. George M. Cohan's classic note on the backstage bulletin board: "Rehearsal Tuesday 10 a.m. to remove all improvements".

Having some familiarity with Alteration from several professional vantage points, I dare not sound too pious. My puritan self tends to see it as a naughtiness usually not so beneficial as even a well-intentioned performer might assume. At the same time, my pragmatist self knows that in skilled hands a bit of rejuvenating can work wonders. Then again, if I do it, you who may not have such skill or taste will want to do it as well, and then where would we be?

The puritanical suggestion here is that if a performer is so bored that they can't find constructive approaches to help refresh their energies, let them leave the play and give someone else a go. To keep the record straight, the pragmatic me blushes at the number of times I should have quit certain shows. Unfortunately, when whimsical Alterations occur, it is usually the audience that is cheated. Showbiz has trouble enough without being white-anted from within.

Of course, if the performer is also the author, director and management of the production, who am I to say nay? Or if the performer has been employed to 'improve' as he sees fit, then the structure of the performance would only be served by the Alterations, which presumably would be designed to benefit the audience.

Advantages: usually this technique is for convenience. Occasionally a more artistic substitution results. And, occasionally, freshness.

Disadvantages: a poor example for others in the company, a tendency to sameness in characterisation from show to show (because we tend to draw on our same stale stock of old tricks), a tendency to self-indulgence, and mangled scripts. And a disarrayed company, full of enemies.

Finally there is *Distortion,* that rehearsal process which so many actors find valuable. We were tempted to name it 'The Kitchen Sink', not because it deals with modern lower-depths realism, but because of what performers may throw into the rehearsal process – everything including the kitchen sink.

Some performers like to build a character, like a snowman, from the ground up, piling bits and pieces together until an illusion of that character appears. Others start with too much and then pare away until what is left is that same illusion, like chipping away marble from a potential statue. Each method has its advantages and difficulties, and each may suit some performers or productions better than others. Sometimes both are used.

The paring-away approach involves initial exaggeration. Overdoing it, even ridiculing it. If you have a natural tendency for *Grim & Earnest* performances or oh-so-sin-*cere* acting, a dangerous embedding of relentless dray-matics often occurs. This technique has been known to stop such ham-handedness before it can begin, by assisting the performer to approach even deep personal associations with something of detachment and humour, and to entice deep values out of hiding in a balanced and fresh way.

You begin with wild and reckless exaggeration, then bit by bit, apply the Joseph Jefferson philosophy of dispensing with the unnecessary, the tasteless, the confusing, the irrelevant, the anachronistic, the straining after effects. Ultimately there should emerge a vital, sleek, strong, integrated and dynamic picture of a person.

The technique of Distortion: actually do too much. Actions, motivation, adjustments, all bigger than necessary. Or totally irrelevant to the play, like dragging in local references. But you know you won't want all of them to remain, so you must be prepared to edit.

One great advantage to this approach is that it reaches for expansive values. For performers who tend to play close to the chest and don't know how to fill a stage, this is a ready antidote. Feelings produced this way seem to contain an exceptional vitality, as if each feeling wishes it could be stretched to include a number of side-effects. In the Performing section, we shall expand on the great

Argentina's comment, "When I dance the role of the slut there is something of a princess about her, but when I dance the princess there is something there of the slut". And why not?

Disadvantages: often not tolerated by some directors and performers, who may not understand that this is a passing process, or may not appreciate that the final product could be rich. And the technique may frustrate attempts by fellow actors who want to develop their characterisations by bouncing off co-workers who aren't so hammy. Over-acting and Distortion do seem hammy. This technique can alienate others, or get you fired.

You also have to watch that you don't fall in love with some of the cute tricksiness of early rehearsals, and refuse to excise the tricks when the time comes. It is tough having to murder your darlings.

One smiles occasionally to hear one actor say to another who has used the technique of distortion as a rehearsal procedure, "You know, you have improved tremendously since the first weeks of rehearsal. I was worried".

WRITE YOUR OWN NOTES

CHAPTER 36

THEY WORK, BUT ...

Suggestions, Hypnosis and Chemicals

SUGGESTIONS AND HYPNOSIS:

The first techniques we'll look at in this chapter are relatively commonplace and innocent devices. They are tools which can effectively produce dramatic results, but if misused can produce undesirable consequences. Such are *suggestion* and *autosuggestion.*

On its most everyday level, *Suggestion* is the process by which we accept direction. It is also the process whereby advice from critics or friends can influence our feelings. Frequently we use it as a preliminary process whereby we let ourselves believe in other motivational techniques.

There are at least four critical factors involved in the acceptance or rejection of Suggestion:

(1) The susceptibility ('suggestibility') of the subject:

(2) The prestige of the suggester:

(3) The specific moral or super-ego limiters or inhibitions:

(4) The ambience in which the suggestions are made.

Within the ambience of a rehearsal studio the director suggests an emotional result to a suggestible actor who has no moral objections to doing what is requested. Chances are that the feeling will occur as requested, since all four conditions have been met. But if any one of these is negative, the hopes of success may be undermined. With two or more negative conditions (you mistrust the director and the studio is filled with scoffing spectators), the odds are against success.

When the factors are propitious, we may find ourselves affected as much by unwelcome suggestions as by those that might help us. Take the case of reading reviews of our performance. We may tell ourselves that we won't take criticism seriously, but what actually happens? Suggestibility: I opened the paper voluntarily, so I must want to know. Prestige: she is an established critic of high reputation. Moral objection: the media have a right and responsibility to publish critical opinions about the arts. Ambience: we're in our own safe room. Thus, it is hard to avoid being influenced by the review, despite our protests.

Suggestion is not a technique we turn on for ourselves. Accepting direction may be an affective process, but it depends on someone else doing it to us. Nevertheless, we need to be aware of the process, if for no other reason than that we can learn to guard ourselves against unwanted suggestion.

Performers are always receiving suggestions, not only from directors, friends, relatives, and critics, but from stagehands, fellow performers, producers, stage managers, agents and managers. Even investors. Some suggestions may be seen as valuable, some not. How you can select which ones you allow to get through to you?

You may choose to elevate their prestige, see the suggestion as moral, and feel comfortable or secure in the circumstances where the suggestions take place. A small cafe after rehearsals can be a very pleasing ambience. Or you may choose to sabotage any of these. By changing any one or two of the preliminary conditions, we may insulate ourselves against Suggestion, e.g. the suggester is an immoral fool.

If we wish to be our own suggesters, thus motivating ourselves, the situation changes only a little. When we tell ourselves to relax, for instance, and the relaxation actually occurs, we are practising a form of *Autosuggestion*. We can call upon ourselves to produce feelings on cue, ranging from shallow to deep. But we must now begin to consider a more ritual procedure.

First, create a pleasant relaxed environment and make yourself comfortable in it. Check that there is no tension. Then say to yourself, and visualise what you are saying, that on this or that cue, a wave of fear will come over you and will last until this or that cue, or whatever instructions you wish to program. Then you may simply instruct yourself to rouse and feel relaxed and well-disposed on the count of ten. You are now post-hypnotically programmed.

Emil Coué had people building their self-esteem by having them repeat, "Everyday in every way I am getting better and better". Such autosuggestion can work. The most favourable ambiences for performing autosuggestion seem to be just before dozing off at bedtime or just as we awake before rising.

If the technique of Suggestion (and Autosuggestion) is so effective, why don't we use it alone for every feeling we need to produce? Partly because the product of such suggestion tends to induce a blanket feeling which seems detached from reality. The suggested results tend to remain steady no matter how much the conditions change, like the girl who kept smiling even as she was run over by a bus. Moreover, in the transition between full alterness and the post-suggestion occurrence, there is a brief 'change of gear' dip, a short blanking-out period. As well, while in the suggested state, one tends to feel out of control as if the will is unable to vary the way we have been programmed.

Suggestion begins to look like a mild form of *Hypnosis*. In fact some practitioners actually regard suggestion as an early stage of several levels of hypnosis. But full deep Hypnosis, or deep trance, is more powerful in every way than Suggestion. The side effects from Hypnosis are much as noted for Suggestion, only tenaciously more so. Moreover, Hypnosis remains a phenomenon which as yet has not been adequately explained.

There are many phenomena which we don't fully understand, but nonetheless don't balk at using, because they work and because they're harmless. But the misuse of Hypnosis can result in the most sinister consequences of any technique I know, drugs included.

We frequently hear from stage hypnotists, hypnotherapists, and others that hypnosis is not dangerous, that no nefarious suggestion can take effect if the subject is morally opposed to it or doesn't want it. Theoretically this may well be true, but taken practically it is absolutely false. When the suggestion is cunning enough to circumvent the super-ego, anyone may be induced to do anything. Murder, alienation, seduction, personality reversal, even suicide. Anything. A famous hypnotist – my teacher – warned that there can be instances when a subject may not be wakened from a trance. This I have never witnessed. But I have seen what Caribbeans call zombies. I was assured that they weren't 'disenterred living dead', but innocents who had been drugged and/or hypnotised into slavery. If it is true that they obey only one 'master', then my guess would be that some post-hypnotic suggestion is assuredly at least a contributing factor.

So while professional therapeutic hypnotists reassure us of its safety, this must be seen as relative. Just as we hear of safe medication, even these may prove lethal in wrong dosages or when prescribed by a quack. So with Hypnosis. In the hands of a learned and ethical professional medical person or psychologist, it may in fact prove to be a safe if limited device. But as a theatrical display, party trick or private demonstration, the risks are incalculable. What is more, almost anybody can learn to hypnotise.

What is said here will no doubt raise the hackles of any number of hypno-devotees. But I would be prepared to debate the point with virtually anyone. As a one-time practitioner, I must confess to – shall we say – the mischievous application of this device. For myself, I might allow myself to be hypnotised, but only with an expert friendly witness attending.

Benefits? When handled properly; relaxation, habit-swapping, specific emotional pre-arranged responses (albeit usually shallow), repeatable results, long retention.

Disadvantages: blanket feelings, withdrawal, transitional pauses when going from normal to post-hypnotic, and when abused, infinitely dangerous.

There are so many other motivational techniques to choose from, that my own list of priorities would place this one last.

CHEMICALS:

We might ask, "Why list Hypnosis as a motivational technique, if it is so risky?" Firstly, because we've undertaken to list and describe *any* accessible device which has the potential for altering the performer's emotional state. And secondly, although we must consider the moral and ethical implications of what a performance can do to an audience (or another actor), the techniques themselves are amoral.

Both the surgeon and the hit-man know how to stick a knife into a living person with full awareness of what is being cut. What the hit-man does is immoral: what the surgeon does is – or ought to be – moral. For the surgeon to apply that skill as presumably did Jack the Ripper makes him indeed a hit-man. What is not the same as how, when or why to do it.

So when we list Hypnosis as a motivational technique, we are studying one of the (reluctantly) acknowledged ways we may shift feelings. Another problematical way is through the use of drugs. And here too it is necessary to emphasise the enormous pitfalls. And not, we hasten to add, for moral reasons. Like Hypnosis, drugs represent a certainly effective motivational technique with many and great functional disadvantages.

There is no doubt that our emotional state can be altered chemically. And each chemical has a more or less specific and predictable effect. Here are a few of the common ones:

Caffeine — stimulates and alerts
Alcohol — frees inhibitions, slows reflexes
Nicotine — first stimulates, then calms
Marijuana — frees inhibitions and imagination, exaggerates feeling responses: can befuddle coherence
Aspirin — mildly sedative and analgesic
Barbiturates — strong sedatives
Mandrax — very strong soporific
Heroin — very strong sedative and powerful analgesic
Amphetamine — strong stimulant, heightens alertness
Cocaine — very strong stimulant
Diazepan (Valium) — muscle relaxant and tranquilliser

L.S.D. — hallucinogen
Magic Mushroom — hallucinogen
Most other drugs of fashion are some variant of these.

Under the control of a responsible professional adviser, one should have no trouble with any of these for therapeutic needs. And here too we know countless instances where a therapeutic device got out of hand. Outside the prescription area, the uses of any of these should be regarded with utmost suspicion and caution. And when relied upon for helping to motivate an actor or performer, even more so.

Consider again the rationale of motivational techniques. They are there to ensure that whenever we need to call up a feeling that isn't happening spontaneously, we can turn to them for help. Feelings of all shapes and sizes will be required, like colours of a painting – perhaps large areas of one colour, fine details of others, perhaps a saturation of some colour tingeing everything. A wide range of feelings requires a wide range of sources: rarely can we expect the full variety from one source. We need to be free to shop around for the products we need.

The major problem with drugs, from the performer's point of view, is that most of them have only one kind of product to sell. And if you are affected by them, it is for the duration of their effectiveness. A line of cocaine will surely bring out something akin to the hyper-mania you may need for one scene, but what of those moments one scene later that require simple gentle warmth or profound withdrawn grief?

One performance after a sleepless night battling sciatica, having taken a single dose of Valium to give some relief to the cramped muscles, I was unable to conjure sufficient aggitation to justify a scene where my action was to storm and blast my daughter's suitor. No technique was strong enough to provide sufficient noradrenalin to justify raising my voice, much less grinding the suitor into the ground. I've gone without sleep many times, and I know it wasn't sleeplessness that affected me. The Valium – whose effects can last 24 hours – just had me too laid back. Here was an affront: "So what?" said the Valium.

With few exceptions, drugs tend to provide a blanket effect for the entire performance. And sometimes a blanket effect can be useful. For instance, we know a stage level of energy is generally higher than the everyday level; we use more than the average adrenalin. So what about drugs that help release adrenalin through the performance? Fine. Except that some scenes will generate sufficient adrenalin by themselves. When the medication is added to natural adrenalin, it is an invitation to overact. We end up with much more than we need.

Some drugs are adrenalin-like in effect but don't have a long duration. If taken as called for, you may find that you can shape their energy flow to your performance. Caffeine for instance, in cups of coffee or tea and cola drinks or chocolate, has found general acceptance among even puritanical performers. But even here there may be lurking traps.

Three other factors should be known about drugs: one is that every drug has an effectiveness time curve. It peaks in maximum effect at a certain time and tapers off at a certain rate. If that peak and slope can be accurately timed to the needs of your performance, you *could* be making the chemical work for you.

The second is that the body develops antidotes against the introduction of foreign chemicals. Consequently you may find it necessary to increase the dosages progressively to achieve the same results.

Third, there are no free lunches; you pay for what you get. Every introduced chemical changes the chemistry of the body. The delicate balance of bodily biochemistry which keeps us in the state we call good health is interfered with. No matter what the drug-blurbs protest, *any* chemical which is not of the same chemical nature and proportion as the body's biochemistry, will inevitably have some side effects.

It's OK to inject insulin where there is a shortage of natural insulin. But anything unnecessary for our delicately-balanced biochemistry causes some upset. It may be so small in proportion to the benefits derived that doctors may say – "to all intents and purposes, and on balance" – there are no side effects. Regrettably, many of even these tiny side-effects are cumulative. They can stop you performing altogether.

When we consider these, together with such attendant problems as addictions and allergies, not to mention the expense that some of these chemicals put us to, there is little reason for putting drug dependence high on our list of motivational techniques. Unless medically-prescribed, my observation has been that limiting drug intake to one or two cups of tea or coffee and, when really needed, an aspirin or Panadol, is about as far as most performers need to go.

As for what has become (in some quarters) the socially-mandatory quick swig or lingering sip of alcohol, I am the sworn enemy. Even one dose and you are affected. Yes, you may feel more relaxed and your reflexes may have slowed down so little that the change is hardly measurable. But when reactions on stage may determine the difference between safe and unsafe, even between life and death, any slowing of reflexes can be dangerous. Racing drivers wouldn't dare. Pilots are fired if they are known to have even one. Acrobats, circus flyers know the lethal potential. Performing in theatre is also a high-risk job.

In my own career, a broken nose, chipped elbow, cracked ribs, dislocated back, whiplash neck, broken instep and immeasurable bruises attest to performers whose timing was just that much off. They often said it was only one drink.

One of the finest talents I ever worked with died too soon from destroyed liver and kidneys. Some of the most gifted performers I know can only deliver a fraction of their capability. The greatest singing actor of his time killed a man on stage when his dagger kept going that extra fraction of a second. After that he really hit the bottle in earnest. Destroyed.

I have been associated with the Ensemble Theatre in Sydney for thirty four years, and we've always had a rule: no drinking for three hours before the show. The spirit of the rule means that if somebody is even slightly uncoordinated from chemicals taken five or six hours before the show, they are in default. Equity ruling notwithstanding (which specifies cause for dismissal must be based on the actor virtually staggering), we would still fire an actor for defaulting twice from company rules.

After the show you may do what you like, but certainly not before or during. The Ensemble is an intimate theatre, and the audience is in a position to see the difference between someone nimbly responsive and someone just a bit off.

When this ruling became known to the profession, it was widely predicted that the theatre would soon close down for dearth of actors. "Who would be prepared to work under such conditions?", they laughed, as they downed another. Indeed, many actors were accustomed to drinking as a natural function of performing, and some theatres tolerated or even encouraged imbibing during the show.

For the record, the Ensemble has performed seven or eight shows a week, fifty-two weeks a year for thirty-four years. We are the second-longest running professional theatre in Australia, and the longest surviving unsubsidised one.

A sobering thought perhaps.

WRITE YOUR OWN NOTES

CHAPTER 37

SEMANTICS

He sits at the table eating. But how colourful is the action to eat? We might add an adverb like 'ravenously'. Or we might have chosen other, verbs for this behaviour like – *feed, partake, breakfast, regale, feast, carouse, tuck-in, cram, bolt, gluttonise, gulp-down, wolf-down, peck, ingest,* and a few others. But with the help of Peter Mark Roget's ***Thesaurus*** – the only required book for Ensemble Studios' students – we decided on the verb *bolt*.

Why should we have bothered, when to bolt one's food might look much the same as to cram, or gulp down, or wolf down? The answer is that it would not feel the same to that performer. In order to play the action "to eat", but with a particular quality, the performer could well have sampled those other words. Cram? No, sounds too greedy. Gulp down? No, too frenetic and desperate. Wolf down? Too ferocious. Bolt? This one suggests hurry and urgency. It suits the character, and it turns the actor on. So "bolt" it will be.

Observing our early rehearsal process may seem like looking in on a scholarly session on *semantics*. Performers struggle interminably in deciding whether this provocation is because the character is playing the action "to accuse" or "to confront" or "to set-up" or "to challenge". Some might think that so much time taken out of four-week rehearsal period is suicidal. But the case is otherwise. Getting a clear idea of what it is everybody is supposed to be doing to one another means there need be little discussion once they are on their feet. And it often suggests ideas for staging, which may become some sort of implementation or contrast to what was decided that first week.

There is also an economic or logistic bonus in this, since the first weeks can be rehearsed in any small room. The larger set-size space is necessary only when performers get up on their feet to block the show.

Using the first week of plotting to find the emotive verb also saves having to go through another reading in which one could note the specific adverbs: 'happily', 'eagerly', 'frantically', and so forth. Having chosen the verb 'bolt' we have already provided the quality of 'frantically' or 'hurriedly'. And we may also have provided a few subtle overtones that the adverbs wouldn't suggest. Perhaps somebody bolting their food might also feel a touch embarrassed at being seen doing it. So to cover their embarrassment, they may also bung on a bit of self-ridiculing exaggeration. Using the emotively loaded verb 'to bolt' lets us pick up some bonus touches of embarrassment and clownishness.

The advantages of Semantics approach: simplicity (provided the technique works for you at all). Expeditiousness, since you get the juices flowing early in rehearsal, thus giving them a chance to be worked in, modified, or swapped for something better in plenty of time. And, as we mentioned, a potential for richness.

Disadvantages: if the process works for the performer, we can see no disadvantages. Perhaps if the basic association undergoes some changes during the run, these emotive verbs could change their loadings. It should be remembered that the choice of words is specifically tailored to the reactions of that particular performer. No word automatically conjures up the same reaction from different people. One person's 'bolting' may suggest panic at being late for work: to another it may sound like that party game that was so much fun.

Semantics is a broad-spectrum technique that can invoke a very wide range of associations and their feelings. Incidentally, that ability to find that one inspiring word usually marks a director as being especially good.

CHAPTER 38

RITUAL AND MAGIC

The backstage behaviour of some performers can raise the eyebrows of the uninitiated, or shock them speechless. Wander unannounced into certain dressing rooms, and you could find perfectly normal and highly gifted people sitting on the floor cross-legged, eyes closed, chanting a mantra in front of a small idol in which a stick of incense burns. Or you might see a mascot or good luck charm on their dressing tables, or a charm which gets slipped into a pocket before going on stage. Sometimes they pray, or perform a ritual similar to the secret handshakes of clandestine societies.

One famous performer I knew chewed gum before each performance, and always parked it on the inside of the proscenium arch when she entered. You knew the number of performances from the count of parked gum, and perish forbid anyone should remove a piece. Her routine and her gum were inviolable.

One superb performer kept a poltergeist. Perhaps she was kept by one – it was difficult to decide. She talked to it quite openly in the dressing room, and although I never heard replies, she seemed to. Her 'friend' served a number of purposes. It could relax and prepare her for going on, and console her when she came off. It could also serve as a scapegoat if anything went wrong. On one occasion she came on stage without a necessary personal prop. She bluffed her way out of the difficulty, but after the scene she stormed back into her dressing room, slammed the door, and the reprimand she administered to her friend for having mischievously hidden the prop could be heard along the corridor.

Some touch wood before going on. Some talk to photographs. Some kiss their images in the mirror. My own was to touch my pants zipper, collar, and head, while saying "Fly, tie, sky". My rationalisation was that I was ensuring the correct arrangement of my clothes and hair. But after one performance when things did not go well, it occurred to me that I had not gone through my ritual. Not that my hair or clothing were askew, but I felt that the bad performance was a result of failure to perform the necessary ceremony.

Ask any performer whether they are superstitious and the likely answer will be "No" (while they knock on wood). But let anyone whistle in the dressing room or put new shoes on the dressing table or sing Tosti's ***Farewell*** or mention ***Macbeth***, and more often than not the transgressor must perform certain rituals akin to exorcism if not atonement – just as a lark, of course.

Everyone says, "Of course I don't take those things seriously". Always the disclaimers: let us not seem to be depending on anything other than our own resources. Are we not ourselves omnipotent, omniscient magicians? Do we not dispense magic each time we give an autograph or an autographed photo? Or answer fan mail? We must not allow ourselves to be seen – even by ourselves – in a penitent position. Having someone say "Good Luck" to us might be seen as admitting that we need luck, or that they are superior magicians who have the power to confer luck upon us. We insist that they say "Merde" or "Break a leg" so that we can prove that our magic will prevail.

Every theatrical will tell you of instances where luck made the difference between success and failure: advancing their career or causing it to slide. "One minute earlier, and I would have got the job". Some see luck as the ultimate motivation. Whatever the scene calls for, if you are lucky it will be there. Many an actor's belief in his intuitive resources depends on the ultimate intercession of luck. "My intuition didn't work tonight. Back luck!" Or "I was lucky tonight, everything came together". Mind you, with the right magic, we may summon luck on cue. How many rabbits have surrendered their feet for such a conviction?

What are these mysterious fortunes that can weigh heavily? Are they impositions on us from another sphere? Are they spirits that one might appeal to? Are they intermediaries to a super-spiritual force? Are they forces within us? Since we don't know for sure, many actors believe it's a good idea to cover all bets: Astrology, spiritualism, magic, yoga, transcendental meditation, and perhaps a dollop of conventional church-going.

It can't hurt. And at least there is the acknowledgement among people engaged in a very earthy, no-nonsense, iconoclastic, occasionally cynical pursuit, of some spiritual functioning in their own psyches. So if you see a theatrical whose neck chain bears a crucifix, a star of David, a star and crescent, a mandala, a tiki, a crystal, and some other configured pendant ... well, as the man said, "That's showbiz".

CHAPTER 39

GAMESMANSHIP AND INTERPERSONAL CHEMISTRY

The first rehearsal is convened. There sits the cast waiting to begin. They enthusiastically greet others familiar to them. Equally enthusiastically they introduce friends to strangers. Prestigious names and important show titles are innocently bandied about. Some have brought candies to share around. They're not wearing the clothes they'll wear tomorrow, which can endure grime and sweat. These are image clothes. Chosen to impress.

But who? The director? They already have the jobs. The audience? There is none. Surely not each other? Surely indeed each other!

This is the first foray into Stephen Potter's one-upmanship. Who in this company will cap the totem-pole? Who will rank second? And so on down to the groundlings, who have in fact already been chosen and are called ASMs – assistant stage managers, the theatrical equivalent of a copy boy. But beware! The rule is never be nasty to those beneath you, particularly ASMs, who may one day be directors.

So everybody is nice to everybody else, but with an edge of jockeying and sparring. "I hear our director is almost as good as my last one (important name deftly dropped)". "My last leading lady (more important name off-handedly but audibly mumbled) says he's a stickler for getting the script away early". A third joins in, "How did you manage to cope with her? She was my understudy once and I wonder if she's more secure these days?" Crunch two in one go: advance one step.

Jockey, show-off, bitch, brag, undermine, butter up – but nicely! Sweetly, gently, carefully. You don't yet know about the political commitments within this cast. Careful what you say about the director, producer, backer or PR person: the one you are talking to could be a bed-mate of one of them. Or of several.

Your definite position on the totem pole will not be finalised for a while yet. The way you work, or socialise, or retreat during rehearsals will contribute to the design. And of course when the reviews come out there could be a scampering reshuffle.

Mind you, even before that first rehearsal jockeying has taken place. Agents demanding certain billing, salary, dressing room status, travel conditions, personal dresser, cast approval, etc. But beyond that and within the company, the group makes its own arrangements.

This phenomenon is a definite feeling-shaper. How you rank with each other will affect not only your backstage behaviour but that onstage as well. And if one is not aware of the traps, the results can be most amusing. How often the brief but crucial role of the policeman who comes in at the climax is given to the ASM to save a salary. And to see this 'policeman' trying to overcome obsequiousness as he roughly arrests the leading man is the stuff of which dining-out stories are made.

Being aware of the pitfalls permits performers to take advantage of their accepted status on stage. If a performer has to play the action 'to top' another who is three faces above her on the pole, what an opportunity to reduce the other's status. The motivation is quite simply, 'You've been throwing your weight around backstage. Take this as a reminder that I can clamber all over you if I put my mind to it'.

Certain actions in a play are easily motivated through *Gamesmanship,* if they fall into categories relating to domination or status. Actions like 'to undermine', 'to bitch', 'to show off', 'to make peace', 'to intercept', 'to champion', 'to dismiss'. Provided, of course, that the status of the person you are supposed to 'bitch' or 'champion' conveniently expedites what you would like to do to them. Then, what an opportunity to do it from behind the camouflage of the scene.

But Gamesmanship is not confined only to exploiting an existing phenomenon. We can arrange the phenomenon to order, and the above action 'to top' gives us the clue. Topping is a device for ensuring that a sequence of exchanges can be played in such a way as to build the phrasing of a scene. Your partner does something. You match them with some dynamic that goes one better, they go you one better, you better them again, and so on. Thus the top topper topples and replaces the other's position on the totem-pole. This can be played as the action (either mainline or supplementary) 'to top': or other actions can be played with a 'toppingly'-coloured adverb, such as 'tantalisingly' or 'one-up-ingly'.

There is usually no complexity about playing a simple action such as 'to top'. To arrange for the out-ploying type feeling, simply turn it into a game. No soul-searching required to see it as banter, fun, recreation. What does it take to get a game of gin rummy or chess going backstage between scenes? The resultant quality of such an approach to topping is usually one of deftness, lightness, mischievousness, whimsy, wit, or good-natured banter.

Topping can be motivated by other techniques, like possessiveness, survival, challenge, or latent aggression. These will make the quality of topping far more serious. If you want World War III, one of these will probably serve better than Gamesmanship.

But the exploitation of already-existing Gamesmanship within the company is the most common approach. It can be used to affect the phrasing of a scene without topping, but to provide a variety of colouring. Take a group scene. Try seeing each of your fellow performers in terms of their status in relation to yours. Let it affect you. Then, with or without a prompt from an additional technique, relate to them. You will find that you will reveal different attitudes toward each person with almost mercurial nimbleness, thus providing colourful variety.

The stuff on which Gamesmanship feeds may be found almost everywhere in a company: if the company takes individual curtain calls, our conception of status is reinforced every performance. What is the bowing order? Who gets most applause? Who got a round of applause on their entrance? On their exit? The longest or loudest laugh?

We mentioned before that critics can upset a company's totem-pole no end, sometimes completely destroying a company, sometimes just an individual actor. Some actors, having received glowing reviews, may feel they are no longer part of the totem-pole but are flying somewhere above it. This can result in total isolation from the rest of the cast, leading to self-indulgence, over-acting, disassociation, and – ultimately – artistic suicide. Of course the play suffers.

One arguable axiom in showbiz is: If you want to ensure that it will be a while before you work again, receive an Oscar or critic's citation. One explanation offered is that now an artist will surely make themselves unaffordable. Perhaps managements assume that actors think they hover above the totem-pole. Sometimes an accurate assumption.

One of our reasons for establishing the Ensemble Theatre as a non-star company was to head off some of the worst effects of inevitable Gamesmanship. To a large extent this has succeeded, although often the audience makes its own stars, as do critics. Still our commitment to equality of treatment (and billing, and – very important – salaries) helps to nullify some of the star treatment actors sometimes get from critics and audiences.

So at the Ensemble, Gamesmanship is not a significantly important reference point for motivation with us, or at least we try not to let it be. But what *is* a definite motivator is *Interpersonal Chemistry*.

Long-standing friendships. Marriages – current or ex, legal or defacto. Common interest bonds. Budding friendships. Or simply what seems to be the inexplicable rubbing each other the wrong way, or warmth at first sight. This chemistry is so much an issue that, when auditioning, no matter how good individual talents appear when they present themselves, or how well we know them to have performed at another time, we will not finalise the casting until certain people have met and read together.

This final callback is crucial, though not everybody, particularly agents, appreciates the need. "You know her work. She did brilliantly with you before. Why even think of auditioning her?" We try to explain that with Jack she was magic, but who knows what will happen with Joe. Often we have caught impending trouble just in time. Once or twice, when this procedure was by-passed, we regretted it.

Of course this chemistry changes as the show goes along. But by then we know more about what's going on between the performers, and can sometimes find antidotes if the chemical reaction yields poison. Often a romance starts, blooms, sours, becomes a triangle. Each stage has its own chemical reactions. One brilliant performer kindled sparks with a certain opposite number. First week of rehearsal, they were dynamic. Second week they were sour, but he and another girl sparked in their scenes. A few weeks later that was sour, and he and some other girl related warmly. Before the show opened he had gone through every girl in the cast, and the opening should not have taken place. Individually they were very good to brilliant. As a team and in small combinations they were awful. It was a long time before he was used again. And at that, duly cautioned.

Recognising that Interpersonal Chemistry can affect emotional responses, how do we convert this phenomenon into a technique?

Basically by deliberately creating the chemistry. Surely, if Interpersonal Chemistry were analysed we might discover some of the details that inter-react. Factors that rub us soothingly or against the grain could be someone's pushiness, obsequiousness, indifference, arrogance, hypocrisy, race, colour, religion, sex, obesity, svelteness, handsomeness, plain-ness or even some unnamed characteristic with prior associations. But even without such analysis, it could be worth trying a few gambits simply empirically.

For example, how often do people playing opposite each other find excuses for going out for a cup of coffee? Or discuss the last book or play they may have shared? Or joined each other in sports or outings? Or shared reminiscences? In other words, break the ice and observe what swims underneath.

Another would be impromptu deliberate signals. Your estranged fellow actor has just been taken over the coals by the director. What would happen if you gave that actor a conspiratorial wink or even muttered a few words like "He does that to everybody. Don't take it personally".

Conversely, if you wish to alienate the fellow, why not snigger or share a bit of bitchery behind the hand with some other bystander. Within the victim's sight of course. This is closely allied to the Ensemble Effect, but is not quite the same. One way of alienating a person would be simply to not invite him out for coffee when others have been.

Which leads us to a pitfall. One inadvertent cultivation of Interpersonal Chemistry is when groups become so exclusive that they form cliques. Ginger groups? Fine. Other kinds? Beware. One clique begets another. Soon there is no show.

On the positive side, deliberate approaches have led to intimate but transitory pairings known as 'two for the road'. Sometimes everlasting marriages. Such associations may even manage to help the play.

When carefully undertaken – with sincerity – there is no telling what may occur. If you are well versed in psychology, you may engender precisely the results you aim for. If on the other hand you are like a kid with his first chemistry set, who knows what may happen in the test tube. But rather than smoulder unhappily, almost anything is worth a try.

CHAPTER 40

BUILT-INS

Possessiveness, Survival, Fear, Jealousy, Challenge, Latent Aggression, Personality Compensations and Psychoanalysis

The following groups confront personality characteristics more directly. Just by living this long, each of us has in-built a whole range of likes and dislikes, drives and predispositions. Why not use them as they have been using us?

POSSESSIVENESS AND SURVIVAL: JEALOUSY AND FEAR:

The first pair of these techniques, and their two by-products, could be seen as manna to the most pragmatic of performers. They are concerned not with questions of ethical behaviour nor philosophical purpose, but with the bottom line, with the big question: what's in it for me? For many performers, and for all of us sometimes, the important thing about performing is that it should be a self-satisfying, self-advancing, self-asserting job.

Not even here, as you might guess, is it all selfishness. But before outlining these two processes, let's touch on what they may generate in us as feelings.

Some of them are pretty essential ones. For example, determination. Even more than courage, determination is the key driving force for a performer throughout a working lifetime. The legend of the tortoise and the hare is nursery stuff compared to the amount of determination any successful performer will need just to stay in there.

Courage is another. How many rebuffs can the performer take before quitting? The number must be infinite. Loyalty, dedication, pride, ingenuity, toughness – all of these essential characteristics of the performing artist can be generated by recourse to these techniques. And one convenience about these is that they needn't be rehearsed, merely assumed and believed. Of course, the longer and deeper one believes them, the more zealous one may become. (That zeal may even lead to a dangerous fanaticism, which we'll discuss shortly.)

Possessiveness, which is sometimes called Territoriality, may be seen under two aspects: individual and group. Individual Possessiveness includes such things as: my role, my scene, my speech, my costume, my reviews, my space onstage, my self-expressions, my showing off, my billing, my dressing room, my conditions of travel, etc.

Think for a moment of what the achievement of each of these has meant to you thus far. Think again of the possibility of losing them. Think also of improving them. Surely a small secret voice in each of us is concerned with personal advantage. You may not discuss it with anyone, but in your own heart of hearts you may come to the point where you say, "Dammit, they are mine and I am going to keep them, make the most of them, polish and improve them, and defend them". And saying this you will no doubt find that you have generated some of the appropriate feelings.

But another set of feelings may be introduced if what we claim to possess is usurped by someone else: ***Jealousy.*** A powerhouse! (Some have suggested that this is a potent technique in its own right: I prefer to see it as the other side of the coin of Possessiveness.) This can lead to feelings of desperation, spite, anger, even violence. But ultimately by the time it is usable on stage, it will have been watered down to the aforementioned courage and determination. Whatever competitiveness that remains may often calm down to the other technique, gamesmanship.

Group possessiveness: our team, our company, our group expectancy (what the public or group has come to believe about us), our gang reinforcement ("We can get better if we can only have ..."), national pride, etc.

Let's pause for a moment on the topic of national pride. It is one thing to say "See, as Australians we can put a show together that is as good as anywhere". It is quite another thing to say, "Only Australian plays and performers should be permitted in Australia". If the standard of our group (national) work is of world quality, we have two choices. One is to join the world, to show them our work and to have access to theirs. Another is to play at barriers: you keep to yours and we'll keep to ours. Since the theatrical arts are probably the most effective means of creating mutual insights internationally – even if we don't always like what we see – the game of national theatrical barriers seems unnecessarily spiteful.

This unfortunately can be one of the sets of feelings generated by Possessiveness. The more polite version of these may be made to look like Competitiveness or Challenge.

That brings us back to Possessiveness. As a technique it tends to be inward looking, which means that if it were our sole or primary technique, the theatre could lose its potential for warmth and compassion. Fortunately, this technique serves mainly as a garnish to a whole range of others whose concerns do not lead to narcissism, jingoism, and artistic incest.

Another point should not be missed. It is important not to blur the distinction between individual and group Possessiveness. Too often, 'I' hides behind 'We'. Personal advantage much too frequently pretends it is group advantage in order to get innocent others involved in championing what is actually a private cause. How often we have seen some strong figure embark on some self-serving project and seek social approval by rallying the community to make his project a 'common cause'. Once that cause is endorsed, the strong figure steps forward to claim his personal advantages, only now with general approval. Even if the group does discover this belatedly, they may not be able to go back. We see this with all manner of endeavours such as those of playwrights, actors, film-makers, entrepreneurial bodies, funding bodies, politicians, industrialists ...

The related technique of *Survival* is at least far less devious. We can divide it into four categories:

Personal: my livelihood depends on it.
Familial: family to support, kid in medical school, mortgage to meet.
Associational: others in the show have to survive as well.
Professional: my career is in the balance, and 'you're only as good as your last show'.

Here we are looking at the commercial value of the artist, as opposed to the ego or prestige status we considered under possessiveness. Sometimes the two overlap, or we may trade one off against the other. This happens when a performer whose Survival drive is uppermost goes from a show in which she had top billing to another that gives third, fifth, or lower billing but for considerably more money. Conversely, some performers driven by possessiveness will work for less money to achieve higher prestige or better billing. Working on Broadway frequently meant less money than one might get doing the same show in stock or on the road, but the prestige of that magic street name could be worth more than the difference in salary.

Survival can determine your choice of specialisation. There are people who work exclusively as chorus or extras, who go from job to job and seem never to be unemployed. They don't care, or say they don't, about a higher profile, glory or any of that, because what they gain in security and longevity more than compensates for the possibly meteoric transience of stardom.

The attitudes that go with Survival can help engender feelings such as conscientiousness, friendliness, warmth, co-operation, efficiency, and a refusal to be intimidated by surrounding conditions. It may also generate intolerance at the bumbling or inefficiency of others. Sometimes it cultivates such proprietary feelings that one begins to see oneself not so much as an employee but more like a member of the board of directors.

Often the topic of Survival is referred to by its other face – *fear*. On opening night, are we thinking as much about the positive aspects of Surviving, or the fear that we may not? Two sides of the same coin, but fear tends to evoke slightly more desperate responses. These can include selfishness, irritability, even paranoia.

A less frenetic example of fear of unemployment is when a rehearsing actor asked the director "Why am I walking upstage at this point?" And the director replied, "Because you are paid to".

Techniques such as Possessiveness and Survival lend a touch of earthiness to the lively arts, useful for those performers whose tendencies are too ethereal. Some say it makes for a more realistic profession. Possessiveness and Survival may be seen as substantial incentives behind the unionisation of performers. Survival calls for cool tradesman-like principles: a practicality which it is too often assumed that actors are devoid of. Many an actor believes that too, and prefers to leave all that business to agents and managers. Or is it laziness?

Of the two, survival may keep us in there longer, but possessiveness (for some performers) is the more compelling and omnipotent driver. So compelling indeed that it may slip out of control, into the realm of neuroses. Careful ...

CHALLENGE AND LATENT AGGRESSION:

These two techniques are as outgoing as the previous two were reflexive. The preoccupation is on the job at hand, there's less of the reminder "What's in it for me?" True, *Challenge* does call for a degree of watching oneself, and honest self-monitoring: "How far can I go before it becomes deadly?" But what we watch mainly is what it is that is testing us.

The instinct behind this is the one that encourages us to adventure when we are young, testing ourselves against nature, others, invented dangers. We find out what we can do as we defy death, and we often simulate death-challenging circumstances to find out. In later life, when death itself might be expected to come at any time, there would seem to be no real need to invite the Reaper any closer. Yet that reassurance of courage still needs to be there, lubricated and ready for use when the time comes.

So from time to time we take chances with our security. If we have a secure reputation for delivering the goods in one area of work, we may say, "I'm typecast. Must break this type and try something else: show the world that I can do something else". In so venturing we forsake the security of certainty for the risk of failure, and it doesn't take many failures for the public and one's peers to forebode that the end is nigh. But if we succeed, we are enabled to say, "I am not earthbound. I can still fly freely. And I have courage!". That feeling seems to me second in importance only to the quality of determined commitment. And when courage and determination gang up, success should not be far off.

And then, having succeeded, we find also the precious bonus of versatility. The audience-performer relationship seems to function over a time-span in a peculiar but predictable pattern. The audience, once it has set a performer high on a pedestal, must now topple this demi-god from the pedestal. Of course most performers resent having worked so hard only to be set up as a public sacrificial offering, but some elude it by nimbly changing into something the public hasn't yet seen.

When Sinatra had established a great public reputation as a singer, out came the machetes and crowbars. So Sinatra did a fast shuffle, risked his all as an actor, and won. And then, when his new career had reached a stage where he looked ripe to be toppled again, he danced right back to singing. There he remains at this writing, too formidable to tackle again, lest the public be made to look foolish once more.

An artist must have a good sense of timing, as well as considerable courage, to undertake a challenging career-switch. They might synchronise the break just in time to start a new angle to their careers. One of Australia's finest performers, Lorraine Bayly, found it wise to do just that when her identity became inter-woven with that of her motherly character in the TV series ***The Sullivans.*** So she tackled a musical in which the image of wholesome family unifier gave way to that of Madam of a brothel. Then a contrasting down-to-earth characterisation of a cool sophisticated lawyer in another series. Then on stage, a record-breaking season as a foul-mouthed alcoholic nymphomaniac in ***The Gingerbread Lady.*** Each was so successful that the critics find it hard to decide which pedestal to try displacing her from.

On a smaller scale, one is faced with Challenges within a play, like choosing between a risky-but-spectacular and safe-but-dull pieces of business. Or between an action which brings richness to the interpretation but also risks having the audience misinterpret the character, or one that makes it certain there will be no misunderstanding albeit the character will seem a bit shallower. Will you risk the danger?

One distinction between a good performance and a performance of genius is that the latter usually provides some element of danger, but one which, by its brilliance and daring, may illuminate the character or relationship in a way that the safe pedestrian four-square approach rarely can. Like the sequins on Chaliapin's upper eye-lid when he sang Mephistopheles, tiny strokes that could have brought ridicule, but when they were applied by the master provided illumination.

Sometimes when I'm directing a play I get a flash of 'inspiration' and ask an actor to carry it out. There's usually a pause, then a tentative "You really want me to do that?" In most cases I am apt to say, "No. Bad idea. Forget it", because the performer looks as if he wouldn't have the courage to make the challenging bit his own. He might do it, but it would always look like an apologetic "Sorry, but the director insisted I do it this way".

But if it is someone like the brilliant Brian Young who has asked, the answer is usually "Yes, please". He always takes the Challenge, makes the idea his own and more often than not the results vanquish the doubts. Brian is one of the most courageous (and under-publicised) actors to be seen anywhere, and is capable of genius performances because of his ability to accept and integrate Challenge. A Tasmanian director talked with awe about a piece of business Brian had worked into his performance in ***The Philanthropist***. As I understand it, he had been eating breakfast while sitting in an armchair, and upon the entrance of a girl he put the unfinished meal on the floor at his feet. He then rose, kicked over the bowl and its contents and, without diminishing his persuasiveness, proceeded to clean up the mess exactly on cue. Evidently, he proportioned his behaviour so that the clean-up actually provided an additional dimension of bumbling *without* distracting from the main task. "Dangerous", said the director, "but he carried it off, and I don't know how".

By itself, Challenge can be relied upon to stimulate courage, and perhaps curiosity. And of course Challenge can stimulate further challenge. As an auxiliary technique it can be the can-opener for involving a whole range of feelings via other techniques. That is, if you are reluctant to use Emotion Memory, you can employ Challenge as a sort of dare to yourself to try Emotion Memory. And if you rise to the challenge, you can thereby access a whole panoply of emotions that can be unleashed by that technique.

Challenge is thus in that group of auxiliary techniques like If, Procrastination, and Circle of Concentration which are sometimes referred to as 'can-openers'. Preliminary techniques which pave the way for others to follow.

Aggression, strictly speaking, is simply a degree of drive or forcefulness. But by common useage it has become linked with Hostility. Let's look at both: how they differ and how they combine. Unexpressed or latent Aggression, along with Challenge, should be familiar to football coaches and their players. It's the sort of motivation which the fans also exercise on players, and one that many players use to psych themselves for the competition. It is the granting of licence or encouraging activation of the killer instinct – even if we tell ourselves that we don't have one – and extracting from it the portion called aggression.

Given adequate motivation, every one of us could kill. But most of us in most societies exert a range of controls on this instinct which makes it relatively safe for living together in communities. Our conventional defence mechanisms – repression, suppression, substitution, sublimation, acting out, and so on – prevent that instinct from breaking out and endangering each other. Some repression is so thorough that we would never admit to ourselves that this capacity exists.

Comes wartime, and a careful program is instituted to dislodge this instinct from its minders and irritate it sufficiently so that the impulse to kill is readily accessible and acceptable. Hostility dominates. The big problem comes after the war, when the society has to try to get the worms back into the can. The products of the killer instinct are so powerful and generate so much steam that once they are released they are very difficult to control.

Amongst theatricals however, when aggression and hostility are generated, the release is in measured proportion to the need for the required amount. It is not so much opening a can of worms as punching a hole in the can and letting out just as many worms as you want, then putting a cork in the hole. Next time, just remove the cork. No need to worry about supply: you know how worms multiply.

The hole-punches are in some way similar to wartime techniques, but fortunately more akin to football pep-talks. The coach may say, "Get out there and kill them", and we spectators say, "You'll murder them". Theatricals may bolster each other with "Lay them in the aisles", or "Go fight the giant". And while the coach sends them out for bodily encounters, actors go out to engage 'them' in the battle of wills and wits. Having won, we may then pronounce the penultimate citation: "We murdered them".

If you look closely you will spot a larger distinction. The language may sound the same, and we are both appealing to the killer instinct, but what the coach requires is drive plus hostility, and what performers want is usually merely drive. Not the hostility, but the attacking quality, the initiating, persevering, persisting quality. Adrenalin, not noradrenalin. Admittedly, some actors, spoiling for a fight, might prefer the latter.

Much work in theatre is, as lawyers say, adversarial. Competitive. Getting into classes and remaining there usually involves auditions, examinations, assessments, which compare you with others and yourself. You compete, even against time. Going to agents or auditioning for jobs, you compete. When you get the job, you compete for salary, billing, etc. At first rehearsal you jockey for company status, in plotting actions you arrange for conflict: your costume even is a mild form of competition called contrast.

And the audience: overcoming the attitudes it comes in with is, as Hammerstein says when he describes the audience as a Big Black Giant, different each night. It can be a laughing, weeping, talking or sleeping giant.

> Every night you fight the giant,
> And maybe if you win,
> You send him out a nicer giant
> Than he was when he came in ...

The ethos of competition is built into our profession, it comes with the territory. Any expert in competition will testify that the ones who emerge triumphant have to display the killer instinct. But we *do not kill*!

A great swimmer tells of how, for days before a competition, she would not talk to her competitors, not even to team-mates who were competing with her. In that time she would find ways of converting her competitors into virtually enemies all, to be annihilated. By the time she took the plunge, she was killing them off, we suppose.

How do performers psych themselves for war on stage? How do we turn on a normally murderous function safely?

One way is by quietly brooding and cultivating a few paranoid attitudes about the other in the cast: "I'll show them", or "Wait till I get out there: they won't know what hit them", or "I've been saving the big one for opening night. They think they're so good, let's see what they think when I let fly". "They've been walking around as if they own the theatre: I can't wait to see their faces when ..." But you can invent your own. You know how – you've done it often enough. Unlike Gamesmanship, which is fraught with mischief or humour, this technique takes the gloves off.

Another is to employ some other technique as auxiliary to justify to yourself that you have the power and they are vulnerable and fair game. They have you in the gun as you have them. Kill or be killed. Paranoidal? Indeed.

You might try performing little rituals or telling jokes at 'their' expense. I recall a news-reel clip of British soldiers on their way to the Falklands fiasco, sitting round in the bowels of the ship laughing and singing of how they are going to get themselves "a spic or two". I hope I heard them wrongly. Invent little poems or songs about 'the enemy'. Draw caricature sketches. Play demeaning one-upmanship games with them backstage. Undermine them. Ignore them. That sort of thing.

Then – and most importantly – after all the drumming and war talk, remember that *it is all a game!* Here we veer sharply from the path of war or other hostile encounter like football. Here we filter out the hostility as much as necessary, leaving a strong clear flow of aggression. What is equally important is that the aggression must never swamp co-operation to the extent that the stage is full of soloists, each in their own telephone booth. When we remember that it is a game, we can use Aggression for the high octane rating we impose on whatever feelings the scene calls for. It places us in a position of authority, with a secret belief that we can cope on our own if need be. But in this case, we bring our omnipotence to bear in a common cause: to fight the giant.

Keep in mind that this technique could be wasted, in fact contraindicated, on some performers who are already so loaded with aggressions and hostilities that it could get in the way. As with all techniques, you use only what you need.

As the Gurkhas never draw their razor-sharp kukris out of the sheath unless they are certain that they will draw blood, so it is with techniques, which must be handled with good taste, judgment and care. And none more so than Aggression.

Advantages: provides drive, energy, vitality, attack, authority to elevate behaviour to stage energy level. Also helps provide the extra drive behind otherwise mild feelings as may be required for building a phrase.

Disadvantages: aggression often brings with it a degree of unwanted hostility. The two are not the same. It is as possible to overpower or kill someone happily as it is to rescue someone angrily. Drive and hatred are not necessarily linked. Think of the fun some people have, hunting and killing defenceless animals. The aggression we tap from the killer instinct need not be accompanied by hatred or even anger. But then, if you *want* the two together, you may invite them both. It's your scene.

PERSONALITY COMPENSATIONS AND PSYCHOANALYSIS:

We have seen some techniques that produced results instantly, and others like research that could take years before a feeling-change could occur. This section gives an instance of each.

Personality Compensation is another way of saying 'taking advantage of our neuroses'. Of course this presupposes, first of all, that you have some neuroses to take advantage of, and secondly, that you are aware of them. It may be that you are one of those rare people who are devoid of even one little neurotic hang-up: if so, this technique is not for you. And it is not for you if you aren't honestly aware of the hang-ups you do have. Mind you, if a director detects some you do not know about, he can play Svengali and take advantage of these by Trickery. But if the technique is to be self-administered, you have got to courageously confront the monkeys on your back and put them somewhere you can call on them as required.

Two of the most active monkeys are Jealousy and Guilt. They have been known to change lives. They are important enough to merit chapters of their own. But essentially, they are more appropriate here.

You need a scene of jealousy? If you happen to carry a dollop of unresolved sibling rivalry, you can simply believe that whatever it is you covet has been given to your brother/sister. Guilt? The scene is going badly: it's your fault. You need to appear hyperactively obsequious, like somebody trying to make sure they are noticed by the important people at this party? If you know that you strive excessively for ego-gratification you can just imagine that unless they pay attention to you it will prove beyond all doubt that you are an inconsequential nothing. In one unguarded moment when Olivier was asked what was his most important motivator, he is reported to have said, "Look at me, look at me, look at me!" It seemed to have worked well for him until a period later in his career when he found it terrifying to remain on stage by himself. Perhaps he was uneasy about what he thought they saw, in which case some other neurotic drive might have taken over.

You can exploit such hang-ups as ego-gratification needs, sibling rivalry, Oedipal compensation, exhibitionism, narcissism, compulsive or obsessive determination, and the need for revenge or retaliation, to name a few. Whatever the bugs, they can be used to help motivate an action. You can imagine satisfying the hang-up, or frustrating it. Or, beyond imagination, you may actually act out some involvement with your neurotic habit.

If for example you love what you look like and can't leave yourself alone (narcissism), in a scene where you need to feel good you can arrange to have mirrors or shiny metal objects or plates of glass available for you all over the stage. Or if you need to feel insecure, have none – and if a mirror is required by the scene, arrange to have it fogged over so that you can't see your reflection.

One performer I knew was an obsessive picture-straightener. Wherever he went, he couldn't help straightening whatever hung on the walls. His friends suggested he ought to be barred from art galleries, so famous was his compulsion. In one scene where he was required to feel angry and frustrated, he arranged for the photos on the wall to be set askew by the slightest amount, and forbade himself to straighten them. It drove him wild.

In order to understand and come to terms with your neuroses, you might consider spending some time with a psychologist, psychoanalyst or psychiatrist (head-shrinkers – or shrinks for short). Once you are in the clutches of a shrink, you run the risk of losing your neuroses, which is one reason why so many American actors go nuts trying to decide whether they should undergo shrinkage.

The more one studies acting and performing, and the more varied the occupational demands, the greater the insight into what makes people tick. Along the way, theatricals discover that they too are people, despite what is written on their pedestals, and putting one and one together they may discover that they have been learning about themselves as well. What they then find is not always what they thought or hoped would be there. Including doubts as to whether they belong in this profession at all.

At this point, many consider trying the super-motivational technique called Psychoanalysis, which is supposed to be capable of virtually overhauling all your feelings. And that's where angst sets in: after all, it takes years, it isn't always successful, it can put you through hell, which is also like what it costs, and you never really know what will emerge at the other end. Will you lose some of those precious idiosyncrasies which make you so unique? Will you lose a few of the golden keys of motivation that you now count on? How many? Which ones?

"I expect it will free me up in areas I can't go into now because of traumatic blockages. But will it be worth it?" Decisions, decisions! If you weren't climbing the wall before, now could be the time for it.

For a performer with the sorts of hang-ups that make access to a broad range of responses impossible or unduly difficult, Psychoanalysis can work wonders. Given, of course, a proper match of accessible patient and good reputable, suitable shrink. Despite the theatrical myth that we need our hang-ups, it is even more useful to dispel as many hang-ups as possible. As some of us have found, a personality block doesn't simply keep us from accessing a single set of attitudes, a block usually obstructs an entire system of roads. Getting rid of blocks can open a whole network of areas in the psyche, each turn and side-path of which is potential treasure ground.

Nevertheless, to those who have not been out and returned, the prospect can be daunting. And I would hate to see the couches of the relatively few properly qualified shrinks cluttered with relatively healthy actors, each hoping to unleash only one or two more motivational resources, when there are so many truly sick people in need of those couches. Still, there is much to be said for the well striving to remain well and get even weller. The complete regimen of legitimate psychotherapy, for those who need and are prepared to go through with it, can open rich reserves for the actor-performer. But one should be certain that it is indicated.

But what is to be said about all those illegitimate offspring of psychoanalysis or psychotherapy, most of which promise the same results and more? Wherever you look you can find some group, cult or practitioner who will offer to untie your knotted psyche and release such hidden powers that now you too can kick sand in someone else's face. We have seen any number of people seek solace or other benefit from the widest range of sources, from ***Readers Digest*** inspirationals to ***Chorus Line*** confessionals. Regrettably, many of these half-baked sources tend to create problems more serious than those they presume to address. Before you hand yourself over to a self-proclaimed miracle worker, best to examine their claims and credentials under the microscope.

Having said that, let me now admit that Ensemble Studios does introduce student actors to some aspects of illegitimate psychoanalysis, if for no other reason than that they may be less susceptible to charlatans and their blandishments. When they've worked together for about a year, some group inter-dependence tends to form. And about sixteen months into the course they are invited to participate in a specimen 'group'. (Note the word 'invited': such groups are purely optional.)

They are invited to talk frankly and intimately about themselves, their history, their aspirations, their belief systems, fears, desires – anything they feel they can share with this group. The group leader invites confidences, but is careful not to direct, prompt, summarise or judge. And often the results are startlingly dramatic. People start with free association or random incidents and stumble onto insights, often abreacting their blocking traumas completely out of existence.

Occasionally what starts out as psychoanalytic outpourings becomes psychodrama, using drama to arrive at personal insights. Students act out incidents of their lives, or re-enact them for another crack at the problem (often with spectacular success). And sometimes these enactments evolve into socio-drama, which explores inter-personal relationships. The effect on the group tends to be no less dramatic. Not only do they offer support, but they find themselves confronted about their own secrets. It can be a dynamic experience.

It must be remembered that whatever material emerging from the participant must be voluntary. Wrenching personal revelations out of each other is little less than rape.

One should watch out for the 'too easy' revelations, the anecdotes too eagerly shared. Often these are at least partial lies, much in the manner of the oft-repeated hard luck story, the repetition compulsion. But the freshly-explored recounts are usually quite distinctive and fruitful.

Another caution involves the question of discretion. To some extent, a group of this sort tends to close ranks and remain protective of any confidences mutually shared. But almost inevitably, given time and the appropriate circumstances, word gets out and juicy (and embellished) morsels circulate through the school and the profession. And perhaps the best insulation against this is no insulation at all. The actor should be prepared to know that his confidences may become public hearsay. We should be able to take this into account before joining in the game, and refrain from playing unless we are fully resigned to that eventuality.

In the matter of confidence, the actor should refrain from implicating defenceless non-combatants. At least one group was severely disrupted when one woman insisted on enumerating and naming the string of men in her guilt-laden life, and just happened to include the boy-friends, fiancés and husbands of about half of the others in the group. For these reasons, as well as the non-qualifications of the leaders of such groups, I am not overly fond of this procedure. So when such groups do convene, I preface them with a precautionary orientation not unlike that preceding their study of drugs and hypnosis.

But some of our best teachers swear by the procedure, and demonstrate extremely positive benefits to students in their groups (including the occasional student's decision to get out of show business). Such drills have been known to release feelings of courage, compassion, anger, guilt, love, spite, and many others. Inhibitions have been dropped, as have addictive habits of several sorts. But most interestingly, this game helps answer one of the most plaintive appeals one hears from actors: "Why hasn't anybody told me?"

When actors present their scenes in class, the group discusses what they saw and heard, and comments on the skills involved. And too often, the comments become evasive and circumlocutory. The actor is then left with the feeling, "They liked it, *but????*' That 'but' could be some personality trait that the group was reluctant to mention. Signs of over-reaction, hostility, homosexuality, obsequiousness, lack of aggression, memory lapse, self-delusion – the sorts of traits the group supposes would be too invasive or confronting. So the actor goes on believing she is progressing albeit with some inner doubts. Then one day, one of the group blurts out, "Why do you persist in singing: don't you know your voice is awful?" And the poor wretch who has been aspiring to musicals all this time asks, "Why didn't somebody tell me?" A no-holds-barred group might have saved her months of effort and terrible humiliation were she to audition for some musical director. But what price frankness!

These special results from that psychoanalytic group could hardly ensue in such a way from a group convening for the first or second time. The year and more of growing camaraderie seem necessary. And because of that familiarity, some of the more negative side-effects which beset so many so-called Therapy groups are absent. Yes, it isn't too hard to spill your guts to total stangers, but the results are not the same. And although the leaders of the groups are not qualified psychoanalysts or psychiatrists, neither are they delving into interpretations nor presuming remedial procedures. If the student discovers benefits, fine. If not, at least the group usually consolidates more supportively. And inevitably, some people discover that what they glimpse in themselves might warrant professional attention. At one time, the rumour circulated that the school "drives people nuts! Look how many students attend therapy groups!"

Other approaches to personality-probing are more dynamic, more imposing and directed. Such approaches that promise Nirvana are out of bounds to our teachers. We all know of the one-to-one counselling that may take place at the behest of either the student/actor or the teacher/director: "I've got a problem", or "See me in my office". Occasional teachers and directors, not burdened by loads of integrity, have been known to be compelled by extra-theatrical appetites to play at psychoanalyst. So what starts out as a problem-solving session has been known to turn into a problem-creating one. One voyeuristic director can almost be relied upon to explore the sexual histories or fantasies of actors, justifying such efforts as an exercise in 'trust'! Presumably, if they trust him with their intimacies, they will subsequently perform better. (Actually, sometimes they do!)

How many directors see themselves as Svengalis, or Pygmalions, or Dr Frankensteins? They treat actors as if they were there to be manipulated, shaped, or actually created by them. For the actor's betterment, of course! And it is true that in many cases the actor does benefit in some way. But what starts out as an attempt to improve the personality of an actor by plumbing his psyche, often results in a relationship of bondage. Inevitably, where an actor is not in full control of his functions – personality or otherwise – we have a partial zombie.

Psychoanalytic insights can be priceless. *Know thyself* is an eternal truth. But we must keep an eye on the process of learning about ourselves. And another eye on the skill and integrity of the teacher.

CHAPTER 41

OTHER TECHNIQUES

Well, that constitutes as many distinct motivational techniques as we have been able to classify. Does that mean there can never be any others? Of course not. Even as you read these, no doubt any number of you have been saying at some point, "Yes, well, what about the procedure I sometimes (or always) use?"

If you do have one that is unique and you are prepared to share it, please get in touch. This is, after all, an interim report of as much as *we* know at the moment. We hope that readers can help us all extend the field of available understanding about acting, just as we have learned from our own students who from time to time have said, "And what about ...?". But before wasting costly postage, have a good look at yours and check it against our list. Is it possibly a mixture of two, three or four of the ones already listed: or actually another variety of one of them?

In fact, we have been considering two more for the list: one a procedure which you and we have known about for years, though until now we have regarded it more as a mixture of other techniques. It is the process whereby groups frenzy themselves into a state in which (1) they no longer worry about themselves, (2) they unify their behaviour: (3) they increase their energy until it can be out of control.

We do it in group warm-ups before the show, but we see what looks like the same phenomenon in war dances, Japanese company- personnel unifiers, slogan chanting, protest marches, etc. In this process, one person starts the drill and others pick it up and repeat it. The strength of the process seems to depend on the number of people involved, the frequency and duration of repetition, the complete unison of the repetition, and the simplicity of the procedure.

For a long time we thought of this as a mixture of Contagion, Psychological Gesture, Imitation, Hypnosis and a few others. But unlike the others, here there is an obvious surrender of rationality in exchange for automatism and excitement. In this one, people think for themselves less, and may find themselves carried along to a point of great emotional expression. We saw it in Hitler's *Sieg Heil!* and we see it in revivalists' clapping of hands, the Ayatollah's fist-beating-the-air masses, lynch mobs' chanting, and the rhythmic shouting at protest marches. I know that the feeling was there when I paraded to the beat of a drum and the blare of a band in the Air Force, when I became another robot, ready to take orders and man a gun on cue.

What shall we call it, if it continues to seem unique enough for a name of its own? 'Mass Auto-induction'? 'Group-reinforced Hysteria'? Well sometimes it ends in mania. Or even a schizoid kind of depersonalisation. In any event, it is still under the microscope. We watch as groups of performers get out on stage before the show and do some movement and speech exercises in unison. It makes them feel good, relaxed, warmed-up, reliant on each other, and more excited than when they started. Maybe we'll just list it as Technique 45, and leave it to you to dispute.

The other somewhat fuzzy technique is one that Alfred Lunt was said to favour. We might call it 'Isolation' but it seems suspiciously like a combination of Reality and Autosuggestion. It is the technique of 'focussing' one's tension onto some more or less unobtrusive part of the body. In his case, he would take all his nervousness and deposit it into his hands, for example. So while those hands might shake or tighten, the rest of the body could be cleansed of nervousness. Convenient no doubt if one could arrange to keep the hands pocketed or behind one's back. No doubt one then also avoided cups of tea. The process is not far removed from that primitive ritual of heaping one's transgressions onto some sacrificial animal (a scapegoat) then obliterating the sins along with the animal. Come to think of it, perhaps this technique does contain a smidgen of ritual as well.

As we reconsider the list, we realise there is certain to be a division of opinion among readers, ranging from "I've known this all the time but have called it by a different name", through "Oh here's one I didn't know", to "I give up! Now we're expected to act by numbers". We're not too concerned if you disagree with this or that aspect of our classification: any attempt to make information more precisely accessible is bound to evoke disagreement about the accuracy of some parts. But if the question is, "Should this list have been compiled at all?", we have to defend what we've done.

Yes, the list is useful to many theatricals. It has been requested by literally hundreds of people. And we know that it has proved itself immeasurably at Ensemble Studios. Its practical and proven usefulness to actors is our primary justification for providing the list of motivational techniques.

But for a long time I've harboured a secret fantasy which I now make public. I would like to see this information leaked to the public at large. Giving away our trade secrets will not disadvantage us with our audiences. Knowing about the inner workings of music or painting has not destroyed the audience's appreciation of those arts: rather it has served to improve their appreciation. And with more refined critical faculties, they have been better able to sort out the poseurs and the mediocre from the genuine and capable.

I would love it if those who in everyday life deviously use acting techniques to pull the wool over our eyes may be seen to be doing it. If we don't mind being had, so be it. But if we feel they do these things to unfairly exploit or victimise us, we should be able to expose them, or at least catch them in the act.

To use our understanding of the art of lying in the search for truth: what a switch! And, as I said, it's a fantasy.

CHAPTER 42

FORMALISATION

How do we know someone is playing an action? Unless it is a completely inner action, the only way to tell is when we see and hear it being carried out. How do we know someone is undergoing an emotional response? Only by what we see and hear of body language or sometimes more explicit physical reactions.

What we see and hear is form. In other words, any behaviour or stimuli that can be sensed. If you can smell it, touch it, weigh it, arrange it spatially, taste it, it is form. Moving or standing still, if the senses can recognise it, it is form.

Actions and motivations take a lot of preparing. But unless we can see or hear the results or both, they are unrecognisable. When actions and motivations reveal their physical trappings, we say they are now 'physicalised'. Shaking hands requires a gesture. Sadness may reveal itself by tears. How otherwise could we recognize thoughts or feelings?

Physicalisation would be our first category of classification of formal components. It means formalising otherwise imperceptible occurrences. Actions and motivations are not the only sneaky things we make apparent. Stage effects must also be apparent. There is a phone ringing. Someone needs to answer it. How do we know? We hear it. A gun fires. How do we know? We can't see the bullet. But we can see the fire, smoke and recoil. And hear it of course.

We have classified at least nine other categories of form:

Elaborative: decorative detail like clothes and makeup: supplementary detail like dialects, limps, twitches, idiosyncrasies, posture, co-ordination, tempo-rhythms, habitual behaviour, self-satirising mannerisms, comments on personality, unique telltales of internal conflicts, etc. In other words, touches of customary behaviour and habits that identify the rest of the personality not covered by action-motivation physicalisations. Details that help define the character, which take up where actions and feelings leave off. Those which flesh out the character.

Dynamic: any form capable of attracting attention and interest. Bright colours: exotic artifacts: spectacular jewellry: unusual walking, talking, standing, sitting: swearing and blasphemy and borderline social behaviour: emotive words like traitor, crackpot, communist, fascist, the flag, the people, un-American, un-Australian, tax-cheats, peace, nuclear: dramatic scenery: weapons: medical implements: elaborate scientific apparatus. Elements which are appreciated for their contribution to the theatrical phrasing of a show. Attention-getters.

Aesthetic: any form which relates to the pleasure principle. Lush music, beautiful sights, sounds and movements, beautiful voices. Also raspy, ugly or irritating or otherwise abrasive behaviour for creating displeasure. Bizarre forms and kitsch can be included. Also beautiful or irritating scenery and costumes: these appeal almost directly to feelings of pleasure or displeasure, not designed to draw attention to themselves.

Narrative: forms which tell a story either by their presence or sequence of arrangement. Many a documentary on rivers, forests, the sea may prove captivating without the presence of a single person or even, sometimes, a narrator or titles. These appeal directly to our intellectual or logical appreciation.

Artistic: by itself not offering any form of its own, but rather the arrangement and organisation of other forms. Their sequence, timing, emphasis, phrasing, taste in selection. These trigger a portion of our intuitive function I would guess relating to information installed since childhood. There are some who will unquestionably assume that one may be born with intrinsic taste, for example the nobility. Anyway.....

Ritual: usually irrational, but appealing to another branch of the intuitive functions, religious rituals, marriage, funerals, harvest festivals, spring festivals, magical hocus-pocus, processions, commemorations, traditional and sacrificial forms and so on. Jungians might suggest that what is revealed here is some manifestation of the 'collective unconscious'.

Sensual: (perhaps read sexual) sexually provocative. As erotica, dancing, perfumes.

Customary: forms relating to certain periods of history: fashions: national dress: national music: artifacts.

Functional: implements of certain trades, skills, occupations, hobbies, sports or habits.

One might ask, where do 'manners' come into this? Manners usually relate to a smidgen from each of the ten categories all mixed together. They are designed to conform to community mores.

Now that we have them, what do we do with them? We use them. We design with them. We activate and exercise them. We create with them. Just as with a good symphony where different lines of music are entrusted to different instruments, but all come together to serve the whole composition, so with other formal components.

A number of formal threads can co-exist to add up to a stylistic whole. The scenery can tell us one part of the experience, the costumes another. The sound, whether dominant or underscored, says still more. The movements, grouping, lighting, tempo-rhythms, phrasings, juxtapositions, use of space, all contribute. Stage effects like revolves, trucks, walk-ways, treadmills, drops, projections, smoke, water effects, strobe or UV lighting, masks, make-up, acrobatics, parades, fight sequences – all are there to be used in implementing the impact of the production on the audience.

At one time theatres would be packed out at the prospect of a snowfall scene on stage, a swimming pool or Peter Pan flying through the air. Now that's old hat. Lasers, explosions, entrances from a high wire, scenery rising from the ground. And yet they come. More and more trickery and productional sleight-of-hand.

Why?

The cynical might suggest that the more spectacular the gimmickry, the more the director seems to have needed to conceal the paucity of the script or performances. I know there was a time when some actors seemed not able to achieve the dramatic requirements I set for them. My usual back-stop was to underpin that scene with appropriately emotive music or other effects.

In time I trusted the actors more. Recently, the only music I used was before, between and after acts. Are they better actors or am I more trusting? Or am I in fact depriving the audience of some extra dimension they may feel they rightly deserve? Possibly yes to all of them.

It would be wrong to generalise that the only time one resorts to formal effects is to remedy defects in the story or acting. Most theatre operates on several levels at once. The range of contrapuntal lines range from simplistic, as in street theatre or busking, to opera, which to me is the ultimate fusion of the lively (and other) arts.

And needless to say, so many aspects of form have become refined over the centuries that now experts have sprung up, each specialising in one branch exclusively.

Thus we have musical directors, scenic designers, sound designers, lighting designers, costume designers, choreographers, make-up artists, dialect consultants, technical consultants, historical consultants, all manner of special field specialists, and hordes of executors and artisans employed to bring the work of these experts into being. Naturally, each branch could become so involved that their expertise could require a lifetime of learning and polishing. So the poor actor-performer might be excused if he is not held responsible for more than a small portion of the overall picture. Nevertheless, that portion he does confront must be handled with considerable skill.

How much is left to the actor? Certainly the bulk of physicalised and elaborative form. Then, a bit of everything else, depending on the specific job in hand. Sometimes the director takes charge almost completely of such categories as the artistic, the aesthetic and the ritual. Understandably so, because of all the pigeonholes, these are the hardest to evaluate from onstage. The picture can be best appreciated from where the director sits. Add to that the dynamic. So often what the actor may judge as a dynamite piece of business is, from the front, a fizzer or tasteless. Beyond these categories, responsibilities might be shared between actors and directors.

Certainly, the actor is beholden to deliver the right dialogue, dialect, cues, timing, age adjustments, idiosyncrasies, staging, business, use of props, phrasing, volume, enunciation, inflections and be adorned in the right wig, make-up and costume. So for these he must take the fullest responsibility. In rehearsal and in performance. And presumably, before leaving acting school, there should be at least a moderate competence in all these skills. From then on, his proficiency should be expected to improve by virtue of conscientiously approached experience, as well as with the help of the occasional discreet hint from the more seasoned professionals in his company.

The consideration of form in greater detail than is encapsulated here, should fairly involve a virtual whole library as well as that lifetime of experience. Always we must keep in mind that the audience is god. And the only way they can partake of the theatrical experience we have worked to bring them, *is through form*. To what extent mental telepathy might contribute remains open to question.

Like myself, many a director, faced with the dilemma of choosing between two actors, one expert in form but poor on content, the other expert in content but poor on form, will generally speaking go for the actor good on form. At least with him, the audience will see and hear what's going on, even if they may miss out on the empathy. The director can usually find techniques to compensate somewhat for content shortcomings. Such cosmetic techniques are not so readily available for deficiencies in handling form. Yes, they can give the mumbler a wireless mike but his poor articulation may prove inadequate even for that.

Notwithstanding this cop-out in deferring to other sources a more comprehensive study of form, some general observations must still be made here.

Firstly, there is a danger in expecting form to substitute completely for the absence of proportional motivation and action. It is still possible to see productions in which the actors are displayed as in animated tableaux, each picking up their cues mechanically the moment the previous actor finishes, all elocuting their words clearly and colourfully, but nobody scoring off anybody else on stage.

It is somewhat like a costume hung on an animated shop-window mannequin. You can see what it's supposed to be, but it is devoid of heart and mind. The audience can identify, but the director might have to underpin this with emotive music in order to coax a fragment of empathy from the audience.

In the olden days when the only known stage techniques were how to handle body and voice, such external performances used to be known as 'working on technique'. We now call this 'Indicating': going through the motions of actions or feelings. Now that we know of content techniques as well, there should rarely be any excuse for not fleshing out the costume with heart and mind as well as body.

Among the pitfalls attendant on Indicating is the tendency to 'post in one's performance', to let the voice and body take off on their allotted rounds while the mind is elsewhere. I have known at least one actor to work on stage with the ear-piece of a small transistor radio stuck in his ear-hole while he gathered racing results. Never missed a cue. In fact, between cues he might occasionally whisper the results to others on stage who were equally devoted to the performance.

Of course it is expected that one's Circle of Concentration can scurry all over the place. But theoretically, this should be in the interest of serving the performance.

Those of us who have had to work with actors set on automatic must have tales galore. Like one actor lapsing and skipping a few speeches or even pages, but the other actor remaining oblivious, still picking up his cues with the same programmed sequence of speeches, which now have nothing to do with what the lapsed actor is saying.

Some actors *actually* insist that others should behave in such a way as to not disturb the verbal and kinetic patterns these actors have designed for themselves. Even looking them in the eyes could throw them. If you must look at them, you had to confine your gaze to a spot in the centre of their foreheads!

Alas, such going-through-the-motions has not disappeared from the stages of the world.

Another observation about the indicated performance is its tendency to draw upon theatrical convention rather than life or originality, sometimes even on earlier characterisations or readings. When one examines what one is expected to imitate or abstract, the indicator is at least expected to observe all the formal trappings of, let's say, the real feeling. What does real crying look or sound like? Let the 'going through the motions' at least try to look convincing. But so many actors don't even bother observing the real thing. They may in fact confine their observations to what another actor did in similar circumstances, or even what they themselves did in another performance. They may fall back on theatrical convention. Perhaps not as extreme as the back of the hand to the forehead. But how often do we see the eyes wiped with nary a thought to the running nose?

Yet another caution concerns clutter. It is possible to have so many eye-catchers and 'significant' tricks going on that it is well nigh impossible to identify the relevant or important material from the busy-ness. Mobiles, mechanical contrivances, processions, lifts, revolves, flying effects, smoke, strobe, cacophony, thunder and lightning flashes against garish scenery – the poor actor hasn't a chance. Once an opera set was made of gold lamé'. When the lights came up, the audience was blinded. There were actors on stage, but who could see them?

There is also a danger of being caught in the battle between designers. So often designs are conceived not so much to serve the play as to one-up another designer.

And the same caution should be observed for the performers, who can become so tricksy and cute with form that we can't find their content. I have had great difficulty finding the few observers who could tell me the story line lurking in the Australian production of Cats. The more formal technology we acquire, the more we seem to need to show it off.

In summary, while content ingredients rely on what humans are, have been for ever and expect to be until Armageddon, formal ingredients continue to evolve. Every new technology provides theatre with fresh possibilities for a new formal device. It is quite on the cards that human-kind probably has more formal tricks up its sleeve than even nature, beautiful sunsets and the Grand Canyon notwithstanding.

Behind that issue may be the philosophical questions, how come we have the capability to create as we have done? Are we vying with nature? Are we here to take up where nature left off? Or what?

WRITE YOUR OWN NOTES

PART 2

GETTING IT ALL TOGETHER FOR THE AUDIENCE, THEN

PERFORMING

WRITE YOUR OWN NOTES

CHAPTER 43

ACTING AND PERFORMING

We are now ready to evaluate more objectively: aren't we? Our comments on acting are no longer confined to "I liked it" or the converse: are they? Every chapter alerted us to something else to observe on TV, film or stage: didn't it? Let's do a checklist. Suppose that there on stage is an individual who:

(1) is relaxed
(2) is dynamic
(3) plays clear and clean actions
(4) has proportionately motivated his actions
(5) makes smooth transitions between each action
(6) has characterised formal and content details thoroughly and consistently
(7) is alert
(8) can play multiple supplementary actions
(9) has designed 'dangerous' or surprising moments
(10) can switch smoothly between mainline and supplementary actions
(11) can relate with concentration to props and other people onstage, both as sources of motivation and as objects for manipulation
(12) has adjustments that seem completely worked in, as if second nature
(13) does not 'play' those adjustments
(14) does not 'play' his feelings
(15) does not 'play' his characterisation
(16) can adapt to accidents without disturbing either the characterisation, relationship or the direction of the scene
(17) has the ability for multifaceted moments where, for example, the words say one thing, the actions another, and the feelings yet another
(18) can display several levels of feeling at once
(19) shows restraint and relevant good taste
(20) looks 'loaded'
(21) prepares where he came from and where he is going
(22) in sense-memory scenes, allows for full impact from the invisible other, as for example listening to the other voice in a telephone conversation
(23) when addressing an audience, always relates to the audience or camera as an object of an action, and sustains this as a subtle supplementary action when not directly addressing the audience

(24) is warm and sensitive
(25) has easy command of timing with others on stage
(26) knows how to conceal the art
(27) knows how and when to play big and small
(28) has complete control of voice and body
(29) is uninhibited in revealing private aspects of his nature
(30) has used extraordinary creativity in constructing the character and relationship
(31) can control personal idiosyncrasies or habitual mannerisms so that each characterisation can be unique as may be required
(32) carefully matches his response to the stimulus as it unfolds
(33) can exercise the 'ensemble effect'
(34) knows when and how to vary dynamics other than big and small
(35) can find humour in sadness and vice versa
(36) knows how to 'play against'
(37) does not 'gild the gold' or 'paint the lily'
(38) does not comment on his performance

Would our response be,"Now *that's* acting!"? Mine would.

If, on the other hand, we watch a presenter who:

(1) has authority
(2) has complete command of the audience and can read it quickly
(3) is readily identifiable on some level
(4) is clear on at least one level of impact or communication
(5) has good timing relative to the audience
(6) phrases well
(7) plants and pays off subtly
(8) directs out attention, and misdirects it where concealment is called for
(9) has personal appeal
(10) has sustained consistency of all the acting elements
(11) is economic and efficient
(12) is vocally and physically adequate or aesthetic or both
(13) can execute surprising or dangerous elements
(14) has a proportionate relationship with other people and props on stage
(15) has adapted comfortably to the medium or size of stage or auditorium
(16) can dominate or yield according to demands
(17) has crisp and courageous attack
(18) has unselfconscious skill in stagecraft
(19) does not fool around on stage with private gags or business that the audience might not share
(20) is prepared to give every performance his best shot

Then we are inclined to say, "Now *that's* a performance!"

Acting and ***Performing*** are terms that are usually used interchangeably. While there are many important links between them, I feel that there are sufficient crucial differences to be worth making a distinction. Many good actors are good performers and many good performers are good actors. But alas, too many are either one or the other.

When this checklist was first prepared, it was innocently assumed that these considerations applied only to 'naturalistic' theatre. In fact they apply to all styles of acting in all media, and often to other fields of the lively arts. One hears of the occasional musician aspiring to many of these criteria.

Please note that in listing these criteria, nothing was said about how much the audience liked the person, or believed in the characterisation. More often than not, observing all the above criteria *could* create an entity both plausibly identifiable and even likable if that character is designed to be so. Liking it or not is based as much on what the audience brings with them as what they experience before them. Shortly we shall discuss this issue in detail.

Just as there are several approaches to music, so with the acting performance. Here are four such, which in practice may be interchanged or combined in the same play.

- ***Indication.*** Here we refer not to the motivational technique but rather to an approach for the whole play. Acting by 'technique'...remember? This is the procedure of going through the motions. It may be as ham-handed as mugging or so subtle as to be almost indistinguishable from the last point below. The usual results may induce sympathy but rarely empathy.
- ***The SIN-cere approach.*** Sometimes called 'grim-and-earnest'. Here actors, seeking to fulfil the author's or director's instructions, tend to play at the results. They try to play the unplayable like feelings, their histories, their characters or the play.
- ***The 'do-your-own-thing' approach.*** Here thrives the actor who is directed by an intimidated director or by one who is content with mapping the staging and leaving everything else to the actors. While whatever it is they come up with may be good and well-rounded, the pieces often don't interrelate. Like pieces from different jig-saw puzzles. Like a sharply focussed, well lighted, artistic souvenir photo of a friend who was captured from the neck down. Perhaps that was all that was memorable of that friend, and perhaps that rounded performance is the only thing worth remembering of the production. But what of the rest of the play? Such acting tends to result in isolation from others in the cast: often referred to as telephone-boothing.
- ***The integrated performance.*** Here the actor tries selflessly to provide the play with whatever is called for, even if this involves great effort. His details are proportional to his own characterisation as well as its relationships. Such an approach has the highest chance of inducing empathy as well as sympathy.

This is not to denigrate nor champion any of these. They can all be approaches of choice, given the appropriate production. But they are as distinct as classical music is from jazz. Regretfully, too often the distinction is lost on an audience unless the observer is particularly judicious. Such judiciousness remains rare.

Let us proceed with details of Performing. Some have described acting as building a fine Swiss watch and performing as selling it. Having created a priceless multifaceted characterisation, it is now necessary to offer it to the public. Here we hope to mount a gem of acting in a setting which ensures that the audience is duly affected by it. There is little sense in the actor feelingly describing the dramatic conclusion he has reached if he mumbles or chokes on the telling words we waited all evening to hear, or mis-times it. We are public servants in the truest sense, so we must be sure that the public is fairly served.

Yes, I grew up in an ambience that misinterpreted Stanislavski, believing him to say that if what we did was 'true', the audience would receive the full impact even if we were inaudible. Then suddenly, about 1945, my peers were in disarray. Stanislavski's hitherto unpublished book, ***Building the Character*** hit the bookstalls. He asked what about the music of the words, the colouring and beauty of the voice, the consistency of dialect, movement, timing etc. These too complement the 'truth' to make it more palatable as well as richer in implication. These are also tools with which to transport tonight's audience. To this day, there are actors who cling to the 'truth-will-speak-for-itself' notion.

There is an art in handling audiences. There is a special skill in ensuring that *this* audience is escorted on an adventure specially suited to them. Then they may better understand the difference between reading a book and experiencing it transformed into sparkling, throbbing, illusion of life. Not life itself but an artistic concoction. The difference between the cacophony of traffic noise and Gershwin's ***An American in Paris***. An Artistic Truth.

The following chapters are about tools for performing.

CHAPTER 44

AUDITIONS

If one dared to generalise about the auditioning process, the suggestion would be to treat it as impersonally as possible. The performer has certain skills to sell. This includes the vitality on which these skills ride. One may approach the auditioner with the same warmth and friendliness as a line-of-merchandise salesman approaches a buyer in a department store.

After friendly greetings, one unrolls one's products, presenting them as attractively as one can, then leaves it to the buyer to decide. "Yes, we can use five gross of those, one of those, and two of these". Or they might say "Very nice but we don't handle that line any more". Or simply "No thank you". Unless you have allowed your skills to lapse or you have arrived drunk, that refusal should never be seen to reflect on you personally. One way or the other. You are selling a product. If your product is unsuitable, no amount of wheedling can justifiably affect the sale. But perhaps you have not kept your skills in condition. In which case you could be displaying shoddy workmanship and you deserve to have your work rejected.

But directors make allowance for nerves to affect a display of capabilities. They can usually see where you have something to sell but allow that this can be an off-day or that nerves have diminished the real show. And usually, they hope *you* are the one they are looking for. The sooner they can cast the show to their requirements, the sooner they can stop searching. You can safely assume that the auditioners are actually on side. In any event, *they are not the enemy!*

Unbelievable as it may seem, auditions are usually more painful for the auditioners than they are for the performers. So you do your best *without panic*. Enthusiasm, energy, friendliness – fine. But not the life and death desperation that often shows too clearly through everything else.

And the material should be well-chosen and prepared. *Short* bits (no longer than four minutes if possible) that display your strong points as comprehensively and tightly-parcelled as ingenuity permits. Then if you are asked to read their material, make it your own, not unlike the Strasberg 'First Reading' (which will be described in the chapter on Rehearsals) if you think the director is prepared to tolerate it.

If, on the other hand, they expect a full characterisation, then quickly assess a scenic action, work in a few handy characteristic adjustments, and, without panic, relate to the person you are reading to, bit action by bit action. *Really relate*. Watch and listen fully to what the person reading with you comes up with, and use it to help launch your next action on them.

One fine director, Sandra Bates, found ways of having auditioners believe they were helping the *other* actor to audition. Such a ruse tends to disarm a nervous actor, open them up considerably and generate a degree of warmth which comes with dedication. Wouldn't it be a good device to make yourself believe that it is not you auditioning but rather the person you are reading with? You are simply helping them out.

And make it an enjoyable experience. And why not? We're here because we chose to be. Nobody forced us to audition, did they? Authority, humour, courage to risk the unexpected. Beyond that, there may be no predicting what each director asks of you. But if you can quickly polarise each instruction in terms of actions, feelings and adjustments, you should have little trouble.

Three details should be expanded here, relating to your choice of your set-piece audition material. This may not be as easy as it sounds.

First, decide what your saleable points are. Your strengths. This in itself may be an extended search. But certainly after a few years of study or working in the profession, the feedback you get can be abstracted to give a fair picture about how you come across doing what.

This is not the same as asking yourself what do you enjoy doing. That may have little to do with your actual ability to deliver. Keeping in mind that the objective of auditioning generally is to get a job, auditioners will be assessing how you actually come across. Not how you wished you came across. Recently we put out a call for a twenty-two-year-old girl, relatively naive and vulnerable. One of the actresses who showed up was about fifty. The years had not been kind to her. She was heavily made up and certain she would pass for twenty-two in an intimate theatre seating 230. Pathetic but true. No, she did not get the role.

Once you have discovered your saleable features, look for a short scene that, if possible, gives those features a chance to reveal themselves for a moment at least. Not only that but also display your ability to transition smoothly and logically from one to the other. And also reveal your capacity to show real feelings in depth. Deep emotion with at least one overlay of feelings or attitude. Like real grief, but fighting it back with a smile. That sort of thing. And always a touch of humour, even if we see it only as a way of coping with a serious situation. But never comment on yourself. Relate to whomever you are playing to, even if your partner is only a sense memory. Like with a phone conversation. And if you can also manage to include a supplementary action in your scene, played without faltering or interrupting the mainline action, do so. That is very impressive. But always action-playing. No image-playing or playing feelings or adjustments.

Actions!

And all this squeezed into under four minutes. OK? Hardly an easy project. Of course most of us will have to settle for one showpiece with one or two such demands missing. In which case, prepare two pieces. Divide the selling points between the two. But always show the best first. Then if they are interested they could well ask, "What else do you have?" It's wise to have two pieces anyway. They may even ask for the second piece first.

You may take years to find the perfect audition pieces. And then as your qualities mature, you may yet start the search all over again.

Secondly, a few warnings. It is generally not advisable to audition for an author his own material. Chances are ***nobody*** can do his writing justice, in his estimation. You risk being rejected out of hand, (unless of course you do fluke it. But is it worth the chance?).

Also do not expect that some great playwright has already written your audition bits for you. You may have to start with a long scene from a play that does contain scattered bits of what you need, and cut it and sew the pieces together, or even join in other bits from the play. Better still, write your own or have someone write it for you.

Incidentally, I am one dissenter who does not believe you should audition for a role, disguised as your idea of the character. Sometimes it does work. Often it presumes to usurp the functions of the director and suggest that you would not be flexible to change. This is how you see the character, so there. Take it or leave it. Oh yes, some directors will take it. I think the better directors might just leave it.

My suggestion is simply: Show Your Wares. Leave it to the director to decide if your qualities can be shaped to produce his concept of the character. You may learn that the director who can detect and appreciate your qualities will be the one who can also exploit them to the best advantage. The others may not be worth working for.

I recall an audition for the role of Sky Masterson when the road company of ***Guys and Dolls*** was being formed in 1951. Big names auditioned. Almost everybody dressed in black shirt, white tie, striped jacket and soft hat. Only one didn't. He got the offer. And not a big name.

When it comes to trying to do something different or gimmicky, I agree with Alan Jay Lerner: "To be good can be different enough". Be courageous and don't be afraid of being unconventional if that is you and relevant. But cute gimmickry could be a no no.

Be clean. As well groomed as you can be. And never defiant or defensive. Open and courteous always. And don't force or even push. Easy but strong and authoritative. And *never* drink or use drugs before an audition. Relax by using motivational techniques other than chemicals.

Remember, there is no shame in not getting the job. Most of the time you and most people flunk auditions. You may be excellent, but wrong for the role. Or the chemistry or contrast between you and someone already cast may be wrong. You might be too similar. There's no aspersion on a Rolls Royce failing an audition when they seek a Harley-Davidson motorcycle or a ten-ton truck.

And thirdly, the question of star quality. Some directors refer to it as ***loading.*** Many look at it as the ultimate mystery. You are born with it and that's final! Why don't I believe it?

The nearest an auditioner might want to come to trying to squeeze into a role would be to prepare loadings. That is, if you hear that the role is a sinister lady, and you are prepared to risk believing the rumour and appearing sinister, it can be done. But will that provide you with that unfathomable loading?

Try this on your friends first. Prepare a really deep emotion of wishing to destroy something. Emotion memory, As If, Usery – some technique that really reaches deeply into you and turns you on. Now, when the juices are flowing, simply adopt an attitude of putting off whatever you feel like doing. Also, do not let anybody read your feelings. And play a mainline action such as 'to welcome' on somebody. Or 'to size them up'. Or 'to read their mind'. A passive, non-committing action. Don't watch yourself! Only them. Let them tell you how you come across. Chances are they will in time without your asking.

The same kind of thing goes for looking mysterious, sexy, mischievous, whatever. Prepare a strong emotion of some dark secret, lusty desire, or just having won the lottery. Then overlay with a disguising, non-committal attitude. And go about your business playing a very passive action on someone or something. Not on yourself! Keep your attention off yourself.

At a rehearsal not long ago, one girl looked unusually radiant. Her scene was written as undynamic, requiring simple actions with rather restrained attitudes. Today it had acquired an extra glowing dimension. After she had left the room, someone whispered "She's in love".

You may well discover that those mysterious loadings can be produced. The more that bubbles beneath the surface, and the less you allow to show through, the more the undercurrent will find a way of squeezing through to the surface. The trick is to generate a strong undercurrent, suppress it, and go about your business of actions on anything except yourself. In fact, the more undercurrents you can sustain, the more loaded you appear.

Look at the so-called stars. Perhaps you might even detect the popping of volcanic bubbles coming through. Born with it? Or which of these tricks are they using? Then, by contrast, the so-called open person seems to let it all hang out. Can you have a loaded but open person? Indeed. Let everything hang out except one secret loading. Experiment for yourself.

Some of the most radiant on-stage people you may find can be quiet and unprepossessing in private. If one takes into account these balances of loadings in relation to coping that gives them that on-stage sparkle, you might see that in private, either they can dispense with their undercurrents or, more usually, they don't worry about the overlay. Or it could be that they can't be bothered socialising, giving themselves a break from performing.

So it could well be that with a bit of practice, you too could be a star!

Auditions, at best, are miserable experiences, for both auditionee and auditioner. Look forward to the time you may not need to audition. But usually the best directors will still insist on auditioning even top performers. Screen tests apply even to the most established. But auditions should not be seen merely as exquisite torture serving little real purpose other than to deliberately humiliate you.

Auditions can be imperative for both parties. Even if he knows your work, the director may want to check out your interpersonal chemistry, also what has happened to you since the last time, and most importantly to look for those special qualities in you that would suit the character he has in mind for you. The last time he saw you, he was looking for other traits belonging to that other play.

And for the successful auditioner, it is confidence-making to know that you have been duly checked out and are deemed suitable. Rehearsals being what they are, there will be many moments of self-doubt. But if the director had faith in you, that can be highly supportive. And you don't want to feel you are in the wrong place. Which is probably the strongest argument for avoiding the casting couch or any other process of bribery for getting the role other than on merit.

Passing an audition or three for that role is like a huge seal of approval. It is uplifting!

Oh yes. PS. It doesn't hurt to thank the auditioner and bid a polite "Goodbye" as you leave. Surprising how often people don't.

CHAPTER 45

THE SCRIPT

There was a time (?) when theatricals evaluated a script by how good or big (or both) were their parts. Surprisingly, there are in fact other parameters. What follows are a few that have been guidelines for me as a director. I repeat, 'for me', as this is only one person's point of view. I insist, it is not a catechism. It would be presumptuous to attempt to tell writers their job. I only compile this as a checklist for those of us who must convert a written script into a living presentation. Perhaps there are also authors who might find in this some reminder of what they may have forgotten. As for the actor, he should know that all these considerations may have to be addressed. And in the likelihood that some component is missed or belaboured, his job may be to make up for the error with his performances. The tools and techniques are in the rest of this book.

This is my approach. I first seek to identify the issue or the ambience of the play. The situation. The story line. One of the finest musicals ever written – ***Music In The Air***, by Kern and Hammerstein – was set in romantic Bavaria. A week or so after it opened, Hitler marched into the Sudetenland. Bavaria was no longer romantic and everyone stayed away from the play. Plays set in Ireland, though they may appeal for peace, may prove disastrous at the box office at certain times in history. This is a serious consideration. We don't expect to do plays for ourselves, and if the audience is absent, we end up doing so.

Then, is it castable and actable? Could we reasonably find a cast to do the play justice? And theatrical? Why should it be staged? Wouldn't it be better, or at least just as good if it were a radio play, a novel, even converted to a musical composition? Staging is very special, bothersome and costly. Why bother if it's not necessary?

Now the spines. What does it want to do to the audience? Make them weep? Laugh? Worry? Feel encouraged or inspired? What? And if it is not clear, can we use it to say something clearly even if the author may be innocent of it or could even object if he knew. As Shakespeare's plays are designed to say almost anything the director chooses.

And the people. Are the characters consistent? In conflict? Identifiable? Do they undergo change as a result of their interaction? And are they rich enough for two spines: one they think they pursue and one they really pursue? And of course is the sequence of conflicts imaginatively developed? Nothing duller than a scene of 'You will!' 'I won't'! 'You will!' 'I won't !' ad nauseum. Conflict can change its shape and exist on a number of levels, often at the same time. And is the result of one conflict germane to the next scene which picks it up from there? And is there provision for subtextual development?

The relationships. Do the characters need each other or can one play a scene solo? Do their relationships undergo changes? Do characters intermingle so that one can find itself involved in several relationships?

And formal design. How germane to the production and strictly set down are the author's requirements? In a musical, there would be no question that songs be sung and dances executed exactly as conceived. But even in 'straight' plays, does the author require the sets, props, business to be exactly as written? And do *these* require specialists like choreographers, musical directors, particular scenic designers? And are they available?

And distinctiveness. Are the characters sufficiently distinguishable from each other?

As for phrasing, are the moments progressively more dynamic as the play proceeds? Does it build? Is the shape of the build in an unvarying straight line or does it occur in waves? How the actors build dynamics is only one factor. Do the circumstances, technical effects or surprise elements contribute?

Is there a persuasion scene where the play comes to a head? The showdown scene? Is that followed by a realisation scene where the cookie crumbles or the bulb lights over the head of the protagonist?

And is the play theatre-wise? Is a character who exits down left required to appear a second later at the head of a staircase up right in complete costume change? Does the play run too long? Too short? Does it plant and develop ideas logically? And are these ideas handled economically? Is everything in it necessary? Is a sentence used when a gesture would suffice? Or a song when a word would suffice? Are there opportunities for subtlety?

And are the scenes relentlessly monotone? Are there moments of seriousness in the comedy and humour in the tragedy? Is there relief or variety?

And do we consider the play optimistic or pessimistic? Is it an upper or a downer? And is it relevant to the audiences we can entice? Is the show easily promotable? And will word of mouth or reviews bring people in? If we really knew we would all make money, so there must be much guesswork in these.

Then of course – can we afford it? This would not be the concern of the actor, but all the other items would be. Because actors are the ones who can ensure that every one of those other considerations that come with the play is attended to as well as feasible. Every one of those issues is a problem that actors will have to deal with either in interviews and promotion calls, in rehearsal or in performance. Actors should not exempt themselves from knowing about such things. Often we are called upon to direct ourselves. So if we must be directors, we had better be aware of almost as much as the director would be.

It is sad, often embarrassing to see actors tolerating a fumbling director. Therefore if the actor is in fact more aware of what seems to be needed, compassion urges us to avoid humiliating the director with one-upmanship. How often do actors have to bite their tongues or suggest tentatively, "George, what would you say to this idea (please)?" George may therefore learn from you, and – who knows – five shows later he may actually be a good director.

CHAPTER 46

REHEARSALS

In other chapters, particularly in the one on characterisation, we have talked about but not adequately pinpointed, the rehearsal process.

This is the time when plans and ideas which have been marinated for perhaps years, actually come together in a hopefully cohesive materialisation. Not that we expect to see the final product at the end of rehearsals. Some say you won't see that until Press Night in the capital city.

Some say you may never see it, as the show may fold prematurely, or that the show is expected to keep maturing for years.

Notwithstanding, the fusion process is called Rehearsing. And the ingredients that must be brought together include special contributions from author(s), director, producer, theatre owner, publicist, scenic designer, lighting designer, sound designer, props department, wardrobe designer, fabricators of lights, audio, costumes, scenery, props, sometimes composers and musicians, rehearsal studio proprietors, transport companies and myriad backstage managers and workers to install, move, maintain, organise these contributions.

Oh yes, and performers. (When performers become too proud of their contributions to theatre, they are sometimes reminded of the recent costing breakdown for the average play. All items of expense were listed in order of expenditure. And where in the list did the performers come? Second from the bottom, one ahead of toilet paper.)

Each of these ingredients is cooked up separately in areas of their own, and the resultant stews gradually brought together in one mess, usually creating the maximum mayhem around the time of dress rehearsal.

That's when the performers and the scenery come together with costumes, photographers, stagehands props etc. This is the time when directors and producers prove their professionalism. Often they delegate the bulk of the headache to the stage manager, but much remains for them to test their sanity.

This is when Moss Hart coined his immortal aphorism. In New York, dress rehearsals could run through the night almost to the time of opening. One pre-dawn, at a time in history when shaving cream commercials generated some slogan about 'five o'clock shadow', Moss surveyed the sleeping performers draped across stall seats, the stagehands forcing a 6 foot flat into a 4 foot space, the costume designer tearing strips off the wardrobe lady as well as one of her costumes, electricians relocating yet another lamp and quarrelling as to which circuit it should relate to, the new ground-cloth being hammered down and a photographer tripping over the old one in an attempt to pose the half-awake leading lady in a door frame which was only half painted.

And to himself as much as to posterity, Moss sighed, "What you need is five o'clock courage!"

It is then when those dozing performers could perhaps be dreaming of those halcyon days only four weeks ago when their greatest problems concerned their pecking order.

The performers work initially in a department of their own. They convene in rooms, studios, on stages not necessarily their own, in theatre foyers. Some highly creative rehearsing for ***Brigadoon*** occurred in the women's toilet.

Particular procedures are determined by the director and the exigencies of that particular show. There is also a strong determinant in the factor of whether the show involves stars or is primarily an ensemble. Also how powerful or prestigious is the director.

Another critical determinant comes from the so-called 'workshop' production, which may have a degree of looseness not unlike acting school exercises. A star production may have the veto if not the actual directorial initiatives in the hands of the star. Workshops may relegate to the director the functions of ringmaster or traffic cop or social director on a cruise ship. It can be anything or virtually nothing.

I should like to describe one man's approach to an ensemble company. It is an intermediate procedure from which the reader can extrapolate variations befitting their own needs or biases. And here I assume a straight play. A few observations will be added for the special problems of musicals.

First rehearsal, people are introduced, including stage managers, producer, assistants, perhaps designers, publicity people, maybe the author, and of course the performers and director. Then scripts are distributed and each performer clearly identified as to role. Please note: my own idiosyncrasy favours performers *not* having access to the script before then if at all possible. I prefer that the company develop their characters and relationships together. If a performer gets a script earlier, there is sure to be a strong set of preconceptions about the play, his and other characters. Such prejudices are hard to shake and more often than not impair the production.

Then, the cast reads. But the process is one which is an adaptation of perhaps one of the most valuable contributions Lee Strasberg made to my theatrical perceptions. We call it the Strasberg First Reading. It should be stressed that while many directors use it, mostly overseas, the approach is strange to many Australian actors who find it slow, cumbersome and unnecessary. Conceded, slow and cumbersome for some people feeling their way, but for those with some acquaintance with the technique, quite brisk. And fruitful in the extreme.

The rules are:

(1) Only look at the script when some signal suggests it is your line. Otherwise, leave yourself accessible to be talked to.

(2) When it is your line, look at a bit of what you have to say that you can make *some* sense of. You personally. Not the character. We haven't formulated any character yet. Nor do we know about the situations within the play. This we will know later. For now, all we know is we are sitting around a room or at a table, and trying to use the words in front of us for communicating with each other. People to people.

If the first portion of the speech reads "Will you have one?" this might be the opportunity you sought to offer a sweet to the performer you are expected to address. Do so as you say the words. Then the next portion of the speech is "I don't like drinking by myself". What can you refer to? Oh yes, perhaps this is a way of inviting that recipient out for a cup of coffee during the break. Signal to your friend that this is an invitation as you read the line. Try and make them understand you even though you use no additional words. And wherever possible, make the words refer to something that they have a fighting chance of understanding. Note, the first sentence served a piece of candy while the second implied coffee and a chat. Fine. For the first reading they needn't connect.

But at least you are talking to each other about *something*. And the other person is feeling his/her way onto your wavelength. Communication on a deep warm level is being established on first encounter. We don't often find people in many plays relating to each other so well even after long runs.

Now you finish reading and look expectantly at the other person, who has been looking at you, remember? They get the signal that it must be their turn, so now they look at the script. *You don't!* They look at their first words which say 'How's your liver these days?' Liver? Why ask that?

But rule three says you can transpose words to mean something else, always striving to make your ideas accessible to the other person. Now he spots your wedding ring and, knowing the strain which showbiz places on marriage, asks "How's your liver these days?" probably indicating his own wedding ring finger or yours. He transposes the word liver to mean 'marriage', and even hoped to clarify his interrogation with a bit of mime. But that is not actually necessary. You on the receiving end try to work out what he or she means. Maybe you can. Maybe you can't, but you try. Then next line.

Ultimately you come to a line that you just can't seem to fit into this game without taking minutes of time. Forget trying to justify it. Just read it as if you can't make tangible sense of it, so here are the words anyway. That was rule number four.

Rule number five deals with common references. Suppose a line occurred which read 'Are you dependable?', and the reader made it imply something sexual. The group probably catches on and laughs. The next time that word 'dependable' occurs, the reader may capitalise on the common understanding and get another laugh. Great!

By now, certain benefits can be seen to accrue. Firstly, you are familiarising yourself with the play while *avoiding* preconceptions.

Secondly, we are establishing an early group rapport which may expedite or rearrange the expected pecking order, but serves as a group unifier, breaking down reserve.

Three, by opening up to each other, we can all discover (and this is particularly useful to the director) unexpected personality traits which may be exploited in drawing up the characterisations. Or sometimes we recognise traits that will have to be plastered over so that certain characteristics do not show.

Finally, the group may discover that they will have already gone a long way toward memorising the script! Yes, on that first reading. Because, while this was not a primary objective, they have been employing Mnemonic Association. This technique is used in memory training.

So what time you may lose on a somewhat faltering first reading, you more than make up for by not fumbling as much at later rehearsals. But as suggested earlier, with some experience in the technique, it is almost as quick as a radio-type reading.

Having dragged our way through the first reading, which could take all day, we then invite discussion.

Second phase of rehearsal. Maybe second day. What do we think the author wants to leave with the audience? That they have had a good time? That they now know something they didn't before? If so, what? The feeling of having been purged in some way? If so, how? A message? An inspiration? A show of feelings? In other words, the spine.

Then, we discuss each character's identity and how it relates to the spine. Typically, each performer will tend to see his character as nuclear to the play. So what's new there? Every department in the entire production will most likely see the play as revolving around their contribution.

Here is where the director's tact and authority have their second trial. The first was casting.

The director elicits each person's precepts or assumptions to try to integrate certain results.

(1) They have to fit in significantly with the decided spine.
(2) They have to be significant figures of potential conflict.
(3) They should contrast each other and provide variety.
(4) Whatever each prefers to think of themselves, only one character or relationship is the nucleus. That is the one who speaks on behalf of the author.

Or more truthfully stated, the one that speaks on behalf of what the director thinks is the author's spine.

If the author is also the director, the decision is easy. If the two are separate, then indeed one could expect separate points of view. Ultimately, unless the author is alive and has a clause in his contract permitting veto or final say in directorial choices, the final decision is the director's. He is not producing a read script with gestures. He is producing a theatrical presentation. And every department undergoes modification to accommodate the overall presentation *according to his concepts.*

If the author can't speak for himself, there is no argument, though noisy coffins can be sometimes detected.

Discussing characters: each character acquires a spine of his own. Even scenic actions for each. And now every character is discussed in terms of physical detail. Dialects, age adjustments, hair style or wigs, special mannerisms or idiosyncrasies etc. Not that the ideas are finalised now. Most ideas will grow during rehearsals. Today we may have certain firm ideas, but the rest are simply set in motion. We will discuss the progress of these ideas from time to time.

Now for the plotting.

What is your character doing in this first line? You guess, and the discussion involves the whole group. Finally a verb or verb-like term is chosen. A bit action. The character is setting up a victim for a practical joke. We write in the left margin "set up". And if it is a long speech with several actions, each bit is noted.

The next character's actions are discussed. Can we ensure that they conflict with the previous one? If not, what behaviour could be brought into conflict? Feelings? Adjustments? We note these non-actions in the right-hand column.

We make sure that the bits are characteristic of these characters. Also that the conflict leads the phrasing of the scene upward. And we examine the possible needs for supplementary actions.

We see actions in relation to where they may be leading, and allow for planting of ideas which may pay off several scenes later. If the author has provided no such planting we may introduce some supplementary action. Many a play has been saved thanks to such devices.

Relationships are gone into in detail, and actions selected characteristic of these.

Always the director has the final say.

We sit sometimes for a week, plotting every solitary bit in the whole play.

Then we read the play again, simply playing actions. No dialects, or other characteristics. Just actions.

While this plotting has been going on, each performer has been doing homework. This involved working on the characteristics we decided upon at that second rehearsal. We explore and begin to acquire speech patterns and dialects, posture and walk, special physical skills like lifting, taking falls, fighting etc. Research comes in here as well. All this interspersed with the random publicity call TV and press or radio interviews or promotional lunches.

Then another read-through to check on the feelings contribution to the actions. If semantics and intuition have not provided us with the appropriate feelings, then we scribble a few adverbs into the right hand column. What valuable reminders these scribbles will prove to be later on!

Now up on our feet for blocking. This will be done in two stages. The first is general geography. On this speech you should walk to here. Sit during this one. Turn on this word. Exit on this one. That door, not this.

These instructions are noted in the script which may have been dismembered and glued into a larger notebook. Or if the manuscript has space for scribbling, that's where you write. Between dialogue, lines and arrows over dialogue. Draw pictures on back of pages if they are blank.

And during this phase we *do not* play actions. Just recite words mechanically to synchronise with staging.

Then for blocking step two, we add fine touches. The director usually contributes the most to stage 1. Now the performers are encouraged to contribute most to stage 2. It is part of the fleshing out process.

Now we start the fine staging with the actors playing their actions. Now the show starts to come to life.

Shortly the scripts are out of their hands. Only with prompts from the stage managers, they combine feeling their way with memorising the mechanics.

And here is where what we have been drilling as homework comes into the rehearsal. Those things which must eventually become habitual are drilled until they are. Those things which must remain freshly-prepared each performance are kept refreshed with trials of different motivational techniques.

Now the props are there and perhaps certain bits of costume which will need to be worked in. Boots, tight skirts, trailing and hoop skirts, sword belts, capes, hats, gloves.

Finally we are ready for dress rehearsals. Before that, at least one technical run-through with lights, props, sound effects or underpinning, timing of quick costume or makeup changes, dark adapting eyesight so that one can enter and exit during blackouts, checking the colouring of makeup in those lights, finding the exact mark on the stage where a special light will come up on them.

And the dress rehearsal itself! Well, it is often said, "Good dress, bad opening". Which rarely gets challenged as dress rehearsals are rarely good. Not that anybody really goes out of their way to louse up a dress rehearsal just so that the opening should be good. The one presiding rule of most dress rehearsals is Murphy's Law: If anything can go wrong, it will. And here we see how irrevocable is that law.

But we battle through, and – before the press gets to us – throw in a few previews. Which are really rehearsals with audience, and where the performers try out their supplementary actions on the audience.

Then the press arrives to tell us how long we expect to run.

And the cast gets notes after the show for quite a few performances after opening. Sometimes additional rehearsals.

Then the show is in the full charge of the stage manager.

If it were a musical, time would have to have been allotted for dancing or singing calls for each number or scene. Choreographers, choral conductors, conductor, rehearsal pianist – all working at the same time in different locations.

The director popping in on each from time to time. Discussions. Changes. Sometimes tempers flare. Sometimes resignations.

Bit by bit these are fused. Orchestral rehearsals. Then dress, without and with orchestra. More complex but qualitatively similar.

You may well ask "Why are you describing a procedure that most directors don't follow?" True. Procedures are as varied as are directors and this is mine. Directors may start by reading. Or they may start by getting everybody on their feet from day one. They may simply block, or expect the full performance, complete with characterisations, at first encounter. Or they may simply say to the performer, "Go ahead. I'll tell you when I don't like it". That last breed of directors, whose chief function seems to be to ensure that performers don't bump into each other, can be called Traffic Cops. There are other names for some of those listed above, including 'genius'.

Marvellous results can accrue from almost any approach. It's not always how you start but how you finish. So long as the right ingredients eventually find their way into the production, what's the difference how they got there? Now there's the rub, and also the answer to that question. *So long as the right ingredients find their way into the production*.

The process I said was my preferred approach is an idealised one which tries to ensure, in a logical sequence, that all the ingredients will be there. In a sense, I suppose what I was doing was listing what I think the right ingredients are. It should be confessed that in certain circumstances, I may not rehearse exactly as outlined. If some performers already bring emotional loadings to the process which need no further discussion, or have grasped the spine, or if they do not need some of the benefits of the first reading, we may dispense with any of these steps.

The larger problem for the performer than which comes first, talking or blocking, is what does the performer do when he feels the need for some additional drill, skill or insight, and it is not allowed for during rehearsals? Quite simply he has more homework to do.

If you discover the benefits of plotting actions, but the director does not allow for these or even frowns on them, you still can acquire them if you really want to. At home, you can plot your own, with or without a fellow performer. You may also arrive at an arbitrary spine to provide a common direction for your bit actions. With others in the cast over a cup of coffee, or by yourself if they are inclined to think such preparedness is precious or an admission of your lack of acting talent. You may simply do it without the director. (That also goes for the acquisition of any of the other essential ingredients.)

Only don't confront him with it. Just go about your business and let him tell you what results are or should be forthcoming. Then in your least provocative and most professional manner arrange to give him whatever he believes should be there.

From all this it might be assumed that I believe the director is always right.

Yes!

If for no other reason than that the concept, which may be vague or firmly visualised, of the entire production is his. You are not in a position to see the overall which includes not only you but others and lights and sound and scenery and laser beams and smoke and and and ... He may not be good, but he is always right. At least until the producer fires him.

There is a school of thought that every bit of direction is a basis for argument. Dispute everything. With my favourite approach to rehearsing, almost all disputes have been resolved in the first week. The belief is that the more completely performers feel privy to the overall scheme of things, and absolutely clear as to their own contribution, the more cooperative they tend to be. Exceptions are rarely found.

If you don't like what the director is doing, leave the show if you can. Otherwise do it as he requires and get out when you can, vowing never to work for him again.

One performer who barely tolerated my direction decided privately that, come opening night, she would do her own thing. Being theatre in the round, I wanted her long speech to be delivered from the corner of the stage so that she could command the entire audience. Came the night, and on cue we brought up the special pin-spot which illuminated that corner. But she had decided to go to centre stage where she thought she would be more prominent. As the only light on stage was in the corner, she could be discerned only as a vague figure. There she stood delivering her loooong speech, in the dark.

The last time I saw her working in the theatre was as an usherette, in a dark auditorium.

WRITE YOUR OWN NOTES

CHAPTER 47

CHARACTERISATION

In earlier chapters, whenever the topic of characterisation recurred, inviting details, we would pull up and say "Later". Later is now.

In truth, now I should say "Later" yet again. Because this topic deserves a book in its own right. Perhaps one day, given more time and audacity, more of the itsy-bitsy details should be noted. The best we dare attempt in this chapter is some overview plus a consolidation of other references in this book.

Characterisation for the performer is creating a plausible illusion of a character for the audience. How plausible? Depends.

How naive is the audience?
How prejudiced are they?
How close are they?
How forgiving are they?

The ultimately plausible characterisation would have all the personality and physical traits of the original person or idea, *and* be projected in a manner authoritative enough to mask the distracting effects of the medium.

With such a definition, could it be assumed that if an actor- performer came on stage with a good characterisation of some living person, and at the same time that living person joined him, the actor-performer could seem more plausible than the original?

Indeed, that very thing can happen!

Of course if Al Jolson came on stage with his superb impersonator Larry Parkes, there would be no mistaking Al Jolson. Because Al Jolson had learned to work in theatre and face audiences when Larry Parkes was just being thought of.

But place some self-effacing inventor on stage with a good character actor who had been portraying his life, and the realities of a public display would tend to make him cover up some aspects of his personality and probably bluff or accentuate others. His inexperienced presentation of himself could look misleading in comparison to an authoritative performer who had rehearsed so that no unnecessary cover-up were necessary.

In private, the real person would relax and look like himself. In public, the experienced actor would be able to portray what the original looks like in private. And that is the person this play is about: not that self-conscious, edgy, apologetic, overly-smiling fellow who bumped into the proscenium arch on his way offstage.

Those wildly flying-around building blocks of self-consciousness destroyed his stage-image. It is this kind of argument that one thinks of when one hears that a good painting or a good photograph can look more like the person than her or himself. Well ...?

Earlier, we used an example of real peasants onstage looking like real peasants while the actors looked like phonies. How do we reconcile these arguments?

Three answers.

(1) The peasants were required to do what peasants do. So doing it provided actions, which minimised stage nerves. And so they did their actions with peasant skill.

(2) Peasants spend a lifetime drilling and co-ordinating muscular, personality and social patterns of behaviour. They were well rehearsed by life itself. By contrast, the performers, whose preparation time would have been the length of rehearsals plus the season's run thus far, *must* look comparatively under-rehearsed and usually shallow or obviously stereotyped. The performer's acknowledged handicaps.

(3) And a group of peasants provides its own group reinforcement, again minimising nerves.

All adding up to a lot of convincing building blocks.

But, if one asked a solo peasant to act out a prepared scene from a play, there would doubtlessly be a real difference. That skill, we can assume, would not have been learned.

Again, characterisation is an illusion. Putting aside for the moment make-up, costume etc, this illusion is designed by choosing, shaping and mixing together particular proportions of body and voice, action and motivation characteristics.

First, we study the person to be characterised. I prefer physical details first, but this order of priority is optional. Height, weight, sex, colouring, hairstyle, age, historical period, occupation, state of health, hobbies, special features, impediments or mannerisms including dialect, education, nationality where it applies, social status, familial status, fluidity, strength, vitality, endurance, flexibility, balance, musicality, special skills, tempo-rhythms. Now a number of these items seem to be misplaced in the category of physical characteristics. Like, education, nationality, social status, familial status. Why? Or, why not?

Because these may well have conditioned physical mannerisms. Education and social status can effect poise and co-ordination, particularly as revealed in manners. National traits may be particularly distinctive, based on customs of dress and mannerisms as well as manners.

I recall three separate characterisations, each requiring a shrug. Petruccio (Italian) threw his arms apart and upward, rotating his palms to heaven. Hajj (Arab) raised his shoulders. Tevye (Jewish) retracted his neck like a turtle, with the slightest cocking of the head and lifting of the shoulders. One wouldn't do for the other.

Then we list personality characteristics:

- The character's spine (unless the director wants this done under his scrutiny).
- How intelligent is the character? How emotional?
- How sensorily sensitive is the character? Intuitively?

Then what predispositions to certain feelings in response to whatever circumstances we find in the play? How would this character feel if insulted, for example?

- What predisposition to certain actions regarding those same circumstances? What would he be inclined to do?
- What inhibitions or other restraints would be characteristic?
- What sort of coping or defence mechanisms tend to show? Violence? Humour?

Perhaps some psychoanalytic classification if the character is so readily definable.

And then of course, the personality traits that could be consistent with such a classification: Captain Queeg with his constant toying with ball bearings (***The Caine Mutiny Court Martial***) as a paranoidal preoccupation, comes to mind. Strictly speaking, it is really only necessary to know what and how characters behave within the framework of the play. Other detailed information may be interesting but not absolutely necessary.

I recall asking a lovely old actress how thoroughly she knew her character. "Darling" she said, "I know what she had for breakfast". I thought that was marvellous, but couldn't recall a breakfast scene in the play. Or even one that would take into account the prelude or sequel to breakfast. I believe the legendary Group Theatre insisted on detailed research for their characters. The story goes that sheaves of written background were prepared for the butler whose only appearaned to proclaim "Dinner is served!" (Or was it a messenger delivering a note? I can't imagine The Group doing plays with butlers.) If any of that helps in any way, great. But I do wonder how much of that kind of preparation is nothing more than mental gymnastics.

Leading into and leaving the play should be thought of, (characters should be seen coming from and going to somewhere to do something), and of course, what transformation occurs in the character during his journey.

How often we forget that the character is exposed to two hours of influences during the play. And how the character relates differently to different characters, objects, places, food, etc. should all be allowed for. Every stimulus *must* affect him in some way. How can anyone remain unchanged after a sequence of influences? Particularly as within those two hours we may have telescoped a whole imagined lifetime of experiences.

Every character should have undergone *some* transformation by the end of the show. Some plays call for big changes – like the elder Germond in ***La Traviata***, or Othello. Some call for the subtlest of metamorphoses – like Puck, or the one-line butler. But *some change!*

A small hint in planning that change. Look at the endpoint. What has the character finally arrived at? See if you can't start the character's climb as far removed from his final position as possible. If he ends up as a goody-goody, see if he can't seem to be utterly rotten at the beginning. Or vice versa. But remember to plant the seeds of the character-to-be, so that the metamorphosis does not seem to occur implausibly or abruptly. This gives the actor the opportunity to run a bit of gamut. The wider the range, usually the richer and more empathy-inducing the character.

Then one might explore artistic impositions. Would Imagery help? Are there enough of these mannerisms and characteristics to fit under some umbrella concept? Do these traits add up to a bull of a man? Is she rather feline? Or a clucking hen? If so, we can add little touches that might not actually be found in the script. But perhaps some animal, or abstract trait can help conceptualise the character so that we can gain greater insight into this person than if we actually met them in person. One woman's protrayal of a seductress came to sensual life when she noticed that so many of the traits she listed made the character a bit kittenish. So she added a purr-like quality to her speech and the illusion was complete, though nothing in the script or direction suggested purring.

Olivier – incidentally known for his occasional disparagement of 'method actors' – says about his preparations for Othello, things like, "I should walk like a soft black leopard ... a bell ... sometimes your body can become a bell".

Likewise, tempo-rhythms can add an artistic quality providing conflict, variety, insight. Take the hen-like image of a character. Not only might she modify her voice to suggest a mild clucking, but the rhythmic pattern of her speech and movement could be broken up into little irregular parcels of behaviour. Quick-quick-quick-pause-slow-quick-slow-slow-quick-quick. Then, because somebody she relates to has their own pattern of tempo rhythm, the two characters contrast and provide variety.

Plan some colour saturation for your character. Clothes, hair, tinge of make-up. Of course consult with director and perhaps scenic and lighting designer. Your contribution must synchronise with all the other artistic bits and pieces.

Then, having made that never-ending list, trim it if you can to artistic essentials. Often, less is more. Get to the nitty gritty with your selections, just putting a pencil-line through the rejects. Perhaps one or two of them might be worth recalling as you go along in rehearsal. Don't avoid the risky or dangerous ideas if you think they can illuminate or enrich without detracting from integrity. Therein can be one difference between great and merely good.

Now, to apply the list. Of the characteristics left on, check off those that will need to be cultivated by asking, 'Which of these traits are different from my own?'

If your character tends to become impatient when someone does the wrong thing, and so do you, the performer, don't tick that trait. You already have it working for you. Only check those mannerisms you have to go out and get.

The checklist completed, now ask yourself: "Though I might not normally sit in the chair the character's way, can I learn to do so easily?" If the answer is "Yes, a few rehearsals should do it", fine. That's how that mannerism can be worked in. But if the answer is "No" some other avenue might be explored, for example some motivational technique. This is preceded by another question, "Under what circumstances might I sit this way?" Maybe an As If: "as if I have a painful boil on my bottom" might do the trick. But if you ask, let's say, "How can I arrange to pause and weigh up before answering questions? Because I think and reply quickly by habit, I don't think it will be easy to slow down as the character must". Now you will have a different approach to the problem. Simple drilling or motivational technique may not fix it.

Scan the possibilities. How can you make yourself slow down that way? Obviously you rehearse it with pauses. But the pauses are most likely to seem empty. They won't look like transitional beats at all. One trick I used was to spell out in my mind the last word that my partner said. Then, when that became too easy, I spelt the word backwards. Then when that fatigued I'd count the letters in the word. Later I would pounce on whether there were odd or even numbers of letters there, and then check them. That device worked for the long run of a show. It slowed me up and the pauses were full of sorting-out type thought that, I was assured, the audience took to mean I was thinking about the play situations. Not a bit. That was me, the performer, doing a bit of sorting out that fitted in with that part of the characterisation.

Sometimes you can pre-arrange all the elements during rehearsal. Other times you simply note what the results are intended to be, moment by moment, and leave it to your professionalism to make them happen during the performance. The choice is individual.

Now let's consider phrasing and dimensions, at least to the extent that your character contributes to these. When does your character carry the ball in the scene, and when is the character helping or hindering? Have you provided your character with the power, mass, bulk, drive, authority or whatever dynamic ingredients that make the audience believe you can take responsibility for the story line or scenic action of the author? Or if you assist or interfere, is your character structure just formidable enough for the task and not so much as may overpower the one carrying the theme at this moment? It is possible for an Iago to swamp an Othello if each is not proportionately designed. The choice of mannerisms, actions, feelings go to contribute to the illusion of inter-relationship.

Recently a play was destroyed because of the performance of a bully and one of his underlings. The play hinged on how terrifying the bully is as he re-arranges people's lives against their will. In a contretemps with one of his supposedly obsequious followers, the follower – veering from strict direction – treated the bully with contempt and went so far as to make a rude gesture at him. The bully stuck to what had been rehearsed and did not flatten his insulter. From then on, the bully was ineffectual and the play meant nothing.

How does one beef up a character? One way is to provide strong feelings and actions when there is conflict with a strong opponent. These can be composed almost like a piece of music, to ensure more and more sparks will fly as the scene progresses. For example, one can start out with a moderately strong action impelled by a mild motivation. Then, moderately strong action with a moderately strong motivation. Then increase motivation. Then elevate the action. Then one, then the other, making sure that each step permits you to top the resultant dynamic of the other.

Or, another design is to play a big action with a mild feeling. Then, try again, only this time take the action down one notch while putting up the feeling by two. Next time, action down one and feeling up two more, repeating the tactic until the action seems almost innocently casual, but the feeling is hair-trigger-deadly.

In the event that your character has to increase in dynamics, but you don't have a chance to engage in strong conflicts, there are other devices.

One is referred to as a 'tripod' approach. An action is chosen that is far away from a feeling and equally far away from an adjustment. Like the legs of a tripod. A man can be reading the papers (action) casually (feeling) while eating a sandwich (adjustment). Each, as you can see, is not imperative to the others. Then as a particular item catches his eye, he slows down on the eating and feels less casual. Gradually he is not eating at all and is very worried about what he reads. Perhaps in time, his mouth which had beed used for a habit like chewing is now used to frame the words "That's me they're writing about"!

What has happened is while each department was doing its own thing, the person looked moderately interesting but not really worth worrying about. Gradually as it became a case of 'all hands on deck', those divergent legs of the tripod came together at the peak in one solid mass of metal. All elements worked together to increase dynamics. You see this often in simpler form when someone is walking along reading a paper and suddenly stops while still reading.

Then enriching of characters to improve their dynamics includes the ability to structure characteristics in depth. We have been looking at modifying characters as they move along in time during the scene. Some of the strongest structuring can be designed for a moment of stillness, as with multifaceted responses. Why is it necessary that a character is seen responding to anything with only one set of reactions? Reading a paper, meeting a friend, tasting a new dish, why does it have to be simply with interest, happily and enthusiastically respectively? Why not something more superficial than interest as well as something deeper? Why can't the newspaper item not only interest him but bring out a touch of irony, like "I told them this would happen but the stupid bastards wouldn't listen", as well as suppressed anger, like "so they fired me for talking out of turn".

It was from my wife Helen that I first heard the phrase 'Grim and Earnest' to describe the simplistic mono-dimensional responses of so many *dray*matic portrayals we are doomed to look at. Even anger, remorse, jealousy can usually afford to be tempered by an additional feeling that takes account of people looking at you at this moment, your own self-esteem, and even the coping factor. Which nasties want the world to see them as nasties? For that matter, isn't any kind of wearing one's heart or image on one's sleeve kind of suspicious?

Many actors – even performers – plunge into their big dramatic scene at such a headlong pace, licking their chops in anticipation of the tatters of passions they will wade in, that they forget to consider how blinkered or tunnel-visioned that scene might seem to the judicious. Oh, the pit may lap it up. "Now that's acting!" they may say. And the actor will have had himself an "orgy of self expression", to quote Mammoulian.

But don't look for empathy, because it will rarely be there. Empathy is reserved for those in grief or turmoil who exert some effort to help themselves, who try somehow to cope. With courage, laughter, minimisation, somehow. Thus those additional dimensions which provide the depth we seek and the dynamic richness we treasure. Remembering "The drunk does not try to stagger", people swept away from normal composure by any stimulus, seek to regain that stability.

Plan into your characterisation the primary responses and the secondaries as well. However... If the scene calls for a departure from fully the lifelike, we may have to deliberately thin out the character. For example, much of comedy depends on some aspects of distortion, ridicule, dehumanisation, disproportion. Enriching characters may work against that kind of comedy in scenes like these.

Comedy where the characters are more rounded can benefit in other ways from an enriched characterisation. Portraying many of the characters in plays by Neil Simon or Alan Ayckbourn, only requires an enriching touch to turn audience laughter to audience tears. Likewise, remove some identifiably human dimension and we can get a laugh.

Then as to phrasing the character, learn to connect the bits as the character would. If the character is a slow or stodgy one, you can design each action to start only after the preceding action has been fully completed. If the character on the other hand is a smooth mover, you can prepare each action just as the previous one is winding down. As one is petering out the other is cranking up, so there is always an overlap.

If, yet again, the character is mercurial, plot a lot of supplementary actions and have the character nimbly moving from one to the other as well as continuing the mainline smoothly, and the illusion is one of competent quick-witted busy-ness, mental agility and the like.

In shaping the phrase, assuming the play like most expects an upward build of interest, plan your bits to be progressively more dynamic. Use a fair attention getter at the beginning of the scene, cut back a bit, then build in waves, the strongest actions, or feelings, or adjustments toward the end. Then the next scene picks up the dynamics where you left off, if possible. All the items can be planned as part of the characterisation.

We are not simply portraying a life-object on stage. We are trying to ensure that the character has a reason for being on stage. Unless the character is going to contribute to the dynamics of the story or spine, why don't we save a salary and simply talk about him? We are involved in a time art. Yes, there are those who think that frozen character studies are an end in themselves. Is that not better left to the still photographer or the documentary makers? And even they prefer, as they say, something dramatic about their characters. In other words, to see the characters applying themselves in some conflicting encounter. And as we are doling out these encounters in two hour adventures, on average, there has to be much art and guile in spreading that encounter over that time while keeping the interest of the audience. The characterisations must do their part.

Having sketched the overview and pinpointed where this or that impact should occur, this would be the time to ensure that *every bit action* is noted. As mentioned, we usually write the verbs in the left margin of the script. What is the character doing every moment of the play to help realise the outlined plan? Now we arrange that the dialogue is going to be the means by which each action is played. With the help of staging of course.

Can we now assume that having planned the things the characterisation needs, then away we go in clear sailing? Devoutly to be wished. Now we look at those details that are classed as adjustments. Dialogue, business, mannerisms, dialect, age and health adjustments, tempo rhythm, vocal melody and range, inflection, posture, gait, gesture. And at a particular phase of rehearsal they can be drilled quite mechanically. We pay attention to them to the point where they are completely memorised, where they are second nature. Automatic. During performances we should ***not*** have to think of them. Unless of course there is an accident. A fluff. A mistake. Then for a moment pay enough attention to these to get back on track, and forget about them once more.

And this would be a good time to remind ourselves of one omnipresent consideration: ***aesthetic appeal!*** Beauty wherever possible. Or at least, attractiveness. Wrap any 'moment of truth' in sugar and it becomes more ingestible. Beauty and grace in voice and body can make even the nastiest nastiness more accessible.

I don't want to plow on without some mention of two of those adjustments:

Firstly, dialects. There are many approaches to working these in. These range from the phonetic, or perhaps a recollection of having used it oneself, to research involving recordings, or living amongst such people or having someone who actually uses that dialect read or record your script for you. Most performers of my acquaintance find several prototypes if they can and distil, by careful listening or phonetic notation, some concoction from them all. What do we do about Elizabethan English? If we could, we might track down some communities purported to still reside in the Ozarks who retain that very dialect. Otherwise, be guided by whomever you guess to be most 'expert'.

But the dilemma of accuracy of dialect and intelligibility for our audience must ever challenge our judgment. What do we do if the authentic dialect remains unintelligible to the audience for which the show is designed? My own vote is for diluting the dialect. When ***Brigadoon*** went into rehearsal, the cast included one authentic lowland Scot replete with burr. He was released within the first few days of rehearsal. For unintelligibility. Yet there is the point of view that says, "To hell with the audience. I want the real thing regardless." Well ...

Secondly, there are the considerations of age and health: probably that portion of characterisation that most performers relish most. How we love to stagger and cackle our way into decrepitude! From time to time, we convene special classes we call 'Physiology for the Actor'. One day we may make such a course constant and compulsory. Because therein, one discovers the actual changes that may be manifest with growing older, various health complaints, and even the pharmacology of some usual drugs and chemicals.

Not everybody may need dialects or geriatric mannerisms. But the plea here is for knowing that one can find out about both if one is sufficiently resourceful. And one should go for accuracy first before deciding how authentically they will be portrayed in the final presentation. Each poison affects people differently. Loss of muscle tone with aging forbids quick elastic change of directions in movement. Arthritic complications limit range of movement. All these should be considered even though we may decide to keep the behaviour within artistic bounds.

Back to the sequence. Meanwhile, we are trying our actions on each other, trying out different transitions and phrasings, discovering where supplementary actions can be useful, and making sure that what we detailed can come together. Now also is the time to work in different feelings to impel and colour these actions. Try spontaneous generation of appropriate colours. If they fail, speculate on what techniques or combination of techniques will make them happen.

At this point, larger considerations of direction need to be considered. But by now, your characterisation should be well under way. There is modification yet to make, but that will occur during rehearsals. What your partner throws back at you, or how your partners respond to what you do to them will cause touch-ups here and there. The director might tell you, 'The way you are hammering her, and her apparent vulnerability makes you look too brutal. Cut back on something'. Then there is a search for what was meant by 'something'. Ultimately, you fix.

Now we get into make-up and costume, polish your facility in handling the props and work in the set. More touch-ups.

Finally the audience gets into the act. Again the director will probably point out that what was intended to affect the audience a certain way is not working out. A touch-up here or there might rectify. That's what try-outs are about. In the old days, we could afford to go out of town for a few weeks. Now the show previews in town before the press gets to it.

Then the character has only to grow in richness as the show runs.

With a clear appreciation of the components of characterisation, and with 45 motivational techniques to draw upon, there should *never* be any excuse for a characterisation going stale.

Even if the show runs for twenty years.

CHAPTER 48

RELATIONSHIPS

This consideration has been implied in most of what we have looked at so far. When we think of actions, motivations, adjustments, conflict, or serving the audience, putting aside those infrequent moments we are dealing exclusively with ourselves, we are involved in relationships. One might even say that when we deal only with ourselves, this too can be seen as internal relationship. So why are we bothering with a chapter exclusively on this subject?

In the interest of overview, we may find it pertinent. For example, we may choose to plan a relationship or let it happen. If we choose, we may say they are brothers, sisters, parent and child, husband and wife, boss and employee, officer and enlisted man, performer and director, cop and robber.

If we choose to let it happen, we may simply generate a situation which allows people to play actions on each other. After a while, the audience may discover they are friends, competitors, fellow sports, political allies, political antagonists, lovers, and the list goes on. If this approach is successful, their attitudes to each other may both imply and reflect those relationships.

But we had better consider what time may do a relationship. Have we not observed couples at a party who virtually signalled they were newly acquainted? Others groaned to anyone with half a mental ear that they had been together a looong time. What were the telltales?

Generally new associates tend to cater to each other more. They explore each other. They couldn't be absolutely certain of the other's needs, whims, sensitivities. A bit of walking on eggshells. Much eyeballing. By contrast, older associates tend to take each other for granted. Not necessarily in a dismissive way. Simply, there is less need to explore because they already know. Maybe not everything, but enough to feel secure with easy address. They could tease each other more frankly. They could swear good naturedly at each other. Or pillory each other publicly with jokes at the other's expense. Or simply seem to ignore each other. Or if a certain remark is passed by others, they may quickly or knowingly glimpse at each other. An inside joke they share? Also, how often does one know what the other is intending to say even as the other only has just started to speak? Then is there interruption? Overlap?

Then there are considerations of estranged relationships. How do they feel about the possibility of reunion? How do they feel their new friends are reacting to old associates meeting again? Is there a desire to keep the old association secret? How do they mask their reactions from others?

Then watching relationships transform before our eyes. From what to what? And when performing them, how do we keep those initial relationships or transformations fresh every performance? As a show runs, backstage relationships change. How do these affect the onstage ones?

What are the problems of husband and wife playing in the same company? Or opposite each other? Or ex-husband and wife doing either? In the musical ***Kiss Me Kate***, some attempt is made to both exploit and explore such a relationship. Happily, the script says!

And what about multiple inter-relationships? Shortly, we will look at the 'three scene'. But for the moment, think of a scene played by characters A,B, and C. While you (A) play a mainline action on character B and a supplementary action on character C, what does C think of what you are doing to B? What does B think of what you are doing to C? What do they think of each other? What do onlookers think of your relationships with B and C? What do B and C think, being observed by onlookers?

Such awareness is the enemy of blinkered or tunnel vision. It is the friend of the wide open circle-of-concentration. The ability to embrace multiple relationships provides the mechanics of designing and carrying out a whole range of social graces. It makes it possible to enact a faux pas, where for a moment you were aware of only one level of understanding and suddenly realise that your deed can be seen as foolish or insulting from another point of view. It also permits portrayal of relatively omniscient characters like diplomats, kings, gurus or Christ himself.

See the advances theatre has made. There was a time when the only consideration was the self-expression of the character alone. Anybody else within earshot didn't matter, so we assumed they vanished or we just pretended they didn't hear. Then we progressed to the 'two scene', and still on-stage onlookers were expected to look the other way. Now we are at the stage where we must account for whomever is within earshot or in view. What next? Intergalactic communication? This chapter does not suggest easy answers. It simply raises the questions. Elsewhere in this tome, you may stumble on clues about which tools may be employed in finding the answers.

But one general procedural observation should be made nonetheless. The image of charm, warmth – what's your name for it? – comes from deep relationship. If you wish to create the illusion of what's-your-name-for-it, listen attentively to your partners. And when you address them, don't talk to their ears. Talk to their mind's eye. Vivify your concepts for them. And as you communicate – ***read their minds***. Do they need what you are offering? How? What are they thinking as you offer? When is it unclear to them? Clear? When have they had enough? Are they offended? Amused? Tailor everything so that it fits them perfectly. ***Cater to their needs!***

My director-friend previously referred to places so much emphasis on the degree to which actors commit themselves to each other, that she is almost prepared to overlook otherwise-flawed performances. Devoting yourself to the needs of partners, besides helping them, opens in you a kaleidoscopic display almost impossible to synthesise mechanically. Of course, if your character is cold, detached or colourless, avoid these very procedures.

These are considerations to remember as you frame your own characterisation, plot your actions, rehearse and perform. These as well as that other outgoing involver, "Whenever possible the object of your action should be your key motivator", keep you open. They then should go a long way toward creating interpersonal sparks on stage as well as avoiding the hideous trap of the self-indulgent Telephone Booth performance.

CHAPTER 49

JUSTIFYING ARBITRARY DIRECTIONS

When I commenced acting those several years ago, it was by guess and by gosh. Sometimes the results were acceptable to director or audience. Hoping to increase the frequency of those instances, and having a somewhat scientific bias in my thinking, I embarked on a pursuit of getting to the root of things behavioural and theatrical.

Thus it was that I was taken in hand by one who had worked with Boleslavski, Ouspenskaya and had auspicious names among his peers. Names like Henry Fonda, Josh Logan, Margaret Sullivan, Gail and Hester Sondergard and the like. This was Bob de Lany. It was he who taught me to Identify and Believe in the Situation. Also to trust my responses. And as the situation moved me to behave, so to go ahead and do. Virtually to live the life of the character. "What fun", thought I, "I can live a thousand lives in one lifetime. Freedom!"

But two disturbing things came to my attention. When, as the character in a play Bob was directing, I responded as the situation seemed to invite me to do, often Bob would veto my results. "No – do this instead", he would insist. "But I feel like doing that", I challenged, flinging back at him his own teachings. Always he won and somehow I had to end up doing some things my character (and I) didn't seem to like doing.

The other disturbing observation was that when Bob directed himself in a play, he did what he had been insisting I should do. Whatever he conceived for his characterisation was pretty much what he ended up doing in performance. Ideas of his characterisation guided the feelings, the choice of actions and the staging. If other actors' similar approach dictated their behaviour as well, that was fine *until* what they did and what he did clashed. Then *they* would have to change. He rarely did. In other words, his performance was the nucleus of the production and the others had to work around him. A bit like the actor-managers of old, whose instructions to others in the cast might be "Read your lines loudly and clearly, don't bump into the furniture, and keep out of my way". (I hasten to qualify that I never saw it as a function of ego, but rather one of superior artistic judgment. I still do.)

But when he was directed by someone else, he took the most arbitrary directions imaginable like an obedient pet. He would start out doing his thing, but upon receiving contrary instructions, reversed just as quickly and did something else with as much conviction. It was then that I began to doubt hand-me-down platitudes or generalisations. He was saying in effect "Do as I say, not as I do". And I was now replying "Why should I? Just because you are telling me what you were told by somebody who was told by somebody else?" Why base my performance on the mandatory 'Living the Role', and expect to do what I think my character would do when the performance actually ends up with me doing mostly what the director wanted me to do?

Early indoctrinations are not easy to shake off. I lived and worked with the paradox for years, espousing fealty to 'the rules' but practising other techniques behind my own back. Then when working with Howard da Silva years later (it was at my behest that he began teaching), some of his exercises brought the solution to the problem.

The answer to the problem seemed to be, that we had been innocently assuming that there was only one optimum approach to 'truthful' acting. That is, how the 'character' felt moved to behave. There were actually several, and they could depend on what was deemed the nucleus of the production concept. It could be actor-centric, director-centric, maybe even author-centric. It depended on who held the whip.

If the star or some other actors called the shots, the play would have to shape itself around their wishes, inspiration or comfort. If the director did, then whatever you thought the character should do, the director had the veto, or even dictated the terms from scratch. If the author had it in his contract to determine whatever nuances he wished, then that's how it had to be done.

If the whip-cracker says "Stand on your head, wiggle your ears, clap your hands while you whistle 'Dixie'," you do it. With authority. And that means literally make it look as though you initiated it and have good reason for doing it. And this is how indeed I have found the situation to be over the fifty plus years of immersion in active theatre.

The exercises Howard provided involved the 'justification of arbitrary commands'. Simply, it meant given a piece of staging, make sense of it. Given arbitrary words to say, make them your own. Given business to do, integrate it as necessary. And the problems he assigned were complex. Do a half dozen things, include certain set dialogue and justify it all in one integrated scene.

By justify, he meant not merely an intellectualisation of an idea. There had to be proportional feelings and all. And we had to make every bit of form absolutely necessary. If one component could be removed and the scene was not impaired, then that bit had been too loosely interwoven. It became patently obvious that rigid dogma could become a millstone around the neck. We are told that Vakhtangov split from Stanislavski over this very set of issues.

Vital acting – contrary to purist thinking – can be generated by starting with arbitrary staging and formal requirements, then building the details of character and relationship to suit those demands. Never have I, since then, been able to take seriously the actor who, upon having been given a direction, tells me he can't/won't/wouldn't do that as it doesn't fit in with his idea of the character. My reply is usually "Stretch the character a bit and squeeze the direction in. Or change the character". Our production is not going to be limited by the boundaries of how actors conceive their characterisations.

Those exercises. A simple one to start. Stand in that corner, walk to the centre of the acting area, sit on the ground, turn around 360 degrees while still sitting, rise, hop on one foot to the opposite corner. You may mime props, use personal props or articles of clothing, but don't do any more or less staging. Make up a single issue type scenelet. Try to believe in it. Take a time limit of three minutes to prepare it. Do it. Later the problems become more complex and the time limit shorter.

One student decides this is a schoolroom where young children are going to have a children's festival. There is a hopscotch design chalked on the floor between centre and a corner. But the area in the centre, from which contestants start has not been marked out. She is the supervisor who must check out the games as well as remedy final unfinished details. She walks to centre, sits on floor, and using herself as a large compass, swivels around on her behind holding out a chalk to mark the circle. Then checks out the hopscotch for size to ensure the youngsters will have a fair pattern to work in. Thus she hops to the corner on that pattern. That seems to fit the rules.

How tight a story is it? Not bad. Can you think of a better one? Then do, and really ***need*** to do it. Now act it out.

Invent another example with four or five requirements. Then start adding dialogue. Some sentence borrowed from the newspaper will do. Then graduate to having to give a precisely imitated reading of that line of verbiage. Take from the newspaper, for example, "fifteen people were killed on the roads this weekend". Have somebody read that line to you with their own emphases, inflections and intonations. You copy that reading precisely as given to you and make it your own. And make it consistent with your chosen character and situation.

Then take some of the same instructions you invented, only this time rearrange their order. Find some quite far-out instructions to challenge each other with. Keep them safe please: no sword swallowing or balancing on window-ledges. As you will find, this is a superb exercise for stoking our imaginations. Not only those of the people having to carry out the tasks but also those inventing them. Indeed, one variation in this game is that after the challenged students have carried out their ideas of the instructions, the person who issued the instructions has to carry them out as well.

Then as one exercises, one becomes accustomed to accepting directions, no matter how far-fetched. Hereafter, let no one say that acting requires no creativity!

About those readings! That's a touchy one. I was raised on a motto, "Please don't give me a reading". The great Helen Hayes was said to freeze up if she were given a reading. Then one day, it occurred to me that as most of my income derived from musicals, every time I tackled a song I was being given a 'reading'. A song really ties you down to every sonic nuance. Not only inflection, but pronunciation, tempo-rhythm, key, phrasing, timbre – the works. And with all that, we are doing things with these words, emotionally-charged things. Imagine the musical director playing the song for me and I say, "Don't tell me how these words should sound. I'll do it as I feel". Or "Just tell me what I'm doing with these lyrics. The melody and inflection will take care of themselves naturally". Richard Rodgers' ghost would curse me with instant tetanus.

Australian performers might sometimes be unfamiliar with regional American lilts and pronunciations, especially of certain idiomatic phrases, and then I find it mutually beneficial to give them a 'reading' of a line. I can't recall a single nervous breakdown as a direct consequence.

Taking a reading need not be confined to a study of enunciating idiosyncrasies. It can also include the formalisation of a specifically-motivated task. In Neil Simon's ***Gingerbread Lady***, I wanted the accuse-evade exchange between Evvy and Jimmy to have a certain childish singsong quality which each of them picks up from the other and advances a step further. "You were whispering", "We were not whispering", "You were whispering" "We were not whispering: we were talking softly", etc. That lilt was designed to keep the scene light. It needed it. But it also insinuated a hint of immaturity in these two apparent adults. Without the specific reading, the direction would have beaten around the bush forever. Fortunately the actors were disciplined as well as skillful.

The easy custom of being able to take direction of any kind is the enemy of artistic rigidity. One should not expect a production to bind itself to the convenient techniques of the actors. Yes Judy Garland got away with it in ***A Star is Born***. When she felt like working she did. But the rest of us lesser mortals find we must use our techniques to serve the play. The play is not there to help us exercise our techniques nor pander to our limitations.

Given an arbitrary direction, the performer asks "Now which buttons do I press to ensure that I can come up with those results?"

Yes, there are times when certain of the director's choices of results can be disputed. But you had better be able to see the play objectively, at least as well as the director, before engaging in that one. We assume you think there is a better way to serve the play, and there are polite ways of going about such disagreement. But the disagreement should be automatically terminated if what you are really trying to serve is yourself at the expense of the play, or if you are simply looking for a lazy way out of having to rise to a challenge.

CHAPTER 50

STYLE

The sight of a Broadway goddess fleeing in terror at the sight of an acolyte is the stuff of comedies. And yet that almost describes the response of the magnificent Agnes de Mille whenever she glimpsed the balloon over my head perpetually inscribed with *that question*.

That question was 'But Agnes, what *is* style?'

At the time, when theatre buffs talked of style, they inevitably spoke of Agnes de Mille. ***Oklahoma!*** was distinguished by its style, as had been ***Rodeo***, as subsequently was ***Carousel***. Agnes' style was indelible and characteristic. Yet each show had its own style as well as hers. One rehearsal break, worn and distraught, cornered with no possibility of escape and fending me off with a desperation akin to thrusting a crucifix into the face of a vampire, she rasped, '*The Formal Design!*' And the secret was out.

But it seems that not everybody got to hear of it. Some still talk about style with a vagueness normally reserved for other cliché's like 'It works' or, 'It moves', 'great timing', 'slow', 'I liked it', 'brilliant', 'dull', 'not to be missed', 'Disaster', and my own favourite non-committer, 'interesting'. Not that a concept like timing is not objectifiable. To an intelligent observer, one can measure the quality and quantity of a timed delivery. And so can one testify to components of style. But, too often, those who grasp at these terms rarely know precisely what they are talking about.

Secretly, I'm not sure that Agnes had a clear, intellectual concept of what she was famous for until forced to encapsulate the process. Her definition, hurled almost as an invective, seemed to catch her by as much surprise as the delight it produced in her assailant.

Formal design. How simple. With design, we examine details of size, colour, configuration, balance, proportion, placement, rhythm, perspective, contrast, consistency, inter-relationship and emphasis, to name a few that come to mind. Until now, we seem to have been pre-occupied with elements of content arranged artistically. Motivations implement actions. Actions are phrased, interwoven, and parcelled into scenic actions. Scenic actions are strung together into the over-all action of the play, etc. Content design, which we call the *spine*.

For some, this might have seemed novel, particularly if the concepts of accessible content were unknown to them. Customarily, such observers might only have been able to recognize formal details, even if these were sometimes difficult to analyse. So far, this tome seems to have dealt mainly with content, and now seem to be returning to more customary and securely familiar territory.

With Agnes De Mille's crystallisation, we can see that *style is to Form what Spine is to Content.* It is a pattern which prevails from beginning to end. All formal components are consistent with and supportive of the whole. They contain formal ingredients which are – or can be – abstracted, heightened, phrased, shaped, interwoven, grouped, contrasted, etc.

Looking at that particular production which excited the theatre world and prompted the persecution of the Mighty Agnes, we may glean a few particulars. ***Oklahoma***! burst like its punctuation onto Broadway, March 31, 1943 and the subsequent fallout irradiated every lyric theatre on the globe. To this day, it is the subject of musings and analyses, some of which are probably accurate. Let us here add to the babble.

The plot was boy meets girl, etc. Nothing novel. The setting was the recently – purchased and more recently squatted Oklahoma territory where farmers and cowmen jockeyed for advantage. (No allusions to its dispossessed or any other trivial overview. Not an Indian anywhere.) Thus, a natural sub-plot suggesting there could be ways in which 'the farmer and the cowmen should be friends'. In the tradition of most musicals, they inevitably succeed. They inter-marry. Love conquers all. So far, what's the fuss?

Oh yes, it becomes readily apparent that there was no opening chorus. So? ... In Victor Herbert's ***'Naughty Marietta',*** the opening is a solo town crier. Other musicals can be cited. Revolutionary? In its way, yes: along with that Ensemble Effect, the special dominant distiction of ***Oklahoma***! is its extraordinary dramatic integrity carried by an equally consistent style.

Dramatically, it is a tight play. Perhaps not as tight as some of its successors but quite tight. That is to say, remove some scene or portion and the show should falter. In a loose play, remove almost any segments and they may not be missed. In fact, musicals were notorious for their inter-changeability. A composer had a song he was fond of. It might have to be off-loaded from a musical because the show ran overtime. No worries. It would most likely find its way into the next musical on hardly any special pretext. A song is a song. If it sells copies, well that's it, isn't it?

It might be told that one of the best (I thought so because I shared the routine) songs in the show was dropped in rehearsal, because the brilliant director Rouben Mammoulian couldn't integrate it into the dramatic flow. It was seen as simply time out for a tin-pan-alley hit number. He has only recently been forgiven. But he was right as usual.

In later years, my work involved presenting potted musicals in a theatre restaurant. ***Oklahoma***! was one. Try as I might, the only bits that seemed to be even remotely expendable were a few down-in-one-crossovers. (That is, when the curtain drops on a scene, there is often a short scene in front of the curtain to keep the audience diverted while the set is changed.) Usually, these are seen as obvious padding but sometimes function in selling some otherwise extraneous song, routine or talent. At any rate, I think my potted version cut the full-length running-time by perhaps ten minutes.

And as for its form, firstly it was lyric. That is, a musically or poetically heightened form of expression or communication. People talked to each other in song, mime, dance.

Then it was also realistic, wherein the characters and relationships were not very remote from lifelike.

Then too it contained segments of fantasy – as the dream sequence.

Then it mixed the fourth wall convention with full frontal presentation. Or should we say that it retained that mix. Musicals have done so forever. But with tightened integrity of concept, such conventions are more difficult to justify. Consider when characters become deeply and privately involved with each other, as if there were no eavesdroppers, how readily can one justify addressing the audience directly? How smoothly can you get the audience into the act?

Consider a simple stylistic challenge. Fusing realistic behaviour with lyric. Cowboys danced one segment where they arrive as a group. How to enter? They might have run in and headed for the girls. They might have jetté-ed in like Nijinskys flying through the air with their legs in a split. Or they might have slid in on their knees as Michael Kidd so brilliantly had men doing in ***Guys and Dolls*** years later. Which of these or anything else could catch the flavour of macho cowboys?

Agnes abstracted a formal design from how these men worked and travelled – indeed often where their affections lay – and brought in the invisible horse. The horse was more than some formidable beast. It determined how the men dressed, travelled, sat, walked, and stood. It bound men in a community and often determined their laws. Capital punishment for horse-theft, but murder often defensible. And in the auction scene, the ultimate sacrifice Curly makes to gain access to Laurie's basket (sic) is to bid, – yes, his horse.

So, when the cowboys arrive, they are doing 'bells' in unison. That is, they are leaping up, swinging legs to one side with knees bowed, and clicking their heels in mid-air. Then they land and repeat the move on the other side. In the dream fantasy, this move becomes even more formalised, occasionally more grotesque. And, of course, when the cowboys simply stood around in the non-lyric segments, they retained the bow-legged stance with thumbs hooked in belts, arms rounded in a torso reprise of the below-the-belt parentheses.

The entire production retained such, and similar, motifs, playing with them, interweaving them, heightening them. In the dream sequence when Curly confronts Jud, the now earthbound Curly becomes ineffectual against the striding Jud whose familiar terrain is indeed the earth. And even gunfire cannot compensate for Curly's vulnerability when off his horse.

Agnes handled her stylistic components with the mastery of a great composer threading musical figures into a symphony.

And how to label the style? What should we call it when there are elements of realism, lyricism, fantasy, fourth-wall manipulations, etc? The resultant style, because of its integrity, cannot become detached from the show itself. One would have to call it the ***Oklahoma***! style. As Kazan's directorial concept of ***Death of a Salesman*** gives us the ***Death of a Salesman*** style.

In these instances, we recognise such integrity that the production can no longer be loosely pigeon-holed. Musical styles, farce styles, burlesque styles, even Shakespearean styles. Are these not very loose-fitting envelopes into which we try to cram myriad productions, each of which deserves an envelope of its own?

True, we do run into trouble when, from behind the smokescreen of so called experimental (often read as 'I-haven't-a-clue-what-I'm-doing-but-I'm-sure-its-important-and-it-makes-me-feel-good') theatre we can put together a potpourri of components which may possibly be explainable to ourselves but which may so often produce confusion on top of innocence. One is reminded of a little kid with his first Chemistry Set enthusiastically mixing mysterious chemicals in a test tube and producing an occasional coloured solution. What and why remain a mystery, but he ended up with something 'different'. 'Innovative', I believe is the word some funding bodies may use when fumbling for criteria. The wheel which is rediscovered is too often square.

Again, as Alan Jay Lerner said, 'To be different is not the same as being good. To be good can be different enough'.

A tightly-integrated style is certainly one tell-tale of what makes for a 'good' production. A good formal design, usually born of some elements of content, inseminated by a fertile creative mind, can so consolidate a production that it will have to be seen as a single entity. By the judicious of course.

At this point, I must buy an argument with some respected acting aficionados who insist that style can *only* originate from content. While it may be the more desirable approach for some of us, it is completely possible, feasible, practical and creatively integratable to start with an imposed style, and find the subsequent content to fill it out. Think of a ballet which acts out a story set to abstract music. Just as it may be preferable to tailor clothing to a human, we also know that an article of clothing can be designed and made, then somebody found to fit into it with no substantial alterations to the clothing.

Many a fine production has been conceived and produced starting with a formal design. Many a fine lyric has been written to fill out the music which was written first.

In Australia, most of the better imported shows are purchased as formal designs. The production has to flesh them out with content. When theatre companies apply for the rights to certain shows, they may not acquire the rights to the script without also having to commit themselves to the overall production, costumes, set design, staging, sometimes even poster design, because the written play itself was not necessarily what succeeded. No doubt this practice may be seen as unfair. Is it not conceivable that my stylistic presentation of a script might not be an improvement on the Broadway or West End original concept? Conceivable indeed. But many an author may not wish to risk it. The original was forged with an enormous budget, trial and error, the finest talents available in the big ponds, and even at that they maybe came close to failure. Can they rely on continuous royalties if the show gets a bad review from lesser-advantaged presentations? They can cite many examples to support this view.

Yet there are instances when a courageous touch of originality have actually improved the import. How to breech the impasse – is a puzzlement.

CHAPTER 51

DIRECTION AND MISDIRECTION, PLANTING AND POINTING

George M. Cohan wrote and directed a play with, the story goes, a good second and third act. But the first act, because of complicated exposition, was boring. So, on opening night, the curtain went up on an empty stage. A man entered, looked around, went to the desk, opened a drawer, took out a revolver, checked that it was loaded, heard someone coming, put back the handgun, closed the drawer, and innocently chatted to the lady who entered.

All first act, the background to the plot was described. At interval, the audience speculated, "She's going to kill her uncle", "No, it's the paternal grandfather who will shoot the maid's illegitimate son – his grandson". "No, ..." At the bell, the audience raced back to their seats, where they remained to the final curtain. The gun never again appeared. Nobody shot anybody.

That 'pistol in the drawer', has become famous as an example of the device, 'to direct attention'. To infer. To tantalise. To whet one's appetite. In other words, to escort the audience's attention from one image to a possible next, a key device of a time art.

It is also a superb example of the process of *planting*. Only in this instance, there was no relevant tag or payoff.

If you were standing in front of a painting in a gallery, you might want to peruse it at your leisure. But if it is a conducted tour, the guide has to pull you away to the next painting so that he can get back to escort the next group. So the guide might say, "However, his real genius came to the surface in this next work", or some such. And you will be tempted to move on. He directed us toward the next item. Performers do this all the time. Or else the audience would drag behind.

That pistol in the drawer was at the same time a great example of *misdirection*. Sending us for a trip up the garden path so that we are out of the way while the house is robbed. A diversion. A wild goose chase. A cover-up.

A good bit of Misdirection must also be a good bit of Direction. Whatever is up that garden path must promise to be fascinating. Naming the function 'direction', or 'misdirection', really depends on your main reason. Do you want to draw attention *to* something or *away* from something?

One rather underhand use for these twin devices was exemplified by the way the bass Chaliapin visualised that mouse walking along the foots, thus distracting from the tenor's aria. This particular application of the two is called 'fly-catching', probably because it was first named when an actor, during someone else's big scene, persistently tried to swat an imaginary fly. (Sometimes that cruel technique has been mistakenly called 'upstaging' as chapter 6 points out.) Nevertheless it is a good example of 'scene-stealing' using direction and misdirection.

The process usually involves Plants and Pointers. A Plant is the concept you wish the audience to notice however subtly. A Pointer is a device for drawing attention to a plant or any other theatrical component or direction. The most obvious Pointer is merely to point with your finger. Provided of course, that you have straight fingers.

Another Pointer is your direction of looking. We refer again to the practical joke of standing on a corner, looking up at a building or the sky. Someone is bound to get caught. Of course, as with all pointing, the more pointers, the more directed is the attention.

A standard Plant, on the other hand,is a dynamic action, motivation, concept, form or happening. Remember, dynamic is another name for attention-getting. In this instance, the dynamic prop or happening is also insinuating or suggesting. It contains a built-in promise. Somebody produces a gun. We know that guns don't normally get flourished like pocket-combs or lipsticks. Before a gun is produced, there is usually some life or death reason. So, when a gun is seen, we can be forgiven if we wonder whose life or death it is. Anyway, we are left to speculate.

When a conjurer makes an egg disappear, then with one hand makes a few mystical passes, showing first one side of his hand, then the other, we can be led to believe that the egg will reappear in that empty hand. Particularly, if he keeps looking at that active hand as well. He is both planting an idea and pointing up his hand. Now, while we peer suspiciously to detect how the egg will be retrieved, his other hand is probably sneaking a bird from under his cape. Here, direction is employed as misdirection. It keeps your attention away from where the bird is kept, and from the free hand of the conjurer. In addition, the idea of an egg reappearing was planted in our minds. And when a bird appeared, we realised that a joke was played on us. He has pulled a switch on us.

Dialogue is often a pointer. Something as simple as "Here he is now", can cause people to expect and pay attention to his direction of entry. But probably the most constant and effective pointer is also the most subtle. A thoroughly performed action on another person, or on any object other than oneself. Take a line like, "Oh my God, did *you* do that?" Out of the mouth of a vocaliser, someone in love with the sound of his own voice, it could well be a *dray*matic reading. We might be impelled to either keep looking at him as if to say, "Well read", or turn to one another to comment on his eloquent 'acting'. It becomes 'a speech'.

Coming out of the mouth of a strong action player, we will be tempted to turn to whomever it could be directed to, to see what the answer will be. The way the action is played becomes a pointer. Watching an audience watching a pair of strong action players is like watching the crowd at a good tennis match.

It probably hasn't escaped your notice that the fully committed action *also* serves to plant. Haven't we noticed how quickly and expectantly we turn to the player *receiving* the ball? What is it we expect this tennis player to do? Miss? Score? Then whatever does happen fulfils the planted notion or frustrates it. So too with actors.

There are many devices in theatre that are used as pointers, many of them technical. Lights, costume, staging, sound. The major real changeable component in the development of theatre would seem to lie in the area of novel techniques for creating dynamics. Subsequently, these can become pointers. Actions and motivations would seem to have remained constant throughout history. Only the new technologies, with which the same old actions are carried out, seem to change. When spectacular movements of scenery and people, laser, quadraphonic or multiphonic sound, smellorama, smoke and strobe have done their bit, something else will come along to play with.

One instance of a lighting pointer might be mentioned. In the play ***Angel Street***, (later filmed as ***Gaslight***), there is a scene where the detective has been helping the distraught wife. Suddenly they hear the husband returning. The detective must not be found here, so he quickly gathers up his personal effects and is about to sneak out. However, he has forgotten his hat, which is on the table. He seems to be managing to get out *just* as the husband is about to appear. But Abe Feder, my old lighting teacher who lit this show, had devised the subtlest of spotlights to just emphasise the forgotten hat. I believe no performance went by without people in the audience calling out, "Your hat! You forgot your hat!" Which of course was retrieved in the nick of time.

Some attention should be given to subtle pointers which intend to underscore a point, but which do not necessarily direct or misdirect. They don't have to promise anything, but they do give emphasis to words, ideas, or objects.

In fact, their use is called 'pointing up'. A gag, a name, an idea is nudged to the attention of the audience or any other recipient of an action. Indeed, the most obvious device is actually a nudge. Or saying one word more loudly or 'significantly' than the others. Or with a wink. Or a too-long look. Yet in adept hands, it can be as subtle as the most insinuating poetry.

In the hands of most of us, it can look arch, nudge-nudge, wink wink, heavy-handed, just plain tasteless or patronising. As if the performer continually appeals with, "Did you get it? You know what I mean?" It takes considerable practice to lean deftly on a word or phrase, so subtly that it seems to be a throwaway. The difference between fencing with feathers or bludgeons.

There is a truism that every play has its key scene, every scene has its key speech, every speech has its key sentence, and every sentence has its key word. The ability to bring these out, or point them up, without revealing your machinations, is the work of artistry.

The difference between subtle bitchery and sophomoric sarcasm.

The difference between true satire and ribald burlesque.

The difference between fine and rough.

Once you have mastered how to point up on a throwaway, there is little difficulty with handling pointers of any size. Including those for directing and misdirecting.

When you can deftly reply to the squelcher "age before beauty", with the topper, "pearls before swine," without sneering, rubbing it in, hammering it home, or taking a bow to any onlooker, you may be getting the hang of it. Without that skill, Dorothy Parker, Oscar Wilde, Noel Coward, or even Moliere may be replicated too ponderously.

A good throwaway is hard to time. If a laugh does occur, it might not be right away. The audience may not know fully the implications of what has been said until perhaps a little while later. So, when they do laugh, it may interrupt a speech further along. If on the other hand, you have added just the slightest pointer to the throwaway, you tend to get the laugh out of the way at the proper time. More on timing later. Other devices for pointing up may include: a short pause before or after: a quick look out of the ordinary: a slower, more spelled out reading of the words: an interruption in the flow of behaviour: a move on the line: coincidentally producing a prop: a shrug: a smile: slight variation in volume or tone: or a special emotional colouring. But *subtly*! All these, if not delicately handled, can often be seen as a comment on one's own behaviour. This is *always* tricky unless the character or scene is supposed to be seen that way. Generally, comment on what others do if you must, but beware of commenting on what *you* do, like laughing at your own jokes. Or patting yourself on the back. Or nodding approvingly after having done something. Or stamping your foot, or grimacing or snapping your fingers in frustration if you think you said the wrong thing, or something the wrong way. That's for amateurs and bad professionals. Why? Because if nothing else, you are drawing attention to your crafty wheels turning. What's more, you are depriving the audience of the adventure of responding to you as a function of discovering the natural evolution of the scene. You are force-feeding a prefabricated response down their throats telling them how they should react, behaviour which to the judicious can be patronising, offensive and generally off-putting.

In summary, pointers for directing the attention to relevant elements that assist in clarifying the unfolding of the play are germane to the time art. Not that they do not exist in other arts. But they are dispensed differently. In a painting, for example, at first glance, the eye may be caught by a bright object, dab of colour, intriguing image or symbol. Then as we look at it, some line in it leads our eye to another point or mass not quite as attention-grabbing but still somewhat noteworthy. And as we turn our attention to it, some element points us to where nearby is still another eye-catcher, then another, until our attention is finally brought around to some detail which perhaps summarises the essence of the painting.

In the process of arriving at that more subtle point, the eye has moved over some rhythmic pattern, the rhythm itself insinuating some emotional associations. With the average Botticelli, the eye will have taken a sensuously curved route. In ***Guernica***, the eye zigs and zags. Each attractive point functions as a pointer to provide the painting with rhythm and movement, much as they do in theatre. But in a painting, they are there all the time waiting for the viewer to discover them at leisure. With a time art, the artist doles out the points to be picked up in the artist's design of when, Now, then, – wait for it, – now, then, quickly now, now and hold it – wait – wait, NOW.

Now 'planting' is what the pointer often points at. We may plant an idea for immediate consumption (like the set-up for a gag) or for a delayed assimilation (where the audience says, later in the play, "Of course. *that's* why she didn't want to play tennis in the first scene. She'd just had an abortion!") Or we may plant so subtly that the idea registers only in the subliminal unconscious, like promotional signs around a sports field.

We elaborate on this in later chapters. For now, let it be said that one has to take into account four considerations at least.

- How dynamic is the concept to be planted, in its own right?
- How soon and significantly do you want this to register in the audience's mind?
- What possibly distracting elements are there in the scene?
- How much effort in planting or pointing up therefore would be in order?

By itself, a handkerchief is less attention-getting than a gun. A supplementary action played on a dynamic object will suggest less immediacy or urgency than a mainline action. As will a lower key motivation.

A gun produced in an arsenal crammed with guns is not generally noteworthy. A gun produced in a church or a library is. But even if you want to draw attention to a drawn gun in an arsenal, perhaps you can do it extra quickly or slowly, or with a flourish or a shout. The tightest productions tend to pay special attention to the pattern of plants and pointers, particularly if all kinds of twists and turns are involved. Ideally, nothing should seem dragged in, fortuitous or just convenient. Every noticeable development in the production should be preceded by the earlier planting of the seeds of that development.

Imagine a tightly knit murder mystery where the baddy is finally exposed and is about to escape when, by a strange coincidence, a policeman *just* happens to be passing by and drops in to sell tickets to the Police Ball. If neither the policeman nor the Ball had earlier been planted somehow, what a cop-out. 'Contrived' we may want to say.

There is the argument that says that the whole idea of deliberate pointing or planting is unnecessary. If you are clear in your own mind of what you are trying to communicate, then the formal shape of things will take care of itself. This might be seen as a similar argument to a songwriter saying if you find the right lyrics, the music will compose itself. And yet so often this seems to be proven correct. It would seem that the simplest allusion to some idea could get a marked reaction from an audience without the actor having raised the subject before.

In such instances there will have actually been planting, but not by the actors. The audience may arrive pre-planted by everyday circumstances. All then that is required with a primed audience is the tag. Like a one-liner. If a politician is believed to be the reason for a depressed economy, say, the mere ironic mention of that person may have all the effect intended.

So much satire depends on the prevailing state of the audience. When one matches the tags with the pre-planted state of mind, the play can be seen as 'right' for that audience. One definition of the classic play is that it brings to the surface attitudes in us that life itself has planted in virtually everyone. Who doesn't have a built-in worry about death, being replaced, mutilation, sterility, rejection, etc?

So though the actors have not done the planting,they should still be aware of the audiences' loadings. Otherwise the plant itself may get the response reserved for the tag. "What an audience. They're laughing at the straight lines." Maybe the scripted plant were better mumbled. Maybe the tag is no longer necessary. Maybe we can get another laugh from the tag. We must size up our audience.

Finally, we must consider that portion of direction-misdirection which was clumsily solved by introducing a just-happened-to-be-passing policeman. This is the 'tag'. In a drama, often referred to as the *payoff* or the *denouement*. That is what finally transpires after the key or crucial pointed-up plant has undergone its last twist and turn, often within a range of some expectancy.

In some drama and in most comedy, the tag occurs as an unexpected development. In which case we may refer to it as a 'switch', or 'gag' or sometimes 'pay-off', 'though these are more frequently talked of only in comedy. The tag can be thrown away, deftly but clearly, or may require a degree of flogging. So much depends on the number of plants and pointers, how heavy and how recent.

Casey Robinson, the screen writer responsible for some notable contributions to the Golden Years of Hollywood, believed every film should have a theme, motif or what we refer to as a spine. To ensure that the audience had sufficient clues to help prompt an awareness of the spine, he always posted at least three flags. The first would be a plant early in the film with some character tossing in the words almost as a throwaway. Then about halfway through the film that motif might be pointed up perhaps as part of some passing joke. Finally, at the end we might get it as a seriously stated summary or musing. The tag.

See if you can't find these in the next TV re-run of ***Dark Victory***, ***King's Row***, ***Snows of Kiliamanjaro*** or even ***Casablanca***.

WRITE YOUR OWN NOTES

CHAPTER 52

COMEDY, DRAMA AND TIMING

Call this ***The Tales Of Two In A City***.

A certain performer never managed to appear on Broadway, although he auditioned well and was often given the job. But during rehearsals, the axe always fell. If it wasn't that his scene was cut, it could be because he was too good in his scene with the star. Or he refused a personal 'invitation' from the director. Or the show closed in rehearsal. Always something. He was regarded as jinxed.

So, when once more he was cast, he decided to break the jinx. For every terror-filled minute of his five-day probationary period he avoided every pitfall. And at the end of that period, he was still in the show.

He arrived home to find all his friends eager to celebrate the breaking of the jinx. "But," he reminded them, "they still have until midnight to fire me". So everyone sat around glumly filling in the hours, and sure enough, 11.55p.m. there was a knock on the door, and a voice called, "Telegram".

His friends urged him to forestall going to the door until the legal time expired and they would be witness ... "No", said our friend. "What will be, will be". So he went to the door as his friends sadly retrieved their coats.

Suddenly there was a shriek from the door followed by hysterical laughter, "Hey, fellers ... my mother died!"

There is the other instance of a young guy from the small town of Hillville in Ohio. He was an only child living with his mother. His father had abandoned them when he was three years old.

She had supported the two of them as a charwoman at the town hall and by taking in the occasional bit of laundry. She had insisted that he had the talent to make it big in the theatre, for which he did seem to show some talent. So when he was eighteen, she packed him off to New York, insisting on funding him from her own earnings.

The boy was obviously in two minds about all this but he accepted on condition that if, one day, he did make it big, he would more than compensate her for her sacrifice.

In New York he studied, augmenting his small subsidy from home by washing dishes, sorting mail, and occasionally gaining a walk-on role in some nondescript off-off-off-Broadway production.

Then it happened. When he was twenty-one, he was spotted doing his brief bit in such an off-off-off Broadway production and was offered the juvenile lead in a Broadway drama.

He was unable to get his mother on the phone, but did manage to contact a neighbour. Then it was that it was hinted – with great reluctance – that his mother wasn't well, that she had long ago lost her job scrubbing floors, and was earning her way, and his, doing much more demeaning work. But he was sworn to confidence.

So when he finally did contact his mother, they spoke only of his great break and just in passing she admitted that her tired voice was due to just a "touch of flu" and she'd be fine shortly. Then he did the noble thing. He offered to come home.

She tearfully insisted that all past efforts would have been wasted if he did. He must persevere! This was the great once in a lifetime break! He gave in.

They talked only once during rehearsals. Her 'flu' was hanging on a bit longer than she expected. But she rallied him on.

Opening night seemed a triumph! However, no one could be sure until the reviews came out. He stayed up all night to catch them and – sure enough – his career was heralded and properly launched. So early in the morning though it was, he phoned his mother. After ringing for several minutes, a female voice answered. But it wasn't hers.

Now, we have two stories. About different people? They could be the same people with a story told differently. Oh, a few small details are pulled around. Dramatic licence. But do they produce the same effect?

What's the difference in the telling?

Comedy and drama are made of the same stuff.

Drama presents a worrisome, or threatening, or guilt-laden situation in frank confrontational terms. Here is the problem. Solve it if you can. The consequences of misjudging or otherwise not succeeding in solving the problem(s) can be more dire yet than they are now.

In drama, there is a fighting chance of salvation. Usually somebody wins out. In tragedy, there is only a slight chance. Doom seems a foregone conclusion. Usually nobody wins out. In most comedies almost everybody wins.

When the audience identifies with these problems and or the people involved, they make the issues their own. Chances are that the audience came in with these very problems or some equivalent.

A woman needn't have scrubbed floors to maintain her family in order to identify. She might have simply missed out on some small pleasure so that somebody else would benefit. That could be enough for her to identify with a charwoman putting her son through school and into a career. And an enactment will bring to the surface a lot of unspoken and possibly unrecognised turbulence that was never resolved. Even a small inner conflict can fester and irritate if it remains long repressed. And a guy needn't have had this much sacrifice put his way in order to tap the latent guilt that most children can feel. The mere fact that parents have supported them at all can be enough for identification!

So when we tell or act out a drama, we point up those emotive concepts that accentuate sacrifice, humiliation, disability and possibly ultimate reward. We try to misdirect the attention from details that could minimise or defuse these in any way. Oh, just an occasional ironic touch of lightness to imply coping with difficulties. But not too much. One can cope too successfully.

Right into comedy.

In comedy, we also start with identification. But in comedy, we disarm the threat. Either by making the threatening situation less dangerous, the threatener less effectual, or our ability to cope more invincible. Like Superman, Indiana Jones or Crocodile Dundee. We are more able to pluck the barb. We can make injury less hurtful, humiliation less permanent, (or else it is happening to the other fellow) and even death, or the threat of death, can seem like fun and socially presentable.

If somebody falls down a flight of stairs and just lies there in a pool of blood, that is something most of us would rather not have happen to us. But, if they fell down a flight of steps, arms and legs flailing, and at the bottom they got up, dusted themselves off, and maybe even kicked the stairs before strolling away unharmed, that can be funny. Likewise, slipping on banana skins, tripping over furniture, falling in the water. If presented in a way that we thumb our noses at death, we have reduced a threatening incident to a harmless one.

One physiologist friend described laughter from comedy as follows: if you are startled, you gasp. If you feel relieved, you sigh. If both stimuli come at you virtually at the same time, you have diaphragmic convulsions. That emerges as either panting or laughter. Whether we believe it or not, it sounds nice. In any event try to find anything you think is funny but without something about it actually involving a very serious issue. Threatening, in fact.

Whatever we laugh at seems to relate to some subject which, if taken seriously would generate in us fear, guilt, anxiety, dislocation, confusion, insecurity, disgust, or some such. Even puns would relate to a threat to our ability to communicate coherently. Suddenly words no longer mean what they are intended to mean. That's like going mad. Then if the pun also insinuates some forbidden associations, such as sexually repressed ideas, they are all the funnier.

The skills and techniques for handling the wide range of comic situations is a discussion beyond the limits of a few paragraphs.

But a few general observations can be made for handling an average comic moment.

First, select or identify a topic which could represent a threat to the audience targeted. In other words, know which bits are expected to be exploited for humour.

Second, point up the threat in the setup of the joke.

Third, time the assimilation of that inference. Give the audience just enough time to get as much of the point as you want them to. Usually, that means involving them in the seriousness of the plant, but leading them up the garden path as to how the threat will be resolved.

Fourth, pull the tag or punch-line which defuses the threat just before the group twigs. Usually, this is the switch. Generally, the most effective tags are told innocently. Or with the attitude of "This *is* how you interpreted the issue, isn't it? Because that's how I meant it. So why are you laughing?" There is another attitude that some employ on the switch, and that is "I caught you that time, didn't I? Wasn't that funny?" This one I find often employed in dramas where someone makes an ineffectual joke in a feeble attempt to lift some depressive out of their doldrums.

The more repressed the threatened association, the greater the possibility of laughter. It remains for the comic to explore that possibility.

In material already written for comedy, the performer's skills involve making the right choice of which ideas are threatening and may need pointing up. Or even planting. Or which ideas actually may hint at the defuser so that one may direct attention away from that issue and avoid tipping the gag. And, of course any other idea we might want to point up which can be used for possibly embellishing the misdirected idea. Like a smokescreen. Or a decoy.

Fifth, do nothing to defuse it before the threat has been adequately established. A good gag-killer is to announce "This is a joke", or, "This is funny". That would be perhaps second only to reciting the punchline before telling the gag. In other words, don't telegraph the gag.

Sixth, gags are best told if they are designed to amuse the listener rather than the speaker. Try to catch the listener off guard. Try not to laugh at your own jokes, or comment in any other way on your telling of them. And don't force or overpoint. And this relates to spoken, visual, situational, one line, and any kind of comedy one can think of.

And don't expect to become a funny-man from reading a book. There is nothing that will spare you from making it happen in front of audiences. We all have to lay our own eggs. These words are merely guidelines – you may even discover that they might not apply in your case.

And as for drama. Just don't pluck the barb. If anything, sink the threat deeper. Drama is the attempt to resolve some threatening situation, with barbs intact.

Generally, drama brings to the surface situations and issues that cannot be avoided or relieved by escape into fantasy. But there is nothing in the dramatic play that says one can't *try* to escape into fantasy. To remain a drama, the trier just doesn't succeed in laughing it off.

How heavy do these situations have to be to rate as dramas? Maybe not heavy at all to start with. Because a drama will build. By virtue of conflict.

All theatre needs conflict. So, even if there is a dispute about which TV show to watch, so long as conflict persists, the argument should increase in dynamics. The characters may not succeed in kidding their way back to peace. The loading in the arguments is always serious or important. Murders have been committed over disputes about which show to watch. Fencing one's way out of serious issues with real, sharp swords can identify drama in comparison to comedy's fencing with a feather versus a rubber sword.

How does timing relate to a moment of drama?

Similarly to the way we toy with the audience in comedy. But before there is the need for the equivalent 'surprise' timing to be done, we should set up the circumstances. Sometimes the situation is planted in a way virtually the converse from the playing of comedy. It is not unusual to decide that where in comedy the values are heavy, in drama we can make them light. And in comedy,where values are light, in drama we might make them heavy. I suggest you read this paragraph again after you have finished this chapter.

Otherwise, procedures applying to drama approximate what applies to comedy. A typical dramatic moment might be dealt with as follows:

First, deal with considerations that are not threatening to the audience. An important identifiable problem, but soluble.

Second, lead the audience toward a promised solution.

Third, time the acceptance of the solution.

Fourth, spring disaster or some conflicting obstruction that frustrates the easy solution, and which *can* be threatening to the audience.

Fifth, don't promise disaster during the setup.

Sixth, try to win audience empathy. Make them sorry for you. Unless it is a quirk of the character, *don't feel sorry for yourself*. If you do, the audience will tend to think you are feeling sorry enough for all of us. No need for us to feel sorry as well. If you wish to win empathy *try to cope*. Don't wallow, don't suffer, don't wear your heart on your sleeve.

When you do manage to feel deeply miserable as a result of the dramatic upset, play against it. Try to find the funny side. Under no circumstances gild the gold, paint the lily, nor gild the lily. Empathy comes best when you generate the real, deep suffering but *try to cope*. If you honestly try to lift a piano the audience will strain on your behalf. Trust playing against the grief!

And do remember Argentina's pursuit of opposites: the touch of the slut in the queen, the touch of queen in the slut. To which we might add, the seriousness in comedy as well as the comedy in drama. Otherwise it can become Grim and Earnest. Of course, if that's what you want ...

Apropos timing, it is a constant source of bemusement how so many cognoscente throw that word around. "What great timing!" one often hears as one leaves the theatre.

Thinking back to what they refer to, one is often unable to endorse the observation. One can remember a whole string of moments when the performer walked into laughs, let the audience get ahead of him, anticipated a cue. But one does recall how clearly various pointers along the way were delivered. And fairly subtly at that. One would be led to say that the pointing was expert while the timing was actually lousy. In the absence of clear parameters, words lose their meanings.

What then is timing? It is the recognition of the amount of time for a given response to occur, usually as intended, and the skill to proceed with the next moment at that point of completion. What responses are we talking about?

It can be a response to an action, in which case we might perceive that the objective has been satisfactorily achieved. It can be response to an adjustment or a feeling in which case we must quickly judge what it is we believe is an adequate response.

It can be a response to a by-product, a visual effect, an accident, a costume. Virtually anything that can affect an audience will have to be taken into account if we expect to control their progress through the play. Or put another way, anything that took time to affect the audience, and where that time had to be allowed for.

Even the simple example of the curtain going up on a spectacular set which causes the audience to gasp or applaud. If dialogue is spoken at that very moment of applause, it well may be lost. That is bad timing. One should even consider giving the audience a bit of extra time to be affected by the spectacle.

Much of the stimuli we know we provide deliberately. But, if the audience laughs because a performer inadvertently tripped coming onstage, we must still allow for the laugh. We cannot continue speaking while they are laughing because they simply will not hear us. The speech is wasted. *Don't walk into a laugh*! Let it take its course. How the voice of early vaudevillian friends rings in the ears: "Wait for it!"

A special point should be discussed here. How long do you ride out a laugh?

Some say you wait for the laugh to reach its peak, then as it starts to diminish you read your next line. Some say, wait for the laugh to finish completely. Then go on. Some prefer to plough on regardless of laugh or no laugh.

My vote goes to waiting it out completely, *Unless there are special circumstances*. If you have a strong voice, a PA system, expendable dialogue or simply visual business with which to cut across even moderate laughter, you risk frustrating the audience so that for the next while they are asking each other "What did he say, what did he say?" Or if you are trying to squelch their laughter so that they can save some of it for a better gag to come, OK. But let's save such tricks for another book.

Space forbids properly discussing actors' responses to audience responses. Let's simply generalise and nibble around the edges.

The following responses can be quite obvious even to the inexperienced: applause, laughter, a gasp, weeping, fanning themselves with programmes, whispering or talking together, calling out, walking out of the theatre or deadly slow clapping. One fellow went a bit far during one of my performances and died.

More often than not, the responses are so subtle as to require guesswork. Often we want the audience to simply comprehend what we say to them. Or to see our point of view. Or to interpret what we say in a special way. What signals can we reliably count on that will tell us "They got that, now go on"?

If we can see and hear any portion of the audience clearly, we might detect the same sort of body language we can recognise in a face-to-face encounter. Subtle nods, smiles, frowns, moving of the head, thinning of lips, looking away, sitting forward, slumping back, stillness, general agitation, and the like. Many of these can be detected in intimate theatre out of the corner of one's eyes and ears.

But blinded with lights and with an audience further removed, one fumbles more. We may find ourselves having to guess by the varying qualities of silence. Yes, it does range from dead silence to faint restless murmurs and squeaking of seats.

To help us in our guesswork, we tend to first call on our friendly pointers. We try an early foray by nudging ever so slightly one of the potentially important issues with a certain degree of explicitness. Then listen for more obvious responses several speeches down the line, responses which depend on the clarity of the earlier speech. How much of the audience seemed to cotton on? Only the audience down front? Maybe you aren't loud enough. Turn up your volume a bit. Now we are getting some more obvious responses from most of the house but not the back: speak louder.

Are we getting scattered responses from everywhere in the house? Maybe we aren't allowing enough time for our points. It could be an averagely obtuse house. Perhaps we aren't nudging the key lines hard enough? Too hard? We hear groans, or their responses are less frequent as we spell out more. Yes, sounds like too hard. We are over-working.

Right, we have come to some equation about what set-ups it takes to activate the audience. Now for the time aspect. Given that they now think that something is shocking, how long before they gasp? Several seconds? That could mean a slow house. Instantly? A quick house. Even before you have finished the speech? You may be overpointing. You could be telegraphing your punch. Giving it away too soon in some way. Or they simply could be a very quick house. Or they've seen the show before.

Bit by bit you get the measure of the audience. Or, if others have been on before you, listening to them settling in with the audience can save you considerable effort. You may know the audience before you step on stage.

Almost every audience will provide the performer with some accessible touchstone areas where he can get their measure. Granted, some audiences would seem to be almost totally feed-back devoid. Like some matinee audiences mentioned earlier. In which case one might point up and time the material as if the audience were full of certain average people you know of similar age and background. One very fine performer, when he found it hard to define his audience, imagined it was full or Rotarians.

That is a problem in radio and TV. How does one emphasise or time one's communication attempts without actually perceiving the feedback? One of the best radio men in Australia, Robert Peach, imagined he was talking to his wife. Talkback radio has done wonders in helping radio personalities to acquire some norms against which to average output. Television and radio audiences are often prompted to laugh and applaud, not simply to make the sponsor think his money is well spent but to provide feedback, albeit phoney, to help the performers' timing. Even canned laughter can be useful.

Most of the time we find pointing and timing working together. Sometimes each does a successful job. While it is pointing that suggests what is the key issue, it is timing which allows for the audience to comprehend that issue to the extent that you want them to. If you want a cursory appreciation, give them less time than for a deeper appreciation.

Now, let's see these work.

Remember: you set up an identifiable situation. Or if it is already there, you point it up. Then after giving it a chance to sink in, you pull the tag.

Did we ever finish the tale of the young actor who's mother funded him until he got his first big break? Anyway ...

This woman's voice, which answered his mother's phone, told him that she had just bought the business from his mother who, in the past two years, had managed to establish the most successful brothel in the county: that his mother had just run off with the sheriff who had abandoned his wife of thirty two years and their eight children: that his mother would be phoning him from Mexico in about a week: but she had left a message to tell him that there was no truth to the rumour that she was the secret backer of his new show.

WRITE YOUR OWN NOTES

CHAPTER 53

THE IMPOSSIBLE SCENE

Let's look at a 'two-scene'.

This is where two characters relate to only each other. And each character has a choice of objects onto which he can play some action. He can play on himself, he can play on the other actor and he can play on their relationship. And on props of course.

Obviously, the other actor is a clearly defined object. As this actor is played upon, his responses can be clearly seen. Thus, the way the action is played can be clearly guided by those responses.

Playing on oneself is a bit trickier. One may try to persuade oneself to take a sickie. But one's conscience can make itself felt in reply. However, perhaps not as clearly as one detects feedback in another person. Nonetheless, quite detectable.

Playing an action on a relationship is trickier still. Let's say it is a friendship. This is shared by both participants. Suppose I want to enrich the friendship. I might say glowing words, but the results of those words are hard to detect in that ephemeral bond between us. But I see a bit of it in my friend and some in myself in wavering surges of enthusiasm. But I can visualise a concept of friendship, which may be getting richer as I talk. A faint image, but still, discernible.

Assuming we leave props and other objects out of this exercise for the moment, we can see that I can play on three possible objects (me, my friend and our friendship) and so can my friend (himself, me and our friendship). Between us, we can choose between six possible objects of actions to engage in a scene. And having them available doesn't necessarily confine us to playing on them one at a time. I could be playing a mainline action on him while at the same time playing supplementaries on myself and our friendship. It would keep me busy, but I'm sure I could do it. And I trust so can he.

That is, if we wish to engage in a *rich* and *versatile* exchange. No more baby-stuff here. No more either/or. Mainlines ***and*** supplementaries, all being juggled at once!

A moment later we switch. I play a mainline on myself, like to recall the message I neglected to give him, while at the same time playing supplementaries on him (to apologise) and on our relationship (to keep it from snapping). He pulls similar switches, and we are making artistic music. He of course chooses to conflict with me on at least one level. Maybe he plays the mainline 'to chide' me, thus conflicting with my supplementary on him – 'to apologise'. At any rate, the possibilities for structuring our scene with gross and fine detail is not unlike two pianists, each simultaneously playing piano and an harmonica. Four hands and two mouths, all harmonising. Wow!

Silly? You ain't seen nothing yet. Silly though it seems, this is what two very skilled actors can in fact do. And the results can be entrancing.

But now, let's add just one more character. How much more busy can this – we'll call it a 'three-scene' – be? Shall we guess: half again as busy? Brace yourself. Let's refer to them as Characters A,B and C.

Character A can play on:

(1) Character B
(2) Character C
(3) Himself
(4) The relationship between himself and B
(5) The relationship between himself and C
(6) The relationship between B and C
(7) B and C ganged up against him
(8) B against himself and C as a gang
(9) C against himself and B as a gang
(10) The relationship between himself and the ganged up B and C
(11) The relationship between himself ganged with B against C
(12) The relationship between himself ganged with C against B
(13) The relationship between himself and the entire gang

And that's only Character A's mainline choices. Let both B and C operate similarly and we could have any 3 of 39 possible objects of mainline actions being impinged upon at any given moment.

Offering the actor such a range of choices should be welcomed. But then if we add supplementaries, it could mean that each actor would have to keep one mainline and twelve supplementaries going at all times. And then of course control their switching from moment to moment. And all of them locked in synchronously. Who will volunteer to try this?

I don't know of any actor capable of sustaining more than about one mainline and five supplemenary actions at any apparently same moment. (We know supplementaries are quickly juggled bits and not really simultaneous.) So who can learn to exploit the full potential of a three-scene?

Not I. But what we can do is, that in knowing that each of those objects is available to be played upon, we can dance around and land on any of them when useful. This offers us versatility galore and rich virtuosity for the taking. A trio can sound like a full orchestra. Even without involving ourselves with props, each of us has the choice more than a dozen objects with objectives to match.

Even the mainline-plus-one-supplementary conflicts played between A, B and C can give an overwhelming impression if controlled. (Let's ignore gangs and relationships for the moment.) Mind you, they must be truly interlocked conflicts. For example, A has to play an action on B, like 'to accuse', and on C 'to sabotage'. B could play 'deny' on A and 'appeal' to C. C could play 'to disassociate' on B, while trying 'to ingratiate' on A. You might care to draw a diagram on paper: then you can see conflicts between each of them, as each plays one of their actions as a mainline and the other as a supplementary. Then when they switch, mainline becomes supplementary and vice versa.

Not many authors can write a good three-scene. Simply because there are three people in a scene doesn't necessarily make it a three-scene. More usually they are 'ganged two-scenes', (two against one) with no flexibility for swapping around. Or else they are tug-o-wars: one in the middle being pulled in two different directions, but no interaction between the pullers.

And even if authors did write them, not many actors can play them. Not well enough, I hasten to qualify. Unknowingly, most performers are only a hand-span away from being able to play three scenes. Because the process of performing can be seen as *almost* a three scene. The audience is the third character. Mind you, they can't be relied upon to offer conflicting actions, but every now and then, such conflicts do happen.

At any rate, being aware of the rich potential of the three-scene, performers should feel free to explore their relationships in depth and theoretically should never feel they have gone as far as they can go in a play. Even if the author has not written them as such, it is often possible to conceive most trios of actors as three-scenes. All it takes is a little clever action-plotting and the skill of playing supplementaries.

With a challenge like that, how can anyone ever get bored no matter how long the play runs?

And should you ever plumb the depths of keeping a dozen or so actions going at once, there's always the four-scene.

WRITE YOUR OWN NOTES

CHAPTER 54

THE PERFORMANCE

Having studied for years, humiliated ourselves begging for work, at long last auditioned successfully, found an agent who contracted well for us, rehearsed for about a month to design and refine a whole catalogue of inventive bits and warm relationships in a sauce of tantalising incidents, we have finally arrived at that moment of truth. The well-prepared production. And now we are ready for that other moment of truth: ***The Performance***!

So all there is to do is to simply recreate what was achieved in rehearsal. Right? Well ...

In more doctrinaire days, there lived a mystery. If, as Lee Strasberg said, 'acting is responding to imagined stimuli', and there are so many great responders around, how come we aren't splashing around in a sea of great actors? Why is it that wherever we look, we aren't discovering great actors? Perhaps we might forgive the uninitiated average show-watchers for not recognising these fantasy-responders. But surely the average experienced theatrical should be able to spot them.

In which case, how come such universally-accepted top theatricals like Noel Coward get offside? How come he is purported to have left a Brando performance of ***Streetcar*** saying something like "A wonderful performance. I wish I knew what it was all about"? It was a comment on the dialogue. He couldn't hear much of it.

It was partly in answer to criticisms of this sort that Bobby Lewis reminded us "It's never good to be impressive but not clear". I don't think he was talking about the skill of creating enigmas and red herrings which deliberately mislead or confuse the audience so that all comes clear in the end. (With such skill Bobby has made a specialty of directing Agatha Christie's whodunits for TV.)

I think he may have been referring more particularly to the 'private' performance. It was I who was giving it at a final rehearsal. I was rendering a 'moment of truth', so intimately that no one past the third row could possibly know. Seeing all the subtleties much less hearing them would have been a feat of deduction for 95% of audience. *But I was truthful!* I was indeed responding to those imagined stimuli.

Let's be fair. Even people in the back rows would know that up there on stage, there was an actual happening. A total moment of involvement in cause and effect. Very much like one might observe out on the street when one sees one or two blocks away an actual altercation outside a pub. We know that people are squaring off for a fight, but we haven't a clue what it is all about. We can't hear their voices and the contenders are turned away from us or hidden behind each other. No opportunity to take sides if we wanted to.

True – one needn't see faces to recognise the rest of body language. But each portion of the body carries different portions of a message more tellingly. We are accustomed to depending on faces for certain parts of messages. Those may be the very parts we may most need to know at a certain moment.

I am put in mind here of the performance too often encountered, where the play builds to a moment of revelation, and the actor comes to the crunch so personally moved that when he utters the telling words we have waited two and a half hours to hear, they are strangled or mumbled to passionate extinction and we never know the payoff unless we then read the play or talk to somebody who sat in the front row. All the more exasperating when other evidences testify that here indeed *was* a moment of inventive, possibly exciting truth, but we were not allowed to share it!

Actually, the above sentences should have referred to *artistic truth*. Because the entire performance is structured on lies which – as Harold Clurman said – are "Lies like Truth". But in these unclear circumstances, one should baulk at employing the adjective 'artistic'. Something in the art is missing. That portion which deals with communication with the audience. What is absent is *display*, if that is not too disruptive a notion.

There are performers, as we said before, who regard the audience as a necessary evil. They intrude upon the actors' indulgences. They are there only to make the salary possible or to endorse what great actors these great actors are. Audiences should be humbly grateful that they have bestowed upon them the privilege of being allowed to witness these artists do their thing.

It is these who have bamboozled the rest of us into going along with their obvious philosophy that audiences were invented to serve the artist. While this may have indeed been true in certain ancient court theatres where, when some important noble lady insisted on displaying her new voice with wardrobe to match, others at court attended out of political survival. Or in church theatre, where to not attend imperilled one's soul. Such social injunctions persist to this day but mostly on opening nights. For the rest of it, and though it may sit uneasily on some of us, we come to the painful recognition that *we theatricals are there to serve the audiences*. That we cannot deservedly accept fullest credits for skillful, artistic truths unless a goodly portion of our artistry concerns the art of ensuring that the audience gets whatever it was they came to get. As fully as the design of the concept intended.

If there is a message in the play, let it be reasonably clear. Reasonably, because some in the audience may be slow on the uptake. If we over-flog the message, we alienate those who are quick on the uptake, who will then feel patronised. Every audience requires its own balance of subtlety versus explicitness.

Our job includes finding that measure. If there is a plot, likewise let it be clear. And, if an actor is undergoing a magic transition of indecision, let sufficient clues be accessible to all the audience so that if they can read clues, these are there to be read. And if they couldn't read clues any better than they would in everyday life, let them be surprised just as they would be in everyday life. Tailor the degree of access to order.

The art of *acting* involves turning ourselves on. The art of *performing* involves sharing or offering the results. The two do not automatically go together! Remember those actors who say, "If I create a moment of 'truth', even an intimate one, it will automatically come across". My own reply is "where and to whom?" In front of a camera, with a microphone 18 inches overhead and the camera pre-angled for optimum view and effect, most likely that assertion is true. But in theatre? Even in intimate theatre considerations of sightlines and volume are vital. For the average proscenium theatre, seating around 1,000 people, some intimate performances may just as well be played with the curtain down.

Sound, unless focused and reverberated, diminishes as the square of the distance. In other words, what can be just heard in the second row of an open air theatre may be lost in the seventh row. And where one may catch a noble profile if one is sitting centre in an auditorium, people to one side of the audience may be looking at the actor's full face, while someone on the other side may have a prize view of the actor's earhole.

And even at that, we are not simply going to leave it at the audience's access to the actor. While that may suffice for many plays, (those that are designed mainly for allowing the audience to experience our doings by peering over our shoulders,) there is more. Considerably more. And the artistry of handling all this and that 'more' is what converts an actor to a performer. *We are conjurers*! We create illusions for the entrancement or edification of the audience. Our acting is not an end in itself.

Along with the skill of manipulating ourselves and our fellow performer, we must acquire the skill of manipulating the audience. Sometimes we let them know they are being manipulated. As when we directly address an audience. Sometimes we pretend we don't know they are there and make them believe our pretence. But whatever we do, ultimately, *it is for the audience*. Some will read this statement as if I had said that everything we do is designed for the lowest common denominator in audience appreciation. *No* – not at all. One can be aware of different levels of access and arrange to communicate on each of those levels.

If all we were concerned with was simply seeing and hearing the actors, then most productions could end up as play-readings with gestures. Fortunately, we do not stop at that. There is a continual flow of gross and subtle details to fill the scene. Some of this detail is aimed specifically at the intellect of the audience. Some at their heart-strings. Likewise the audience's imagination and senses are catered for. And there should be enough accessible clues for a discerning audience to be able to recognise the work of the geniuses amidst a cast full of others.

What's so distinctive about a genius' performance? The genius manages to deliver, with complete authority, the widest and/or deepest range of elements in what seems to be the most compact – perhaps seemingly simple – package, and in a way that conceals the wheels. He often chooses some disarming incident of revelation so that the audience acquires illuminating and surprising insights while being caught off guard.

In ***Victor Victoria***, Julie Andrews establishes that she is starving. But the play is a satiric comedy. Also it is necessary for her character to be seem as a person of uncompromisable principles. Yet the script calls for her to offer her body to her disgusting landlord in exchange for a meatball. She would have to be pretty hungry for that. In which case, comedy could blur into drama. With a piece of business not much less ingenious than Charlie Chaplin eating his boot in ***The Goldrush***, the hungry girl scrapes at the droolings of gravy on the landlords bib and licks her finger in ecstasy. We laugh but we get the message and we empathise with her. I don't know whether that was an invention of the script or the director or some actor on the set. But if it was something Julie Andrews threw in, I would vote for endowing her with the touch of genius. A confirmed genius (like Chaplin) could be counted upon to deliver many such touches throughout his performances.

This would seem to be the appropriate moment to discuss that other phenomenon which most of us non-geniuses aspire to: the Inspired Performance, which even a good craftsman may occasionally render. Theatre aficionados often return to see the same production several times in the hope that this time they might catch that once-in-a-lifetime event. One might compare their avidity with those audiences who return to circuses in the hope that this time someone will fall off their trapeze.

What is this inspired performance? Certainly it is different from the others, which may range in quality from fair to excellent. But does the actor change staging? The script? Readings? Emotional loadings? Actions? Costumes? What?

That depends. If the production offers 'star' liberties to the performer, any or all of those may be pulled around during the actual performance. Both in kind and in depth. And on those inspired nights, perhaps they all fall together in a more coherent or illuminating way. In which case one might reasonably ask "Why can't that same new-found combination be retained for all performance?"

Because often, the performer himself may not know what actually transpired 'chemically' (or organically if you prefer) when these elements mixed this way for the first time. Thus the popularity of Alteration as a motivational technique. Performers use this one not only to keep fresh, but often to try to recapture a moment or a scene that once came to life in a very special way.

But there is the other end of the spectrum of performer's permissiveness. Suppose we may *not* deviate freely from what has been rehearsed. Just as the violinist playing a Brahms concerto may not take it upon himself to intersperse a few spectacular bars of the Tchaikovsky concerto. When we are not free to deviate, changes can occur here too. But they are of a more subtle variety. But effective and, I venture to propose, identifiable. A note played on a violin made by Stradivarius sounds not only the fundamental tone, but considerable richness of reverberation. The same note played on a $10 special reveals the fundamental note alright, but very little of rich reverberation.

Back to people.

Don't we know what it is to be mildly surprised as opposed to startlingly surprised? Mildly in love as opposed to passionately? Mildly angry as opposed to ferocious? But we also know what it's like to be *casually* mildly surprised as opposed to *seriously* mildly surprised. Two examples:

(1) Your next door neighbour whom you don't think is much of a brain has just been promoted to an executive position. Oh? Well, good luck to him. (And his company!) I didn't think he had it in him. Then it passes. In one ear and out the other.

(2) Down the street, we pass the postman who waves some letters. The inference is obviously that he has some mail for us which he will drop into our letter-box. Later we return home to find no letters. Also mild surprise. But we may keep on about it. It may stop us as we start to walk away. We may return to the box and look around on the ground. Or ask the family if anyone has emptied the box. Our total being may become preoccupied, even though we weren't expecting any important mail. Yet the issue is still a mild one: nowhere near a matter of life and death. But it has set in motion a whole lot of reverberations.

In performing, we meet big and small situations. The big ones can normally induce the startling, passionate or ferocious responses. As we did with the mild responses, let's ask of the strong ones now, how casually or seriously should the balance of our responses be to these.

We see a fetching photograph of a most attractive person. We are apt to feel, even as Jimmy Carter admitted he was capable of feeling, a strong lust. Then we turn the page and engross ourselves in a science-fiction story. No, we don't go on and on lusting over that picture. We'll lose no sleep. It was a quickie. But it *was* powerful while it lasted. And while it lasted, *not every bit of us got into the act.* Much of us could stand aside and remain detached. We retained more than enough clear mind to be able to move quite smoothly onto the next object of attention.

Now the ordinarily good performance can be full of such moments. Strong or weak involvements. And enough of ourselves responding to each to give it the required quality for a moment. And we have little difficulty moving along. Because the associations that these kindle will tend to be relatively few or casual. They do not seem to remind us of something which in turn reminds us of something which in turn reminds us of something else. We reverberate not unlike the cheap violin.

But the exceptional performance finds each moment setting in train a whole range of associations. Some conscious and many not. I smell a rose. Not only does it have a lovely smell, but now I also wonder how many variations in colour there would be even in the same variety, and do all roses bloom with the same design, and also, I wish my wife could smell this – I'm sure she'd love it, and isn't it sad that the rose blooms so briefly and then must die, and so must I and lose forever the capacity to smell roses or anything, and also, when I die I *will* smell but in the other sense of the word, and also, but then I might end up as fertiliser for perhaps some roses, and also, is not nature wondrous with its cycles of life and death, and also ... These associations could all occur within a few seconds.

Thus the average actor's response to a rose of "Oh yes, very pretty" is as nothing compared to the multicoloured bitter-sweet-comic responses of one who has allowed a simple encounter to resonate in many chambers. Like the sound in a Stradivarius.

And the richness of the moment involves both the performer and the audience so deeply that, when the next bit occurs, chances are that it catches us all by surprise. Like being interrupted in the midst of an interesting discussion. Also it takes a strong hand on the steering wheel to turn us toward the next bit. Like it was when we found no letters in the letter-box. Then, even as we sat down to make a phone-call, part of us still wondered "Did I mistake the postie's signal?" or "Did he put it in the wrong box?" or "Did someone steal the mail?" or, or, or ... A less sensitive responder would have discovered the empty mail-box and have done with it. No complexity of responses requiring that strong hand.

Understanding this, can we improve our chances of giving 'inspired' performances? I think yes. But we must remember that many resonating associations are unconscious. We can go for the conscious ones deliberately, assuming we are disciplined and nimble. But the unconscious ones have to be invited. Perhaps this was what Stanislavski meant when he suggested that truthful (relevant?) associations helped cultivate the soil in which inspiration could take root more readily.

At this point, you might well ask, "So what's the difference between the inspired performance and the genius one?"

As I see it, the difference is fundamentally in the choice of what one is performing. If the design of the role or the play is exceptionally demanding or multifaceted, and one carries that task out inspiredly, that to me would be genius workmanship. But if the task is relatively simple, when that is carried out exceptionally well as described above, full credits for an inspired performance and, as I see it, little more.

Surely it should be acknowledged that being able to build a cathedral single-handedly and brilliantly could be seen as a somewhat greater achievement than building a brilliant dog-house. Even the passing observation about that moment from ***Victor Victoria*** might be seen as building a microscope with which to see life (a cathedral), as opposed to what might have been done by another performer who simply looked at the gravy stains and was affected (a dog-house?). That might be seen as building a good magnifying lens.

So, while all that might be gleaned from a moment where an actor allows himself to become fully involved in some strong make-believes, the shaping and phrasing of that moment with the one before and the next one may not simply be determined by his own whim. The audience is in the act. It tells him when and how to proceed. Once again ours is a 'time art', and the moments need to be doled out the moment the audience is receptive to the next portion. And we help shape that receptivity.

We lead the audience along to anticipate. Then when they are sufficiently convinced that a certain event is about to take place, we may pull a switch on them and they are surprised. And, if they laugh, we wait out their laughter. If we go on regardless, their laughter may obscure our next words. They won't hear them and so it goes.

What? Actors must concern themselves fully with what's on stage *and* also handle an audience? Indeed, to be a performer. One simple approach is to regard the audience as yet another actor, or group of actors if that helps.

Sometimes, we must decide if the play works better if an audience remains divided, as opposed to having become unified into one mass mind. Most shows work better with unified audiences, thus most theatrical pre-performance ritual is designed to unify the audience. The playing of the national anthem, causing all to rise as a mass. Or the dimming of the houselights. Or warmers illuminating the decorous curtain. Or a spectacular set inviting the audience to applaud: these are all unifiers.

But supposing the audience did not succumb to those tricks, and we *want* them unified. Then it may fall to the performer to unify them. The most usual gambit is to do something which is *sure* to make them respond simultaneously. If that works, then you can handle them as one person. Otherwise, you'll have to work them around by other guile, and here again is where experience works for you.

Once you can see the audience as a single entity, then every performance is ... yes, a potential three-scene. There. Our old friend the three scene has come home to roost! Without skilful three-scene playing, even on a shallow level, the would-be performer still remains at best merely an actor. Acting we can do in private. In business. In salesmanship. But when we are required to work on stage, we must be performers.

True – an audience can become absolutely entranced with a whole range of behaviour on stage that would seem to be non-manipulative. A dog wagging its tail, a baby carried on in an actress's arms. These are dynamic components from which a performance may be constructed. But let's see the dog time a sequence of moments so that the audience is systematically led along a predetermined path. Only then are we watching a performing dog.

Now the question. If we respond to audiences in order to manipulate them, where is it we are taking them? Wouldn't it be easy and natural to let them take us? They just laughed. Let's give them another. Obviously they like to laugh and I feel good to know I helped amuse them.

But oops! the script calls for now to jolt them with a shock-horror confrontation. Better not let them laugh here, or at least not for too long. The truth is that we are locked into a pre-design. And we have got to conform to the author's imaginary tale. And the director's imaginative concoction. And our own creative inspiration from rehearsal. We have certain words to stick to and certain staging, certain actions, certain feelings that are now quite arbitrarily part of a design. And what we give and take with an audience is within the framework of that design. We are bound to a play which says to the actor "Given these arbitrary tasks, under what circumstances could you plausibly make them your own?"

Not only did we have to come to terms with that problem in the rehearsal stage of planning; now in performing, we must keep an overview which ensures that we take the audience on our trip and never allow them to take us on theirs.

So what happened to our definition of acting? It has now grown up as the actor grows up to become a performer. And in so doing, we add one more element of imagination. As actors we believed in imagined stimuli. Now as performing actors, or actor-performers, we may add another element of imagination. Now as performers, we are engaged in producing and selling imaginary behaviour achieved by responding to imagined stimuli.

The performer is the filling in a fantasy sandwich. The author (and director) dreamed up the required behaviour. The actor-performer must arrive at this mythical concoction using his special skills. And then he must put it across plausibly and persuasively to an audience. The performer plays the middle against both ends! The actor-performer's mind is a very busy place. Not only must he find appropriate references to turn himself on, but he has got to be sure that the results are the appropriate ones for the play, *and* that the way in which all this is affecting the audience is the way intended.

An actor not bound by play or audience might simply say "However the imagined stimulus involves me, so be it. Let her rip". But a performer may have to say "Given these arbitrary required results, what must I do to ensure I come up with the appropriate responses to encourage those results?" Then when actually performing, may have to add, "And given this *real* stimulus of an audience and *their* responses, what imaginary contortions of my behaviour should I arrange to expedite what I have to do to them?"

Sounds awfully complicated? Actually, no more so than improvising part of a scene. Or piloting a rocket ship to the moon.

WRITE YOUR OWN NOTES

CHAPTER 55

THE AUDIENCE AND ETHICS

"That's a lousy audience. I'm gonna walk through this performance." "No, I find it a good house." Which is it?

Do we judge them by how well they recieved us? Are we dependent on the Ensemble Effect of their approval? How often, when we have gone back-stage after seeing a show, have we heard actors say "God ... you didn't see it tonight! You should have been here last night; it was a great house". What is usually meant is that, for certain reasons, that performance was more buoyed up by that audience. The moments that got laughs last night didn't tonight. So that makes tonight's a lousy house?

Aside from the reminder that actors are there to serve audiences and not vice versa, perhaps our complaining actors should look to their own skills. *How well did they read tonight's audience?*

When we improvise in rehearsals or as part of our training back in acting school, we strike problems. Not the least of these is, how well do I know my fellow actors, dare I impinge the full force of manipulation upon them? Might I not go too far? Not far enough? After a while, when we have learned more about each other, the game gets easier.

Because in the game of acting, the person you play upon tells you much about how to go about it. Their signals back to you when you try bouncing an idea off them can have you scampering all over the mental court to retrieve their return. Picture hitting a tennis ball against a brick wall. You can arrange how the ball will bounce back to you. But hit the ball to another player across the court. In the event that they do get to the ball, you will have tried to arrange it so that the ball is returned where you can hit it again. But they will try to ensure that you falter. They will dictate where you now have to run to return the ball if you can. And of course, the better you know your adversary, the more you may predict their behaviour and reasonably anticipate their and your next move.

The finest actors I know have – to belabour the analogy – great control over the ball. They serve well. They scamper nimbly. They have practised playing close to the net and far back behind the base line. Their racquets, their clothing are efficient and well suited. But every game, every match will be shaped specifically to exploit the weaknesses of their adversary. What good the power serve against someone who's specialty is returning power serves? Why continue to lob the ball over the net to someone who is known for his ability to leap and his enormous reach? Your adversary will always determine the special way in which you exercise your skills. They will tell you why to hit that one to their backhand. Obviously because their backhand is weaker.

Once more – wherever possible – the object of your action should be your key motivator.

Back to improvising with an audience. But we don't know this audience. How do we get onto their wavelength? Firstly, as a result of experience, by osmosis.

I made a peculiar observation on tour, once, that I arrogantly assumed was unique. The moment I got off the train in this sequence of sometimes one-night stands, I knew something about the people in this town. They could seem formal, relatively uptight, completely unrestrained, jovial, casual, driven, friendly, hostile, innocent, whatever. The way people behaved in the streets, the street signs, shop-fronts, the way traffic behaved, the way people dressed, cleanliness of the city, noise, they all added to give an impression. And I knew generally how the show had to be played that night, and even how it would be received. Imagine the blow to my ego when I subsequently learned that almost every well-seasoned performer learns that as a matter of course.

In fact without touring, if while still in the dressing room one can hear over the intercom the sounds of the assembling audience, one can get a fair measure of what one will actually find when the curtain goes up. The way the audience may or may not call out or laugh loudly, or murmur, or clump downthe aisles. Reverberations may offer clues of a full or sparse house. Or where the bulk of them are seated: close to the stage or far back. Or even the quickness of their responses by the nimbleness of exchanges.

Then of course, there are those telltales as described earlier. Even without any analytic dissection, many experienced performers will have learned to size up audiences, as they will assure you, intuitively. Or one may presume the temper of the audience by briefing or by customary expectations.

You will certainly know when an opening night is upon you. In which case you perform not so much for a lay audience as for a panel of judges and an enormous, sometimes stacked, jury. Or, you may be told that the house has been bought out by a special group as a fund-raising benefit. Gird your loins and be prepared to access perhaps, if you are lucky, a third of them. The rest may well be there as a duty function and would probably be happier elsewhere. The real challenge is in winning over the other two-thirds as well. Such a house is usually hellishly difficult to unify.

A regal or vice-regal occasion: be prepared for no easy responses for quite a while. Most of the audience may not be watching the stage so much as watching royalty. And only when it is patently clear to the watchers that the royals have relaxed and are enjoying the show, it is as though a signal has been exchanged that it is now OK for the rest to do likewise. Which they then dutifully do.

Midweek matinées. Even to this day these may be regarded, as Louis Calhern purportedly coined them, as Death in the Afternoon. (Unless of course they were deliberately bussed in.) Tired shoppers. Pensioners. Naive out-of-town visitors grabbing whatever tickets remain unsold at the agency and with no clue about the show. All have contributed to the tradition of a not very demonstrably responsive kind of audience. Actors, not necessarily performers, frequently regard such shows as simply making up the obligatory number of eight performances weekly. Were they more sensitive, or truly performers in the finest meaning, there would be no inclination to walk through the performance. The audience would be given full measure.

I recall one seemingly deadly matinée of a supposed comedy, and was astounded to discover afterwards a long queue of little old ladies lined up for autographs. I dared the tactless tactic by suggesting that from their response it seemed that they must have hated the show. "Oh no," said one, "it was so funny that it was all I could do to keep from laughing out loud". The others concurred, and never again was I tempted to walk through a matinee. Nor any other performance, I hasten to add.

Then of course, there are the reaction performances. These are not so much reflections of any special quirk in audience behaviour – unless it is quirky of them to buy tickets for the performance after press opening. This reflects more on the let-down many performers can't easily control, having shot their bolts the night before. No doubt the press opening was given a bit more than full measure (after all, a verdict of 'not guilty' means one eats regularly a while longer), and with the best of intentions, many an otherwise fine performance the next night may seem a trifle spent. We do try, but if we just happen to leave out a few crucial speeches or spill the coffee on her subsidised costume – let's simply assume Thespis has a hangover.

No audience characterisation is complete without mention of the 'actively participating' audience. Here is where theatre-going becomes a vehicle for the audiences themselves.

Opening nights, of course, when shows are expected to start late because the house manager can't tear the audience away from the society page photographers. Many a staircase has been obstructed by fashion-bedecked posers arranging themselves where the press can spot them. And the so-called Diamond Circle at the old New York Metropolitan Opera was just that on gala occasions. More diamonds on display there than Tiffany's had in its vaults.

Fan clubs and claques still hold forth at opera and ballet. There would be little doubt that many are there expressly for the opportunity to rise to their feet, stamp, and "Bravo" or "Brava" until they are hoarse. And the solo bows of the cast seem to be designed to cater to these audiences. Alas, so often these enthusiastic displays bear little relationship to the actual quality of the performances.

Audiences attending cult theatrical presentations may not be far behind. It would seem there is as much 'scripting' for the audience's behaviour at ***The Rocky Horror Show*** as there is for the performers. And the brilliant Barry Humphries usually ensures that a goodly segment of his audience wave their gladioli in rhythm.

And certainly, audiences at burlesque Victorian melodrama are expected to barrack and even throw things. Almost always good clean fun, depending on what they throw. When the Ensemble presented ***The Drunkard*** in-the-round those many years ago, the audience was actually provided with bags of peanuts along with their programmes. On one occasion, a youngster in the front row hurled his missiles with such ferocity that we feared for the eyesight of the villain or the audience on the other side of the stage. We sent an usherette to ask the kid to cut it out, or at least toss underarm. She returned helplessly to inform us that the kid was the son of the actor playing the villain. We consequently switched to popcorn.

On the other hand, there are audiences who seem determined not to respond under any circumstances. As previously mentioned, when some worthy charity has bought up all the tickets to be resold to kindly sympathisers at inflated prices – then the actors are truly tested. Squirming, grumbling sometimes snoring may be heard. And the ticket-purchasers are often embarrassed by their companions' disinterest. And most of them wishing they had simply donated the money instead. Often, so do the actors.

No doubt there are other audience encounters where one can be forewarned and one does what one can to suit each. Friends or talent scouts in the audience. Some famous personage has died. War has been declared. In Australia, horse-racing results may affect an audience, as can other sporting events. But at least we know what to expect, and prepare accordingly.

Another way of getting onto the audience's wavelength, and here could be the ultimate display of theatrical mastery, is the instant psychoanalysis. When intuitive spontaneity of judgment and fatalistic resignation to the inevitable fail us, we may then turn to Readers' Digest psychoanalysis.

Whatever happened to this funny bit? Nobody laughed. Was the subject matter too touchy? Did I work too hard? Did I play the house? Was there a distraction or was I not clear enough? Or ...? Any number of funny things might have happened to the audience on their way to the theatre. And while we may deduce some of them right there and then, we may only catch the results as we perform, and have to fall back on a broader evaluation or audience-performer relationship.

One 'right-there-and-then' incident concerned the audience at the tryout performance of ***'Allegro'*** catching the faint whiff of smoke which the performers could not detect. In this instance, the audience's restlessness and inattention confused the actors and actually prompted Richard Rodgers – who had been in the audience watching his show – to stop the performance and explain to the audience that the auditorium's air conditioner (which does not vent onto the stage) was picking up smoke from the side alley where some adjacent restaurateur was burning off his non-edible garbage. Only then could the performance catch the audience's attention. Without him, the performers would have had to persist until the smoke was thick enough for them to stampede.

It doesn't take a well-trained psychoanalyst to assume that audiences can be terrified of fire, which is reasonably to be found where smoke comes from. But it does take a bit of insight to assess less blatant confrontation. Let's consider. Who is the audience?

A group of people assembled for some vicarious adventure.

Why did they come? Because we advertised? So does the local mortician. Because of what we advertised? Well, what was it we advertised? When the production of ***Cold Storage*** was in prospect in Sydney, we advertised the humour and indomitability of people under stress. Good advance bookings. In Melbourne, the play was promoted as an adventure in a cancer ward with two dying patients. The show died, even after good reviews.

Does that mean that the topic of death is death to a play? In Melbourne at that particular time, perhaps. At another time and place? What about ***Death of a Salesman***? Or ***Death Takes a Holiday***? Classic successes as well as successful classics. But no doubt, somebody in the front office had a few worries about the title. Until the good reviews and profits rolled in.

What is it in the audience psyche which at one time shuns any notion of death, and at another, relishes the idea? Perhaps in the Melbourne incident, some clue may lie in the fact that at that time, there was considerable publicity being given to cancer, carcinogens and threatening details of survival rates and therapeutic problems. Therefore, strictly speaking, it may not have been confrontations with death itself so much as the idea of death from cancer.

As this is written, there would seem to be hardly a play, film or TV series or serial in which there is *not* some confrontation with death, often violently. In one locally produced soap, ratings rocketed the night it was known that one of the well-loved characters was to die. But devotees of that series could fairly anticipate that the death would be, if not romanticised, at least cushioned.

In tentative reply to 'Why do they come?', the audience comes because they feel the *need* for something they believe will be on stage. Our advertising may spell it out or simply hint at it. But they won't keep coming – no matter how much is spent on advertising and promotion – unless that need is promised fulfilment.

What are the audience needs? For example, if they are to accept a death scene, should it be made horrific, realistic, comic, romantic, ethereal, noble or how? At different times, different things.

So, what have we got in the audience? People fulfilled in every department? Not likely. There are too many departments and too many people to assume that any community will be peopled only by the totally fulfilled. In any given community, usually there are enough people with a need in common to support and/or justify a show which addresses their particular need.

The audience is made up of people in need!

And what can we do about that? Shakespeare said "... the purpose of playing, whose end, both at the first and now, was and is, to hold, as 'twere, the mirror up to nature: to show virtue her own feature, scorn her own image, and the very age and body of the time his form and pressure ..." Haven't we come a long way since Shakespeare? Only in external detail. In style. The fundamental human has never really changed. All instincts have been there no doubt since Adam and Eve let them all hang out.

If we can get the measure of what some substantial portion of the community seems to require, does that mean we automatically have a hit on our hands? Not likely. Simply better odds. Not all theatricals are equally skilled at holding up the mirror. In other words, we may not be 'good' enough. But probably more significantly, perhaps our material is not seductive or tactful enough. Or occasionally, too tactful.

Popularity or acceptability is generally more a reflection of rightness rather than goodness. How often we rankle at the poor quality of certain shows which nonetheless pull the numbers. When one compares these with shows whose subject matter may be relevant to a tiny minority, but whose quality of presentation may be superb, the flops may well be more frequent among the 'good but generally irrelevant'.

But wouldn't a brilliant performance, by nature of its multi-facetedness, have something for everybody? Most likely. Except there are times when hardly anyone in the community may be found who wants to know about some of the facets the artist reflects, and most need a great dollop of one or two special virtues heavily concentrated.

For example, what plays succeeded during World War II in England, even at the height of the blitz? Escapist, sensory unrealistic razzamatazz *and* murder mysteries. One could easily acknowledge the need for the glorified Army-camp concert, but bodies all over the floor? Wouldn't this be another way of trivialising death, which was ever a terrifying confrontation, and in Blitz-time enough to send most people mad with terror were they to look at their prospects frankly but humourlessly?

There is no doubt that their spirits were maintained not only by the enormous straight-forward courage of the populace, but perhaps as much by the British ethos of falling back on theatricalities. Not only the films, radio plays and theatre plays, but also the long tradition of theatrical ritual (as in pageantry). And the humour and satiric or ironic allusion in everyday life. Cockney rhyming slang is a case in point. Nothing important is described actually as it is. The more significant references are presented poetically in an obliquely commenting phrase. Thus the female partner in a marriage is not 'the wife' but rather 'the trouble and strife'.

Dramatising but slightly obscuring truths is what theatre does expertly. And dare we say, theatre could well be the chief repository of such skill. But dramatising is *not confined to theatre*. We refer of course to the time-art of dramatising. Face-to-face acting out. Not via books or paintings. The doctor suggesting to a patient with a serious ailment that the treatment almost assures positive results usually is acting. His objective is to instill hope if not confidence. A detective quizzing a suspect may be acting to frighten him into a confession or at least to incriminate someone else. And each will have used a different approach.

So too do professional actors select their approaches according to what needs to be done. One approach we use is by choosing a particular acting style which we assume is best for this special adventure. And, in a sense, it is not too far-fetched to think of acting styles as somewhat equivalent to modes of travel.

If we choose a superficial, indicated approach, with the barest outlines of characterisation and the faintest smatterings of insight into the characters, and where the entertainment value is constantly assured, we might think of a tour on a cruise ship which stops for a day or so at a number of ports. Your every pleasure is catered for, and you periodically catch some glimpse of those strange 'foreigners'. Shallowest encounters. Good for responses of sympathy.

The other extreme of acting approaches offers multifaceted characterisations. At best, with details of extreme depth and breadth. This would be like living with families in their homes in other countries. Deep encounters. Here is the best chance of generating empathy. Between these two extremes are the countless hybrids.

One particularly trendy approach is worthy of note. Some call it the 'noncommittal approach'. In these times of self-service, the do-it-yourself petrol station mentality seems to have permeated showbiz as well. This is where the character does or shows nothing, and the audience is expected to project to fill in everything. This glorified indication technique (no need to generate appropriate feelings) actually does sometimes help to induce empathy. Here is reading into behaviour whatever one needs to as there is no explicit evidence to suggest otherwise. This one is like travelling to another country, and spending all your time holed up in the international-style hotel. You know there are natives about, and you can rely on hearsay or use your own imagination as to what they are like but you haven't actually met any. Then when you return home, you may confidently expound on their peculiar customs.

If the performer has chosen wisely his particular acting approach, the audience identifies with him and, depending on the performer's skills and the audience's vulnerabilities, vicariously lives out the situation with him. In fantasy of course, they respond to an acknowledged make-believe. The other people in the audience provide the on-going reminder that it is indeed all make-believe. Moreover, the force of numbers, the darkness of the auditorium and the sitting shoulder to shoulder, provides the audience with the moral and emotional reassurance of protection that invites each person to drop his guard. Thus the audience is made more vulnerable. Or suggestible. And the social imprimaturs of theatregoing provides an additional aura of legitimacy which often enhances the play's seductiveness. We haven't quite regressed to the naive stage we once were at when it was common to say 'It must be so because I read it in the newspaper'. But we do get taken in by a well-tailored production.

The theatre has always been a much more insidious persuader than even newspapers. We have more successfully instilled our teachings because the audience usually didn't realise it was being taught. Remember Casey Robinson's aphorism, "The audience does not like to be taught, but they love to learn." As some evidence, have not theatrical similes become natural inclusions in our language and thinking? We refer to the Brutuses, or Cassiuses, or Iagos of this world, or that somebody upstaged someone else. Or they made quite a scene. Even the word 'obscene' was a theatrical term referring to something which should only occur out of public view. (Ironically,the original Greek theatre which gave birth to the concept regarded only one behaviour as obscene. Death or the act of dying. All else was, as it were, on-scene including nudity and explicit sex acts.) Art and life borrow from each other.

Theatre has been used as a great persuader partly because it could function on so many levels and could be sneakily seductive. While one hand could be shaking your hand, the other hand could be picking your pocket. Hitler knew it well. So have so many other shakers and movers of the social scene. There is nothing exclusively good or evil about the theatrical arts themselves. In themselves, they are amoral. Like a knife. In the hands of a killer there is destruction but in the hands of a surgeon there may be salvation.

But the performer must be prepared to guess whether what he does is designed to help or hinder the social scene, or groups of people. Of course, at best it remains a learned guess. It would usually be hard not to know. How much guesswork is involved in evaluating offered commercials: one promoting cigarettes, the other safe driving. But sometimes we guess wildly wrong. And again, occasionally there is an obvious risk that, while the show may prove inspirationally beneficial for many, somebody out there may be incited to destruction, as for example with ***Clockwork Orange***. So sometimes we gamble. But whoever practises theatrical arts on an audience must be prepared to bear the consequences of their acts, however they turn out.

Acquiring performing skills is no less innocent a pursuit than buying a rifle. Until and unless the theatrical acquires an ethical responsibility regarding the way in which these devices are employed, both possessions can be potentially perilous to the rest of us. And rather than get to the point where theatricals need to be licensed like possessors of fire-arms, would it not be better for us to re-examine our skills and resolve to act in a socially responsible manner to the best of our abilities?

Regardless of how skillful or popular a performer becomes, if he allows himself to push cigarettes or some other such questionable product on the pretext of "I'm only an actor doing an acting job. I can't be responsible for how others may be affected", then is not that performer in the same category as mercenaries hired to raze defenceless villages and machine-gun survivors? After all, they are merely burning down a few homes and firing at moving targets.

Simply doing their jobs.

WRITE YOUR OWN NOTES

CHAPTER 56

GOOD VERSUS RIGHT – TELEVISION, FILM AND STAGE

In the chapter introducing the distinction between acting and performing (chapter 43), we ran through a couple of checklists of possible criteria for evaluation. These lists would surely have bewildered all but a handful of students. Those of us who have gone into the subject in great detail are relatively few. The fact is that the judgement of good acting or performing (or both) is still decided generally by non-students who may not know or care about such pedantic criteria. Careers and cultural maturity hang on those decisions.

Who, other than students, is to say what is *good* acting?

Everybody.

Ask anybody. They will comment about what they last saw on TV, film, or maybe even the stage. And there's no hesitation in assessing the quality of acting of this person or that. Sometimes they volunteer, 'I really like him'.

Sometimes this statement comes from the corner where we have driven our poor commentator, with questions like "But what makes the acting good?" Having fended you off for a bit with replies like "Well, because he is", and "I've seen a lot of acting and his is good", or, "Everybody knows what good acting is", then "Well, he was real", "He was natural", likewise, "I could believe he was that person", maybe even, "Well, the critics said so", – finally, the cornered plea "Well, I liked him". So there!

Most performers can display scrapbooks full of 'mixed reviews.' One learned critic says "An inspired performance. Brilliant", while another equally respected says of the same performance, "Disastrously misguided. Ruins the play".

As for plausibility, the character may seem totally believable to you but your neighbour thinks he is artificial. Who do we believe? Is there no objective finality of assessment whereby the eager performer might be given his report card, 'A', for brilliant, 'B', for excellent, 'C', for good, etc? Or even some multi-phasic breakdown which assesses various aspects of the performance in relation to each other and finally to some norm? Or are we doomed to the inevitable "I liked it" – "I hated it" classification.

Dare it be proposed that objectivity can be sought and even found? And that subjectivity be seen as an evaluation of 'right' rather than 'good'? Right for you, that is. Right for our times, our community even. That is to say suitable, relevant, identifiable, pleasurable, and other adjectives of appropriateness. Perhaps the presentation touched on some pre-planted attitudes: aired some unspoken worries. And with the help of a little publicity it becomes popular. But it may not be good.

Of course it's quite on the cards that something 'right' might also be 'good'. But 'good' might have to be measured by other yardsticks.

We have only to look at our earlier example, junk food. Some impartial bodies have measured these foods against their yardsticks, and pronounced that most of them were not good nutritionally. The food salespeople and producers wouldn't or couldn't tell us that. Who are these impartial bodies? Nutritionists, medical people, health experts and their laboratories.

Now remember, we are only talking about food. It took a whole slew of experts who will have studied the subject scientifically and earned their qualifications in *objective* determinations. Against them, we pit the judgments of those who vote with their tastebuds or bank accounts. Who should we believe?

When it comes to buying a car, do you make the crucial determination by the state of the polish and upholstery? Or do you seek the advice of impartial mechanics and automobile associations? Or do you believe the salesman?

Is it accidental that 'right' is so consistently associated with the ready, the convenient, the superficial? How often can 'right' withstand the scrutiny of a careful examination?

One thinks of the facility of so much modern advertising where virtually *anything* can be sold provided it is presented catchily enough. Consider the transience of fashions and trends, and the ease with which these are snatched up, and just as avidly traded in, by even the highly intelligent, sensitive and, one would think, discerning amongst us. How glibly slogans and catch-phrases are adopted by so many.

One is put in mind of some lyrics of a song (which did not become popular) ... "In this world of overrated pleasures and underrated treasures ..."

So often, it is the external trappings which are the come-on for right. This is not to deny that flashy packages might contain actual treasures. They sometimes do. In which case, what the package promises, the contents actually deliver. The kind of contents that can withstand close scrutiny. Yes, a pretty gift-wrapped box can contain a real and good diamond.

The inability to differentiate between right and good has changed history. Entire nations have been traded for baubles and trinkets.

When you wish to determine the state of your health, the condition of your car, or how good your business was last year, you don't go to well-intentioned but inexpert consultants. And yet when we want to know how good a work of performing or acting is, it is astounding whom we consult.

Remember the suggestion that how good something is might be measured against its own yardsticks. A one metre cut of timber is best when it is precisely one metre. But a performer is *not* a hunk of wood, despite the occasional similarity. The performer and his performance would probably rank as the most complex partnership in any art-form ever contrived.

Where would we start to measure delivery against aspiration?

That ear-splitting silence is the sound of countless theoreticians and working theatricals thrusting their parameters of objectivity onto us for discussion. Therefore, as an act of either desperation or audaciousness – perhaps a bit of each – I offer my own criteria for your dissection. Be my guest.

My own parameters are quite simply based on measuring the effort against its own undertakings. There is no need to comment on how gracefully the quadriplegic danced or how beautifully a mute girl sang. We need only assess whatever was attempted.

We ask: what is it, what does it attempt to do, and how well does it do it?

This trilogy of questions applies to the whole as well as to each of its component parts. The 'it' can be a whole project such as an attempt at a character, a scene, a relationship, a spine. 'It' can be the components which are used to build the whole, and include dialogue, dialect, staging, business, co-ordination, isolation, endurance, balance, tempo-rhythm, gracefulness, beauty, strength, flexibility, versatility – all these as bodily functions.

Vocally, 'it' can be resonance, volume, timbre, tonality, flexibility, range, articulation, dialect, vocal mannerisms and impediments.

Mentally, 'it' can be actions, concentration, choice of techniques including motivations, transitions, judgments, discipline, relatedness.

Attitudinally, 'it' can be authority, loadings, openness or vulnerability, neuroses, idiosyncrasies, courage, determination, charm.

Intuitively, 'it' can be imagination, creativity, consistency, versatility, unconscious techniques, inspiration, devotion or dedication.

So when we look at a piece of acting, we find ourselves looking at big 'its' made up of a lot of little 'its'. And to the question, 'What is it?', we usually have little difficulty identifying about half of that list.

However, with a bit of prompting, we learn to distinguish 'isolation' from 'co-ordination' and 'imagination' from 'creativity'.

To the next question, "What is 'it' supposed to do?", here we find ourselves deducing the contribution the little ones make to the big, and perhaps come to some conclusion about the big 'it'.

If the big 'it' were the story line, the spine, the scenic action, the style, etc., the little 'its' can help tell the story, clarify the spine, structure the scenic action, keep the style consistent etc.

Then if we look closely, we may discover that some of the small 'its' are superfluous. If we test the story line, for example by asking, "Now this small portion, how does this contribute to the story?" We speculate on a coherence. Then we can ask "Do most of the other components contribute to that same story?" If yes, then the portion we are looking at is at least consistent. Then we ask, "What would happen to the story if we removed it?" If the story can remain absolutely intact without it, it may be superfluous. But before demanding that the actor remove it, let's be sure that it is not a keystone in the structure of some other perhaps large component, like the spine.

Then, having decided that all the bits belong, comes the hard part. How well do they work?

When it comes to evaluating physical components, there are many trained or intuitively-judicious people who can spot a clumsy pirouette or hear a note off-key. Centuries of critical awareness has armed much of the populace with those yardsticks. But who will spot the half-completed action? Or an indicated feeling? Or a three-scene relationship cleanly fenced? Or two or three layers of feelings being simultaneously sustained and shaped? Or the dynamic components that go to build a phrase?

These are skills most of us have yet to learn.

Does this mean that we pedantically critical people put every action, feeling (and how they fit together) under an electron microscope as they occur? Yes and no. Sometimes the quality is blatantly self-evident. But also we are trained to recognise the misfits by intuition. We watch a TV show and suddenly an alarm rings. Something jars. What was that? We fund the impression and usually discover a boo-boo.

As my friend Rod Power said when he perused parts of this manuscript for psychological inaccuracies, "I suddenly twitched". This when he came upon one of my brash, half-baked generalisations relating to the field in which he was expert. And so too those of us attuned to precise craftsmanship and artistic arrangements may twitch or be jarred.

"Why", you might well – indeed should – ask, "should anybody else twitch according to your criteria?"

I never said that these were rules descended from the mount. These are *my* yardsticks. But what are yours?

If we both see the same performance and you summarise thumbs down and I say thumbs up, rather than engage in "He is" – "He isn't" all night, let's first discuss the criteria. Then, we have a better chance of checking out when the performer measured up and when he didn't. But at least the discussion has taken us deeper into an awareness of human nature which, Shakespeare suggests, acting is all about.

Ultimately we might have to settle for how right the performance was for each of us, and agree to disagree about quality.

But if the performer gets wind of our discussion, he too might wish to benefit from it. If he hears that someone suggested that he wasn't following through with his actions or not motivating proportionately, he would have a choice of responding with "So what?" or perhaps, "Hmm, I thought I was playing cleanly. Must check out my performance again". But at least he will know what succeeds or fails to impress in accessible terms. We would be referring to behaviour he could do something about if he so chooses. But what could he reach for if we had said 'Good'. Or 'Bad'. What could he fix?

If this sounds like a cri de coeur, it is. Most actors I know are desperate for guidance, reassurance, acknowledgement – *some intelligent feedback*. Strangely, the usual critical approval or audience applause seem generally inadequate to their needs. These actors are experts in their fields. They know how to pull the wool over people's eyes. Even critics'. How can they share insights with those they have manipulated? And most actors *would like to improve*!

A very real dilemma the actor faces is the difference between the language of subjective appreciation used by audiences and the objective jargon used in engineering their performances. He usually wants the kind of detail few audiences can give. Or if they can, they might refuse lest their appreciation of the play is diminished or they risk disenchantment.

The customer at the counter anguishes over the choice of Ma Griffe, Shalimar, Opium or Joy. The perfume chemist deliberates over Attar of Roses, Oil of Jasmine, Indole or Scatole. He tries to conceal his chemistry, as well as his concern that the woman at the counter should *not* know that Indole and Scatole are the aromas of human faeces. But if the actor wants *intelligent feedback*, he must be prepared for the audience to be able to recognise and discuss Indole and Scatole.

With respect for your unqualified friends, could you rely on them for such a penetrating assessment? And what critics do you know who actually know as much about acting as the average motoring columnist knows about cars?

Until recently, acting was a subject that could not be seen in detail. All that even so-called experts could do in assessing a performance was what some of us still do in assessing an automobile. Walk around it, kick the tyres, stare blindly at all the machinery under the bonnet, sit in the driver's seat, twist the wheel a bit, reach for the gear lever, and maybe ask for a spin around the block. You may not notice the trail of engine oil or the smoke pouring out of the exhaust nor can you hear certain worn gears grinding because of the sawdust the salesman has packed into the differential.

The performers' syntax and analytical details, eager to be gleaned, have been around for three quarters of a century. This book only *begins* to catalogue the list. And look at the size of this monster of an opus. Armed with even this, let's look at the stage again. Let's look at some mythical performance in a who-dunnit.

What is it? It is a performance in a drama, the spine of which seems to be 'crime does not pay'.

What is this actor's performance supposed to do? It is supposed to give a well-rounded and multifaceted characterisation of a detective who is here to solve a crime of murder. This murder is actually something he was responsible for. He himself was the murderer.

How well does the performer do it? Let's look at the details. Were all his actions integrated with that character? Oops. Something jarred. (I twitched.) When he entered and the audience applauded (he's the star, you see), a smile flashed across his face and he looked at the audience and nodded. A whoops indeed! His motivation got away from him, he played the action to acknowledge the audience. Is that consistent with a well-rounded characterisation? No. What else. Oh yes, when he was in the room with his accomplice and one of the people being interrogated, he handled the three-scene extremely nimbly. He kept a mainline going on one, while operating on the other with a supplementary. And when he switched, he reversed the priorities. However, the others did not play very cleanly their conflicting actions back at him. What else? ...we can do a checklist of actions. Then feelings: how proportionally did he motivate? Again, measures of integrity. How much of what he did contributed to a unified spine?

Well, he played one action 'to blast' but he did not seem to be proportionally angry. He showed telltales of complete composure only a second later. No carry over. Therefore, the anger was most likely phoney. But wait. Was that supposed to be real anger? He is actually the murderer. Much of his interrogation is a charade. Window dressing. No, unreal anger would actually be appropriate at that particular moment. Now that could be a clever touch or an accident. Let's see if there are further clever touches elsewhere. Yes, there were. Bravo. There is skill at handling subtleties.

Now here's where some clever phrasing took place. He played the action 'to concede' (a backtracking action, remember, which invites dissolution of conflict) but kept up the conflict by providing a feeling of resentment. That action continued for some time and yet the phrasing increased in dynamics, because he kept amplifying his resentment, which was later underscored by his randomly picking up collected porcelain pieces and putting them down, and finally dropping one at a climactic moment, which not only broke into fragments, but also pointed up his losing of composure.

Good direction perhaps, but certainly good acting in that he was able to carry it out so smoothly and proportionately. Neither the feelings nor the business drew attention to themselves until the crash.

And so it goes until the final summation. But which sub-editor would tolerate a critic's copy if he wrote all that: provided he did of course.

Keeping his assessment brief, he might get away with it: a clearly-integrated spine which could be called, 'getting away with murder',strong on relationship, subtle as well as expansive playing, generally-consistent adjustments – particularly dialect – very wide-ranging action and motivational control, nimble, capable of phrasing with smooth transitions. Particularly notable is his ability to phrase by apportioning various values to both the dynamics of motivation and action. Superior authority with masterly physical and vocal control. Deserving of the applause which greeted him, I would venture (subjective, please note,) and therefore that small transgression at his entrance, forgivable.

Still a lot of words but don't we merit them? But for the fact that it may be customary, why must we assume that it is properly acceptable to deal with a performance in simple 'thumbs up, thumbs down' values? We don't do that with players of cricket, football, baseball, tennis, or with swimmers. We discuss for hours the finest details of how so-and-so has improved or gone down the drain, and the merits and comparatives of this participant or that. Page after page of newspaper space and countless hours of radio and TV are committed to detailing the subtleties and nuances of who placed the ball where and how. Should not the performer receive similar consideration?

To repeat ad nauseam, his is the most popular, intricate and perhaps demanding art of them all. His commitment to his profession could be for a lifetime, learning and polishing as he progresses. How dare we dismiss his artistry with a simple "good", or "bad"?

Of course, one can and does summarily encapsulate a performance as good or bad if one is in a hurry. But one should be prepared to back up that summary with knowledgeable detail. Many a doctor, when asked for a summary of our state of health, may also say "good", "pretty good", "not so good". But he will have to cite chapter and verse when asked "Why?"

Three quick observations.

One is a reminder that a performance has got to be measured against its own play and intent. We can't condemn a certain actor for handling the comedy badly in a play that allowed for no comedy. Or for not staggering after a few drinks when the whole point of his character is to prove that he showed no visible effects from drinking.

This means a certain degree of play analysis – rather production analysis – to determine what is expected for that play. Some plays demand burlesque, so good naturalism would be inappropriate. Some plays demand breaking through the fourth wall so unless they do, their playing may be inappropriate. You must be guided by a careful appreciation of the production's intent.

Another point has to do with a performance beyond the satisfactory ones. Beyond into the realm of brilliance or genius even. Here, one should consider not only what serves the play in a competent measure for measure. Here we are concerned with issues of aesthetic philosophy which encompass the very drama of life itself.

It is possible to give a wonderful performance which is so particular to this play that even the most judicious could find no flaw. But given a truly great performance, then one may find moments of illumination that provide extra dimensions to the character that are enriching beyond our customary experience, and may even be extrapolated to reflect insights into all of humanity.

This one finds in great works of art of all kinds, and alas, sometimes in performing. I say alas, because, as we said before, unless the performance was recorded on film or video, it died the moment it was born. And of the people in that particular audience, relatively few might have savoured the magic moments. The remainder might have taken the magic for granted.

The performer does not portray life in the ordinary sense of the word. The situations he works within take events which in life might normally take place over several years, and these are condensed into two hours. They also give us glimpses of people's inner workings with advantages of time and specific clues that few people in real life could expect to experience. In everyday life, we may have a group of friends for years. And, one day, only one of those friends may discover some deep dark secret about another in the group. In theatre, 1600 people know it every night. On TV, millions are made privy.

And, among these little flashes of personal revelations, the genius occasionally surprises us. A touch of feeling, a passing supplementary action, a well-worked-in adjustment, can give us an insight as if by a flash of lightning.

I recall one play about a girl coming back to live with her parents after her marital break-up. In passing, the father took her elbow and the girl looked down. The tender but tentative way in which the father held the elbow a slightly extra moment of time, and the girl's reaction suggested incest and possibly why the marriage broke up. The rest of the play confirmed the guess.

Knowing this, let it not be thought that any old extra bits are necessarily enriching.

So much of theatre is cluttered to the gills with cuteness, extraneous trickery, effect for effect's sake, self-indulgence, and outright pretentiousness, each claiming some mystical significance and relevance. Gaudy costume jewellry trying to pass for diamonds!

Point number three. The tools for acting, are basically the same for stage, TV, film, radio, sideshows. Actions, motivations, adjustments. But the tools for performing make it possible for you to adapt to each medium. One asks you to manipulate the audience, in another the director and editor may manipulate the audience. One asks you to beef out the voice, don't worry about matching. Another asks you to keep your voice down and match the other person sharing the same microphone. Each medium places its own conditions on how you exercise your acting. And the skilled craftsman should be able to accommodate each demand.

Of course if a camera operator asks you to move a step to the right and you oblige by stepping stage right, valuable production time may be wasted as you are lectured on the difference between stage right and camera right. But a motivated action in one medium is a motivated action in the others. And a speech impediment in one is the same speech impediment in the others. You work within the frame in each. You relate in each. You phrase in each. Make clean transitions. The same in each.

But how you sell the product will vary. Remember, the only way the audience can read what is going on in you is by what you show physically. Remember also that every muscle in your body changes with every feeling. So in a film or TV close-up, your face fills the frame. The audience can now read every small but magnified twitch. It is only the face muscles they can see. Now on stage, the larger frame is filled by your going from one side to the other. Now the audience can see and interpret the movement of every muscle in your body. If you feel angry, yes, your face will be affected. But so will your legs, arms, back, neck even your pace. So you will walk angrily, sit angrily, gesture or turn angrily. All we need to do is allow the actor to move about the stage to fill the proscenium frame. And of course make the angry voice more intelligible to fill the theatre. Otherwise a "truthful" film performance is no less "truthful" than a stage one.

But the ability to accommodate each frame comes with experience. And the more one gains fine quality experience in each medium, the greater the skill one acquires in handling that medium.

Surprising?

WRITE YOUR OWN NOTES

CHAPTER 57

EMPLOYMENT – CONTRACTS, AGENTS AND UNIONS

One young talent in Australia pulled some strings and thought he would now work in the United States: the big pond. Young though he was, there was something Faustian in his willingness to pay his way if he couldn't earn his way. So, the strings he pulled on led him all the way to Las Vegas. And he was suddenly aware of the conditions.

Sure, they could arrange the union cards for him. Sure, he would work. But he would be owned. He would work where he was told. He would earn whatever they decided he should have. He would be managed, advanced, and always committed. No get-out clauses.

He panicked and swam back to the small pond before the deal went through. Telling other theatricals of his escapade, there seemed to be little shock reaction. "What else is new?" one said.

Theoretically, the performer is a solo industry. He is a self motivated, self employed, self-product. He works when he chooses (when work is offering), pursues work when he chooses, bargains for special conditions, keeps himself in condition, studies as he sees fit, holidays likewise: a one-man industry.

That's the theory.

But not usually having a business training, he hires an accountant, and being too modest to promote himself or too out of touch to know where the jobs are, he hires an agent. Then when he gets the job, he contributes the services of his own talents and designs. And to strengthen his worker affiliations, he joins a union.

More theory. Because the facts are that while the accountant may indeed work for you, you are beholden to all the others. The agents may audition and choose *you*. The employers lay down their conditions of employment and you had better toe the line, and the unions do you a favour in letting you join whenever they choose to do so. And there also, you must toe the line.

You pay nominal dues to the union, approximately 10 percent of all your earnings to your agent, and let's hope you are lucky enough to get a good one. The other kind may not get you much work, so what's 10 percent of nothing? And if you can land a good personal manager, or you need a publicist, you may kiss goodbye to up to another 50 percent of your earnings. Before tax. Special clothes, arrangements if you are musical, photos, brochures eat up more again. And the length of employment may vary depending on any number of factors, not the least being the success of the show.

You work while most in the community play and vice versa. In fact you work so that they can play. You lose your private life, unless you are very cunning and invent one for public consumption. Your ego gets distorted in both directions. You cross class barriers in your associations, and you are often lionised. (We sometimes joke that we are in the demi-god business.) You become an authority or consultant on social, political, recreational, and communication issues, which in fact you may know nothing about. You may become a diplomat for your country, or even president. You often stop to ask "What am I doing here?" It's a mad, mad, commitment you have taken on. Ultimately, your commitment takes you over.

So when young Faust, who chose to swim in the big pond, described how he might have been owned by the mob, nobody blinked. At least he would probably be working regularly.

The performer is an artistic journeyman. Sometimes his work is seasonal, sometimes even recurrent, like going back to the same rep (or stock) company each year. Mostly it is totally irregular. Sometimes you get a long stretch of constant employment as in a TV series or serial or a long-run stage show. Sometimes, you tour or travel. Sometimes you stay put. Mostly the jobs are short stints – a day here, a week there – wherever in the world they may occur.

There is a bitter irony here. The lively arts are probably the most successful boundary-crunchers of any human endeavour. We communicate with people everywhere. Human emotion knows no barrier such as may be erected by politicians, religionists, and traders. So, one would think that the theatrical might require no work visas. But when one wishes to work in another country, one then discovers that, sorry, there are barriers after all. But the politicians and traders did not provoke them. The barriers are usually forced upon us by our fellow theatricals in those other countries. Yes, one can recognise a certain logic in this. As one can in the long-term disagreement between the factions in Belfast or Beirut.

The techniques of discovering where the jobs are, and how one may apply for them is usually left to delegated experts, those theatrical agents, who often collude with your manager, if you are prestigious or organised enough to have one.

The basic difference between the two, is that the agent usually has a pool of actors, several of whom might apply for any going role, and the agent must liaise most frequently with managements. In fact, one often suspects that a few of them could sometimes be more devoted to the managements than to their performer clients. If they can provide the managements with X number of talents, each bringing in 10 percent of their salaries, (and the higher-priced the talent the better of course,) often that may be all they are concerned about. Whether you or somebody else from their stable is among that number may be otherwise irrelevant.

Your manager, on the other hand, has only you as a one of a kind. There may be several others in the manager's stable but one of each kind. One leading man type, one character man type, one leading lady, and so forth. Or you might have a manager all to yourself. They don't fill jobs. They find jobs for *you*. They look after you: your grooming, development, progression in your career. It is they who may refuse a job your agent offers if they think this could be a retrograde step in your career. They *really* own you. Their percentages can be anything. And they may also employ publicists, hairdressers, groomers of several sorts, do all your travel arrangements and see to your comfort and well-being. They may even support you between engagements. Then, of course, you have accountants and legal advisers. Many a manager is both.

And naturally, you must hold the relevant union tickets, paid up and in good standing. If you are really interested in the general issues of employment, you should *actively* participate in your union. Don't leave it all to the officials. Or you might wish to become one yourself. Reagan did. It is so easy for cynical practices to spring up anywhere in showbiz, and unions are not exempt. At least twice during my sojourn in showbiz I was involved in dislodging questionable union officials.

And the contract for any engagement – do *not* work without one – may be a standard union format with a few special conditions, or may be one tailored exclusively to you. In either event, be sure of what you are signing! If in doubt, consult the experts. All unions have legal advisors, if your own is out of town or something. There have been times when I took an extended engagement on a handshake. Contracts followed to keep the records clear. But those were situations of extreme trust and I advise anyone thinking of acting similarly to be most cautious. Since one of those most trusting 'handshakes' nearly came unstuck, I doubt that I would rely on that sort of thing ever again.

As for you, the performer, *never* allow yourself to get out of condition. Physically, vocally, mentally, emotionally, creatively, socially. You are hooked into a lifetime of hypochondria. The moment you drop everything and take a holiday where you blister and get fat, is the moment the job of your lifetime comes along requiring smooth skin and svelte figure.

Of course, if you are prepared to set aside some periods in your life for switching off from the business, it's your choice. But know that getting back into condition is much tougher than staying in it. And with the passing years, such a process becomes infinitely tougher yet.

Another caution. *Don't bitch anyone* in the business. Career's are such that this year's wardrobe lady is next year's producer. If you must deride someone, pick on people who do anti-social things like kick dogs, or push paraplegics off buses.

A reputation for responsible, ethical, professional behaviour is a most valuable credential. Your prestige makes a difference in how you are valued by management, profession, and public.

And in that regard, you should learn to distinguish between publicity and notoriety. Becoming famous by committing mass murder doesn't necessarily improve your professional status except among murderers. There are some among us who will use anything or anyone to get their names published or broadcast. Such behaviour tends to boomerang in time, and the damage done to others along the way may often be absolutely catastrophic.

People who write autobiographies implicating others: people who blackmail: or lie about their credentials laying claim to what rightfully belongs to someone else: people who engage in public scandals unheeding of the repercussions upon innocents: they deserve no work in the profession. Yet we know they get it and often stay in for quite a while.

But when comparing their lives and careers with others who can manage professionalism without personal exhibitionism we usually see chalk and cheese.

This is not even to suggest that the performer's private life has got to be anything like saintly. Far from it. Live as fully as your tastes or heart dictate. Your private life remains truly your own business, despite the attempted intrusions from press, fans and public at large. This plea is that those of us who so desire be able to keep it private. As suggested before, if it seems judiciously advantageous to provide the public with a private life background at any time, one can still keep one's own life to oneself by fabricating another 'private life' which can be designed not to disadvantage anybody.

Some actors were born in three different places at three different times, depending on who was interviewing. And if it could be advantageous to say you are dating so-and-so, better check with so-and-so first to ensure it is going to be all right and equally advantageous to them. Otherwise, you might have so-and-so's beloved bashing your head in.

What else as a hint to keeping happily employed? Oh yes, prepare another career. Anybody in showbiz should have a second string to their bow. What will you be doing the 90-95 percent of the time you are not on stage? The rent must be paid. Will you depend forever on unemployment benefits? Some performers work behind shop counters 'between jobs'. It is almost a slogan in New York's Macy's Department Store that the sales-person attending you was probably the star of the Broadway show you saw a few weeks ago.

Some actors work as waiters, office cleaners, taxi-drivers. Some are pharmacists, nurses, stenographers, computer operators or even programmers. I know of doctors, lawyers, ministers, teachers who think of performing as their primary occupation, but who engage in their other fields as part-time workers.

And why not?

When going for an audition, you need all the actual confidence and authority one can muster. And nothing is quite so confidence-making as the knowledge that you don't need the job anyway, because you already have one.

Then as a bonus, your work in the everyday world minimises the tendency to become professionally incestuous. You can enrich your insights from real experiences rather than draw on each other's replicas of life. And also, no skills are wasted on the performer. There comes a time in every career when you are called upon to come up with a skill which you just happen to have because you have trained in just that. The axiom which is indeed a truism is "The fuller the life you lead, the more there is to draw upon".

And another axiom with which to close the chapter: "Never say you didn't know it was loaded". How often in murder or manslaughter trials do we hear how someone was killed with what was assumed to be an unloaded gun? In showbiz, that excuse is a phoney.

You must know that at the beginning of a career, you may be tempted to grab any job offering in showbiz. "Later", you think. "When I can pick and choose, I will see to it that the only job I accept are those I believe in. Those that I can use to champion my own convictions. Those I needn't feel guilty about." You think.

It can't be repeated often enough: you will be held accountable for the possible consequences of *anything* you do. Every presentation is capable of mind-bending. Perhaps I keep harping on this subject because of my own guilt. I shamefully admit to having directed cigarette commercials, which I am morally opposed to. But at the time, I was prepared to risk approbium and even the finger of an invalid pointing at me saying "You persuaded me to have my first smoke and now I have cancer". If someone were to say that to me, I should have to plead guilty. I knew the dangers, but at that time in my life, I justified risking other's lives. I assure you it is a rotten load to carry around.

Then there are people who prostitute themselves to get around an otherwise impossible series of bad fortunes. But the memories remain as does the accountability.

Recently in Australia, two international incidents occurred as a direct consequence of so called satiric TV skits. Much rationalising, chest-thumping, innocence-claiming all around. And naturally the popularity of that show zoomed way up. One wonders about the actors' thoughts if, for example, resultant trade embargoes threw hundreds of workers onto the unemployment market. Would the performer continue to believe, "This is a free country. We can say whatever we like", without some small awareness of their contributive responsibility? Would they yell "Fire" in a crowded theatre?

Let's hope they are more aware than that. Of course, how they come to terms with their self-awareness is another matter. But let's draw a long bow for a moment. What if some of the people subsequently unemployed rioted, someone was killed, a legal action was taken against those fomenting a civil disobedience, and the actors were drawn into the action. Then if the group of actors were found guilty of some sort of contributory negligence or fomenting, and each actor fined or even imprisoned, who would rally to their cause with "They were merely doing their jobs as actors"?

You might rally to their cause.

Not I.

WRITE YOUR OWN NOTES

CHAPTER 58

TROUBLE-SHOOTING

Here are a few classic problems thrown up by students and performers over the years. The handy replies offered are one or two out of no doubt dozens of possible answers. These are solutions we have seen work over and over, and they may serve as a convenient starting point from which performers can ultimately derive their own salvations.

These are not to be seen as the ultimate answers! They are merely some we know can work.

At the same time, you may find in these issues some thumbnail reminders of techniques described in greater detail in earlier pages.

Q. What do you do to relax before going on?

A. ***Physically***: Sit or lie down. Scan each group of muscles from toe to head. As you isolate each group, flop them so that they are flabby or contact the bed or floor. Check from top to bottom to top. Then with the least amount of effort, get up. If you are standing, slump over from the waist letting your head and arms dangle. Then slowly from the lower back, slowly straighten, then higher on the back then higher until you are erect with no tension.

Mentally – Emotionally: Experiment with motivational techniques that take your mind off yourself and convert any identifiable threats into friendly concepts. Keep in mind this is play-time.

Q. Now that we relax, where do we get energy?

A. Now do a series of physical warm-ups which provide you with proportional energy to what the scene requires. Then motivationally, prepare your opening actions with important motivations, and resolve to have fun throughout. Thereafter, keep attention away from yourself!

Q. In a big theatre, how will the audience recognise subtle emotional changes?

A. ***Don't*** pull faces or gild the lily if this is what you are tempted to do. Motivate yourself strongly, but ensure that you have prepared staging that requires you to employ as much of your body as possible. If there is a choice of walking two steps to a chair, or to another chair ten steps away, choose the ten steps. Every portion of your body will communicate a small fraction of body language. All portions combined give a larger cumulative effect and reveal clearly how you feel. The more you relax, the more transparent you become. Trust it.

Then if it is still not enough, try a stronger motivation. If that still doesn't work, you have two choices. Either indicate (go through the motions of a feeling response) or simply play the actions with whatever feeling you do have and leave it to the audience to read into your behaviour what they want to see. It's nowhere as good but better than nothing.

Q. How do you make contact with someone who doesn't look at you?

A. You go ahead and look at him. Use Usery, Just Like, As If to interpret that he is actually involved with you but either too shy to look, or that he needs to relate to the audience instead of you, as if they are his security blanket. By forcing yourself to relate to him, you may well yet seduce him into relating to you. Obviously we assume your appeals to the director or stage manager are fruitless, and talking to him about it – *tactfully* – has produced no results.

Q. My partners could use some advice, I think. They are deviating from the performance and missing out on some clever touches they could add.

A. Unless there is a touchy issue that could cause trouble unless confronted (like inadvertent upstaging, or the habit of drinking, or eating garlic before the show, where a quiet diplomatic hint might just do the job) ***don't give uninvited notes to your fellow workers.*** If the opportunity presents itself to discuss the play, and each of you diplomatically can hint a few mutual polishing possibilities, venture these at your peril. Otherwise, talk to the director or stage manager. On the other hand, if they ask for assistance, again you may do so but at an awful risk.

Q. I find myself anticipating. How do I break the habit?

A. By anticipating. Only now, anticipate something other than what is about to happen in the play. This second approach is applicable for every moment of a play. When you play an action, commit yourself *fully* to the attainment of the objective. You will be so focused on anticipating that objective, that whatever else intercepts your action will catch you by surprise.

Q. I suddenly find my motivation not working. Help?

A. It is impossible to do anything deliberate without motivation. You are motivated now. Otherwise you wouldn't be calling for help. But what you mean is you haven't tailored your emotional drive to the quality which the play calls for. But you can still play the action with whatever motivation you actually do have.

At the moment you may feel lost, inadequate, desperate. Those are feelings nonetheless and you can play a whole range of actions (almost all) driven by those feelings. Let's assume the action to be played is 'to accuse'. The desired feeling should be 'smugly'. So you can't get 'smug' on cue. Can't you continue 'desperately' until you get back on line? How much difference would it make to the characterisation? Make a quick assessment. If the compromised feeling is expected to change your character appreciably, better to *Keep a poker face* and let the audience imagine you are feeling what is needed. But if you guess that the swap would not be critical, use what you do feel.

More often than not, your authority, which would come from the knowledge that you can carry on regardless, could fool the audience into believing that for that moment, that feeling belonged to the character. Capitalise on whatever feelings you do have, and get on with playing actions. These tell more about your character than an occasional stray feeling. Only as a last, last, last resort, indicate.

Q. I find myself losing concentration.

A. Back to action exercises and Circle of Concentration work. Master this skill by practice, practice and more practice. It is imperative. Often, a bridging device to tide you over is to involve yourself in minuscule details about the object of your action. It usually forces focused concentration.

Q. The audience throws me. Do we have to have them?

A. They are the people you tell your story to. There is no professional theatre without them. They have come to you for transport. Conjure with them. Mould them to your requirements: they are putty in your hands. Surprise them, amuse them, sadden them. But never allow yourself to think defensively about them. They have asked you for help to gladden or depressurise their lives. Does an ambulance driver run away from an accident victim? Rescue them. They might put up a front of being aloof, secure, independent. That could be a front indeed. They wouldn't be here if they were actually that self-sufficient. Love them, pity them, help them, don't fear them.

Q. I don't think I'm getting my fair share of publicity.

A. Is this a result of something your agent or contract overlooked that others' agents didn't? Or is it bias on the part of the publicity department? Or is it what is actually most common in show business: that journalists and interviewers have their own preferences as to whom they interview?

Your publicist might have tried to circulate equally enthusiastic material about all of you. But the journalists being appealed to for free coverage may be attracted by the blurbs about others for any number of reasons. If that is the case, find something more newsworthy or invent some gimmick. Otherwise live with it or hire your own publicist. However, they *must* work in conjunction with the show's publicist or there is trouble. If the reason is the first two possibilities, see your agent.

Q. What do I do about getting bored with the show?

A. Explore your motivational techniques. Something *must* work for you to ginger up your enthusiasm. Otherwise, if your contract permits, and you are quite prepared to join the pool of some 90 percent or so of unemployed actors, consider leaving the show. Your boredom surely does nothing to enhance the audiences' appreciation of what they paid to receive.

Q. One of the others drinks before the show. Not enough to qualify for the dismissible state of drunkenness. But they breath fumes over me and their co-ordination is just this much off. What can I do?

A. If possible, a quiet word to them. If necessary a word to the stage manager. If crucial, a word to the director or management.

Working onstage is both delicate and dangerous. Careers can be made or shattered, not merely for the drinker but also for those relying on him. Also, the physical damage that may be incurred is unlimited. There was a time in New York when accident insurance premiums for performers were in the same classification as for steeple-jacks. Working with performers legally or illegally drugged is a possible risk I know I do not wish to encounter any more. Most physical damage I have incurred was directly traceable to drinking, and not my own. I would rather quit a show than have to work in one where a drinker is so placed as to do me possible damage. But if you wish to live with it, know it is a risk.

Q. What do I do about a chronic upstager?

A. Is he doing it deliberately? First, a tactful word to him. If to no avail, talk to the stage manager or director. Again, if that doesn't work, live with it and play your lines out front if it won't hurt the show. But you may wish to do what so many do at the risk to the show: engage him in a one-upmanship duel. Mask him. Stand between him and the audience. You might try fly-catching on his crucial lines. Or a stifled yawn. But I wouldn't recommend the ancient remedy of broken glass in his cleansing cream. Unless really, really necessary. The game of upstaging the upstager leads to too many absurd consequences.

If he upstages accidentally, a quiet word to him or to the stage manager. Then if still unsuccessful, leave on his dressing table a brochure of some professional acting school.

Q. My workmate has bad breath. (Or doesn't bathe.)

A. If it is too tactless to drop a hint in discussion with him, a word to the stage manager. Only as the very last resort, leave on his dressing table a bottle of mouthwash or a cake of deodorant soap. It usually works. After the initial humiliating shock.

Q. What about blocking on dialogue?

A. Here's where knowing what actions you are to play pays off once more. You may forget the words but you will rarely forget the intent of those words. Continue to play the action in your own words until you and the others steer back to the script.

If it is you who has blocked, stick with the action. If it is the other who blocked, adapt your words to accommodate his ad-libs but try steering him back to the actions and strict script. *Don't* whisper the words to him that he is supposed to say. The nearest thing to that kind of prompt is to spoon-feed him his situation plus words. Something like, "Of course I don't blame you for looking stunned. When you get your voice back you can then ask me where did I think I will go now, and I will be quite frank with you". Which is usually prompt enough for the forgetful one to then say "Right. Then tell me where do you think you will go now?" Which was about what he was supposed to say before he whited out. Help each other.

There is another kind of forgetting which can be a bit more troublesome: recurrent blocking at the same point in the play. This is almost always a sign that the unconscious mind is not happy with something you are about to say or do, because it is reminded of a repressed guilt, fear or some such. All the rehearsing in the world is not going to fix it. Even if you force yourself to say it by writing it on your cuff, that mischievous unconscious will revenge itself by making you stumble somewhere else. You may block, twist words or sentences, make faux-pas or just break out in cold sweat.

Yet there is a remedy. Track down whatever it is at the root of that fear or guilt. If you look back at the game we played in chapter 32, where we dug for repressed memories, you might try that. Otherwise a frank discussion with an intimate friend or a psychologist could help. But *not* a priest or minister. Experience suggests that many hangups are the result of an unconscious belief that religion or morals have been betrayed, and too frequently those associations become accentuated by discussion with people who embody those principles.

Sometimes, and this can be one of those rare occasions, a hypnotherapist can help. But the therapist would have to be aware of your vulnerabilities: you may not be ready to confront those ghosts. Also you may find yourself simply swapping one hangup for another. But get to the root of it somehow and the blockage should vanish for good.

Q. And if someone misses his entrance?

A. Ad lib of course. But a transition action. Some bridging idea that could account for being left alone on stage. Something like, "Thank God I've got a few moments to work out what I can say to Murgatroyd before he gets here. Now I hope I have a clear picture of how things stand. I'd hate to make a fool of myself by going off half-cocked. As I see it, Murgatroyd is not to be trusted. Yet I must do business with him as nobody else seems ready to lend me money. But he can trust me. Maybe people have poisoned his mind against me. Well here he comes, and I shall have a chance to find out." This last portion as the actor recently released from a jammed toilet cubicle stands in the wings nodding his head and hurriedly adjusting his costume.

If the actor remains locked in the toilet, go as far as logically feasible, then play it like the end of a scene, walking off toward the stage manager's desk whispering "Pull the curtain!"

Q. What about performers who muck about trying to break you up?

A. Use it. Turn it to your advantage. Twist its significance to serve your moment-by-moment purposes.

Q. What about forgetting personal props?

A. Knowing what the actions are, where these props are expected to serve, improvise without them or find substitutes. Only rarely may you ad lib an exit to fetch the prop. That's a last resort. To make sure you don't forget them in the first place, it is a good idea to make a check list of props for each entry, and tick off each one before going on. The list, stuck on or actually written on your mirror is a fairly standard way of doing it.

Q. And how do I cover coming on in the wrong costume?

A. Improvise some whimsical justification, like, "Why isn't everyone else in costume, or is the party tomorrow night?" You *may* get away with it. We have had stagehands in overalls wander onto period sets, when they thought they were checking a tangle in the flies behind the backdrop. They miscalculated by one drop, coming on in front of it, eyes scanning the flys. Everybody laughed, then we got back to the play. Some of these gaffes can't be swept under the rug so it is best to acknowledge it, have the laugh, then back to the show.

Q. How to deal with a domestic tragedy? I'd rather not work tonight.

A. Sometimes it is wiser for your understudy to go on, but then at other times it might be better for you to go on. Where it can load your scenes opportunistically, use it. It's a good cathartic, letting off steam.

Where it can't be used, find good compensating motivations which serve in keeping your mind off the problem as well as keeping the performance going. The problem of your working around your own grief is not as difficult as it sounds. What should be looked at at such a time is the disposition of somebody who has been left at home with no such distraction. Perhaps it could be more useful to skip the performance in order to stay with them. Or even bring them to the theatre with you. Every circumstance may suggest its own solution. Remember, there are no medals for false heroics.

Q. And an injury or attack of illness?

A. Make a quick assessment. Don't be foolish in this. Do you think you can continue safely with a few small accommodations? If so, make them as unobtrusively as possible but send for a doctor and have him standing by. If it is serious, it would be foolhardy to continue. Let the curtain be rung down and *rush* to the hospital if it is safe to do so. Otherwise, ambulance, doctors, whatever.

When "The show must go on" was coined, it was by the business manager. Sometimes there is more to be lost by the performer, in personal damage, than any amount of personal or professional pride could compensate for. And your co-workers will think no better of you if you behaved as a dying hero. We are all expendable, and alas won't be missed for long. Somebody else will replace us and the show will go on regardless of whether we lost our lives making a gesture or whether we did so being carted off to hospital.

It is a sad fact of life and death in the theatre that the earliest responses one hears upon learning that so-and-so has met with an accident onstage may not be "Was he badly hurt?" but rather "Who's his understudy?" No need for the beau geste. Salvage the pieces.

Q. What do I do when directors say they can't hear me? Everybody tells me I've got a beautiful voice.

A. Beauty is not the same as volume. A small beautiful voice may not travel very far, or cut through an orchestra. The problem may be an adjustment one, an action or a motivational one, or a combination. Pin down the problem by specific questions of the stage manager or friends in the audience. If adjustment: strengthen voice with more exercises: be sure to do a good warm-up before the show: review where your mouth is aimed at various times (e.g. if you are talking upstage or into the wings, you must rehearse turning up the volume to compensate): keep in mind ambient sounds like music underpinning your speech or crowd noises or sound effects where you again must rehearse speaking louder. Just rehearse, drill, make it automatic and, except for the warmup, let nature take its course.

On the other hand, if it is an action problem, you must remember to play supplementaries on the audience at all performing moments. Or mainline actions if it is direct address. And talk *for* the people in the back row, strongly enough so that you hear some reverberation coming back at you. Mind you, if inaudibility is caused by poor theatre acoustics so that there are dead spots in the auditorium, there isn't much *you* can do about it except find out where they are and advise your friends not to sit there.

If your feelings are getting in the way of audibility, remember to include an eavesdropper as part of the reason for the scene. For example there are people in the next room who will be your witnesses if something happens here. Or the show is being recorded for posterity but they are insensitive microphones and poorly positioned. Or everybody on stage is hard of hearing. (Just watch out that you don't exaggerate the lip movements). Find your own As If.

Q. My volume is OK, but they still can't make out the words.

A. Have you checked the reverberation of this theatre? You may have to slow down and enunciate more carefully. But be careful. When slowing down, there is also an associated tendency to quieten at the same time. Keep up the volume, but find some action, adjustment or motivational solution to slow down as we did with the previous question. Also be sure you haven't got into awful speech patterns, like swallowing the ends of sentences or running out of breath.

There is another trap you will remember: that as one becomes more emotional, so the voice and speech mechanisms may tend to tighten. We can lose enunciation and volume that way. Also the closer you are to your partner, the quieter you will tend to be. Compensate. The audience pays to see and hear everything. No cheating.

Q. How do we cope with dressing-room pilfering?

A. That's a killer. Company morale is destroyed more quickly by backstage thievery or kleptomania than probably any other way. Suddenly you can't trust anybody. Firstly, never leave valuables in your dressing room unless you have a secure drawer or locker. Always leave money, watches, jewellry with your dresser, stage manager or to be locked in the safe out front. Don't get lax, especially on pay day. The thief may be a member of the company, or an outsider. Just don't give them the opportunity.

If the loss is larger than pocket-size, report it instantly to the Stage Manager. A search may have to be made at the stagedoor or other exits. In some instances it should be a police matter. However, be sure it is a case of thievery rather than absent-mindedness! But don't take it into your own hands to confront suspects. Leave it to the Stage Manager or police. A company thief may be summarily fired and possibly arrested.

Sometimes one discovers the motivation behind the deeds and sympathises. Sometimes, as a result, more humane action may be taken. But caution here. You may fix the situation or exacerbate it. Be wise. But even having remedied an emotion-caused incident, don't leave temptation in anybody's way. The next time something disappears, it can be worse with first suspicions going to the previous perpetrator. And it may not be that person. Lock up all valuables!!

Q. What do we do about a temperamental 'star'?

A. Temperament is one of those terms which may describe self-indulgence or perfectionism or shades in between. If in fact it is recognised as an outburst from somebody who has patently sought excellence and explodes in rebellion against being asked to deliver or tolerate mediocrity, I suggest we live with it. In fact, I would harbour a secret respect for such people, though part of me says they might have found more tactful ways of solving the impasse. But if it is temperament of the petulant, self-seeking variety, treat them as you would any other spoiled baby. They may grow up in time. Often you won't see them around for very long. There are usually others around who can do the same job without unnecessary hassles and managements know it as well as you. Of course if it is the wife, husband or bedmate of the director or manager throwing their weight about, either live with it or find another show.

Q. I am well on my way to becoming the consummate craftsman. My mind, imagination and feeling functions flow pretty freely and my voice and body do what they are told. Yet, people I trust tell me I do not yet produce great art. What do I need to become the consummate artist?

A. The way the question is framed suggests you are not yet ready for an answer. One day when you ask, "What do *they* need?" or "What does *it* need?", you will already be en route to the answer without being told. Poets and philosophers might be inclined to serve up a pat panacea and perhaps call it ... *Love* ... Some say ... *Total Commitment* ... or *Complete Selflessness*. That could be because they have encountered great works of art which seemed to reveal one common denominator. The total absence of the artist's own ego. The work seemed important or adored for itself or for what it could do for the recipient of the work, or for others.

I too have seen 'great' work by Duse, Chaplin, Kathe Kollwitz, Ulanova, that Bunraku-za Master Puppeteer, Segovia, Picasso, Michelangelo and many to me unknown Japanese artists. Their greatest work seemed to be acts of total selfless commitment.

Let's not fall into a Sophist trap. All cows are female, but not all females are cows. Great art is apparently selfless. Does that mean that if I don't think of myself at all, the ensuing work will be great? Not necessarily. But my guess is the odds on 'Yes' will be greater if:

- Your craftsmanship is up to efficiently and accurately responding as the spirit moves you to serve the play.
- That your love, passion, desire, dedication, commitment – or however you call it – for the work or its effect on the audience is great and totally without thought of direct self-benefit. Great enough to complete the work and walk away. That the objective of your mainline action is not self-serving. Psychologists may tell us there is no such state. Perhaps they haven't standardised their testing procedures on the right samples.

The way your question is asked suggests self-service, self-benefit, even self-improvement. Necessary stages in any artist's development. But even if now you said, "Right! Now I shall do something to make a statement", it would most likely still not be great. The term 'make a statement' seems still to focus on the maker and his process. When one day, consummate craftspeople discover an entity outside themselves that must be served, the great work should not be far away.

Q. I don't have a working problem. I'm unemployed.

Q. What did you expect, security? Join the club and KEEP TRYING!

Q. The more conscientiously I want to work, the more nervous I become before going on. Help?

A. Nerves are not your friend. Excitement is, but not nerves. Nerves are the occupational disease of the performer. If you want to serve the play and audience best, dispense with nerves *altogether*. We have all heard somebody echo "A little bit of nerves gives you an edge which helps the performance". Bullbiscuits! Excitement does. Adrenalin, not noradrenalin! So look to your motivational techniques to help dispel every bit of inhibiting tension. Of course, if your chosen motivational technique actually happens to be Fear, you may well play those actions. But the cost is usually high. So many other approaches can drive you just as hard, but with fewer shakes and ulcers.

See also the answer to the first question in this chapter.

One readily accessible attitude is often the handiest lifebuoy. I recall the note that Rouben Mamoulian put on the board at that crucial opening of my first Broadway show. "Thank you boys and girls. Now forget everything I told you and go out and ***have fun.***"

How could we forget? It was so well drilled that nothing was left to chance. But he depressurised us by removing one area of obligation which made us anxious. Our fear of letting him down.

And this is probably as good a point as any to round off this magnum opus. Despite the intricacies and serious commitments of dedication and responsibility we may feel about our profession, we should know it can be best served if we avoid the *sin*cere or Grim and Earnest overlays. And we try to approach each performance with that reminder –

Have Fun!

EPILOGUE

What has been left out? Lots. This book should not be seen as a substitute for classwork or experience. At best it is a reminder or guide. At worst, a catalogue. We all know that possessing a Sears & Roebuck catalogue does not mean that we own everything listed, nor that we can buy anything listed, or that having bought makes us an expert in the use of anything listed.

There is much clarification, critical guidance and overseen drilling and experience to apply. There is the customisation to be acquired. That is, matching ourselves to techniques and vice-versa. This is still best achieved by working in groups under the guidance of a capable teacher.

Then having the good fortune to be working with good performers under good directors.

And there is yet much more to list. Each reader is bound to find a few items we have left out. But this is an interim report, in which we skim the surface off three concentrated years of study at the Ensemble Studios and attempt to distil even that into printed words.

We won't be disappointed if dabblers find this book off-putting. All that work and so much to learn! But we would be if the truly dedicated feel discouraged. Please don't be. We need you, as much as you no doubt need good tools for works you want to do well.

You may wonder whether all that sweat will be worth it. Despite the agony in this rotten profession, there is much ecstasy. And the people you work with are the cream of humanity. Who else would strive to work in such a service industry, where most of the time, they are to undergo private deprivation and public humiliation in order to manufacture dreams for total strangers in need of them.

From here on it's over to you. Enjoy.

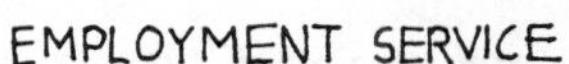

Hayes Gordon *(O.B.E., B.Sc., Phm.G., F.G.A.A., A.A. (Aspirino, Author)*

Hayes claims that he grew up in and around New York from 1941 through 1951. There it was that he studied and worked with some greats, performed in the original productions of ***Oklahoma!, Brigadoon, Sleepy Hollow, Small Wonder, Along Fifth Avenue***, and in the third revival of ***Showboat.*** Interrupted by a couple of years in the U.S. Air Force, even this was spent either propagandising the public in Moss Hart's ***Winged Victory***, or the troops with Army shows, films or lectures on how to hate the enemy.

A confirmed lifelong stirrer, spare moments were devoted to intitiating or activating theatrical training projects for Moss Hart, Howard da Silva and, some say, even Lee Strasberg. Also political ones for veterans and disenfranchised blacks. The resultant skills were to prove useful in Australia.

The preceding 21 years were spent in Boston, where he survived germinating and frequent re-potting as an actor, singer, television producer-director, teacher, analytical chemist, pharmacist, social worker, teacher-trainer and specialist in visual education and project work. He produced, directed and acted in his first TV series in 1940.

In 1952, he was voluntarily transported to Australia, presumably to perform in ***Kiss Me Kate*** for the J.C. Williamson organisation. On that wondrous Pacific island continent of paradox and promise, he became transfixed by the motto 'Fair Go'. Infatuation with both this philosophy and his Australian wife Helen, have kept him here, irascible but happy.

His work on the Australasian stage – ***Kiss Me Kate, Annie Get Your Gun, Oklahoma!, Kismet, Fiddler on the Roof, Annie, Broadway Bound*** – on TV and radio, and in the fields of acting training, directing (over 60 productions ranging from intimate theatre to international festivals and Royal pageants), theatre organisation and psychodrama have earned him the occasional formal recognition, including the O.B.E.

In 1958 he established the Ensemble Theatre, Australia's first successful co-operative professional theatre. This remains the longest running unsubsidised professional theatre in Australia, playing seven to eight performances a week, 52 weeks per year. The acting school, where he still teaches, and from which the Ensemble Theatre evolved, continues to turn out top quality performers.

In 1988, mid-closing week of ***Broadway Bound*** at the Opera House, his health became permanently impaired, making him unable to perform in yet another season of ***Fiddler*** for the Australian Opera.

No longer the governing director of the Ensemble Productions, he nevertheless can be found occasionally writing, directing or teaching, when he is not prowling the streets of Sydney at night, shining a lantern in random faces while demanding "Where has 'Fair Go' gone?"

INDEX

WRITE YOUR OWN NOTES

WRITE YOUR OWN NOTES

WRITE YOUR OWN NOTES